KEEP CALM
YOU'RE ROLLING WITH
GOD

Daily Reminders For Maximum Wisdom, Peace and Happiness

KEEP CALM
YOU'RE ROLLING WITH
GOD

Daily Reminders For Maximum Wisdom, Peace and Happiness

Nikki Bless

KEEP CALM, YOU'RE ROLLING WITH GOD

Copyright © 2017 Nikki Bless

All rights reserved.

No part of this book may be reproduced, distributed or transmitted in any form by any means, graphics, electronics, or mechanical, including photocopy, recording, taping, or by any information storage or retrieval system, without permission in writing from the publisher, except in the case of reprints in the context of reviews, quotes, or references.

Printed in the United States of America

ISBN: 978-1-945558-36-8

DEDICATION

All glory goes to God! This book is my family's gift to Him, from whom all our blessings flow.

Special thanks also go to the best mothers in the world, Mabel, and Janet, the original super moms, and to the best husband in the world, Emmanuel.

My Dearest Mama, may your legacy live on forever throughout future generations, showing that God is not only to be found in church on Sundays but also in our daily interactions with others. You taught me kindness and to ask, *How may I serve?* Following in your footsteps has led me on the path to the most beautiful life. *I am truly grateful!*

My Wonderful Mother-In-Law, thank you for all your prayers, reminding me of the importance of preparing and eating home cooked meals and teaching me that *God is ALL we need.*

My Hon, when I met you, I loved you because you were perfect. Fifteen years later, I know you're not perfect, but I love you even more. Thank you for putting up with me, your also imperfect, God maniac wife! I want to show you every day that God loved you so much that He gave me to you as your wife. I'm honored to spend my life with you and to be the mother of our four beautiful children: Ember (First Place Daughter), Julie (Super Daughter), Emmanuel A. (Emmie) and Emmanuel J. (Joshie).

May God continue to guide and direct us all. Amen.

Introduction

"I BELIEVE I HAVE A MESSAGE FROM GOD TO SHARE WITH THE WORLD"

That was me almost five years ago, seeking my husband's support in starting a Facebook page to encourage people to live happier lives. I'm sure at the time he had no idea what he agreed to, but here we are about to launch our first book, which is a compilation of these blog posts, which I believe are from God's heart to my heart, to hopefully touch and inspire your heart.

It all began one night when my husband, and I entertained a friend at our home in Nigeria. We got into an argument, and my husband and my friend disagreed with me over an issue, and instead of arguing back, I only kept saying, *"Do not judge. Do not judge. Do not judge,"* repeatedly.

Feeling exhausted that night, I went to bed when a strong prompting came over me to get up and continue reading the book *Conversations with God* by Neale Donald Walsch. I started arguing back with the feeling, saying I'll read it tomorrow, but it persisted and refused to go away. I tiredly got up and took the book to our bathroom, as to not to disturb my husband sleeping, when the words *"Judge not"* jumped out at me on that very page. *Talk about freaked out!*

That was the beginning of my *God winks*, which Oprah Winfrey described as "when out of the blue, everything lines up just perfectly." I go as far as describing them as when everything lines up a little bit too perfectly, and I know that it's God reminding me that His invisible Presence is always with me. For me to read those words in that book the very night I argued with my husband and friend about *not judging* was a huge God wink, with Him first revealing Himself to me there in our bathroom. *And, He didn't stop.* The God winks continued for weeks, which led me to have that meaningful conversation with my husband to begin writing my blog.

This book is a compilation of these blog posts, selected by myself and my extraordinary friend, Salzonia, who has been my biggest supporter over the years of writing them. This has been my passionate work for God to share the not Good News anymore, but Great News that we're never, ever alone and that He's *incomprehensibly* with us in every moment of every day and He has the best, *unimaginable* plans for our lives.

I use stories from my personal life as a wife, mom, and person to illustrate

God's intimate involvement in our day-to-day activities. I go from telling you about my most worrisome days to the most hurtful days to the happiest days. Through my joys, hurts, disappointments, frustrations, sadness, worries, problems, and challenges, I've found God to be right there with me. Every time. I incredibly see His hands in every little detail, and it is my hope that through reading my experiences, you, too, will begin to see His hands in your life, as well.

I promise you, no one gets away easy! However, I've found that through keeping my eyes steadily fixed on God, not leaning on my own understanding, but trusting His moment-by-moment guidance, no matter the challenges I'm facing, I always come through them stronger, braver, tougher, and wiser than I was before. I now have this unbelievable trust and faith in God, where I worry about nothing and pray about everything, doing the best with what I feel God would have me to do. Then, *I simply leave the rest with Him.*

He is indeed our best Friend, Father, Partner, Adviser, Counselor, Comforter, Strategist, Helper, Confidant, and Teacher, and He never leaves us. In fact, it was during my biggest hurts when I felt as if He was wrapping His arms around me. Knowing He was with me in those painful moments has even brought me closer to Him. *If the Creator of the entire universe cares that I'm hurt, what is there to be sad about?* It is my hope to encourage you daily, reminding you that we're not going by the ordinary rules of man and that we can live *supernaturally,* close to God. I'm talking out-of-this-world wisdom, peace, joy, happiness, contentment, gratitude, and purpose. I've offered my entire life to Him, realizing that every blessing is ultimately from God.

"Your talent is God's gift to you. What you do with it is your gift back to God" (Leo Buscaglia). This book and these blog posts are all my gifts to Him. I always remind myself that everything is between God and me, not between me and anyone else. I, therefore, work on being my gentlest, kindest, calmest, most loving, merciful, patient and forgiving self and although I get it wrong lots of times, I work on constant and never-ending improvement at becoming the *superhuman* He has created me to be.

I have tasted and seen that the Lord is good and I have something to tell:

"Trust in the Lord with all your heart, and lean not on your own understanding: in all your ways acknowledge Him, and He shall direct your paths" (Proverbs 3:5-6, NIV).

Sign up to receive my FREE daily devotional email: http://werollwithgod.com/sign-up/

Table of Contents

Introduction vii
Day 1 1
Day 2 2
Day 3 3
Day 4 4
Day 5 5
Day 6 6
Day 7 7
Day 8 8
Day 9 9
Day 10 10
Day 11 11
Day 12 12
Day 13 13
Day 14 14
Day 15 15
Day 16 16
Day 17 17
Day 18 18
Day 19 19
Day 20 20
Day 21 21
Day 22 22
Day 23 23
Day 24 24
Day 25 25
Day 26 26
Day 27 27
Day 28 28
Day 29 29
Day 30 30
Day 31 32
Day 32 33
Day 33 34
Day 34 35
Day 35 36

Day 36 37
Day 37 38
Day 38 39
Day 39 40
Day 40 41
Day 41 43
Day 42 44
Day 43 45
Day 44 46
Day 45 47
Day 46 48
Day 47 49
Day 48 50
Day 49 51
Day 50 52
Day 51 53
Day 52 54
Day 53 55
Day 54 56
Day 55 57
Day 56 58
Day 57 59
Day 58 60
Day 59 61
Day 60 62
Day 61 63
Day 62 64
Day 63 65
Day 64 66
Day 65 67
Day 66 68
Day 67 69
Day 68 70
Day 69 71
Day 70 72
Day 71 73
Day 72 74
Day 73 75

Day 74	76
Day 75	77
Day 76	78
Day 77	79
Day 78	80
Day 79	81
Day 80	82
Day 81	83
Day 82	84
Day 83	85
Day 84	86
Day 85	87
Day 86	88
Day 87	89
Day 88	90
Day 89	91
Day 90	92
Day 91	93
Day 92	94
Day 93	95
Day 94	96
Day 95	97
Day 96	98
Day 97	99
Day 98	100
Day 99	101
Day 100	103
Day 101	104
Day 102	105
Day 103	106
Day 104	107
Day 105	108
Day 106	109
Day 107	110
Day 108	111
Day 109	112
Day 110	113
Day 111	114

Day 112 115
Day 113 116
Day 114 117
Day 115 118
Day 116 119
Day 117 120
Day 118 121
Day 119 122
Day 120 123
Day 121 124
Day 122 125
Day 123 126
Day 124 127
Day 125 128
Day 126 129
Day 127 130
Day 128 131
Day 129 132
Day 130 133
Day 131 134
Day 132 135
Day 133 136
Day 134 137
Day 135 138
Day 136 139
Day 137 140
Day 138 141
Day 139 142
Day 140 143
Day 141 144
Day 142 145
Day 143 146
Day 144 147
Day 145 148
Day 146 149
Day 147 150
Day 148 151
Day 149 152

Day 150	153
Day 151	154
Day 152	156
Day 153	157
Day 154	158
Day 155	159
Day 156	160
Day 157	161
Day 158	162
Day 159	163
Day 160	164
Day 161	165
Day 162	166
Day 163	167
Day 164	168
Day 165	169
Day 166	170
Day 167	171
Day 168	172
Day 169	173
Day 170	174
Day 171	175
Day 172	176
Day 173	177
Day 174	178
Day 175	179
Day 176	180
Day 177	181
Day 178	182
Day 179	183
Day 180	184
Day 181	185
Day 182	186
Day 183	187
Day 184	188
Day 185	189
Day 186	190
Day 187	191

Day 188	193
Day 189	194
Day 190	195
Day 191	196
Day 192	197
Day 193	198
Day 194	199
Day 195	200
Day 196	201
Day 197	202
Day 198	203
Day 199	204
Day 200	205
Day 201	206
Day 202	207
Day 203	208
Day 204	209
Day 205	210
Day 206	211
Day 207	212
Day 208	213
Day 209	214
Day 210	215
Day 211	216
Day 212	217
Day 213	218
Day 214	219
Day 215	220
Day 216	221
Day 217	222
Day 218	223
Day 219	224
Day 220	225
Day 221	226
Day 222	227
Day 223	228
Day 224	229
Day 225	230

Day 226 231
Day 227 232
Day 228 233
Day 229 234
Day 230 235
Day 231 236
Day 232 237
Day 233 238
Day 234 239
Day 235 240
Day 236 241
Day 237 242
Day 238 243
Day 239 244
Day 240 245
Day 241 246
Day 242 247
Day 243 248
Day 244 249
Day 245 250
Day 246 251
Day 247 252
Day 248 253
Day 249 254
Day 250 255
Day 251 256
Day 252 257
Day 253 258
Day 254 259
Day 255 260
Day 256 261
Day 257 262
Day 258 263
Day 259 264
Day 260 265
Day 261 266
Day 262 267
Day 263 268

Day 264	269
Day 265	270
Day 266	271
Day 267	272
Day 268	273
Day 269	274
Day 270	275
Day 271	276
Day 272	277
Day 273	278
Day 274	279
Day 275	280
Day 276	281
Day 277	282
Day 278	283
Day 279	284
Day 280	285
Day 281	286
Day 282	287
Day 283	288
Day 284	289
Day 285	290
Day 286	291
Day 287	292
Day 288	293
Day 289	294
Day 290	295
Day 291	296
Day 292	297
Day 293	298
Day 294	300
Day 295	301
Day 296	302
Day 297	303
Day 298	304
Day 299	305
Day 300	306
Day 301	307

Day 302	308
Day 303	309
Day 304	310
Day 305	311
Day 306	312
Day 307	313
Day 308	314
Day 309	315
Day 310	316
Day 311	317
Day 312	318
Day 313	319
Day 314	320
Day 315	321
Day 316	322
Day 317	323
Day 318	324
Day 319	325
Day 320	326
Day 321	327
Day 322	328
Day 323	329
Day 324	330
Day 325	331
Day 326	332
Day 327	333
Day 328	334
Day 329	335
Day 330	336
Day 331	337
Day 332	338
Day 333	339
Day 334	340
Day 335	341
Day 336	342
Day 337	343
Day 338	344
Day 339	345

Day 340 346
Day 341 347
Day 342 348
Day 343 349
Day 344 350
Day 345 351
Day 346 352
Day 347 353
Day 348 354
Day 349 355
Day 350 356
Day 351 357
Day 352 358
Day 353 359
Day 354 360
Day 355 361
Day 356 362
Day 357 363
Day 358 364
Day 359 365
Day 360 366
Day 361 368
Day 362 369
Day 363 370
Day 364 371
Day 365 372
Day 366 373

Day 1 — Live in God, Live in Love

ARE YOU GETTING TO KNOW GOD BETTER?

He's with us and is always guiding, protecting and taking care of us. I'm learning to listen to Him all day long, asking for His direction to make the *wisest* decisions. *He's an expert in everything!*

I asked my son, Joshie, to join me in an appointment with God, and he agreed, and I explained to him about constantly *listening* to God's voice in everything he does.

The simplest way I could explain it was that if you thought about doing something and you get a bad feeling about it (uneasiness, stress), that's God telling you *not* to go ahead with it. However, if you feel good about it (peace, excitement), it's Him saying *yes*, go that way. So, all day long, I'm having conversations with God before doing *anything*.

And every meeting with Him is an opportunity to get to *know* Him a little bit better. Like one reading from a beautiful book, *Encounters with Holiness* by Fr. John T. Catoir, JCD. Coming home from a particularly stressful day, I learned about his father teaching him an acrobatic trick when he was about three years old. They came up with a plan if he ever lost balanced, he would lean forward, and his father would see to it that he fell across his arm and he would then swing down from his father's head. He wrote:

"It worked every time. I gained more and more confidence until I had no fear whatsoever. I mention this story because my father, without knowing it, taught me about trust. I knew I could put my trust in him. I knew he would never drop me. It was a wonderful preparation for my future relationship with God the Father. Instinctively, I was taught to trust God, as I did my own father, and to this day I am grateful to my Dad for teaching me this lesson."

On a *very* troublesome day, when I reminded myself often of using it as an *opportunity to trust God more,* this little story was God telling me that all the terrible situations and trials that I've been through in all my years of life, have been to teach me that just like the father in the story, I, too, can trust Him because He has never let me fall, no matter the challenge that has come my way. *I'm talking Godfidence!*

Dear God, may we all get to know You better. Amen.

KEEP CALM—YOU'RE ROLLING WITH GOD

Day 2 — Live in God, Live in Love

"ARISE, MY DARLING, MY BEAUTIFUL ONE, COME WITH ME"
(Song of Songs 2:10, NIV)

That's our great invitation from God, to live these extraordinary lives with Him as our Guide, Partner, Helper, Counselor, Friend, Teacher, Provider, and Father. *And absolutely everyone is invited to the party!* No matter how badly you think you've made a mess of things, God wants you close to Him. In fact, He has used all my weaknesses and wounds to show all of us a better way of living and thinking.

I love how He doesn't force us to come; it's like He patiently waits in the background for us to remember Him. And unfortunately, that seems to be mostly when we get ourselves in trouble and ask Him to help us get out. Then once we're out, we place Him in the background again until the *next* big problem comes up.

This year, I want you to accept His invitation to follow Him in every aspect of your life with Him taking the lead and not the background role. Like a great friend said to me, "I want to remember God every moment." This is where I want us, remembering God every second and collaborating with Him as to what He would have us to do, where He would have us to go, and even what to say.

We're not going by the ordinary rules of man, and some things He ask will take supernatural strength—like being mentally tough (fearless, focused, determined and refusing to worry), while also being loving and forgiving towards someone you want to choke.

But trust me, when you're able to *let go and surrender* everything to God, handing over all disappointments and outcomes to Him, you begin to experience this *miraculous* life where He not only repays you for any wrongs, He helps you with any problem or challenge you may have and even comforts you when you're hurt.

Quiet confidence will be your strength when you leave situations and circumstances in His hands. I'm talking unthinkable lives already planned for us, which include fabulous adventures, the best people, and off-the-chart levels of wisdom, peace, happiness, and joy.

Start asking, *God, what would You have me do here?* This takes calming down, slowing down, and *listening* to His quiet whispers in your spirit. When you do, a whole new world awaits you.

Dear God, thank You for Your love and constant guidance. Pardon our sins and give us the courage to live the lives You have planned for us. Amen.

KEEP CALM—YOU'RE ROLLING WITH GOD

Day 3 — Live in God, Live in Love

"I'M GIVING UP COMPLAINING FOR LENT"

It was something said by Sal, my faithful friend in South Africa. We've never met, yet she's been so good for me. For example, one year for Lent, she gave up eating sweets, and I joined her in giving up drinking alcohol. This was after my hubby asked me one night if I was turning into an alcoholic. I needed to sober up to write these *crazy* God posts every day.

Years of extreme diets pretty much ended when we embarked on a six-week program of healthy eating called *Eat to Live* by Dr. Joel Fuhrman. Something within me knew she would be someone important to me. *I love you, my Sal!*

And speaking of God connects, I got a comment from a Facebook friend, Karen, who said her appointments with God were at 9 a.m. and 9 p.m. and I got the feeling to ask her about one at 12 p.m. because sometimes they're exactly what I need around that time. She ended up sharing with me a prayer that she loves:

"O God! Refresh and gladden my spirit. Purify my heart. Illumine my powers. I lay all my affairs in Thy hand. Thou art my Guide and my Refuge. I will no longer be sorrowful and grieved; I will be a happy and joyful being. O God! I will no longer be full of anxiety, nor will I let trouble harass me. I will not dwell on the unpleasant things of life.

O God! Thou art more friend to me than I am to myself. I dedicate myself to Thee, O Lord." – 'Abdu'l-Bahá (Bahai Prayers)

The next day, I found myself constantly rereading this superb prayer and reminding myself that *I shall be a happy being*, even as I sat in a prayer room at a bookstore I visited. I entered and immediately felt God's Presence with me there, reading the words arranged on the wall:

"Fear not. I am with you."

We can be happy and joyful beings because God is our extraordinary Helper. *Tell me, what's too difficult for God to handle?*

KEEP CALM—YOU'RE ROLLING WITH GOD

"O God! Thou art more friend to me than I am to myself. I dedicate myself to Thee, O Lord." Amen.

Day 4 — Live in God, Live in Love

"HOW WONDERFUL IS THIS?...

...I get to turn my negatives into huge positives by sharing the lessons with you. Heads held high everyone!" I commented on Facebook.

And speaking of negatives, I had a gigantic ball of tangled hair in my head that I ended up having to chop off a big chunk of it. I was quite upset until I noticed my daughter, Julie, was sad, too, when she saw how down I was about it. I called her to sit on my lap, "Did mommy lose a foot? In everything, give thanks."

That pep talk with her cheered me up! I said to myself, *Nik, what do you have to complain about? You lost some hair. Your family is all here, happy and healthy, so what are you depressed about?* I went to sleep more content than I'd been in a long time, filled with extra gratitude. *God, I'm tremendously grateful for all my blessings!* I have nothing to complain about!

I woke up the next morning still bouncing around with gratitude. My hubby insisted on cooking for us, even though I offered to. He went to the market and brought back fresh ingredients, and we had a super Sunday brunch while watching a Nigerian movie together with my boys fighting over space next to me and giving me loads of kisses. *This is the sweet life!*

Here's the deal: we're rich when we're content and focused on the *positives* in our lives and not the negatives. It has taken me lots of practice to get here, where I'm filled with such gratitude. When my mind goes to thinking about my hair or other negatives, I'm learning to quickly catch myself and change those bad thoughts to good thoughts; Like, *It's only hair. It'll grow back.* (And it has!)

It was another lesson in trusting Him because He knows the experiences we need to grow us into the people He wants us to be. Let's keep our eyes fixed on God, unceasingly thanking Him for all our blessings. *No more complaints! God, I'm grateful!*

Dear God, help us not to take any of our blessings for granted, trusting that You know what is best for us at any given moment. Amen.

KEEP CALM—YOU'RE ROLLING WITH GOD

Day 5 — Live in God, Live in Love

"GOD IS TELLING ME TO TELL YOU"

These words got my attention in a surprising message sent to me on Facebook from Tiffany. She had read a post about someone asking my mom if I go overboard with this God stuff and she wrote the most encouraging words to me. And to be honest, I believe it *truly* was a message from God!

About two weeks before this, watching Oprah Winfrey interview Paulo Coelho, for the first time, I finally understood the verse in the Bible where God says to Moses, "I am who I am," as this verse never made any sense to me. Then that day, I noticed the words "I am" showing up all over the place and that night, I was in complete shock when I opened my meditation book very late and the place that I randomly began reading, quoted this very verse again: "God said to Moses, 'I am who I am.'" *I took that as no coincident!*

Ever since then, "I am that I am" has been my personal reminder from God that He's with me, and it has shown up a lot in the past few weeks. I never wrote about this, and it's been a private thing between God and me. Then incredibly, again out of the blue, I get this message from Tiffany of what God spoke to her to tell me and included were the very words, *"I am that I am."* She had my attention because there's no way she could have known this. Here's the message from God through her:

"My Beloved, I am ever with you. Do not be afraid and do not panic. For *I am that I am (Wink! Wink!)*; I walk with you. I guide you. I understand you. I am with you. And I truly love you more than you could ever understand. Be not afraid of overwhelming troubles that rise up against you. I am your peace of mind. I will cause you to be still when you are stressed and afraid. And time and time again will I deliver you. Keep your hope in me steadfast and watch as I turn things around to bless you beyond what you dream and ask of me. It is the Lord's will that you be glad and satisfied in my house and in me. Amen.

God bless you as you continue to receive confirmation from the Lord that all is well with you."

Dear God, may we never lose hope in You. Amen.

KEEP CALM—YOU'RE ROLLING WITH GOD

Day 6 — Live in God, Live in Love

"NIKKI, READING YOUR POST IS MY APPOINTMENT WITH GOD EVERY DAY"

Said my beautiful, inside and out, friend, Marcela. I called her to tell her the exciting news that I've signed a publishing contract. She's been my cheerleader in helping me to be more balanced after too many years of back and forth extreme diets and weight losses and gains. I've helped her to get closer to God, so it has been a win-win relationship. I cherish and love her and told her that we have a mutual admiration for each other. *God, I'm grateful!*

But speaking of appointments with God, I had a great one. I was listening to a podcast that I'm super in love with these days called, *The Youth Workshop,* Presented by Luke Whyte. That day, Luke interviewed Callum Humphries, a 23-year-old who is an intern with Christian Aid and Callum blew me away when he said, "God is love, and we need to be enacting that in the world. You can't sit back and do nothing." His favorite single line in the Bible was Psalm 34: "Taste and see that the Lord is good." He said that he truly believes God is with us and within us and that God is good and everything around us should reflect that. If it's not showing God's goodness, then there's something wrong, and that's where he takes his inspiration to be involved in making an impact in the world. *Go, Callum!*

So inspired by that, I rushed to my Facebook wall and posted, "'Taste and see that the Lord is good.' Who's rolling with God with me?" Almost exactly one hour later and time for another appointment with God, I thought to listen to another podcast, but after a few minutes, I got the feeling that was not where God wanted me to be for that meeting with Him. I opened my meditation book and began reading the perfect message for me for that day, and as I continued to the next day's devotional, written as if God was speaking to me, I unbelievably read: "Taste and see that I am good!" *Wink! Wink!*

Another God wink, when out of the blue, everything lines up a little bit too perfectly with Him reminding me that His invisible Presence is always with me.

Dear God, may we all come to know Your sweetness, grace, love, goodness and mercy. Amen.

KEEP CALM—YOU'RE ROLLING WITH GOD

Day 7 — Live in God, Live in Love

BE DETERMINED TO ENJOY EVERY DAY

That's where I want us! My kids and I spent the day at the hairdresser, with the girls and me being all enthusiastic about going away from chemically processing our hair to transitioning to natural hair. The boys had such a great time playing that one of my boys excitedly asked, "When can we go there again?"

On the ride home, we played my favorite song lately, *Hold You Down* by DJ Khaled, and as I glimpsed to the back, while stopping at a red light, and there was my son, Emmie, dancing away. I thought to myself, *This is heaven!* The reason I love this song so much is that I imagine the lyrics are what God is saying to me as "hold you down" is slang for saying "to protect someone, get their back, or otherwise support them." *God, thanks for holding me down. I'm wonderfully grateful!*

I've decided Sundays will be my official *Do Nothing Day* because even doing nothing sometimes is the best enjoyment. I woke up to an early phone call from my mom in the Bahamas, and that was the start to a delightful day of just puttering around the house. The girls and I spent hours looking at YouTube videos on natural hair. Ember and I cooked dinner, and as I type this, my son, Joshie, is snuggling next to me watching his cartoons.

And about all those balls in the air, I ain't worried 'bout nothing as I'm confident that God is sticking to His promise... "I will show you the next step forward, and the one after that, and the one after that. Relax and enjoy the journey in My Presence, trusting Me to open up the way before you as you go." —Sarah Young, *Jesus Calling*

Here's the deal: we're always going to have the balls/problems/challenges, but we also have God with us. Let's be determined to enjoy life despite them!

Dear God, may we know true joy that only comes from living a life close to You. Amen.

KEEP CALM—YOU'RE ROLLING WITH GOD

"HEY! I'M BACK TO MY SANITY TODAY"

This was my text to a friend.

I was furious with some people, and I prayed the whole day asking God why I should be nice to them when they're so terrible to me. I tried going to my Tumblr.com website to hear from Him, and I also tried reading all my go-to meditation books, but nothing worked to get me feeling back to my kind, loving, and forgiving self again. *I was extremely upset!*

The kids came home from school and Joshie, my then five-year-old, sat next to me on a loveseat in our living room and laid his head on my shoulder. Next, my then seven-year-old, Emmie, joined us, putting his legs on my lap. And at that moment, I got the answer why I'm to be kind: every blessing is from God, and everything is ultimately between Him and me. Having my two sons snuggled next to me was the reality check I needed.

An old blog post I wrote also reinforced the lesson:

"Guys, we don't go wrong with God when we stay on the high road with Him, being our most loving selves, doing the excellent and right thing you feel God would have you do from moment to moment. I've figured out that this is how He leads us on the path to the best life. It's not between us and anyone else; it's all between God and us. He'll pay you back more than what anyone has taken from you, if you stay on the high road with Him, forgiving immediately, loving extravagantly, and trusting Him to direct you one step at a time.

"He who grows in grace remembers that he is but dust, and he, therefore, does not expect his fellow Christians to be anything more. He overlooks ten thousand of their faults because he knows his God overlooks twenty thousand in his own case. He does not expect perfection in the creature, and, therefore, he is not disappointed when he does not find it."

We can expect disappointments sometimes. And when we are disappointed, we can simply hand them over to God, knowing He's the one to correct all wrongs against us. We simply keep moving forward, being the *superhumans* He has called us to be. *Brilliant!*

Dear God, help us to immediately shake off all disappointments and keep our eyes fixed on You, being an example of Your love in the world. Amen.

KEEP CALM—YOU'RE ROLLING WITH GOD

Day 9 — Live in God, Live in Love

"KEEP YOUR FOCUS ON ME (GOD)"

"You're exhausted in the faith because you're looking at you. The more you look at yourself and the less you look at God, the more you get frustrated at yourself." —Matt Chandler

So true, as whenever I take my focus away from God and begin thinking I alone have to figure out all life's challenges and dilemmas, I get frustrated. Whenever I look back and start thinking about all the negative things from my past and all the ways I've personally messed up, I'm frustrated. Whenever I look into the future and worry how I will handle everything I need to tackle right now and all the other stuff that may come my way, I'm frustrated. But when I stay in the present moment, focused on God, taking life one step at a time, I'm at peace, grateful, strong, brave, full of faith, hope, and joy, knowing God is with me.

I found a Sarah Young book called *Jesus Lives*, and I loved this message:

"Do you really believe in My sufficiency for every situation you may ever encounter? If so, then it makes sense to stop your anxious striving and learn to receive My provisions by looking to Me continually. Each day you face a number of situations requiring My help. Moment by moment I proffer to you the needed assistance. Your part is to recognize your neediness and receive what I offer. My Presence is with you always, providing everything you need. So don't worry about tomorrow's needs. My sufficiency is for a day at a time – today!"

Do you believe?

Our Father, may we never take our focus from You, trusting You one moment at a time. Amen.

KEEP CALM—YOU'RE ROLLING WITH GOD

Day 10 — Live in God, Live in Love

"WHERE DID YOU GO?"

Asked my hubby when a short trip to the grocery store got extended. I had one of those God planned meetings with one of the store's managers. We were expecting guests for dinner, and I needed to get some last minute items. I didn't get the feeling to go all day, but when I felt the timing was right, I left. Coming up the disposable plate aisle, there he was asking me what adjustments/resolutions I had planned for the year. We discussed them for a minute, and I turned to leave before I turned back around again and said, "Don't forget to include God in on those adjustments."

That started a whole new conversation, and he told me that last year was the worst year for him. His wife lost her job, and he constantly told her not to worry. Despite the loss of income to the family, he said they were still doing fine. Out of nowhere, he got bonuses, investments finally started to pay off, and he felt comfortable that they would have enough money saved to last for a few more months, even if she didn't find work. They had a party at their home for New Year's Eve for family and friends saying to everyone, "We may not be where we want to be financially right now, but we're good, and we're thanking God."

Here's the deal: they weren't the only ones who had a rough 2013! It was a tough year for us, as well, and I was happy to see it end. "It was great training," is how my hubby referred to it. When I write that in this life you will have trouble, trust me, I'm speaking from lots of experience, *but it's all training to trust God.*

Like that manager told his wife, that's my reminder for you today, *Don't worry. Put all your trust in God, our constant Companion. He has everything under control.* Take life one step at a time, having endless conversations with Him, asking where to go and what to do, even what to say. That's exactly how hubby and I got through that difficult year. I imagined God was holding my hands whenever I had a tough situation; sometimes, that meant holding them super tight.

Dear God, help us to lean on and be confident in You, no matter the storms that come in our lives, knowing You're with us every step of the way. Amen.

KEEP CALM—YOU'RE ROLLING WITH GOD

Day 11 — Live in God, Live in Love

"WHEN WE STOP FUSSING AND START TRUSTING...

…we'll be able to see that God is more deeply at work in our lives than we ever imagined."

He reminded me of this one day when I was filled with anxious thoughts about the future. Despite having reminded myself that God hasn't let me down yet, I still doubted Him. That was until He had me pull a magazine, *Activated,* from my laptop bag, which had incredibly been there for almost a year, but I never got a chance to read it until that day. There I read a perfect message from Him:

"When God led the children of Israel through the desert, they didn't have a map or a compass or a smartphone with built-in GPS telling them when to turn. They didn't even know where they were going. All they knew was that they were supposed to leave Egypt.

… As they obeyed and followed God, He took care of them. When they ran into a dead end at the Red Sea, He opened a road for them right through the water. When they were hungry, He dropped food from the sky. When they were thirsty, He poured water from a rock. When they didn't know which way to go, He put a cloud in front of them to lead the way.

Yet even after all that, they still doubted God. I never understood why; it was obvious God had been with them all along. Why would they question His abundance and care after He showed them again and again what He was capable of? But then, I do the same thing. God has never failed to provide for me and guide my life, and yet I still end up fretting when the future isn't clearly mapped out.

Proverbs 3:5-6 (NIV) tells us to, "Trust in the Lord with all your heart, and lean not on your own understanding: in all your ways acknowledge Him, and He shall direct your paths." Even if everything is dark ahead, if you feel like you're in a fog (totally me that day!) and you don't know which way to go, if you acknowledge God, if you turn to Him, He will guide you. He will keep you on the right track and bring you through to your personal promised land."

How God planned for me to have that magazine on that very day I needed to hear that message from Him so badly is so beyond me and my brain's capabilities.

Dear God, may we trust You with all our heart. Amen.

KEEP CALM—YOU'RE ROLLING WITH GOD

"I LAY ALL MY AFFAIRS IN THY HAND"

This is where I want us to be with God.

I want us to trust Him with everything! I almost got in paranoid mode when discussing with my hubby the state of the Nigerian currency, which seems to be losing value daily. Then I thought back to the prayer: "I will no longer be full of anxiety, nor will I let trouble harass me. I will not dwell on the unpleasant things of life."

Here's the deal: *I'm trusting God here!* Learning to stay in the present moment, not depressed thinking about the past, or anxious thinking about the future, but in the present where I'm learning to listen to God more and more, as to what He would have me do, where He would have me to go and even what to say. *"Thou art my Guide and my Refuge."*

"I will be a happy and joyful being. O God!" as I suck the enjoyment out of life and all the beautiful people God has blessed me with. "The people in your life are your most important treasures." I got an extra-long hug from my Julie, my then 11-year-old daughter, when I woke her up to get dressed for school. I'm asking God to *"purify my heart"* and let me love others the way He loves me, loving them extravagantly and forgiving endlessly.

I joined my Facebook friend, Karen, and other friends to recite this remarkable prayer nine times a day for nine days, believing every word of it, and it made such a positive difference. I posted it up in my office and at home as a constant reminder that *I shall be a happy being:*

"O God! Refresh and gladden my spirit. Purify my heart. Illumine my powers. I lay all my affairs in Thy hand. Thou art my Guide and my Refuge. I will no longer be sorrowful and grieved; I will be a happy and joyful being. O God! I will no longer be full of anxiety, nor will I let trouble harass me. I will not dwell on the unpleasant things of life. O God! Thou art more friend to me than I am to myself. I dedicate myself to Thee, O Lord. Amen." – 'Abdu'l-Bahá (Bahai Prayers)

KEEP CALM—YOU'RE ROLLING WITH GOD

Day 13 — Live in God, Live in Love

GOD, YOU KNOW EVERY THOUGHT I THINK

That was me freaking out over God, *as usual.* I was having doubts about everything that was going on with me at the moment, a little bit worried and anxious about the future. Suddenly, a thought came out of nowhere, spooking me out even more: *Maybe you're too confident!* I thought of how I'm always fussing my daughter, Julie, for being overconfident about her school work and refusing to study. Then 15 minutes later or so, I needed to use the restroom, but it was occupied, so I had to wait. I opened my meditation book, *Jesus Calling,* on my phone and unbelievably read:

"You have every reason to be confident, because My Presence accompanies you all the days of your life—and onward into eternity."

Wow! God is so *intimately* involved in all our lives. I opened to the perfect sentence for me in that very moment. Here's what else He had to say about all those worry and anxious thoughts:

"Do not give into fear or worry, those robbers of abundant living. Trust Me enough to face problems as they come, rather than trying to anticipate them. Fix your eyes on Me, the Author and Perfector of your faith, and many difficulties on the road ahead will vanish before you reach them. Whenever you start to feel afraid, remember that I am holding you by your right hand. Nothing can separate you from my Presence! For I am the LORD, your God, who takes hold of your right hand and says to you, *Do not fear; I will help you.*"

And this message was confirmed in my other meditation book that I opened for a brief minute when I needed to grab something from my handbag:

God: "I will go before you and level the mountains" (Isaiah 45:2).

Our Father, thank You for Your intimate Presence in every aspect of our lives. May we always trust You and follow Your guidance. Amen.

KEEP CALM—YOU'RE ROLLING WITH GOD

Day 14 — Live in God, Live in Love

"MOMMY, WHAT'S INTUITION?"

Asked my daughter, Ember.

I shared a story from her sister, Julie. It was about a math assignment that she was given and told to stop at a certain point. She noticed, however, there was one more question beneath it. She told me how she paid attention to her intuition (a very strong feeling, a prompting, an impression, a knowing, a quiet voice inside, a communication from God) that told her that she should complete it. She ended up getting a star for excellence for going above and beyond what was expected of her.

Another story was from my nephew, Tope, who recently got a permanent position with a bank. My husband had been encouraging him to go beyond the call of duty, and one Saturday, he was at home resting, when he too got this *strong feeling*, a quiet voice within telling him to go to work and he paid attention to it. Come that Monday, and they had a surprise from their boss, and he was the only one who had something prepared to present because he had *paid attention* to that *prompting* telling him to go to work.

My ultimate and favorite intuition story is when I met my hubby. I was so in love that I tell people that if God Himself had come down and said, "Nik, this is not your husband," I would've argued back, "God, you're wrong! This is my husband!" and 15 years later, I'm still thanking God for that intuition, as He's the best hubby ever.

Moral: Intuition is a greater knowledge from God helping us to live victorious lives in every area. God knows *everything,* including the future. God knew everything about my husband and the plans He had for us. It was like He said to me, *Nik, he is the one,* and honestly the best decisions of my life was marrying him.

You don't go wrong with God, listening and paying attention to His voice. I'm training myself to be sensitive to all His communications/promptings and follow His leading. I consult with Him all day long, no matter what's going on about what to do, where to go and even what to say.

There is *no* situation that will come our way that we can't handle with Him as our constant Guide and Companion.

Dear God, help us take life one step at a time, trusting and paying attention to Your direction in every move. Amen.

KEEP CALM—YOU'RE ROLLING WITH GOD

Day 15 — Live in God, Live in Love

"WE'RE TO KEEP OUR EYES FIXED ON HIM (GOD)"

This was my excellent reminder from my favorite podcast lately on iTunes.com, *The Youth Workshop,* when Luke Whyte interviewed Tom Clark, a youth pastor with "one of the most active and effective churches in the UK."

And, I believe keeping our eyes fixed on God is the greatest challenge of our lives, when no matter what's going on around us, we can keep our focus on Him and what He would have us to do on a moment-by-moment basis. I was telling someone that listening to God's voice is one of the best things we can do. This is how He leads us on the path to the most delightful life with Him, despite the storms, trials, pains, and difficulties, which I'm learning are all a part of His plan to grow us up to be the best people we can be. Nothing bad happens to us when we take all the lessons from the past and keep moving forward, better, happier, and more at peace knowing God is always with us.

Every day, something surprisingly good happens that I know it's from God. Late one evening, I said jokingly to Him, *What's going on here? I didn't get any miracles today.* But when I thought about it, there was something my hubby and I had disagreed on about a week or so ago, and suddenly he agreed with me. *I'll take that as the miracle of the day!*

Here's the deal: My current meditation book, *A Year of Miracles*, is giving me such good advice, and I've taken from it that we should "overlook to overcome." Once we *let go* and put whatever anyone has ever done to us in God's hand, we're putting our faith in God that He will be the one to correct any wrong. I'm going to keep my eyes fixed on God, knowing and trusting that He'll make it all right, no matter what happens to me. Let's stay on *the high road* with Him, being our most loving, patient and forgiving selves.

Dear God, help us to keep our focus on You, putting whatever anyone has done to us in Your hands to correct in Your perfect timing. Amen.

KEEP CALM—YOU'RE ROLLING WITH GOD

"FOR THE LORD YOUR GOD IS LIVING AMONG YOU...

...He is a mighty savior. He will take delight in you with gladness. With His love, He will calm all your fears. He will rejoice over you with joyful songs" (Zephaniah 3:17, NLT).

I'm still thinking about the podcast I listened to early one morning with Luke Whyte interviewing Alan Kahn, who nailed on the head my two big quality of life issues—constant Facebook check-ins and lack of sleep. Alan spoke as if he was talking directly to me because the very night before listening, I sat in my tub praying to God about my Facebook distraction and on top of that, I didn't get to sleep until 2 a.m. because I stayed up late writing and posting to all my Facebook groups.

A week later, a new Nikki emerged with no more staying up late. As Alan advised, I get my proper sleep so that I can face my days with excitement and enthusiasm, not going through them tired and dreary. I have new energy to get my exercise done and to be the best mommy, wife, and person I could be. *I now take my sleep very seriously!* The Facebook check-ins are also way, way, way down, and I feel as if I have a new life.

Here's the deal: I'm amazed how God had the perfect person lined up to offer me advice after that prayer, just hours later. *We don't pray enough!* See what I say about Him always going ahead of us and anything we need being provided to us when we need it?

I feel He wanted me to hit rock bottom with my Facebook addiction. And knowing me, He knew that I would write about it. I'm so happy that my drama became a wake-up call for so many other people who joined me in facing their addictions. I encouraged a lady to hold God's hand when she asked for advice on building the courage to attend some important meetings to get her addictions under control.

"O taste and see that the Lord [our God] is good; How blessed [fortunate, prosperous, and favored by God] is the man who takes refuge in Him" (Psalm 34:8, AMP).

Dear God, help us to "strip off anything that slows us down or holds us back." Amen.

KEEP CALM—YOU'RE ROLLING WITH GOD

Day 17 — Live in God, Live in Love

"A PIECE OF ADVICE I HAVE INSISTED ON REPEATEDLY...

...Be cheerful, always cheerful. Sadness is for those who do not consider themselves to be children of God." —Saint Josemaria

Yes, there are *lots* of challenges, trials, and frustrations we must always deal with but we can still be *joyful* knowing God is with us. I love an old email from a then 21-year-old friend, Seember:

"I stumbled on this passage this morning and decided I would share it with you. I think you should read the whole passage, but this is just a quick photo I took just to give you a glimpse of what David was trying to say to God, as I've noticed that you admire David so much. David thought about God a lot, and he knew that God cared about everything that happened to him. When David felt afraid, he talked to God about his fears (Psalm 59). When David felt angry, he talked to God (Psalm 28). When David felt alone and helpless, he told God all about it (Psalm 68). He wrote down his words of praise (Psalm 47). Often, David just told God how wonderful he thought God was (Psalm 116) when he was joyful.

You are just like David, Nikki. But with you, you try to use your life as an example when you talk to people about God, and that's one thing I greatly admire about you. I enjoy your daily posts, and I always look forward to them because I gain so much from them. By the way, I've learned to forgive quickly and love extravagantly, and I feel at peace with myself.

But today, I want to share Psalm 139 with you; it talks about how God is always around us even when we are not aware He is. He created us in his own image, and we are wonderfully made. After reading this passage, I asked myself one question. *How well does God know me?* How well does He know you? He reads your thoughts, watches you, and knows what you will say even before you begin to speak. Most of all, He knew all about you even before you were born. He thinks of you so often that you can't even count His thoughts. As you begin your day, always remember that God knows whatever it is you're going through because you're constantly in His thoughts. He will never allow you pass through anything that's beyond you or too much for you to handle. As you would say, Nikki, 'worry about nothing and pray about everything.' It has actually worked for me. I worry about nothing these days, and now I am more confident about it because I know for sure that God constantly thinks about me."

Dear God, thank You for Your intimate care and attention to every aspect of our lives. Amen.

KEEP CALM—YOU'RE ROLLING WITH GOD

Day 18 — Live in God, Live in Love

"YOU'RE FORGETTING THE GOD FACTOR"

I said to someone. And, I do the same thing sometimes, not remembering that it is me and God who handle everything that may come my way. It was only this week when I needed to read through some old posts to remind myself that God, the Creator of the entire universe, is my extraordinary Helper in every area of my life. "The LORD is my light and my salvation; whom shall I fear? the LORD is the strength of my life; of whom shall I be afraid?" (Psalm 27:1, KJV).

Here's the deal: "When you make resting in God a part of your everyday life, you'll have abundant joy and inspiration." That's a message from my favorite calendar and where I want us more often, resting in God, knowing we handle nothing alone. We do what a friend perfectly articulated in a message to me: "I have rededicated my thoughts and mindset to always let God direct me on all decisions. I just can't go wrong with Him nudging me along the right path."

It made me super happy that he was getting the important message that God is indeed our Partner and we can trust His guidance for our lives, by doing our best with what He asks of us and leaving the rest with Him, taking life one moment at a time. I don't know about you, but I always want to remember God, having those constant conversations about where to go, what to do, and even what to say, as His direction is the best direction. Even when He asks me to be my most loving and forgiving self because having that off the chart joy, the calendar spoke about, is the best kind of joy to have. I read that even if we only smile, we should thank God, and that's where I am with Him. I give thanks in everything, despite the storms, knowing they are all there for my good.

"I have told you these things, so that in Me you may have [perfect] peace and confidence. In the world you have tribulation and trials and distress and frustration; but be of good cheer [take courage; be confident, certain, undaunted]! For I have overcome the world. [I have deprived it of power to harm you and have conquered it for you]" (John 16:33, AMP).

Our Beloved, may we rest in You always no matter the circumstances surrounding us. Amen.

KEEP CALM—YOU'RE ROLLING WITH GOD

FORGET EVIL, IT'S ALL GOOD AND IT'S ALL FROM GOD

I love how I get to share my experiences, especially when I'm able to turn whatever negative comes my way into positive life lessons we can all learn from. For example, when I think of the most so-called "evil experiences" I've ever had, I thank God for them because they've all gotten me here where I'm this happy, God maniac.

One such "evil experience" got me going to church every Sunday, which ignited my love affair with Him. Another got me to relocate to Nigeria, where someone told me within the first week I was here, "God lives in Africa; He only visits other parts of the world." I think this guy was on to something because it was in Nigeria that I first felt God having conversations with me and we love living here.

Even with a major flop that happened recently, so much good came from it. Sometimes we learn more from our failures than successes if we learn the lessons the experience is teaching us. In life, you get experienced through having experiences.

Here's the deal: forget evil, it's all for our good. Let's continue to walk *bravely* with God knowing whatever He allows to happen to us is ultimately best for us. "God may kill me, but still I will trust Him" (Job 13:15, CEV). These events are all perfectly designed lessons to bring us out of our comfort zones and help us become our best selves—wiser, *stronger (mentally and physically)*, braver, more loving and closer to God. "Often it's said we can be bitter or we can be better." — Marianne Williamson

The lessons seem to never end, but once we learn them, we see a whole new world opening before us. *God, I'm so on to You!*

I'm off to hang out with a friend and to make fruit and veggie smoothies. She's been an extra special gift from God to me in Nigeria. I regularly ask myself what she would do when I'm faced with a decision. Between her and God, they're helping me to become my best self.

Dear God, may the challenges and difficult experiences that come our way sharpen us so that we may become the people You would have us to be. Amen.

KEEP CALM—YOU'RE ROLLING WITH GOD

Day 20 — Live in God, Live in Love

"IN THIS LIFE, YOU WILL HAVE TROUBLE"

There's no doubt about it! I agree with Pastor Rick Warren who said in an interview, "Life is a series of problems. Either you are in one now, you're just coming out of one, or you're getting ready to go into another one." But as I read in my meditation book:

"A yielded heart does not whine or rebel when the going gets rough. It musters the courage to thank Me (God) even during hard times. Yielding yourself to My will is ultimately an act of trust. In quietness and trust is your strength." – *Jesus Calling*

"Simple, not easy," was the correct statement made about getting God involved in more of our decisions and making time for appointments with Him. It takes lots of practice. Even I get mad at myself when I don't get God involved and regret it later. Don't think for a second that this life with God is a problem-less walk in the park. *There will be trouble and lots of it!* For me, it seems as I solve one set of challenges, more show up. But the sweet part comes in knowing we handle nothing alone. God is our unimaginable Helper in every aspect of our lives when we go to Him.

Here's the deal: that knowing comes from developing a relationship with Him. I'm confident and undaunted no matter the challenge that may come my way, doing as much as I possibly can and *leaving the rest with God.* The confidence comes from fighting so many battles where God was with me every step of the way. He instructed me what to do one step at a time with brilliant solutions popping in my head, while I consistently paid attention to the nudges and cues from Him as to what direction to take.

I loved a God wink recently when faced with a bit of a challenge: "I AM with you every step of the way! Let's do this!" We will have trouble in life, and they're not because He's mad at us; it's because He knows what's best to grow us up to be the best versions of ourselves. *His plans for us are GOOD.*

Dear God, thank You for Your intimate involvement in our lives and Your dependable and faithful help in all our troubles. Amen.

KEEP CALM—YOU'RE ROLLING WITH GOD

Day 21 — Live in God, Live in Love

GOD'S CONSTANTLY TRYING TO TOUGHEN US UP

I got kicked out of so many Facebook groups, and it used to upset me – *a lot!* Then, I realized it was God's way of teaching me to handle rejection, again being open to everything and attached to nothing. Dealing with it the first few times was pretty hurtful, but now I ask myself, *Did they remove one strand of hair from my head?*

My meditation book, *The Imitation of Christ*, puts it this way, "But when you begin to perfectly win yourself, and to walk bravely in the way of God, then you will account as nothing those things which first you considered burdensome." God is constantly trying to teach us to walk bravely in His way.

Another time God toughened me up was when He set me up to receive about four traffic tickets at once, and if I was found guilty, I would have had a criminal record. *Yes, God, I'm on to You.* It was all a part of His grand and vast plan to get me to be stronger in dealing with whatever comes my way. Driving to a friend's house one day, a police perfectly set up a speed trap following a curve which allowed him to stay hidden and catch all speeders. I was ordered to go to court, and it was one of the most stressful times of my life. I was pregnant, and because I was innocent, I decided to take on the case myself (I didn't watch all those episodes of *Law and Order* for nothing). Long story short, the judge dismissed all the other charges and I paid the speeding ticket, but going to court and having to speak was a huge growing up experience for me, as I was anxious leading up to it.

Here's the deal: tougher things have since come and gone, and the lessons learned from the tickets incident have all stuck with me. I remember listening to God as I spoke to the judge that day and I even paid attention when the cue from Him was to be quiet. I'm stronger; life is not for weaklings. I practiced the constant conversations with God while being open to everything that may have come my way, taking life one step at a time and trusting God for direction.

Our Father, may we always walk bravely with You as our Companion who never leaves us or forsakes us. Amen.

KEEP CALM—YOU'RE ROLLING WITH GOD

Day 22 — Live in God, Live in Love

I GOT THE MESSAGE–CALM DOWN

I can be quite a drama mama sometimes, but calming down is another lesson I'm learning from a very wise friend. *Do you have to be so right all the time, my love!?!* I wrote, "I've found that I've had to slow down a bit, though, as living a frantic life doesn't give me the opportunity to have those constant conversations the way I would like to have them."

When I'm distressed and freaking out is not the time when I feel God's Presence. The other day I went through something, and it wasn't until I calmed down and asked God, *'What do I do here?'* that I got the perfect message from Him in my meditation book, *The Imitation of Christ* by Thomas A. Kempis. It said, "Although your opinion is good, if for God's sake you leave it to follow another, it will be more profitable for you. For I have often heard that it is safer to hear and to take counsel than to give it." In other words, it's not about having our way all the time, God was telling me. *Nik, your opinion is good, but it would be better for you in this case not to have things go the way you would have them go. Do it for Me, follow this other person's will this time.* It turns out this was the best advice and a valuable lesson; it's okay *not* to have my way all the time. *Wow, who would have thought?*

Let's learn to *slow down* and *calm down,* as that's when we have the best conversations with God. Pay attention to those feelings (your intuition) and go with the decision that brings you peace, trusting God to guide you. He hasn't let me down yet. I'm wondering how many marriages could have been saved from this little piece of advice. *It's okay not to have your way sometimes.*

Moral: learning to calm down has been one of my most valuable lessons. Life certainly throws a lot at us, from one moment to the next, and the times I have not reacted from a peaceful space, I later regret. But when I'm calm, having those constant conversations with God, *asking what He would have me to do,* and responding with His wisdom and guidance, is when things go well, *sometimes way better than expected.*

Dear God, thank You for Your constant direction and involvement in our lives. May we live joyfully, always remaining calm and referring everything to You. Amen.

KEEP CALM—YOU'RE ROLLING WITH GOD

Day 23 — Live in God, Live in Love

"STRIVE TO PLEASE GOD IN EVERYTHING"

Anyone else in need of this reminder? Someone made me laugh when they commented on a recent post asking if my husband had a disability since I was ironing for him. "Whatever you do, work at it with all your heart, as working for the Lord, not for human masters..." (Colossians 3:23-24, NIV) is the Bible verse I'm going with because the blessings from God are off the chain. When I give my best, God gives me His best, and I'm sucking up to Him in every moment. *God, what would You have me to do here?*

Everything is between God and us. My mom is the epitome of this at age 84. She has been the best role model, and I thank God for the times she dragged me to work with her on Sundays to clean her boss' office. My mom always believed in putting in her best.

I followed in her footsteps when it was my turn to go to work. When given an hour for lunch, I took 15 minutes. When told to leave at a particular time, I stayed later always striving to give my best work to my supervisor. And I'll never forget the day my boss came over and said he wanted me to finish my education at the same top university in New York his son graduated. This was after my mom, a single parent, said she couldn't help me to go any further with my college dreams.

And now as a wife, mom, and person, I strive to please God in everything. *He's our ultimate Boss and ALL are blessings are from Him!* This husband that I have the privilege of ironing for is one example of the many blessings sent my way. *I love our family!*

Here's the deal: it's not always easy going where God is directing you. Sometimes, I fight with Him when I don't want to be my kindest, loving, patient and forgiving self. But when I go within and follow my spirit's direction on some treacherous paths at times, I know exactly what it is God would have me to do.

Let me tell you, when I do that, I open my life to such incredible miracles. What He has planned for our lives is beyond our imaginations when we follow Him.

Dear God, help us to acknowledge You and strive to please You in all our ways, even when we find it tough to do so. Amen.

KEEP CALM—YOU'RE ROLLING WITH GOD

Day 24 — Live in God, Live in Love

"THIS KIND GOD, OOH...

...I've never seen your type, ooh! Blessed be your holy name!" was the song we danced to at church one Sunday and this is exactly how I feel. A quote I read recently said, "God's always doing ten thousand things in your life and you may be aware of three of them."—John Piper

One day, I sat in awe of God and these ten thousand things and more that He's always doing. *How could God, the Creator of the entire universe, be so concerned about me?* I think of all the times He has shown me such deep love on some of the worst days of my life, letting me know amid it all, He was right there with me. It's to the point that I say, *God, I lay all my affairs in Thy hand. I will do my best to follow Your direction, in doing what You would have me to do and I'm leaving the rest with You.* I'm talking Spiritual Ninja here, *refusing to worry,* but praying about everything.

I glimpsed at a picture taken of my meditation book on Facebook that had the perfect message, as usual, from God for me: "COME TO ME with all your weaknesses: physical, emotional, and spiritual. Rest in the comfort of My Presence, remembering that nothing is impossible with Me. Pry your mind away from your problems so that you can focus your attention on Me. Recall that I am able to do immeasurably more than all you ask or imagine. Instead of trying to direct Me to do this and that, seek to attune yourself to what I am already doing. When anxiety attempts to wedge its way into your thoughts, remind yourself that I am your Shepherd. The bottom line is that I am taking care of you; therefore, you needn't be afraid of anything." – *Jesus Calling*

"This kind God, ooh, I've never seen your type, ooh! Blessed be Your holy name!"

Dear God, thank You for Your kindness. May we always remember that we're not going by the ordinary rules; we're living supernaturally with You. Amen.

KEEP CALM—YOU'RE ROLLING WITH GOD

Day 25 — Live in God, Live in Love

"I'M GRATEFUL"

The words were printed on a lovely T-shirt we saw on the way out of the mall. Honestly, being grateful is the way for me to feel closest to God. While shopping, my daughter got upset with me when I refused to buy her a pair of shoes she wanted. I've bought so much for her lately, but there she was getting upset because of the one thing I didn't get for her. *Nik, you're guilty of that, too!* I thought to myself. The littlest problem will come up and I'm quick to complain about it instead of thanking God for the so many blessings in my life. *God, no more complaints here;* I'm greatly grateful for everything!

"I AM BALANCE," were the words from another T-shirt, and that was a big God wink at me. I can be such drama sometimes, and I started the morning with the following message to a friend. We agreed that this would be the year we work on being balanced women:

"I'm totally an unbalanced woman! But today, I'm going to be back on track with a salad and smoothie, eating to live! Day 1 again for me! I feel yucky! Love you, my Sal! The year is not over yet! I will get this balanced woman thing!"

¡Ay, caramba! So, to see those words displayed on a shirt the day I was feeling unbalanced was like God cheering me on. "I am balance," is now my new reminder when I feel myself losing balance in all areas of my life.

Here's the deal: God is incredibly involved in every moment of our lives. We may not see Him, but if we keep our eyes and minds wide open, we'll feel His wonderful Presence. *"I am balance!"*

Dear God, thank You for all the God orchestrated moments, reminding us that everywhere we go is Holy because Your Presence is always with us. Amen.

KEEP CALM—YOU'RE ROLLING WITH GOD

"I FORGET, TOO"

I admitted to a friend who complained that sometimes she forgets about God and becomes overwhelmed by everything life seems to be throwing at her. One day, feeling extremely overwhelmed, I locked myself in our bathroom for an appointment with Him. With everything that was going on that day, taking that time to read my meditation book, calm down, and talk to God was exactly what I needed.

Looking at everything from God's perspective, I could sort out with His help what was important and what wasn't important. I paid attention to His voice in my gut/spirit as to what to get done that day and what could be put off for another day. I also felt from Him what I needed to do and what I could delegate to others.

I came out of the bathroom a different person, and the kids and I ended up having a splendid day together, picking up my mom from the airport, who flew in from the Bahamas within 24 hours of me calling her to say I needed her help with them one summer while we were in Florida.

My friend has now set her alarm on her phone to notify her when it's time for her appointments with God. My alone times with God in the mornings, noon and 5 p.m. have changed my life. Like regular food feeds the body, these appointments feed my soul, and I'm constantly reminded that *I'm never alone* and God is so intimately involved in every detail of my life. *He knows everything,* down to every thought I think.

With each appointment, I'm filling myself with God's wisdom, and I find myself making such better decisions that every aspect of my life is better. At work, I'm amazed how the best ideas and solutions to problems magically pop in my head. *Thanks, Boss!*

In my marriage, God is teaching me valuable lessons such as humility and instead of getting upset every time my hubby/human boss corrects me about something, I look to see what I can take from it to improve myself, and I run with it.

My kids and I are bonding on an entirely different level with God teaching me parenting skills, such as being more gentle, calming down, and focusing on their positives.

What time are your appointments with Him? Make them a priority!

Dear God, may we not get so distracted by a busy life that we lose our focus on You. Amen.

KEEP CALM—YOU'RE ROLLING WITH GOD

"NOW THAT WAS THE MIRACLE OF THE DAY"

I jokingly said to God. There I was lying in bed with my three Emmanuels (hubby and two sons), waking up, when out of the blue, my hubby says to me, "Nikki, you're the best wife in the world." This is a miracle because my husband's specialty is in giving criticisms and he rarely has anything complimentary to say. Good thing I was lying down because I might have fallen out!

We used to have arguments about it all the time, and I'd complain, "You never have anything nice to say to me!" With God's help, though, I've grown a lot from the person who longed for praise from my husband or anyone else, and I now focus on running my own race and simply being the best version of myself. *I'm addicted to constant and never ending improvement!*

I loved this quote I read in my meditation book: "We might have much peace if we would not busy ourselves with the sayings and doings of others, and with things which do not concern us. Blessed are the simple of heart, for they shall enjoy much peace." –*The Imitation of Christ*

Hearing a compliment from someone should only add to how we already feel about ourselves. But speaking of miracles, ever since I started reading *A Year of Miracles* by Marianne Williamson, I've been on the lookout for a miracle every single day, and my life is becoming an awesome adventure with God. When I stay in touch with Him and follow His lead, going to Him in the 1,000 decisions I make every day and doing what I feel He would have me to do, is when I experience the sweetest ones.

The miracle of the day before was when I got the nudge from God to call a friend. There I was feeling sad about lots of crazy thoughts, and when I called, once again, it was as if she was expecting to hear from me. It so happened that she had watched a show that very day where she listened to a wife comment about her husband: *Bottom line, I trust him.* And that's the same with my hubby; he has earned my confidence and respect. This had such an impact on me that I called him to see what he wanted to have for dinner, made sure the house was extra clean before he got home, but most of all, it inspired me to be the best wife.

Dear God, thank You for all our many blessings. May we not take any of them for granted. Amen.

KEEP CALM—YOU'RE ROLLING WITH GOD

"I'M GOING TO PRAY; I'LL BE RIGHT BACK"

I said this to my assistant, Sheba. And with everything else I had going on in my mind, including a long to-do list, I found a quiet spot, randomly opened my meditation book, and I was incredibly happy, as I read the following from *Jesus Calling*:

"I (God) am pleased with your desire to create a quiet space where you and I can meet. Don't be discouraged by the difficulty of achieving this goal. I monitor all your efforts and am blessed by each of your attempts to seek My Face."

I found the most excellent book as I searched for a book for my son, Emmie, to read to me. This brilliant, little book, *Intimacy with the Almighty* by Charles Swindol, was all about having a closer walk with God, and it has taught me two important life lessons:

- to simplify my life
- and to have alone times with God.

The alone times with Him started out in the mornings. Sometimes one sentence would be enough for me to feel as if I've touched base with God, but now I'm also having them at 12 pm and 5 pm.

Here's the deal: every time I make an effort to have an appointment with God, mostly reading one of my meditation books and telling Him how grateful I am for everything, I come out with stronger faith and trust, as somehow, He reveals more and more of His Presence and wisdom to me, that when I'm back out in the world. He's my strength and my song, as God goes with me and I know I handle nothing alone. God is my constant Guide, Protector, Helper, Strategist, and Adviser.

He's turning me into a superhuman and areas where I've been weak, He's helping me to become stronger. I have no fear and I ain't worried 'bout nothing, feeling more attuned to what God's Spirit is leading me to do from moment to moment. *And, you can't beat that with a bat!* My sheep know my voice, and that voice is getting clearer every day.

What time are your appointments with God?

Dear God, let us be a generation that seeks Your face. Amen.

KEEP CALM—YOU'RE ROLLING WITH GOD

Day 29 — Live in God, Live in Love

"THAT'S JUST HOW I FEEL"

Was me singing the lyrics of a song I love, and I thought to make that my next post. It's cool how God communicates with us through our feelings. I believe the best way to live is by having these enjoyable, constant conversations with Him, listening and feeling what He is saying to us in every moment. *"God, where would You have me to go? What would You have me to do? What would You have me say and to whom?"* is my frequent prayer and I'm talking the best life with God here. He has the perfect plans for our lives and if we learn to stick close to Him, seeking to please Him by doing the right thing, the excellent thing and the most loving thing in every moment, every example and every experience, we can *relax* and enjoy our life's intimate adventure with Him as our constant Companion/Helper/Adviser/Friend/Comforter/Strategist/Counselor.

Here's the deal: feelings of peace, happiness, or excitement are what I look for before moving forward with any decision. Without any of those, I don't move. I'm even learning to listen and feel what God is saying to me while others are talking to me, as well. Then I go with those moment-by-moment decisions based on God's direction.

My favorite feelings story was when I met my hubby. I was beside myself with happiness and excitement. It was as if God was saying, *Yes, Nik! He's the one!* And 15 years later, I'm thrilled that I made the best decision of my life to marry him after we had only known each other for five months. I love my life with him and our fantastic kids. I'm feeling super blessed spending lots of time with them this summer, and I love the way God is behind the scenes of my life helping me in all aspects. *God, I'm seriously grateful. And...*

"THAT'S JUST HOW I FEEL!"

Dear God, thank You for Your constant direction. You know what's best for us. Amen.

KEEP CALM—YOU'RE ROLLING WITH GOD

"I NEED AN APPOINTMENT WITH GOD EVERY TWO HOURS"

This comment from my friend, Danny, totally made my day when we had one of our sacred telephone conversations. She was so enthusiastic telling me about her appointments with God, and she put me on hold for a bit so that she could grab her iPad and read from our meditation book, *Jesus Calling.* She said, "Listen to what I read at my appointment last night for April 1st and 2nd." And she read them both to me, but she didn't read the accompanying Bible verses that were shared at the end of each one.

We discussed so many great things in that conversation. She's working on a course to improve herself on her job. Things that she was making an idol in her life, she's refocused her attention back on God. She said in the appointments with Him, she doesn't leave until she feels like she has received a high five from God, as I often describe it. *That made the God maniac super happy.*

Fast forward to the next morning, in my appointment with God, and I didn't feel as if I was getting the high five I was looking for from Him in reading another book. I got the feeling to reread the ones she read to me for April 1st and 2nd, and God totally blew me away.

I was a little upset about some feedback in regards to this book, and I decided to rewrite the book's introduction before having a follow-up discussion with the people assisting me with it. At the end of the introduction, I had a quote that I love, but I felt that wasn't the right quote. I changed it to my favorite Bible verses lately, feeling it much better reflected the essence of the book:

"Trust in the Lord with all your heart, and lean not on your own understanding: in all your ways acknowledge Him, and He shall direct your paths" (Proverbs 3:5-6, NIV).

And the Bible verse quoted at the end of the devotional for April 1st that my friend excitedly read to me, but left out: "In all your ways acknowledge Him, and He will make your paths straight" (Proverbs 3:6). *Wink! Wink!*

Day 30 — Live in God, Live in Love

"I NEED AN APPOINTMENT WITH GOD EVERY TWO HOURS"

Once again, out of the blue, everything lined up a little bit too perfectly, with God assuring me that He's my unseen Partner with my life and with this book, as if He was saying, *Nik, HIGH FIVE, you're on the right path. Let's keep going!*

Noticed I *paid attention* to that feeling that the first quote wasn't right. Don't ignore those feelings!

Dear God, help us remember and acknowledge You in all our ways, confidently trusting You, knowing we are never alone. Amen.

KEEP CALM—YOU'RE ROLLING WITH GOD

Day 31 — Live in God, Live in Love

"MOMENT-BY-MOMENT DECISIONS"

Is the response my kids hate whenever they ask about our plans. I'm learning this is the best way to live, though, keeping all plans tentative and seeking God's direction on a moment-by-moment basis to help us make the best decisions as to where to go, what to do, and even what to say. I have a friend who, even as he's headed to the airport to travel, would turn back if he doesn't feel peace and God's direction. And this is where I want us, always paying attention to God's guidance to keep us on track.

Right before the last elections in Nigeria, my hubby and I debated leaving there and traveling back to the U.S. because of possible threats of violence, but when we consulted God about it, we felt peaceful about staying and decided not to go. Very close to the first planned date, the government unexpectedly postponed it, so if we didn't consult God, we would have probably spent lots of money unnecessarily running away from something that didn't happen. When the final election did occur, we again stayed in Nigeria, and it was historically one of the most quiet and peaceful ones to ever take place. *It was amazing!* God showed up and showed off because no one predicted it to be that peaceful.

Moral: it's about living life trusting our instincts, spirit, and gut to lead us on the path God would have us to go. Problems will come up, but if you remain calm and patient, and pay attention to what God is directing you to do, you'll be amazed how the right solutions or people will show up to assist you. God is the best Strategist in dealing with any problem, and if you practice constantly going to Him in those 1,000 decisions you make every day, He'll direct you, one step at a time and piece by piece, and help you in every aspect of your life.

Dear God, help us to slow down, calm down, and listen to you by paying attention to those feelings as You assist us to make wise decisions. May we keep our plans tentative, remembering Your plans are always best. Amen.

KEEP CALM—YOU'RE ROLLING WITH GOD

THIS QUOTE PERFECTLY SUMS UP HUNDREDS OF MY POSTS:

"As you seek God, you will find Him—His solutions, His comfort, His direction, His endurance, His wisdom, His love."—Maria Fontane, *Mottos For Success*

I had a day when I needed all the above from Him, when the kids and I travelled from Miami back to Nigeria. A problem arose with a work-related issue to start the morning off, and the perfect solution came to mind with exactly how to handle it. *His wisdom.*

I've written before that sometimes these solutions come to me, and I know I'm not that smart. With everything going on that morning in my head, I knew it was God directing me as to the steps to take, and remarkably everything worked out better than I expected. *His direction.*

My hubby asked us to bring back pizzas for him. Going to our garage, looking for something to take the pizzas all the way back to Nigeria in, there was a perfect unused rolling cooler bag that perfectly fit the bill. I have no idea where this bag came from! *His Love and His solutions.* God's always ahead of me and anything I need seems to always show up when I need it. The kids all took turns, proudly rolling their dad's pizzas through two airports.

I forgot to buy garbage bags because we had run completely out and something told me to pick up and look inside a plastic bag in the middle of our hallway that busy morning and I opened it to discover a bunch of garbage bags. *Again, His love.*

Getting all the luggage to fit into the car and still have space for all of us to sit was an entirely different issue. Trying to get the last bag in, I called my Julie to help and as she pulled, I pushed, and we got it in. *Phew! His endurance.*

Our flight was at 4:40 and I wanted to get there two hours ahead of time. Driving into the airport, I looked down at the time, and it was exactly 2:40. I took that as a major God wink with everything I had going on that day, from getting bags packed and loaded, getting four kids ready, and dealing with work-related issues, and to get there at the perfect time was like God saying, *Nik, relax. I got you!* And we had the most enjoyable, trouble free flight. As we got into the airport in Nigeria, someone was holding a paper with my name on it, letting me know my hubby was there to get us. *His comfort.*

Dear God, may we seek and find Your solutions, comfort, direction, endurance, wisdom and love. Amen.

KEEP CALM—YOU'RE ROLLING WITH GOD

HEARING FROM GOD

I write a lot about feelings as the way God mostly communicates with us, pretty much wordlessly, but about four times, I heard a voice. The words always come like as if someone is whispering in my ear. My first experience of it was when I was driving along a major highway one day and the words, "You are loved!" were quietly whispered to me. I got this wonderful, blissful feeling all through my body.

The next time, funny enough, was on that same highway when I was about to change lanes without checking out my blind spot, when again the whispered voice said in an urgent manner, "DON'T GO!" and turns out that there was a speeding vehicle I hadn't seen. Those two words probably saved my life that day.

Another time was when I was pregnant with our last son, Joshie, our little surprise from God, that at first, I was not thrilled about at all. In fact, I was depressed about it. Emmie, our first son, suffered from eczema to the point of always itching and scratching himself until he bled, so the thought of going through that experience again with another child was scary. That was until one day as I walked out of our kitchen, the whispered voice said, "One day you will understand why."

From that moment, I was no longer depressed. I was happy knowing God wanted me to have this child. Joshie is now six, and he has become our little love child from God. Recently after a trip, I gave all the kids awards and Joshie got the prize for kindness. The way he treated and cared for a little friend traveling with us impressed me. He has brought so much joy into our lives, along with the rest of our kids.

Moral: God's always speaking to us—mostly through our spirit, feelings, impressions and nudges of ideas popping into our heads. Also, through books, magazine articles, billboards, and other people. His ways of speaking to us are endless. Our job is to be attentive and learn His voice through spending quality alone time with Him. The more and more time I spend in my appointments with Him, the clearer His voice becomes that I know with one glance at Him, what *He* would have me to do.

Dear God, may we get better at knowing Your voice every day, living happy, peaceful and joyful lives, focused on Your Presence with us in every moment. Amen.

KEEP CALM—YOU'RE ROLLING WITH GOD

Day 34 — Live in God, Live in Love

WHAT A GREAT DAY I HAD

Wow! God is too much! I've been a little bit overwhelmed lately by a big project I need to complete. I'm such a procrastinator, and I looked for every excuse not to get it done. I vented that I've had enough lessons from God who seems to always know what we need to help us grow, but this lesson was such a good one. Are you ready to hear about it? Here it is:

Life is a journey with God, and He uses everything—the good, the bad and the ugly—to help us become stronger, better, wiser and to show us that we *can* trust Him with our lives.

My Facebook friend, Christie, introduced me to *Jesus Calling* by Sarah Young, and although I purchased several copies, I gave them all away because at the time I was so in love with a different meditation book. One Sunday, when my mom was visiting us, she asked me to take her to Wal-Mart, and while I waited for her, I decided to pick up another copy and every day I've been reading a little bit of it and I finally get the message of the book: *God is our constant Companion!*

I've written a lot about having a sweeter and closer walk with God, but this book puts it in a way that I understand and I've seen it first hand in a work project that I'm working on. As I let go of my anxieties and turn the project over to God, asking for His direction, I've found incredible clarity as what to do each step of the way and everything is miraculously falling right into place. And now a once overwhelming project is now under control! Here's only one paragraph from this book:

"You will never be in control of your life circumstances, but you can relax and trust in My (God's) control. Instead of striving for a predictable, safe lifestyle, seek to know Me in greater depth and breath. I long to make your life a glorious adventure, but you must stop clinging to old ways. I am always doing something new within My beloved ones. Be on the lookout for all that I have prepared for you."

Our Father, may we trust in Your sovereign control of our lives. Amen.

KEEP CALM—YOU'RE ROLLING WITH GOD

Day 35 — Live in God, Live in Love

A TRIP TO THE POST OFFICE

It was October 1st and even though I was in the US, I told my hubby/boss that I was taking the day off from work to celebrate Nigeria's Independence Day. I promised some friends to send them my meditation book, *Jesus Calling* and I also decided to send Oprah Winfrey's book, *What I Know For Sure.* Inside a book to my Facebook friend, Salzonia, in South Africa, I started ugly crying as I wrote: "What I know for sure? God Himself was behind me sending that friend request to you."

Sal has been my biggest supporter from the very beginning of writing these blog posts. In fact, she was one of the very first people I discussed writing them with and from day one, she has encouraged me. Over five years later, she's still my biggest cheerleader, this time to finish my book. When I call her sometimes, she stops whatever she's doing so that she could give me feedback on my writing and with specific examples of how they've helped her in her life. *God's too much!*

Next, I'm inside the post office, and I'm talking to the lady helping me send the packages. She asked if I was attending an Oprah Winfrey event happening later that month in our area, and I told her I wouldn't be going, but she should go. She said that she would like to attend, but the ticket prices are too high for her and that she doesn't know her life's purpose. I told her that I believe she does know what her purpose is, but she must find space in her life to do it, like me—the wannabe book writer who hasn't written any books. I gave her an extra copy of the Oprah book I had in my car, and I wrote inside that one: "What I know for sure? We roll with God, and all things are possible with Him. Make it happen!"

Then in line right behind me, a gentleman shows up, and he's holding in his hand his book that was recently published that he was mailing out. The post office lady says to him that I want to write a book, too, and before leaving, he talks to me and says, "There's no coincidence I'm meeting you today. God sent me here with a message for you. Stop procrastinating, stop making excuses, and write your book."

Dear God, give us the wisdom, courage, faith, strength and endurance to fulfill Your purpose for our lives. Amen.

KEEP CALM—YOU'RE ROLLING WITH GOD

Day 36 — Live in God, Live in Love

"REMEMBER TO IGNORE MOMMY, TOO...

... She will mess up my life." Can you guys believe this is from my beautiful, sweet, responsible, smart daughter, Ember? I had a good laugh from my little drama mama. *And I thought I was one!* But she's on to something here, as I believe learning to be a professional ignorer (kindly and respectfully, of course) is one of the best lessons to master. Ember is a super daughter and she surprises me sometimes with her thoughtfulness and caring nature. Sometimes she gets a little crazy on me, but I've learned to ignore her, too. And when she calms down she always comes back, "I'm sorry, mommy." If I allowed the mood of her, my other kids and my wonderful hubby to determine my happiness, I'd be institutionalized by now!

And that ignoring goes for everyone! If my hubby does something I may not like, I try to ignore him because like my daughter, he does so much that's right that when he messes up, I don't make a big deal about it; they're allowed, they're human. *I also do my share of messing up!*

I'm learning to become a gentler and more patient version of myself, going a little easier on everyone in my life. No one is perfect, and not everything is something to fight about. Things will not always go our way or be done the way we want them. Choose your battles wisely. Let's focus on the positives in each other. "Weak people revenge. Strong people forgive. Intelligent people ignore." Truly one of my secrets for living a joy filled life!

And from my meditation book, *The Imitation of Christ*: "Try, my child, to do the will of another rather than your own. Always choose to have less rather than more. Always seek to take the last place, and to be subject to everyone. Always desire and pray that the will of God be perfectly fulfilled in you. Behold, a person so disposed, enters within the confines of peace and quiet."

Dear God, may we be the loving, humble, kind, and forgiving people You would have us to be. Amen.

KEEP CALM—YOU'RE ROLLING WITH GOD

A GOD WINK RIGHT BEFORE TAKE-OFF

Late one night, boarding a flight and walking towards my assigned seat, I started thinking about a situation and how embarrassed I was over it. *I can never show my face again,* I thought to myself (I can be so dramatic!). Just before sitting down, my hubby hands me my cell phone, which he had kept for the previous few hours and said that I should power it off. *Can't you do that?* I wanted to ask, but instead I took it from him and turned it off myself. Then I got a feeling to turn it back on and read a little from my meditation book, *Jesus Calling.* I opened right up to November 14's devotional: "Those who look to him (God) are radiant; their faces are never covered with shame. - Psalm 34:5"

Thanks, God, for the perfectly tailored reminder at the perfect time. *Head up, Nik, nobody's perfect!* God, our Heavenly Father, knows the worst of us but loves us unconditionally. His grace (complete and total forgiveness and acceptance) is freely given to us in every moment. We simply have to accept it, keeping our eyes fixed on Him. Nothing can separate us from His love! We are all on a path of growth and unfoldment so, therefore, we can hold our heads high knowing we all have our failures, struggles, shameful moments, weaknesses and wounds. Whenever I'm not the person I strive to be, I'm learning to immediately accept God's grace, pick myself up, dust myself off and keep going, committed to doing better next time.

"Therefore, there is no condemnation for those who are in Christ Jesus (God)" (Romans 8:1).

Again, I'm in awe of God! There I was feeling humiliated, and He found a way to get me to read that excellent message, proving again how much He loves me, how intimately involved He is in all my moments, and how He incredibly knows every thought I think. God's in complete and total control of everything! I ended up having the best flight ever. Even during the turbulent times when the fasten seat belts signs turned on, I was relaxed, worried about nothing, knowing God was right there with me.

Dear God, as we look to You, may our faces never be covered in shame, remembering that no one is perfect. May we always accept Your constant grace and forgiveness. Amen.

KEEP CALM—YOU'RE ROLLING WITH GOD

Day 38 — Live in God, Live in Love

"DO YOU REMEMBER WHEN YOU BOUGHT ME THIS PURSE LAST SUMMER?"

I said to another magnificent gift/friend from God.

We were buying shoes when I fell in love with a black handbag. "I must buy this!" I said to her, and she insisted that she wanted to pay for it because she hadn't bought anything for me in a long time (by the way, this is the same friend who I have arguments with over who's nicer between she and I). I kept this purse in my closet for an entire year, waiting for a special occasion to use it until I finally took it down to attend the memorial service for a friend's sister.

Fast forward two days later, we're watching the show *Empire*, a hit TV show in the US, that we pay to watch and download all the way in Nigeria. We had started on episode 1, maybe a month before this, and that very week we watched episode 8. Of all the millions of purses in the world, one of the main characters, "Anika," has my exact bag, only in a different color.

Now many of you may say this is a coincidence, but I say it's a God wink, with Him fully reminding me that there are no accidents and He is in complete control of everything. I can, therefore, *relax* and trust that His unseen Presence is a constant behind the scenes of my life. So many times I pulled down this purse, but would always put it back. For me to pull it out the very week, we're watching that episode was my big miracle of the day. I'll never forget seeing Anika holding that purse in front of her for a few seconds so that I could clearly see it was the same one.

Marianne Williamson brilliantly explains what had happened in *A Year of Miracles:*

"The universe is both self-organizing and self-correcting. The invisible hand that makes our heart beat and our lungs breathe is at work on multidimensional levels, arranging not only the extraordinary physical processes that keep us alive, but also what we experience: insights, relationships, improbable meetings, creative moments, falling in love, emotions and consciousness, and miraculous occurrences."

Dear God, thank You for all Your touches of love that remind us that Your Presence is with us in every moment of our lives. Amen.

KEEP CALM—YOU'RE ROLLING WITH GOD

"KEEP LOOKING YOUNGER AND HAPPIER"

I said this to a friend, even though she said I'm looking older (LOL!). God surprised her with twins, and I enjoyed every moment holding them and thanking God it's her, not me that He surprised. I don't see her too often, but it seems as if every time I do see her, I leave a changed person. She always gives me a fresh way of looking at my life. She's very wise and brutally honest, as you can tell, and what she said to me was my big miracle of the day. There I was complaining to her about something I've complained about for years to God, and by the time I left her, I was thanking God for it.

I love all my relationships on an entirely different level lately, and I'm filled with joy. Having my appointments with God have made such a difference. He's teaching me such valuable lessons like humility, patience, loving extravagantly, forgiving endlessly, overlooking the faults of others, calming down, focusing on the positives, enjoying every sacred moment, not sweating the small stuff, and being grateful for everyone in my life. My joy of God is spreading to my joy of people.

I love a book I'm reading, *The Joy of Intimacy with God*, by Dr. Bill Bright. He writes:

"If you are struggling with relationships in your family, in your workplace, or in your established friendships, the first place you should check is how you're getting along with God. As you remain in Him with every part of your being, you are fully dependent upon Him... Your relationships become richer. Your work becomes more excellent."

So true! My relationships have become richer, and I caught myself smiling at work, totally thrilled to be there working with God as my Partner. Seeking His advice on what to do from moment to moment brought excitement to even my most boring work that I hate doing. Ideas flowed as to what He would have me to do. I enjoy the people I work with, and I try to encourage a happy work environment where we give our best, working for God, not man.

Our Father, may our relationship with You grow stronger every day as we reflect Your love in all our relationships. Amen.

KEEP CALM—YOU'RE ROLLING WITH GOD

Day 40 — Live in God, Live in Love

GOD DID IT AGAIN...

He continues to blow me away with His close involvement in our lives. At exactly 10:53 a.m., I had the following conversation with a fellow Facebook blog writer/friend, Vincent:

Vincent: You see, I have learned a great deal from you and your posts. I see that you don't complain about the way others treat you, but rather you live in such a way that it reflects on them how they ought to treat you. They see the light in you and just change on their own. Wow!

Me: You're giving me God winks today because I said to my friend Sal this morning: "Our lights must shine!" We have to be God's representatives.

Vincent: I realized that what God wants for us is to live in such a way that even in silence, someone can be inspired and serve God. Yeah...one day, I can remember now, but I was just thinking, and a thought like a voice came to me, and said, "Look, this thing you want to do, this writing you are doing and teaching others how to live, you must live it yourself because people are watching you, if you don't live it, you are a fraud. It startled me. And since then, I try to watch myself. I have to catch myself doing wrong.

Me: A lady said to me a few weeks ago, "I've been watching you." I was at my children's school fair picking up garbage and doing whatever I could to help, and she was there looking at me. Trust me—they are watching!

An hour later, my alarm for my 12 p.m. appointment with God sounded, and this is when God blew me away as if He had something He wanted to add to Vincent and my conversation. I got the feeling to continue reading from where I last left off in Tim Storey's book, *Comeback and Beyond:*

"The way you act and the choices you make influence everyone around you, even those you least expect to influence. You may not be ...

GOD DID IT AGAIN...

aware of who is watching you, and only years later hear of the impact you had on their life. What will the next generation see in you? What do the people around you see in you? If you want the next generation of believers not to cover or back down, to fight for their comebacks, to cover each other's weaknesses and lift each other up, and to stand strong in the midst of crisis, then we need to show them how it's done. We need to walk the talk. Is what we say we believe what the people in our lives see us living?"

Dear God, May we become a generation of people who are strong and courageous and who support and encourage each other. Amen.

KEEP CALM—YOU'RE ROLLING WITH GOD

Day 41 — Live in God, Live in Love

"HOLD MY HEAD UP HIGH, I'LL STAND TALL"

Were the words I fell in love with from the Boyz to Men's song, *I Will Get There,* while working on my book again until about 2 a.m.

It has to be in a particular format and instead of wasting time complaining about it, I'm doing what my DVD exercise trainer, Shaun T, has taught me – to dig deep, having the endurance for exercising as well for my life. Honestly, I've become very lazy, but I've decided today that I will accept God's invitation to play life at a higher level and areas where I've been weak, I will become strong.

And about this playing life at a higher level, God has challenged me again through the rapper, Prince EA, to answer a vital question: *"Who am I in the deepest sense?"* He spoke about us being loyal to conditioned thoughts passed on from generation to generation. Thoughts that we're so loyal to that we've fought over, killed over, gotten angry, sad and depressed over. *Me included!* I get sad and depressed over the same crazy thoughts over and over again. *I've had enough!* I'm going to the next level of focusing on important goals like bringing humanity closer to God, seeing my children grow up to be the superhumans they're capable of becoming, helping my husband take our businesses to new levels of success, and becoming the most awesome version of me.

That means no more constantly thinking crazy thoughts such as worry, fear, and insecurity; They're not becoming of superhumans rolling with God! Instead we pray, work hard and let God worry, doing our best and leaving the rest with Him. That also means we're spiritually and mentally disciplined to new levels of thinking about our lives, goals, dreams, and aspirations and we're constantly, constantly, constantly catching ourselves when we find ourselves thinking negatively and saying, *No, no, no! We're not going there!* and reprograming our minds with new thoughts with the best and most beautiful outcomes.

We must beat our minds with a stick, becoming mentally disciplined, focused and strong like John Joseph taught me.

I can already see my husband and me at our kids' college graduations and me doing significant work in the world for God. I have faith and like the Boyz to Men song says, "I will get there!"

"Hold my head up high, I'll stand tall. And I swear this time I won't fall."

Dear God, help us to dig deep and become the superhumans You intended for us to be. Amen.

KEEP CALM—YOU'RE ROLLING WITH GOD

INNOCENT, I TOLD YOU GOD IS OUR BOSS

Innocent is a smart, loyal, young man who works with us, and I gave him my whole speech about always putting in your best into everything you do. I tell him to work as if he's working for God, not for man, as all our blessings are ultimately from Him. People can disappoint you, but God never disappoints! A company that you work for today can say to you tomorrow, "I'm sorry, but we don't need your services." However, if every day you went into that company wanting to learn, grow, become better, you can go to another company more qualified for a better position or even start your own business.

I told him how I see myself as my hubby's helper as we work together, and I always want to do my best because I believe that's what God has called me to do as his wife. And because I give my best, God has given me His best! I have a great family, and I don't take that for granted, especially after our last checkup, and the doctor said, "You have healthy kids. I don't know what it is, maybe you have good hygiene, but they're very healthy."

Hearing that from a doctor who deals with sick kids all day made me appreciate that statement so much more. The doctor may not know, but I know that my healthy kids are a blessing from God, including His wisdom about how to take care of them. *God, I'm stupendously grateful!* Now that we're back in Nigeria from a summer in Florida and the kids are back in school, we start cooking at 5:30 in the morning so that they can have a fresh breakfast and lunch with as many vegetables incorporated as possible.

So, a few hours after the speech to Innocent, I was about to leave work when I remembered that I didn't have my 5 p.m. appointment with God. I opened *Jesus Calling*, and the 2nd date I turned to said:

"APPROACH THIS DAY WITH AWARENESS OF WHO IS BOSS. As you make plans for the day, remember that it is I who orchestrate the events of your life."

Seeing that *"BOSS"* show up out of the blue like that was another God wink when once again everything lined up a little bit too perfectly.

Heavenly Father, may we live lives with the constant awareness that You are our ultimate Boss, being the people You would have us to be in every moment. Amen.

KEEP CALM—YOU'RE ROLLING WITH GOD

Day 43 — *Live in God, Live in Love*

"DON'T STRESS LIFE—CAN YOU EXPLAIN WHAT YOU MEAN BY THIS?"

I was asked, after opening up in a previous blog post about a stalker incident that pushed me to move to Nigeria. It was all so perfect that I said I don't stress life anymore. I would like to meet that person and give them a big hug and kiss because they've changed my life for the better, bringing me so much closer to God than I ever thought possible. I believe everything, the good, the bad and the ugly are all there to help us become the people God would have us to be. *God, I'm really, really, really on to you!* And, I'm wondering if we are in control of anything because everything seems to be a little bit too perfect at times.

That night, I got a feeling to download another book by Robin Sharma, *Daily Inspirations from The Monk Who Sold His Ferrari*. And within a few minutes of randomly selecting dates to read, I was freaked out again by the following written for March 25: "You are far greater than you have ever dreamed of being. And no matter what you are experiencing in your life right now, trust that all is good and unfolding in your best interests. It may not look pretty, but it is exactly what you need to learn for you to grow into the person you have been destined to become. Everything occurring in your life has been perfectly orchestrated to inspire your maximal evolution as a human being and bring you into your true power."

Looking back at the whole stalker incident, and the ugliness of it all, with the calls beginning a few hours before I was scheduled to give birth to our fourth child by C-section, I now realize they were wake-up calls to my new life with me eventually relocating my family from the United States to Nigeria to fight for my family. And in Nigeria is where I developed a closer walk with God and began writing these blog posts every day. They were all good, and I needed those calls to grow me up to where I am today. I can now confidently say, "Don't stress life!" because no matter what you're going through, you're going to be okay. It's only God's way of growing you up.

Dear God, may we use all the challenges that come our way as inspiration to become greater than we have ever dreamed of being. When we fall, help us to get back up, dust ourselves off and keep going with You as our Partner and Guide. Amen.

KEEP CALM—YOU'RE ROLLING WITH GOD

Day 44 — Live in God, Live in Love

GOD IS TOO MUCH

While in Orlando on vacation and needing to drive to Miami (about four hours away), the people at our hotel initially said they could help us load our luggage back on top of our vehicle. As some nice hotel staff tried to assist us, a manager came out and said due to liability reasons, they couldn't help us any further. Thankfully, though, they had already gotten the bags on top and strapped down to the point that we could drive somewhere close by for further help.

For a while, we had been planning to go to a certain restaurant for breakfast but never made it, so we decided that very morning we would go. With the bag situation to handle, I decided to drop everyone off at the restaurant. Leaving there, I remember debating whether to go left or right, and the feeling was to go left. On the very next property to the left, was a maintenance guy with a leaf blower. I got another feeling to ask him if he would be able to assist me, and he agreed, taking me back to meet with one of his co-workers, incredibly a former truck driver. They both expertly strapped the bags on top and we made it back to Miami safely.

Here's the deal: this was an important reminder that problems will come up in life, but we don't handle them alone. God is our unfathomable Helper! He placed the perfect people on my path to assist me once again. All those days we debated on going to that restaurant, we picked the perfect morning to go. I'm learning to take life one step at a time, paying attention to God's direction and its so mind blowing to me how *deeply involved* He is in every aspect of my life. It was as if He said, *Nik, you need some bags strapped down? No problem, I got you! Just talk to this guy here!*

"Whether you turn to the right or to the left, your ears will hear a voice behind you, saying, 'This is the way; walk in it.'" - Isaiah 30:21

Our Father, may we always follow where You are leading us. Amen.

KEEP CALM—YOU'RE ROLLING WITH GOD

"STILL?"

It was just the inspiration I needed from one of our biggest customers and my fellow God Maniac after I told him that I'm in the process of STILL working on my book. Funnily enough, I had called my friend Sal, in South Africa, for a needed pep talk to push me to get our book done and she told me to take my time. "That's not the motivation I need right now!" I said to her, laughing, and this unbelievable person, with this one word gave me the push I was looking for.

And speaking of this fellow God maniac, every time I'm around him, I always pick up some valuable lesson. Like the time he blew me away when he said, "I want to remember God every moment." Or the other time he taught me, "God loves the humble." And let me tell you, I write these posts and live my life asking, *How may I serve and what can I give?* and God then seems to ask me, *Nik, how may I serve you?* Remember, we're not going by the ordinary rules of man!

What was the lesson the last time I saw him? To be exceedingly grateful for everything. I gave him a bottle of water and he said, "I'm grateful!" and told me that being extra thankful in every moment of life is so important. So now, I'm not complaining about anything. Instead, I'm grateful for everything and whenever I think about complaining, I switch those thoughts to all my blessings. Even for a smile, I thank God. "When life gives you a hundred reasons to cry, show life that you have a thousand reasons to smile." —Stephenie Meyer

Taking a bath that evening and finding only cold water: *God, I'm grateful!*

Dear God, thank You for the 10,000 things You are always doing for us and may we never take any of them for granted. Amen.

KEEP CALM—YOU'RE ROLLING WITH GOD

Day 46 — Live in God, Live in Love

A BIRTHDAY TO REMEMBER

It started with me waking up about 3:45 a.m. to get out early to go and wait in line to renew Joshie's passport. Ember, who woke up on her own and insisted she would go with us, met me in the hallway. Honestly, I say every day is my birthday, but I felt extra blessed by God with a daughter who stuck with me the entire day and was such a great help. She first kept a space for me in line as I parked the car, and all day she was my little assistant doing her best to help me wherever she could.

It turns out the space she held in line was exactly where God wanted us, next to a fascinating lady, also urgently needing to get her passport renewed. As we sat on the ground next to her, I overheard her say that everything happens for a reason and that got my attention because I say the same thing all the time. We ended up having a marvelous conversation. We were talking about God and at one point, she said, "I don't go to church much, but I know His Presence goes with me." That freaked me out a bit and I showed her my screensaver for the last month or so: "And the Lord replied, 'My Presence will go with you and I will give you rest.'"

For this stranger to repeat the message of my screensaver was no coincidence; it was God letting me know that I was exactly where He wanted me at that moment, with everything lining up a little bit too perfectly!

Later, she came to tell me that we still had at least another two hours to go, if I wanted to take the kids for something to eat. I declined and said I would hang around and not take any chances of missing them calling our number. Instead, we ate some snacks in our car. Once we got back, she said, "I've been looking for you! You said you weren't going out, so I brought lunch back for you and the kids." It felt as if God Himself sent that meal for us that day. I was so touched, and I couldn't stop hugging her and thanking her for her kindness. *It was a birthday lunch sent by God.*

Dear God, thank You for all the angels You send into our lives to remind us that Your Presence is always with us. Amen.

KEEP CALM—YOU'RE ROLLING WITH GOD

Day 47 — Live in God, Live in Love

"GOD'S GRACE IN ACTION"

Was my reply to a friend after she sent me an excellent reminder about God's grace (His help, favor, acceptance, joy and every possible good) in our lives.

It had been a week filled with lots of grace. It was a rough one, but one of the best ones as I was constantly reminded over and over and over again that I'm never alone and God is my extraordinary Helper in every area of my life. *I felt overwhelmingly loved by God.*

Emmie, my then seven-year-old, started racking up lots of "dots" for misbehaving in his class. That week, he asked me to accompany him to his class and see all his stars, *no dots.* Joshie, who used to give me such a hard time in the mornings to get dressed for school, is now the first one going to the car. He too is thrilled about stars and wanting to become the student of the month - at then four years old.

A friend called when I was having a terrible moment, and I didn't want to talk to her because I didn't want any of her *stinking positive advice*, but she kept calling. I started crying because it was as if she knew something was wrong the way she kept calling. She said, "Nikki, what's wrong? You're going to make me cry, too." And it turns out, her stinking positive advice was exactly what I needed. She said, "Keep your focus on God. He can turn any situation around, just keep praying." I told her some silly thoughts I was having, and she said, "You're joking, right?" and those words were the reality check I needed to get back to my senses.

Another friend insisted on seeing me, and she reminded me that I have so much to be thankful for because things could be so much worse. God's grace in action, as I'm in Nigeria away from all my family in the Bahamas, but He has placed some awesome people in my life.

Then it was another person who showed up to assist me with a different issue I had going on; they gave me the perfect advice and once again I was reminded that God is indeed my unfathomable Helper in every aspect of my life. I simply should calm down, do my best in what I must do and trust Him to deal with the rest. Worried about nothing, praying about everything. *God, I'm grateful!*

"Pray, then allow God to worry."

Our Father, may our faith in You grow deeper every day. Amen.

KEEP CALM—YOU'RE ROLLING WITH GOD

Day 48 — Live in God, Live in Love

"THERE WILL BE MISUNDERSTANDINGS..."

"...Every family has its cross, its suffering. Always be the first to forgive with a smile. Be cheerful, be happy."

It was as if God knew I would need this quote from Mother Teresa. My wonderful friend, Sal, whom I've never met, has taken on the enormous task of putting the posts in the date order for our book of daily reminders. I thought the 400 old posts I had given her would be enough, but she said that I should dig some more out and send them to her. Thanks for taking this so serious, my love! Out of the 100-plus I dug out that day, this post, where I included this quote, resonated so much with me, that I reposted it again on my Facebook wall, not knowing that I would need this reminder.

"God didn't say come and carry your beach chairs," as a quote I love says, "He asks us to carry our cross and through it all He will be our Joy and our Strength." Every family has misunderstandings and we all have our crosses to bear, but I look at each one as my assignment from God to show up as the best me possible. And I messed up. I'm gorgeously human.

It took one hug from a special two-year-old that God has placed in my life to remind me how blessed I am. Out of nowhere, he came behind me and hugged my legs. I hadn't seen him in a while, so that hug was extra special as if he was saying, *Aunty Nikki, I missed you!* in his own little way.

God, "Your works are wonderful, I know that full well" (Psalm 139:14, NIV). I will do my best to be a light for you in this world, forgiving quickly and loving extravagantly, knowing that everything is between You and me.

I didn't join my family in the Sunday brunch of diet-unfriendly foods, but I exercised, instead. Afterward, I came in happy with that decision and spent some time laughing and joking with them. I told them that when their dad met me, I was looking good, exercising every day, that when we met, he got on his knees quick and prayed, "Thank You, God, for helping me find my wife!"

"Be cheerful, be happy."

Dear God, may we live joyful lives close to You, despite our crosses, forgiving quickly and loving extravagantly, learning to be patient with ourselves and others, always reminded that nobody's perfect. Amen.

KEEP CALM—YOU'RE ROLLING WITH GOD

Day 49 — Live in God, Live in Love

"I'M LATCHING ON TO YOU"

It's my love song to God. The Creator of the entire universe unconditionally loves and cares about me! *How mind-blowing is that?* And like Mother Teresa said, we can each say that with such confidence. My Song to Him from *Latch* by Sam Smith goes,

> "You lift my heart up when the rest of me is down,
>
> You, You enchant me even when You're not around,
>
> If there are boundaries, I will try to knock them down,
>
> I'm latching on ... now I know what I have found."

And lift my heart is exactly what God did again when I was having a terrible day where I wanted to crawl under the covers and hide from the world. Life can get messy sometimes, and I was feeling so depressed and hurt like the whole inside of me was shriveling up. I had planned a date with a friend, and I so badly wanted to cancel it, but I felt that I should go. I got so busy getting my kids ready that I missed my 12 p.m. appointment with God. As soon as I got to my friend's house, I remembered and decided to go to her bookshelf to pick out something inspirational to read. I selected, of all the books there, Joel Osteen's *Your Best Life Now* and miraculously I randomly opened to the following, as if God had this message planned and ready for me to read:

"Don't let bitterness take root. We all have unfair and unjust things happen to us; that's a part of life. When we are hurt, we can choose to hold on to that pain and become bitter, or we can choose to let it go and trust God to make it up to us."

I read the entire chapter, and I left my friend's house so happy and filled with *joy*, deciding to let go of the pain and trust God to make it up to me. The kids and I then joined my hubby for a fantastic evening having a barbecue with our staff.

God, who are we that You care so much about us? Thank You for Your comfort in our sad and painful moments. May we always latch on to You. Amen.

KEEP CALM—YOU'RE ROLLING WITH GOD

"WHEN YOU TALK LIKE THAT...

...I'm learning to become a professional ignorer."

No, he didn't use my line back on me, my hubby, that is! He sure did, and we both had a good laugh about it. To be honest, I'm very thrilled with my professional ignorer now, and a big reason why is because I'm getting God involved with every aspect of my life, including my marriage. I have my moments, but when I go to God in those 1,000 daily decisions, I'm calming down, choosing my battles wisely, and I, too, have become a professional ignorer (kindly and respectfully), forgiving quickly and loving extravagantly.

"God is our boss," is what I told my assistant today at work after she said that she appreciated the way I dealt with a customer. Again, getting God involved in every aspect of my life, I believe in doing the intuitively right and excellent thing in every moment example and experience and it's paying off. I'm blown away by many new customers that show up to support us, who tell me that friends referred them. *God, I'm grateful!*

"Zero!" was the response of my nephew, Duro, when I asked him to grade me on a scale of 1 to 10 on a fun scale. But, even in the parenting department where I have so many decisions to make on a daily basis, I'm learning to run to God. I have a new strategy to focus on their positives and build them up more often and focus less attention on the negative. They're such great kids, but sometimes tiger mom gets a little carried away with the constant and never-ending improvement stuff.

Moral: Get God involved with every aspect of your life! He is our constant Companion, and His guidance and wisdom is the best. Sometimes it's hard to follow His direction, especially when He's asking us to forgive and be our most loving selves, when we want to attack someone. But, when we stick with Him is when we experience miracles in our lives. As I write this, I'm thanking God for healing my once broken heart. It's not only completely mended, but it's also better than before. I've decided not to dwell on unpleasant things. And it's as if I've awakened to a new life. Trust those feelings, always going with the decision that brings you peace when you think about it and stay on the high road with God.

Dear God, may we keep our eyes fixed on You, seeking Your guidance in the 1,000 decisions we make every day. Amen.

KEEP CALM—YOU'RE ROLLING WITH GOD

NIKKI, YOU'RE NOT HAVING A SUBWAY SANDWICH TODAY

That was me talking sternly to myself, walking past the Subway counter inside BJ'S Wholesale Club. Ten seconds later: "Can I please have a steak and cheese sub on flatbread." The Sriracha hot sauce was calling me, and I couldn't resist! I filled it up with lots of veggies, though, and I shared half of it.

But it's all good because I had a moment with the cheerful, young lady making that sandwich, as by the time she asked me what I wanted on it, I was crying. I was reading Oprah Winfrey's book, *What I Know For Sure*, that I had purchased and one sentence got me all teary eyed. It was BeBe Winans who unexpectedly showed up at Oprah's house one day "after a particularly difficult setback," and said, "Girl, I just came to remind you, you don't have to carry this load all by yourself," after singing to Oprah her favorite spiritual: "I surrender all. I surrender all. All to Thee, my blessed Savior, I surrender all."

This, I took as a God wink, as that has been the biggest lesson of the week for me: remembering that it is God and me who handle everything together, not Nikki alone and simply learning to surrender the details of my life to Him.

I ended up giving the lady at Subway that copy of Oprah Winfrey's book, feeling that everything that happened up until that point was all for me to have that moment with her, such as the long wait time to get a temporary pass to shop at this store, to the time I took to have an appointment with God inside the book section, reading my meditation book, all perfectly led to me meeting her. The excitement and huge smile on her face showed her appreciation for the book and I'm praying that she learns some of the many important lessons I've picked up from Ms. Winfrey over the years. It's astounding how much God loves and cares for each one of us!

And my best and favorite lesson from Ms. Winfrey: *LISTEN* to God by trusting our inner voice to guide us before making any move.

Dear God, may our burdens bring us even closer to You, always reminded that You are there helping us to carry them. Amen.

KEEP CALM—YOU'RE ROLLING WITH GOD

Day 52 — Live in God, Live in Love

"THANK YOU, GOD, FOR THIS GOOD LIFE..."

...And forgive us if we do not love it enough." - Garrison Keilo

I woke up between my bad sleeping bubba boys (my then four and six-year-olds who still refuse to sleep in their room!), and I was so grateful to God for everything. I started kissing Emmie, and he covered his face to get me to stop, but I took that moment to thank God for him and my beautiful family.

The night before, I went to bed complaining about my day, but I caught myself. Things didn't go quite the way I wanted them to go, and my boss/hubby fussed me out the entire ride home on the phone. This time I listened, knowing that sometimes we all must bear some harsh words from our bosses. I called him back a few hours later, telling him how much I love him, even though he's my pain in the rump.

He rightly questioned some decisions I made, but I know him so well now, that I know when he's upset is not the time to discuss anything. When he cooled down, I quietly and calmly justified those choices and assured him that every decision I make is from a place of wanting to do what's best for our family.

Feeling a little discouraged, in one of my appointments with God, I opened my meditation book to the perfect verse: "I have told you these things, so that in Me you may have [perfect] peace and confidence. In the world you have tribulation and trials and distress and frustration; but be of good cheer [take courage; be confident, certain, undaunted]! For I have overcome the world. [I have deprived it of power to harm you and have conquered it for you.]" - John 16:33 (AMP)

Dear God, may we be of good cheer—confident and unflinching—despite our tribulations, trials, and frustrations. Amen.

KEEP CALM—YOU'RE ROLLING WITH GOD

Day 53 — Live in God, Live in Love

WOW! HE DID IT AGAIN

Our customer and friend who changed my life when he came over for dinner one Sunday and every time I served him something, his response was always, "I'm grateful."

Now, I'm grateful has become my constant and favorite prayer to God and I catch myself all day smiling for no particular reason, bouncing around with gratitude for *everything*. I caught myself looking up at a tree and feeling so grateful for it. Instead of focusing on stuff that usually irritates me, I focus instead on being grateful. THOU SHALL NOT COMPLAIN!

Well, he has inspired me again when we sat for a few minutes chatting one evening. He's totally a God maniac, on another level than me. I said to him, "You know how some people run to God only when they have a difficulty or problem?" He ever so calmly said, "No, I don't know. I remember God every moment."

Wow! Guess what? Now I'm practicing trying to remember God every moment, too. Before speaking, I pause. *God, what would you have me to say here?* And throughout the day, I always keep in mind the words of my love song to God: "Anyway that I can please You, let me learn."

I'm practicing (and the key word here is *practicing*) being more focused on God from moment to moment. I'm making God a part of every aspect of my life. That means I have no fear, I don't worry, I forgive quickly and endlessly, I live kindly, I love extravagantly, I'm bouncing around with gratitude, and I live life trusting and having faith knowing God is always with me, letting go and going with God's flow for my life. *God, what would You have me to do here?*

A closer walk with Thee. This is the sweet life!

Our Beloved, help us to calm down, and remember You in every moment. Amen.

KEEP CALM—YOU'RE ROLLING WITH GOD

Day 54 — Live in God, Live in Love

THIS MADE ME CRY

After receiving my daily posts for about a month, a lovely person sent this message:

"Such profound truths Nikki. You are such an encouragement to me. Your love for God is visible in every line. I used to be in that place where I laid it all at God's feet. Wouldn't do a thing without seeking His will. Was lost in Him daily. You can say rolling with Him on a regular basis. Then I became overwhelmed by the incumbencies of work and daily living. It wasn't long before praying became a drag, and then I stopped talking to Him and began running my life on auto pilot, but He has never left me. I feel Him close even when I'm knee deep in sin. He has never left me. So, I ignore and carry on and would only reach out to Him in moments of crisis and confusion, and He always comes through for me. Every. Single. Time. He indeed loves me with an everlasting love.

Today, I decided to recommit to Him, to once again be so lost in Him that nothing else matters. I want to be at the center of His will all the time. Rolling with Him on the regular. I don't know why am sharing this with you, Nikki. But I know your heart pants after God. Please keep me in your prayers and thanks ever so much for the lovely capsules of truth. I'm encouraged by them. Thanks so very much, Nikki. God bless you."

Dear God, today, may we all commit to live a life closer to You. Amen.

KEEP CALM—YOU'RE ROLLING WITH GOD

Day 55 — Live in God, Live in Love

SUPERHUMAN: LET'S DO THIS

That was me at about 6 a.m. one morning trying to motivate myself to exercise, and I'm proud to say I completed my 25-minute goal. *Yayy! Go superhuman!*

But this challenge from God to become super people in the world, not going by the ordinary rules of man, is a big one and it's not easy. Physical discipline and telling my body it will exercise is one thing, but the spiritual discipline of trusting God in difficult circumstances—to love, forgive, and have mercy on ourselves and others, developing endurance and patience in trusting in God's timing when we want to give up—is totally on another level.

And this is why I'm trying not to be upset at a friend who ended her marriage. I even get why she never called me to discuss it because I do the same thing sometimes with a close friend, saying to myself, *I don't want any of her stinking positive advice.* So, I get it. But I also get that when we reach this superhuman level in our relationships, everything changes. To see the innocence in others and not their mistakes, to see all the good qualities and not just the ones we don't like, to accept that nobody's perfect and to love them anyway, and to overlook the unimportant, brings such joy to our lives. I'm not talking about regular joy; I'm talking about supernatural joy and peace that passes all understanding.

I love a text message I woke up to on my phone:

"Difficult times come to test the essence of true love. Love is not just about laughter and happiness. It needs to withstand difficulty to survive."

At about 4 a.m. one morning, it was my pleasure to make tea and toast for my hubby as he said to me, "Nik, I'm sticking with you." I told him that I'm sticking with him, too, and it was such a beautiful moment that I will cherish.

"Keep your eyes open to the beauty that surrounds you. God has placed many blessings upon your path. Gather them with joy."
– Maria Fontane, *Mottos For Success*

"Anyone can find the dirt in someone. Be the one who finds the gold" (Proverbs 11:27).

Our Lord, help us become the superhumans you have created us to be. Amen.

KEEP CALM—YOU'RE ROLLING WITH GOD

Day 56 — Live in God, Live in Love

"I'M STILL TALKING ABOUT YOU!"

I told my friend, chatting over the phone. I'll forever love and cherish her for all the wise advice she always has to offer me. *The woman is incredible!* One Saturday afternoon as I moped around depressed, she said to me, "Leave the past in the past!" Those six words have dramatically changed my life, and I wish I could jump through this page and shake you up if you're living your life focused on events of the past!

Honestly, I know this is a message I repeat a lot, but sometimes I find myself so happy, wondering if you guys are getting the message. This choice to leave the past in the past is a huge part of my happiness, and I want you here with me. It's as if I have amnesia of some sort, focused on moving forward, enjoying the sweet life with God in the present moment.

Here's the deal: We've all had stuff thrown at us in the past, but we can't stay focused on it. The way I look at it is that we're only here for like a mist and then we're gone. Life is way too short to be miserable, even for one minute! Last night I got upset with my daughter, Julie, but I forgave her quickly, and we had a hugging session. I could have stayed angry at her, but what's the point? I told her how I felt and we moved on. I don't want to stay mad at anyone for more than five minutes because it takes me away from enjoying my sweet life. Let's maximize every minute of our lives, forgiving quickly, leaving people in God's hands to deal with. Trust me, He's constantly working on every one of us!

To get here was not the work of one day either! It was always telling myself to shut up when my mind drifted towards the past and replacing the negative thoughts with positive ones, especially when it comes to stuff I've personally done in the past. I remind myself that when I fall off the wagon, to get right back on, committed to doing better the next time. Let's go to the next level of living!

"Do not let the past disturb you - just leave everything in the sacred heart and begin again with joy." — St. Mother Teresa

"Therefore, as God's chosen people, holy and dearly loved, clothe yourselves with compassion, kindness, humility, gentleness and patience." — Colossians 3:12

Dear God, may we remember that we are all just learning this art of being human. May we learn patience and be quick to forgive ourselves and others the way you forgive us. Amen.

KEEP CALM—YOU'RE ROLLING WITH GOD

Day 57 — Live in God, Live in Love

CAN I GET ALL MOTHER TERESA OUT ON YOU TODAY?

I'm such a nerd, getting all excited when I saw a book entitled, *Mother Teresa: Her Essential Wisdom*.

I love her closeness to God, exactly where I want all of us. Here are some of my favorite quotes from that book:

- "I can understand the greatness of God, but I cannot understand His humility. It becomes so clear in Him being in love with each one of us separately and completely. It is as if there is no one but me in the world. He loves me so much. Each one of us can say this with great conviction."

- "When you look at the inner workings of electrical things, you often see small and big wires, new and old, cheap and expensive, all lined up. Until the current passes through them, there will be no light. The wire is you and me. The current is God. We have the power to let the current pass through us, use us, produce the light of the world. Or we can refuse to be used and allow darkness to spread."

- "In God we live and move and have our being. It is God who gives life to all, who gives power and being to all that exists. But for His sustaining presence, all things would cease to be and fall back into nothingness. Consider that you are in God, surrounded and encompassed by God, swimming in God."

- "Don't allow anything to interfere with your love for Jesus (God). You belong to Him. *Nothing can separate you from Him.* That one sentence is important to remember. He will be your joy, your strength. If you hold onto that sentence, temptations and difficulties will come, but nothing will break you. *Remember, you have been created for great things.*"· "You can pray while you work. Work doesn't stop prayer and prayer doesn't stop work.

- "You can pray while you work. Work doesn't stop prayer and prayer doesn't stop work. It requires only that small raising of the mind to Him: *I love You God, I trust You, I believe in You, I need You now.* Small things like that. They are wonderful prayers."

KEEP CALM—YOU'RE ROLLING WITH GOD

Day 58 — Live in God, Live in Love

"EVERY CHOICE I MADE WAS BASED ON..."

"Does this feel right?"

"Does this feel right?"

"Is this going to help somebody?"

"That's not going to help somebody."

Oprah Winfrey said that in explaining why she believed her show was such a success for 25 years. And this is exactly where I want us in our lives, constantly going to God and asking for His input in the 1,000 decisions we make every day based on whether what we're considering feels right or not.

Case in point: I had a tough decision I needed to make and either way I went with it, I knew some people were not going to be pleased. But in going to God for His input late one night, in less than 30 seconds, I felt I knew exactly what He was directing me to do because I felt an overwhelming feeling of peace when I thought about that direction and a sense of uneasiness and stress when I thought about going the other way. I'm happy with that decision, and I know that it could be taken the wrong way by some people *(which it totally was)*. However, at the end of the day, we each have our lives to live and we must make decisions based on what we feel is best at that moment and where we feel God's directing us. *Following God's will is the thing to shoot for! Not other people's will for us!*

Know that you are never alone and God is always directing you. We have to pay attention to that inner voice asking: *Does this feel right? Does this feel right?*

And in going with the decisions that feel right, I believe that's God saying, *Yes, that's the way to go with this.* This strategy of listening to God has helped me in every area of my life. God is our ultimate Boss, and *He's an expert in everything.*

Dear God, may our most important goal in life be to follow Your leading in everything we do, being the people You would have us to be. Amen.

KEEP CALM—YOU'RE ROLLING WITH GOD

Day 59 — Live in God, Live in Love

"WHAT DID YOU GET FROM THAT?"

I curiously asked my daughter, Julie, after she agreed to have an appointment with God with me late one night. And her reply totally thrilled me: "I got that in life there will be many things we can worry about, but instead of worrying, we can trust God."

Woohoo! Wish I could've learned that at age 11! She's so right, though, God is teaching me that more and more every day with every experience that *I can really trust Him with my life* and I'm never alone, and anything that I would ever need is already waiting for me in the future, as He has shown me time and time again. I can, therefore, *relax,* focusing on being *calm* in every moment, listening to God, and enjoying my life's conversation and adventure with Him. *God, what is Your will for me?* is where I want to be, concerned about what God thinks of me, not other people.

One morning watching Oprah's *Super Soul Sunday* on OWN, I got a new way of looking at Psalm 23 which says, "The Lord is my shepherd; I shall not want," meaning I do not need to be anxious about anything because God is taking care of all my needs. I'm learning to be content in every moment, and whatever I don't have, I say that it's God will for me now *not* to have that. This has been such a valuable lesson of not only being content in every moment but being exceptionally grateful for everything I do have and taking nothing for granted.

Let's get closer and closer to God this year. *This is the best life!* Even with all the disappointments, hurts, frustrations, and problems, we can have the peace and joy that surpasses all understanding knowing we have God with us in every moment of every day guiding and directing us when we *relax, calm and slow down, pay attention, and listen to Him.*

Dear God, help us to bravely face whatever comes at us, trusting You are with us in every moment. Amen.

KEEP CALM—YOU'RE ROLLING WITH GOD

GOD, WHY DID YOU HAVE ME MEET THEM?

I've been asking Him lately. It all started one morning I took my kids to Target. Both of my sons had picked out two different toys for themselves, but when we got home, my youngest son was terribly upset that he didn't get the same one as his brother's.

I had to go to work, but on the way home, talking to my hubby, I asked his opinion as to whether I should get him the same toy, as well, because I had never seen him so upset before, keeping in mind that we don't want to spoil them. My hubby said to get it for him, and I stopped in Target after work that day to pick it up.

I remember wanting to use the restroom, and at one point I was about to turn around and go before getting the toy, but for some reason, I changed my mind and kept going for the toy first. I got it, paid, then went to the restroom. As I came out, checking out to leave were some people who I'd been calling for the previous past few weeks, who were not answering or returning any of my calls.

God is so funny because if I had gone to the restroom before then or shopped for some other items, I probably wouldn't have seen them. But God put them right in the checkout lane opposite the restrooms, making sure we saw each other.

Why? I kept asking. In my heart, I feel it was another lesson in being open to everything and attached to nothing. We were close to these people at one point, but after seeing them, I realized that was in the past and things had changed. They had moved on with their lives, and whether we liked it or not, *we were not included.* And, that's life. *No one is in our lives forever.*

It's a harsh lesson, but an important one and seeing them that day, the reality hit home. *Life now goes on without them.* For you, it may be a husband that left, a father that doesn't speak to you, a close friend that doesn't want to be friends anymore. But the Bible says even if our father and mother forsake us, God will never forsake us.

Father God, may we cherish the people in our lives, knowing that one day, we will have to say goodbye to all of them. Amen.

KEEP CALM—YOU'RE ROLLING WITH GOD

Day 61 — Live in God, Live in Love

THE BEST GOD-PLANNED VACATION EVER

One thing I love about rolling with God is that I never know what to expect from moment to moment. A summer was filled with lots of wonderful times all planned by God with lots of winks along the way, reminding me that I was exactly where He would have me to be. I had a surprise vacation for an entire month, and I enjoyed every bit of it as we *kept the plans tentative,* collaborating with God as to where to go, what to eat, and what to do. We Googled ideas of where to spend the day one day and came up with an amusement park. I think I had more fun than the kids, riding bumper boats, bumper cars, playing laser tag, miniature golf, and rock climbing. The bumper boats were my favorite, with us getting completely soaked and spraying water at strangers.

A friend shared this verse on her blog, and I can't stop thinking how this was probably written over 3,000 years ago, but sums up my relationship with God brilliantly: "Instead, You direct me on the path that leads to a beautiful life. As I walk with You, the pleasures are never-ending, and I know true joy and contentment" (Psalm 16:11, VOICE).

Here's the deal: everything is between God and us. That summer I had planned to work, but God took me on this extraordinary vacation that I'll never forget. I focus on giving Him my best in every moment, and He gives me His best, filling my life with tremendous blessings, like the beautiful kids and friends I spent that summer with.

Dear God, may we never take any of Your blessings for granted. May our lives be an example of your love in the world. Amen.

KEEP CALM—YOU'RE ROLLING WITH GOD

"I HAVE A TROUBLED MIND TONIGHT...

...Upcoming doctor's appointment, as well as questions regarding relationships. Worries over my children. Money issues. Oh, I can go on and on," was the comment I saw posted on Facebook.

I love The Messages' translation of Proverbs 3:5-12:

"Trust God from the bottom of your heart;
don't try to figure out everything on your own.
Listen for God's voice in everything you do, everywhere you go;
he's the one who will keep you on track.
Don't assume that you know it all. Run to God! Run from evil!
Your body will glow with health, your very bones will vibrate with life!
Honor God with everything you own; give him the first and the best.
Your barns will burst,
your wine vats will brim over.
But don't, dear friend, resent God's discipline;
don't sulk under his loving correction.
It's the child he loves that God corrects;
a father's delight is behind all this."

Here's the deal: we have the best Partner, Provider, Friend, Protector, Adviser, and Helper ever in God. *These verses are spot on!* We don't have to figure out everything on our own; listen to God by paying attention to those feelings and take life one step at a time, and little by little and piece by piece, He's the one to help you get everything back on track. I'm learning not to get overwhelmed by anything, but instead, stay in touch with God in the 1,000 decisions I make every day, and He hasn't led me wrong yet. Problems that once intimidated me are regarded as nothing now, knowing God is my Partner in handling them.

Moment to moment, I run to God as to the decisions to make, and I always go with what feels right and brings me peace when I think about it, doing my part and trusting that God is doing His part. *This strategy hasn't failed me yet!*

Dear God, remind us to keep our focus on You, and not our circumstances. Amen.

KEEP CALM—YOU'RE ROLLING WITH GOD

Day 63 — Live in God, Live in Love

A BIRTHDAY TO REMEMER (CONTINUED)

A security guard at the passport office that was so rude to me the day before, saw me hugging this woman when she gave me the lunch she surprised us with. I mistakenly came in thinking my appointment was on that Thursday, but it turned out it was the following week. When I tried explaining myself, he accused me of lying. I went back to the first guard I had spoken to and heard him say on the radio, "Don't let her in! She's lying!" I was extremely happy for him to see that even though he was rude to me, here was this stranger being *extra* kind to me and my kids by bringing us lunch and talking with us while we waited.

I felt so terrible about my mix up with the dates, so I asked God in a quick appointment how I messed up like that and I felt He said to me, *Follow where I lead you.* And, He led me on this path with lots of lessons, including to be gentle on myself and others when we make mistakes and to meet this lady who I felt God sent me to recruit to write her own blog. Her stories about God and her life were so interesting that I got goosebumps listening to her.

One story she told was about her mother. When her parents were splitting up, her father destroyed all the furniture in the house. Her mother then had to go and buy new furniture. At the furniture store, she met the owner and they eventually got married and have been together for over 20 years. When this woman got married, this man had become so close to her that her birth father walked her up half the aisle and her step-father the other half.

But this lesson of following God's leading has changed my life. I sent an email to a close family member who feels I allowed my husband to control me in a choice I made:

"I didn't feel God was directing me, and I followed where He was leading me, instead. It wasn't being controlled by my husband, but it was me being obedient and listening to God. I feel He has big plans for me and my marriage, bigger than we know right now. I will keep going where God is directing me, and hopefully, you all will understand one day why I continue to fight for my family."

Our Beloved, may we all learn Your voice and follow You wherever You lead us. Amen.

KEEP CALM—YOU'RE ROLLING WITH GOD

"GOD IS NOT A MAGICIAN"

A good friend and customer told me. I replied, "God's the Ultimate Magician who can make anything happen!" He and my husband were trying to persuade me to be more security conscious in Nigeria, but I'm sticking with my faith in God because He's my security: "God may kill me, but still I will trust Him" (Job 13:15, CEV).

This friend and I always have these God conversations, and I told him how God is intimately involved in all our moments. The next morning, in my appointment with Him, God confirmed He was there with us in that conversation. Sitting outside, reading a Bible devotional of over 700 pages, I randomly opened it to read:

"Scripture scholars tell us that Jesus came for an important mission—to proclaim the good news and make the Father known to the world. And because he did not want anything to distract Him from this primary mission, He had to dissuade people from turning Him into a *magician*. His miracles were aimed at helping people to believe in the power and love of God, and not to take their eyes of the target" (Bible Diary, 2014 edition).

Seeing that word *"magician"* show up and everything again lining up a little bit too perfect was my God wink. I guess that's why I'm not so concerned about my security because God is constantly reminding me that His Presence goes with me wherever I go, and He's a part of every moment of my life.

Just the night before, I had a moment where I wanted to scream, but instead, in having an appointment with God, I saw things from His perspective, and the crazy Nikki that wanted to make an appearance was sent away. I calmly dealt with the situation in a loving and peaceful manner, forgiving quickly, and I was happier for it. God is teaching me the true definition of love, which is not rude or unmannerly.

And, God's wisdom is the best wisdom, so slow down and go to Him in every decision. His ways are higher and better than our ways.

Dear God, may we learn to pay attention to even the slightest glimmers of Your Presence, reminding us that Your Presence is always with us. Amen.

KEEP CALM—YOU'RE ROLLING WITH GOD

Day 65 — Live in God, Live in Love

THIS IS MY TESTIMONY

I love my work! I get to share every day the first-hand testimony of God being a wife, mom, and person in the world today. *And let me tell ya, this is the best life with Him!* In fact, I'm feeling spoilt lately. Like I thought about having something special for our typical family Sunday brunch, and next thing I knew, my husband and Julie were off to the market to buy exactly what I wanted. *Spoilt, I say!*

"Beautiful (inside and out), smart, kind, hardworking, and close to God," is what I told my daughters I'm raising them to be. We spent some time washing and conditioning their natural hair and these times have become an opportunity to bond a little bit more with them. I told them how God has the most unimaginable plans for their lives and I want them learning God's voice and direction early, as He guides them on the most magnificent path He has set out for them.

If someone had told me 10 years ago that I would be living in Nigeria, surrounded by the most wonderful people, *enjoying and loving life,* I would have told them they were crazy. But God knew the plans He had for me, and I'm grateful to Him for exceeding my expectations.

Are you paying attention to the direction God is leading you? You do have a choice, to follow God's always brilliant guidance, or you can forget about God and go your own path, which I don't recommend. Like I told the girls, "Do good and good things happen. Do bad and bad things happen. It's always your choice." Even with challenges that WILL come our way, God is our Helper, assisting us little by little to get through them all. *"Greater is He!"*

Every decision I make, *big or small,* I get God involved. And I can't get over how His wisdom is always on point. I pay attention to those feelings always directing me as to what *He* would have me to do.

Dear God, we're grateful that the plans You have for us are good. Help us to stay close to You and follow the path You have designed for us. Amen.

KEEP CALM—YOU'RE ROLLING WITH GOD

"THIS IS IMPORTANT WORK WE'RE DOING HERE"

Danny showed up in my life early one year when she sent a message to me when her husband was caught cheating, and since then I've been encouraging her to fight for her family. Honestly, though, talking to her has helped me. In my years of marriage, I've always been this fretful wife, afraid that my husband would leave me for another woman (specifically, a younger woman), but as I encouraged her, I encouraged myself that we're to keep our eyes fixed on God. To stay on the difficult high road, being the best wives He has called us to be and to leave the rest with Him.

The Nikki who used to check her husband's phone constantly doesn't anymore. He's entitled to his privacy. The bottom line, though, after 15 years of marriage, I know he's not perfect, but I trust him and that the decisions he makes for our family are from a genuine space of wanting to do well for us. He has earned my love, trust, and respect. Problems we go through only bring us closer together.

But more importantly, *I trust God.* He is my number one love and priority! Even if my husband was to leave me, I'm secure in God. Every day, I do my part in being the best wife I can be, following God's leading. I see the best in my husband. I've surrendered my marriage to God. I've let go of trying to control what happens in our relationship. I keep my eyes fixed on God, taking life a quarter mile at a time and what He would have me to do from moment to moment, being my most loving, patient and forgiving self and I'm happier for it.

I love what I read in that morning's appointment with Him: "God has placed people around us to help us along life's path and hopefully teach us something about Himself. Though we hold them dear, we should hold them loosely. Our children, spouse, parents, and dearest friends, after all, belong to Him. And none of them were ever meant to fill the space that only He can fill. Surrender. You'll discover surprises you would never have known otherwise. And you'll know Christ (God) better than you ever thought you could."

The wiser Nikki holds everyone with open hands.

"Sometimes you have to just let go and see what happens."

Dear God, help us be the forgiving, patient and loving people You would have us to be. Amen

"DO EVERYTHING IN DEPENDENCE ON ME (GOD)"

Was the message from *Jesus Calling* to my daughter when she picked a date for us to read.

This is so where I am. I constantly go to God for everything. The other day my wonderful hubby asked something that the old Nikki would have gotten furious about, but instead, I turned to God and asked, *How can I kindly and respectfully answer this question without getting upset?"* And I did, leaving us to enjoy one of the best and funniest evenings ever, with our kids presenting their case as to why they should have what they want for Christmas.

"Eventually, you will learn to relax and enjoy the adventure of our journey together. As long as you stay close to Me, My sovereign Presence protects you wherever you go" (*Jesus Calling*).

"Eventually" is such the perfect word to describe this journey with God. It has taken lots of stuff to get me here, where even as I drive around Nigeria, I have such peace. And with everything else going on, I have a remarkable coolness, KNOWING I do nothing alone.

"I want to reach for God the way I reach for my phone. When I'm bored, when I'm uncomfortable, when I need answers or entertainment, when I'm lonely and need someone to talk to." — Cory Asbury

"Those who know your name will trust in you, for you Lord, have never forsaken those who seek you" (Psalm 9:10, NIV).

Dear God, may we do everything in dependence on You. Amen.

KEEP CALM—YOU'RE ROLLING WITH GOD

"THANK YOU, MY BUNKA BUNK"

That was me thanking Ember for voluntarily bringing me coffee. I asked her if she wanted to exercise and she agreed. *I enjoyed all 14 minutes of it!* My picky eating sons always give me a hard time about finishing their food, and they kept coming to me while we exercised to show me their plates, asking if they had eaten enough and I kept sending them back to eat more.

I think I enjoyed this time with them a little bit more than I usually would after my appointment with God. I read a book chapter, *Simplicity: Reordering Our Lives* from the book *Intimacy with the Almighty* by Charles R. Swindoll, which stated:

"'Behold, I stand at the door and knock; if anyone hears My voice and opens the door, I will come in to him, and will dine with him, and he with Me' (Rev. 3:20). This is the Lord's great invitation to intimacy; to be alone with Him, to enjoy the pleasure of His company over a meal that nourishes both heart and soul. But can we hear His knocking? Can we hear His voice over the clamor and chaos that all too often fragments our lives?"

I'm good now about my appointments with God, but the chapter asked some important questions:

"Are too many things draining your energy, leaving you exhausted—even resentful? What will your family remember twenty or thirty years from now—a blur of overtiredness, and hurryhurryhurry? Or warm relationships, laughter, hugs, and long, quiet walks and talks?"

Here's the deal: let's work on decluttering and simplify our lives, making space for what's truly important. As I read that chapter, that was exactly how I felt: overtired. How can we simplify our lives a little bit more, so we don't feel like our life is becoming a blur? *Something to think about!*

Dear God, help us to simplify our lives and make space for what truly matters, especially an intimate relationship with You. Amen.

KEEP CALM—YOU'RE ROLLING WITH GOD

Day 69 — Live in God, Live in Love

"FRIDAY FIGHT: ROUND 1"

That's the name of my exercise DVD. And let me tell you, it's a fight every morning between me and Shaun T, the exercise trainer, who has not only motivated me to stick with my exercise, but he constantly says that he also wants us to dig deep into our lives. "NO EXCUSES" is the huge sign on the background wall and his teachings have stuck with me. I'm motivated to dig deep and give it all I got. *The fight is on, baby!*

Getting my book back from my publisher with some tough criticism was not easy to handle. I now have to go back through 365 blog posts, revise, and update them to make the book stronger. This will take lots of digging deeper and discipline. Yes, I said it: *DISCIPLINE*. That's the scary word we all hate hearing, but it's a Greek concept which simply means "to train." I've disciplined/trained myself in a few areas this year, and I'm thrilled I did.

The exercise I hate doing stayed on track. I drank my horrible-tasting veggie smoothie every day, as well, whether I felt like it or not. I joined a Facebook friend in a program of eating only fruits 'til 5:00 p.m. and I added my veggie smoothies and coffee, and it has completely changed my relationship with food.

My appointments with God also take lots of discipline, but in the process, He has changed every aspect of my life. I'm closer to Him, and He fills my life with the best things—happiness, peace, wisdom, joy, gratitude, and contentment. I refuse to worry about anything, and I have no fear, other than some tough moments where I'm now learning to immediately run to Him.

"Oh, how sweet and beautiful it is to see persons fervent and devout, regular and well disciplined! How sad and how afflicting it is to see them walk disorderly, and practice nothing of what they are called to!" *(The Imitation of Christ).*

"Let us strip off anything that slows us down or holds us back" (Hebrews 12:1, TLB). I'll admit I'm still struggling with the Facebook distraction, the lack of focus at times, lots of negative thinking and procrastination. What are your weak areas? Today and every day, I challenge us to dig deeper and do better. "Dream big—very big. Work hard—very hard." – Oprah Winfrey

Dear God, help us to be disciplined in our thoughts, words and deeds. Amen.
KEEP CALM—YOU'RE ROLLING WITH GOD

Day 70 — Live in God, Live in Love

"I TAKE LIFE A QUARTER MILE AT A TIME"

This was such a God wink at me one Sunday when watching only a glimpse of the movie *Fast and Furious 7*, as this is exactly where I'm trying to be: allowing God to lead me one step at a time. I don't have to figure out the next ten steps, only one at a time. I have a notebook now that I carry around with me, and it is a daily list of everything I want to accomplish. I focus on those things that I feel I can accomplish that day only, based on constant conversations with God, as to what's important and what needs my attention *for that day*. He's my Partner in everything, and we're working together on some of my weak issues such as procrastinating, getting distracted, and feeling overwhelmed and worried at times.

And God constantly reminds me that He's with me and there's nothing that will come my way that He and I can't handle together. I now enjoy my life so much more because I'm not concerned about all the big waves that may come. I'm relaxed knowing that with God as my Partner, His solutions and wisdom will help me get through any wave. The waves will always be there, big and small, but with God by our side, we can fear nothing and no one.

But I can't stress enough the importance of the appointments with Him. These quiet times alone with God help us to learn His voice and direction. No matter how busy our lives are, we should slow down and find a chance to develop this most important relationship. As soon as I woke up one morning, I started off reading some of my meditation books, and it was such a peaceful way to start my day, focused on God.

One Saturday at a friend's house, in my appointment with Him, I read about the fruits of the spirit:

"But the fruit that the Spirit produces in a person's life is love, joy, peace, patience, kindness, goodness, faithfulness, gentleness, and self-control. There is no law against these kinds of things" (Galatians 5:22-23, ERV).

The faithfulness was a big one that day. We're called by God to be *loyal, dependable, and trustworthy,* no matter what anyone else is doing.

Dear God, may we learn to take life a quarter mile at a time, not worried about the future, but relaxed and enjoying our journey with You as our Partner and Guide. Amen.

KEEP CALM—YOU'RE ROLLING WITH GOD

Day 71 — Live in God, Live in Love

HAPPY BIRTHDAY TO MY MOMMA

The best thing that has ever happened to me was being born the daughter of the kindest soul in the world: my mom. She has demonstrated to me throughout my life the best lessons, which I would like to share with you today in honor of her birthday:

- *Live kindly.* "To the giver comes the fullness of life, to the taker an empty hand." I'm convinced that all our giving is paid back by God Himself. I've watched her give all to all, and I pray to follow her footsteps by being the kindest person I know.

- *80/20 rule.* Focus on the 80% positives in people, not their 20% negatives. I called her one day upset with my husband, and she reminded me that he has so many good qualities that I should focus on and I did. It changed our marriage. Instead of getting upset when the ugly 20% showed their face, I reminded myself, *80/20, Nik, 80/20!*

- *You can take an entire day to clean a kitchen extremely well, and if you're a street cleaner, be the best street cleaner.* Always hearing this growing up from her, inspired me to put my all in anything I do and do the best I can. I remember starting my first job; I would take a quick lunch break and get back to work. I wanted to hand in my best work to my supervisor.

- *Be humble.* I remember going to work with her on Sundays to clean her boss' office, and she was not the office cleaner. This taught me humility and to ask how may I serve instead of asking what's in it for me. My mom was exceptional in her duties, and she taught me never to do only the minimum. A super woman she is, always going beyond the call of duty.

- *"What you don't have, do without!"* Like the Apostle Paul wrote, "I know what it is to be in need, and I know what it is to have plenty. I have learned the secret of being content in any and every situation, whether well fed or hungry, whether living in plenty or in want" (Philippians 4:12). At a very early age, my mom taught me this invaluable lesson, and I'm forever grateful.

> Momma, I'm everything I am because you loved me.
> May your legacy of kindness and love live on forever.
>
> ***Dear God, may our lives light up all the dark places in the world, reflecting Your love and kindness everywhere we go and in everything we do. Amen.***
>
> KEEP CALM—YOU'RE ROLLING WITH GOD

Day 72 — Live in God, Live in Love

"I LOVE YOUR YARD"

This comment from the Chinese food delivery guy made me smile. "Are you saying that to get a bigger tip?" I jokingly responded. Knowing me, that also was a God wink because I was thinking to myself how much I love my yard and God amazingly knows every thought we think. I replaced about 50 plants recently that line the path to our front door and they lift my spirit every time I see them.

"Are you fully loving everyone and everything in your life?" is my big question to you today. These little plants that I've fallen in love with are teaching me to be more appreciative of everything, including the little things in my life that I would usually take for granted. I want to suck as much from every moment that I could. A few minutes ago, I hung up the phone from speaking to a friend in Nigeria and only a few minutes of talking to her were so special. This morning, my mom and sister surprised me with a three-way call from the Bahamas and every second was priceless.

"I go zero to 100, real quick," were the lyrics of a Drake song I blasted in my car this week driving to work. I cherish these trips, where I have the best time singing to myself. And I'm enjoying the clouds lately for some reason, admiring how breathtaking they are.

Instead of a usual, boring "good morning" to my Julie, I gave her the biggest hug, even taking the time to smell her and tell her how much I love my baby girl. I'm trying not to be so attached to my cell phone and to be more fully present in the everyday moments. Absorbed in every conversation, every interaction, and watching every cloud and plant is now a sacred moment that I don't take for granted.

Let's live our best lives, loving fully everyone and everything and enjoying God's presence with us. Thanks, Oprah Winfrey and Paulo Coelho for this excellent question above. I'm enjoying *Super Soul Sundays* on OWN!

Dear God, help us to appreciate fully the lives You've blessed us with, taking absolutely nothing for granted. Amen.

KEEP CALM—YOU'RE ROLLING WITH GOD

Day 73 — Live in God, Live in Love

"LISTEN TO ME (GOD)"

Was my important reminder when I opened my meditation book, *Jesus Calling* by Sarah Young. Only three words, but they're the key to living the best life. Listen to God in every moment, every example, and every experience doing what you believe He would have you to do in those 1,000 daily decisions. *This should be our ultimate goal in life.*

One of my favorite listening stories happened when I laid on my bed one Sunday morning, and my hubby asked me to attend a trade show with him that I was totally not interested in. I kept trying to get out of going, but hubby kept insisting. *God, what would You have me to do here?* I quietly prayed to myself before answering my hubby again. The feeling I got back was to accompany him and to *do the right, excellent and most loving thing by being the supportive wife.*

Months later, I still can't get over how I ended up meeting a couple that day, who, at dinner, two nights later, gave us the best advice that helped to resolve a big problem we were having at the time. *God, You're too much!* I marvel how God's always way ahead of us.

Moral: *LISTEN!* Some decisions we must make are quick ones, and that's when I try to do what I feel would be the right or most loving thing to do. For example, one day, my mom wanted to purchase something at Walmart. I got someone to help us, and there was another customer behind us who wanted the last of that item that was in stock. I had every right to say we should be the one to get it, but, listening to God at that moment, the feeling was to allow the customer and his son to have it.

Everything is between God and us, and my experience has been that the more I listen to Him, the sweeter life gets, *where I can refuse to worry about anything*, knowing I have the best Partner always with me. *Wink, Wink!*

Dear God, thank You for Your constant guidance. May we always listen to You. Amen.

KEEP CALM—YOU'RE ROLLING WITH GOD

Day 74 — Live in God, Live in Love

"FIND YOUR GREATNESS"

One of the best times of my life was spending the summer of 2012 in London during the Summer Olympic Games. We loved watching Michael Phelps win all those medals in swimming. And it was at the time that he won his 21st Olympic medal that I watched a commercial on TV with the slogan, "Find Your Greatness" and I thought to myself, *Wow, that same greatness that's within Michael Phelps is also within all of us.* We may not all be swimmers, but we all have our special skills, gifts, and abilities that we were each born with.

Here's the deal: there's greatness within every single one of us! The problem is that we don't believe there is. We've believed what people have told us and what we've told ourselves, but today, I want you to know there's greatness within you. And Howard Thurman, an adviser of Martin Luther King Jr., can help you tap into that greatness. He said, "Don't ask what the world needs. Ask what makes you come alive and do that." And, once you know what that is that makes you come alive, you're on your way.

For me, I come alive when I write, but for years, I convinced myself that I didn't have what it takes to be a writer. I now know I don't write alone; as I write, I connect and talk to God. I love how Oprah Winfrey described it, and she's certainly someone who's achieved greatness:

"It's all about instincts! Everything I do is based on my feelings. I'm sitting here right now because I had a feeling this would be a good idea." We roll with God, and He's only created stuff like the sun, planets, galaxies, hearts, and eyeballs. There's no limit to what we can achieve with Him directing us when we trust those instincts.

Would it also take hard work, discipline, and lots of practice and commitment to tap into that greatness? *Most likely, yes!* If success was easy, we'll all be successful, right? Pursue those dreams and tap into your greatness. God's with you all the way!

"Lives of great men all remind us

We can make our lives sublime,

And, departing, leave behind us

Footprints on the sands of time" - Henry Wadsworth Longfellow

"The world offers you comfort but you were not made for comfort, you were made for greatness." - Pope Emeritus

KEEP CALM—YOU'RE ROLLING WITH GOD

Day 75 — Live in God, Live in Love

"STICK WITH ME AND YOU'LL NEVER GO HUNGRY"

My hubby told me.

"My problem with you, Hon, is that you feed me too much," I replied. He's the best cook!

I feel God is saying something similar to us: Stick with Me, and you'll live the sweetest life, filled with peace, joy, gratitude, and contentment, despite all the challenges you may face.

- *But, God, I'm tired.* Stick with Me. Your weakness is a gift, drawing us closer together as you realize I'm your strength. "My grace is sufficient for you, for my power is made perfect in weakness" (2 Corinthians 12:9, NIV). Imagine I am with you and holding your hands every moment.

- *But, God, some people are talking about me and insulting me.* Stick with Me. "You will make small account of words which fly. If you do not desire to please others, nor fear to displease them, you will enjoy much peace." *–The Imitation of Christ*

- *But, God, these problems I'm dealing with are too overwhelming!* Stick with Me, as I direct you one step at a time. I will help you plan your day so that you will do less but accomplish more. Trust Me in every situation, and focus on doing the "intuitively" right and excellent thing in every moment, example and experience. And you will come through each challenge stronger, wiser, more mature, and closer to Me.

- *But, God, this person has abandoned me.* Stick with Me. I will never leave you or forsake you. I am your Teacher, Helper, Supporter, Friend, and Companion.

- *But, God, this person did me wrong.* Stick with Me. Stay on the high road, and I will pay you back whatever they took from you and more.

- *But, God, I've made lots of mistakes in my life.* Stick with Me. "Even your mistakes can be recycled into something good..." — *Jesus Calling*

Our Father, pardon our sins and may we live our lives completely focused on You. Help us to get back up whenever we fall, dust ourselves off, and keep moving forward with You. Amen.

KEEP CALM—YOU'RE ROLLING WITH GOD

"I'M INSPIRED BY OUR APPOINTMENTS WITH GOD..."

"...Every day, God teaches me something new, shows me what I need to work on...," was the comment from my Facebook friend, Diane. *Are YOU having appointments with God?*

"In quietness (spending time alone with Me (God) and confident trust (relying on My sufficiency) is your strength." – Sarah Young, *Jesus Calling*

I can't talk enough about these appointments/alone times with God. This is where we gain our strength and courage to face anything that may come our way in this life—in quietness, having meetings with God. Go to Him and ask what He has to say to you today, and have confidence in Him. As Diane wrote, God uses this alone time with us to teach us and to help us in areas we need help in to make us better people who are better equipped to handle the many challenges that can show up from anywhere at any time.

During my appointments, I go to God asking Him what He would have me to do. I love reading my meditation book, *Jesus Calling*, which includes Bible verses that have brought me so much closer to God, reading my old posts, or going to my Tumblr.com website and searching for "God" to hear from Him. I don't have a set length of time for the appointments and sometimes reading one sentence is enough. There were times in those meetings where I felt God saying to call a wise friend or my mom in the Bahamas and they always seemed to say exactly what I need to hear at that moment. One day, I got my message while reading the Bible and a devotional for kids with my daughter, Ember.

But the strength, wisdom and courage comes in seeking God. I leave every appointment with new knowledge from Him. Life is all about the decisions we make, and when we tap into God's wisdom and incredible insights, He helps us to become stronger in every aspect, from our health, relationships, business dealings, or parenting issues. *He's an expert in everything!* My appointments are mornings, 12 p.m., and 5 p.m., and I stay with them until I feel I've gotten a *high five* from God and can then go back into the world with the confidence that I'm never alone because God, the Creator of the entire universe, goes with me. "One of the best gifts you can give yourself is time alone with God."

Dear God, may our lives not distract us from developing a close relationship with You. May knowing You better be our most important life priority. Amen.

KEEP CALM—YOU'RE ROLLING WITH GOD

Day 77 — Live in God, Live in Love

HI, MOM

I promised you that you'll still hear from me every day, even though I'm not writing the post, and I've decided to include everyone in on it today. I've been having the best time with God lately, always reminded that He's intimately involved in all my moments. For example, the other day when I started to worry about the kids' safety in Nigeria, I opened up to the perfect message from Him in my meditation book a few minutes later during an appointment with Him: "ENTRUST YOUR LOVED ONES TO ME; release them into My protective care. They are much safer with Me than in your clinging hands."—*Jesus Calling*

Hours later, I was sitting in my office in awe of God, thinking about how God knows my every thought before I even think it. At that moment, I got the feeling to open my meditation book and found another perfect message from Him: "I know every thought you think, every word before you speak it."

In yet another appointment with God, I decided to read an old post from some of the ones Sal selected for our book, and I read the old one about my day headed to the airport. I read the part about getting all the bags in our car where I ended that paragraph with the word "Phew," and I smiled to myself saying that word was just the perfect ending. About three hours later, I get a text message from a close friend and, of all words available, she texted only one: *Phew!*

This morning, I woke up paranoid and finally going to God with my worries, I opened to another old post, where I purchased my meditation book for the very first time from Walmart. The cashier and I read a little together from the book, randomly turning to the following:

"I, the Creator of the Universe, am with you and for you. What more could you need! When you feel some lack, it is because you are not connected with me at a deep level. I offer abundant Life; your part is to trust Me, refusing to worry about anything."— *Jesus Calling*

No more paranoia!

Dear God, thank You for Your intimate involvement in all our moments. May our awareness of Your Presence grow every day. Amen.

KEEP CALM—YOU'RE ROLLING WITH GOD

"GOD, HOW CAN I POSSIBLY THANK YOU FOR THIS?'

I asked a few months ago in an appointment with Him, upset about some stuff going on in my life at that time.

The feeling I got in that appointment was that I should thank Him, and I totally didn't get it at the time, but I'm officially and on public record praising God for the entire situation, which has been so incredibly good for me. It was one of those growth opportunities from God and inconceivably He knows exactly what we need to grow us up so that we're mature not lacking anything. And this predicament has indeed grown me up on so many levels, with so many lessons that I'm forever changed, happier, more at peace than I've ever been and I'm closer to God, trusting Him more.

I'll never get over how intimately God's involved in our lives. The big lesson was learning to let go of trying to control the events of my life, which I have no control over. It has taught me to focus on God, not what's going on around me. To do what He would have me to do in every moment, every example and every experience, as this is where I get the best direction in living the sweetest life.

"Be transformed by the renewing of your mind." God's ways are so much higher than our ways and it's not about going with what the world expects, but instead everything is between God and us, not between us and anyone else. *God, what would you have me to do here?* God's our ultimate Boss and when we stick close to Him in more and more of our decisions, life gets so much better.

"Be on the lookout for what I (God) am doing in your life. Worship Me by living close to Me, thanking Me in all circumstances." – *Jesus Calling*

Dear God, may the painful experiences teach us the lessons You would have us to learn. Amen.

KEEP CALM—YOU'RE ROLLING WITH GOD

Day 79 — Live in God, Live in Love

"YE OF LITTLE FAITH!"

That describes us when we allow problems to upset us.

And when we're not trusting God and we think of the worst-case scenarios because we doubt Him. *Is there anything too difficult for God?* God is sovereign over all our problems, and there's nothing too difficult for Him. *Believe this!* When we start to worry is the time we stop trusting God. "God has you in the palm of His hand. He has never failed before, and the good news is, He is not about to start now." We should practice building those faith muscles, and whenever we're tempted to worry, that's when we must beat our minds with a stick and say to ourselves, *No, I'm not going there, I'm trusting and thanking God!*

I want to encourage you guys to find some form of spiritual practice spending some alone time with God. "Prayer is you talking to God and meditation is God talking to you." Like Marianne Williamson explained it makes the radio line between you and God clearer so that whenever any situation comes up, you'll more clearly understand what it is God would have you to do.

And that's exactly what has happened to me since starting to have appointments with God. His voice has become clearer, and I can more easily discern what He would have me to do in any situation. It has given me peace knowing I don't handle situations alone. Ideas magically pop into my head as to what route to take. *God knows everything!* He knows what will happen in the future, He knows the thoughts of others and the motives behind their actions which we do not. And it only makes sense to go to Him whenever we're faced with any challenge and ask, *God, what would You have for me to do?* And then trusting Him to guide you one step at a time.

This is what's working for me! I can live a life of peace knowing I don't handle my problems alone. I have the Creator of the entire universe with me to guide me. Have those alone times with Him and be quick to forgive everyone for everything and be your most loving and patient selves, as this will also help clear that radio line between you and God. *He has the solutions/strategies for all your problems.*

Dear God, thank You for Your Help in our lives. May we always slow down, calm down and listen to You before making any move. Amen.

KEEP CALM—YOU'RE ROLLING WITH GOD

"BEHOLD THAT FOOD, DRINK..."

...clothes, and all that is necessary to sustain the body, are burdensome to a fervent soul. Grant that I may use such things with moderation, and not attach myself to them with too much anxiety. In all this, I beseech you, let Your hand govern and direct me between the two extremes and teach me not to fall in any excess."

It was so surprising that maybe an hour after telling someone that I'm learning from the Buddhists about moderation, I opened my meditation book, *The Imitation of Christ,* and found the quote above. Seriously, I'm so over stuff; too much food, drink, and clothes are burdensome to me! I had lunch with my family, and I ate a little food, and I was very satisfied, compared to years before when I would fill my plate with so much, eat and feel miserable afterwards.

Less is now more. The less stuff I have, the freer and happier I feel. In regards to clothes and shoes, I'm now focused on a more natural beauty style of taking care of my body (losing some weight, as usual), skin and hair, and I'll forever be jeans and tee-shirt kind of gal. "If you do not desire to please others, or fear to displease them, you will enjoy much peace," is what also this meditation book says and that's where I am. I don't need expensive jewelry, clothes, or handbags to impress anyone.

My next project with my kids is to totally go through our house and give away everything we don't need or use anymore. I'm inspired by some friends who have a beautiful home with not a lot of stuff, but very few unique pieces. I want to go through life lighter and freer and to teach my kids that life isn't so much about accumulating stuff, but to cherish what's important in life, which for me are enjoying family and friends and pursuing dreams and goals that on our dying beds we can say, "Yes, I enjoyed a great life with no regrets!" My personal mission is to make the world a happier place by bringing humanity closer to God, one person at a time.

"A simple life in the fear-of-God is better than a rich life with a ton of headaches" (Proverbs 15:16, The Message).

Our Father, may we live happy, joyful and uncluttered lives close to You. Amen.

KEEP CALM—YOU'RE ROLLING WITH GOD

Day 81 — Live in God, Live in Love

"I WISH I HAD A FRIEND LIKE THAT"

Someone said to me. One of the most important things you can do is to surround yourself with positive people and this friend has had such an extraordinary influence on me that I now *know* the value of great friendships. I call her my "Alien" and I pray everyone has one. *"As iron sharpens iron, so one person sharpens another."* More lessons:

- *Be genuine.* People know when you're not. If you want people to trust you, you'll earn their trust and respect over time when they see that you're genuine in what you say and what you do.

- *Quality is better than quantity.* Having a few good friends is working for me as I have a much simpler and less complicated life.

- *Be honest, but not overly honest.* Your friend shouldn't leave your company feeling like they were run down by a bulldozer. We should build each other up, not tear each other down. And just because something comes to mind, that doesn't give you right to say it. *Some things can go without saying!*

- *Accept the fact that tomorrow they might not be your friend, but love them extravagantly anyway.* I'm learning to suck every moment of enjoyment out of all my friends and like anyone else in my life, I must accept the reality that they may not be there tomorrow.

- *Only God's perfect.* Forgive quickly accepting the apologies you never get sometimes.

- *Have quality time together by making space in your busy schedules to be with them.* "To show someone you love them, give them your time."

- *To have a friend, you must also be a friend.* Be the friend you would like to have.

- *Surround yourself with positive friends* who motivate you to be all you can be.

- *Agree to disagree sometimes. Remember the 80/20 rule.* Focus on the 80% positives you love about your friends and be incredibly happy, instead of focusing on the 20% negatives.

Dear God, may we be the friends You would have us to be. Amen.

KEEP CALM—YOU'RE ROLLING WITH GOD

"WE CAME TO LEARN MESSY LOVE!"

Was my message to a friend one Monday after she had an unexpected visitor showed up at her house. I shared with her a post I love from Tumblr.com:

"Dear Human: You've got it all wrong. You didn't come here to master unconditional love. That is where you came from and where you'll return. You came here to learn personal love. Universal love. Messy love. Sweaty love. Crazy love. Broken love. Whole love. Infused with divinity."

On Tuesday, she sent me another message that she's struggling over what had happened that Sunday and asked me to call her. I had another idea, though, for her to pick 10 pages from my unpublished book and see what God had to say to her. She went along with this idea and decided she will read every 20th page starting on page 20 to 40, 60, 80 and so on.

She gets to page 20 and unbelievably of all things there, this exact quote I had sent her the day before. Her response was: "Girl talk about a God wink. After that, I decided to forgive and let go. It just makes me want to cry to see how amazing God is. What are the chances of me going on that exact page first out of all those pages in your book."

And she's not alone in this messy love. I'm sure we all have our share to deal with, but I'm encouraged by God to stay on the high road with Him, becoming the superhuman and superwife He has challenged me to be, practicing endless mercy, grace (pardoning without punishment), patience and forgiveness, being my most loving self. He even sent me a special wink of my own reading a post on Facebook:

"Smile, things are working out. You may not see it now, but just know God is directing you to a much greater happiness." *I feel it!*

Dear God, may we learn all the messy love lessons You would have us to learn, loving others the way You love us. Amen.

KEEP CALM—YOU'RE ROLLING WITH GOD

THE MOST BRILLIANT POST EVER ON FACEBOOK:

"Life becomes easier when you learn to accept the apology you never got." - R. Brault

I was sitting and talking to my fellow God Maniac customer when my hubby walked over to us and said, "Nikki, get up! Leave us alone because you're not talking about anything important here!" Can you believe my wonderful hubby spoke to me that way? I said to the customer, "This is why I don't spend more than five minutes upset with him because otherwise, I would spend my entire life being miserable!" I gave my hubby a quick kiss, and I left them alone.

"Life becomes easier when you learn to accept the apology you never got."

Here's the deal: if this same incident happened maybe only a year ago, I would've spent the entire day or two upset with my hubby waiting for an apology I would never get. Now, I've realized that life is way too short to spend it angry with anyone. My hubby has totally earned my respect for him, and I now regularly remind myself that only God is perfect, remembering my 80/20 rule to focus on the 80% positives I love about my him and ignore the 20% negatives. I'll forever thank Oprah Winfrey for the following story:

"Two monks were walking along the road when one monk stops to help a lady and picks her up and carries her across the road. Five hours later the other monk said, 'Why did you touch that woman? You know we're not supposed to pick her up!' Then the other monk responded, 'I put that woman down five hours ago, but you're still carrying her!'"

"Let us be very sincere in our dealings with each other and have the courage to accept each other as we are. Do not be surprised at or become occupied with each other's failure; rather see and find the good in each other, for each one of is created in the image of God." - Mother Teresa

Dear God, help us be our most loving, merciful, and forgiving selves always, living with one foot on earth and our other foot in heaven. Amen.

KEEP CALM—YOU'RE ROLLING WITH GOD

"WHO ARE YOU NOT TO BE BRILLIANT, GORGEOUS, TALENTED, AND FABULOUS?"

I'm in love with this quote from Marianne Williamson:

"Our deepest fear is not that we are inadequate. Our deepest fear is that we are powerful beyond measure. It is our light, not our darkness that most frightens us. We ask ourselves, who am I to be brilliant, gorgeous, talented, and fabulous?

Actually, who are you not to be? You are a child of God. Your playing small doesn't serve the world. There is nothing enlightened about shrinking so that other people won't feel insecure around you. We are all meant to shine, as children do. We were born to make manifest the glory of God that is within us.

It's not just in some of us; it's in everyone. And as we let our own light shine, we unconsciously give other people permission to do the same. As we're liberated from our own fear, our presence automatically liberates others. You are a child of The Most High God and we were born to make manifest the glory of God that's within us!"

This is why I tell you there are no limits in life. Whatever you want to accomplish, you can. *You have the Creator of the universe walking with you!* Believe this! Go to God as He directs you on where to go and what to do. That's what makes life interesting. Once you start, God joins in. Don't die before you die-pursue your dreams. Do what you love and love what you do! "Who are you not to be brilliant, gorgeous, talented, and fabulous?"

Dear God, may our lives manifest Your glory within us. Amen.

KEEP CALM—YOU'RE ROLLING WITH GOD

Day 85 — Live in God, Live in Love

"WOW..."

It's all perfect! I sometimes feel that life is like a play and the right characters show up right on time to act their part in the drama of our lives. I have so many examples, but here are three that have shown up for me as if right on cue:

- *My friend Nyree:* I was going through a bad time in my marriage years ago when she drove over three hours to support our business and ended up helping me with all her wonderful advice. We spent hours on the phone, and I noticed she was so in love with her hubby. I asked myself why I couldn't be like that with mine. I then decided to put more effort into my marriage, and I now love my hubby more than ever. I needed her positivity in my life at that time.

- *My friend Sal:* I quit drinking one year for Lent when she told me she was giving up sweets. In the beginning, I thought, *I can't wait until Easter (the end of Lent) to have a drink,* but when Easter came, shockingly my cravings for alcohol were completely gone. The Nikki I was back then drinking every day was not the Nikki I am now writing these posts. I'm now high from living a blessed life close to God, not from alcohol.

- *Kevin:* As I filled out paperwork in attempts to deal with a problem due to a mistake I had made, my assistant handed me Kevin's business card and said, "This card came in the mail, and I thought maybe he could help you." It turns out she was so right; that business card showed up right on time as Kevin helped me to sort through a complicated mess. God is too much because I know that business card didn't just happen to come in the mail by a mere coincidence, when I sat there filled out that paperwork that very day. It was God behind the scenes of my life helping me, as usual–we're not going by the ordinary rules of man, remember.

At one point, I remember telling Kevin, "I'm leaving this matter in your hands and God's." I did exactly that and a mistake on my part was used by God to demonstrate that He's with me and for me and I can, therefore, *relax* knowing I have the best *Back-up* in the world.

Dear God, may we be angels for others like the angels that have shown up for us. Amen.

KEEP CALM—YOU'RE ROLLING WITH GOD

Day 86 — Live in God, Live in Love

"BUT THE QUESTION IS: DO THEY GO TO GOD WITH THEIR EVERY DECISION"

Was the message from my friend, Sal, that gave me goosebumps. A book called *The Happy Family* from the Jehovah Witnesses (a must have book for all married couples!) challenged me lately with asking if I'm training my children to have a relationship with God. I threw the ball at her, and that's the question she plans on asking her kids, and the question I'm asking you.

"Your best bet is to stake everything you've got on God, and you'll come out a winner— that's a 100% guarantee!" —Maria Fontane, *Mottos for Success*

Here's the deal: you don't lose with God. And even the times I've asked him, *God, why me?* have been the very challenges that have turned out to be so right for me. I needed them to grow me up and make me stronger, wiser, and trusting Him more. God knows everything, and He knows what's best for each one of us.

While chatting again with Sal, she told me how Jeremiah 29:11 has been showing up all over for her, including in our meditation book, *Jesus Calling*. That verse says, "'For I know the plans I have for you,' declares the Lord, 'plans to prosper you and not to harm you, plans to give you hope and a future.'"

God's plans for us are the best for our lives. I'm sucking up to God, going to Him in those 1,000 decisions I make every day by trusting my feelings and my intuition as to what He would have me to do in every moment, every example, and every experience. *My sheep know my voice.* My appointments with Him are helping me to learn God's subtle voice more and more, and He's helping me become the person He has created me to be. Each appointment fills me with His wisdom and this year, my goal of having a closer walk with Him was accomplished. *Yayy!*

Dear God, may we seek You in every decision we make. Amen.

KEEP CALM—YOU'RE ROLLING WITH GOD

Day 87 — Live in God, Live in Love

WOW! GOD IS TOO MUCH!

For the past few days or so, I've been thinking about someone who's around talking some negative stuff about us. Like the saying goes: "You can please some of the people some of the time, but you can't please all the people all the time." Every time my mind thought about them, I would get upset as to why they would do this. But God, again knowing every thought I think, had the perfect words for me.

I decided to organize some books and found amongst them one of my favorites, *The Imitation of Christ*. I randomly opened to a page and read the following: "Behold, if all should be said against you that the malice of men could possibly invent, what hurt could it do you if you would let it pass and value it no more than a straw? Could they even so much as pluck one hair from you?"

Wow! God's so deeply involved in our lives! He knew the perfect words I needed to read. Here's some more about *Having Confidence in God When Words Arise Against Us:*

"My child, stand firm and trust in me, for what are words: they fly through the air, but hurt not a stone. If you are guilty, think that you will willingly amend yourself. If your conscience does not accuse you, think that you will willingly suffer this for God's sake.

It is a small matter that you should sometimes bear with words, if you are not as yet able to endure hard stripes. And why do such trifles go to your heart, because you are yet carnal, and respect others more than you ought? Because you are afraid of being despised, you are not willing to be reprehended for your faults, and seek shelter in excuses.

But look better into yourself, and you shall find that the world is still within you, and a vain fondness for pleasing others. For since you refuse to be humbled and confounded for your defects, it is plain indeed that you are neither truly humble, nor truly dead to the world, nor the world crucified to you. But give ear to my word, and you shall not value ten thousand words of others."

Dear God, may the negativity that come our way only motivate us to be better, tougher, stronger and wiser people in the world for You. Amen.

KEEP CALM—YOU'RE ROLLING WITH GOD

"WHAT A SHINING EXAMPLE FOR US"

Wrote my friend, Sal, about another friend that I'm learning so much from. It's astonishing how God is so intimately involved in our lives that I believe every moment is incredibly sacred and there's always so much going on; it's like He's up to something in every moment!

Like me sitting at that desk in the U.S., working on an errand for my hubby. And there I saw a calendar on the wrong date at the desk behind me that said, "You shall go to a land flowing with milk and honey." This was after I had prayed for months for God's guidance on whether we should relocate our family from there to Nigeria, despite all the crazy reports on CNN. I took that calendar's message as my cue from God to make that move. Listening to the TV for a few minutes one morning a couple of years later in Nigeria, an announcer incredibly referred to Nigeria as the land flowing with milk and honey. *Wink! Wink!*

Then for me to live in Nigeria and get to be around this shining example of a person, who I call her my alien because it's like she's from another planet, was totally and completely all planned by God, before we both were even born. I get to learn so much from her so that I can pass the lessons on to you guys.

"... but be transformed by the renewing of your mind," says Romans 12:2 (NIV), a verse I love lately. Learning to go to God in more and more of my decisions and calming down and listening and keeping my focus on Him, as my friend is teaching me, has made my life so much more peaceful and happier. *This is the best life with God!*

"I will instruct you and teach you in the way you should go; I will counsel you and watch over you" (Psalm 32:8).

"Direct me in the path of your commands, for there I find delight" (Psalm 119:35). "Let the morning bring me word of your unfailing love, for I have put my trust in you. Show me the way I should go, for to you I lift up my soul" (Psalm 143:8).

Dear God, help us to remember that everything is between You and us, not between us and anyone else. May we do as much as we possibly can and leave the rest with You, KNOWING whatever You want for us is best for us. Amen.

KEEP CALM—YOU'RE ROLLING WITH GOD

"YOU WILL ALWAYS FACE TROUBLE IN THIS LIFE..."

"...But more importantly, you will always have Me (God) with you, helping you to handle whatever you encounter."- *Jesus Calling*

That's where I opened to in my meditation book.

Pastor Rick Warren said in an interview, "Life is a series of problems: either you are in one now, you're just coming out of one, or you're getting ready to go into another one." But the good news is that we face none of them alone. God is our constant Companion, Helper, Strategist, Adviser, and Counselor. No matter what the problem area, He's an expert in it. *Get God involved with everything!*

"I am learning that every day. To be calm and follow His lead," wrote a smart friend to me after I commented that we should do our best and leave the rest with God.

Are you following His leading? The times when I'm stubborn, I intentionally say to myself that I'm not going to God are the times I make situations worse. But in going to Him in my worst moments, He always leads me to stay on the high road, calming down, being my most loving and forgiving self, and trusting in Him that He's behind the scenes of my life fighting my battles for me. I constantly ask, *God, what would You have me to do here?* I then pay attention to my feelings. If I have a sense of peace about going in a particular direction, that's my cue from God to go ahead. *No peace, no move.*

"Blessed are those who have learned to acclaim you, who walk in the light of your presence, Lord" (Psalm 89:15).

"Since we live by the Spirit, let us keep in step with the Spirit" (Galatians 5:25).

Our Father, may we have endless conversations with You about everything. Amen.

KEEP CALM—YOU'RE ROLLING WITH GOD

Day 90 — Live in God, Live in Love

HE'S SO HAPPY THAT IT'S GOD TELLING ME TO WORK HARD

My hubby/boss that is! But to be very honest with you guys, I love my life and work, and this year I'm inspired by God to put my best in every moment, every example and every experience. Whether it's my job of assisting my hubby in our businesses, my work as a mom, as a wife, and in my assignment from God – bringing you closer to Him and enjoying the best life with the Creator of the entire universe as our Partner, Friend, Counselor, Comforter and Advisor. *His love stuns me!*

"O Lord, You have looked through me and have known me. You know when I sit down and when I get up. You understand my thoughts from far away. You look over my path and my lying down. You know all my ways very well. Even before I speak a word, O Lord, You know it all. You have closed me in from behind and in front. And You have laid Your hand upon me. All You know is too great for me. It is too much for me to understand" (Psalm 139:1-6, NIV).

And working with God as our Partner gets the best results: "As you seek God, you will find Him—His solutions, His comfort, His direction, His endurance, His wisdom, His love." - Maria Fontane, *Mottos For Success*. It doesn't get better than that. I smile to myself when the best solutions to problems casually pop into my mind, and I know I'm not that smart. *The solutions are all supernaturally from God!*

Here's the deal: I have learned to stay in the present moment, *God, what would you have me to do now?* And then when I'm finished that, I listen for instruction on what to do next, simply by paying attention to my feelings, nudges and impressions from Him. A big *YES* and feelings of peace are God instructing me to move forward, and *no peace or doubt equals NO move.* Something as simple as to make a phone call or not is a conversation with God, as I allow Him space in my life to direct more and more of my actions.

"Since I (God) am your Strength, I can empower you to handle each task as it comes. Because I am your song, I can give you joy as you work alongside Me. As you walk in the Light with Me, you can have one foot on earth and one foot in heaven." – *Jesus Calling*

Dear God, may we be the people You would have us to be in every moment by learning to calm down and follow Your leading. Amen.

KEEP CALM—YOU'RE ROLLING WITH GOD

Day 91 — Live in God, Live in Love

"LET'S HAVE AN APPOINTMENT WITH GOD!"

I said to my Julie, my then eleven-year-old sweetheart before she left for school. I grabbed her daily devotional for girls and randomly opened it for us to read together. The Bible verse quoted for that day was John 4:16: "God is love. Whoever lives in love lives in God, and God in them."

She asked if that included loving her sister, Ember, even when Ember is mean to her. I asked, "Everything is between you and who?"

She reluctantly answered, "God."

I told her how He has blessed me so much and how no matter what anyone does to me, I practice staying on the high road, and I'm living the best life with Him. I told her we should love others so much that they wonder why!

I love having these appointments with God with my kids. The last one with my then seven-year-old son, Emmie, about having good habits. I asked him to give me an example of a good habit, checking to see if he understood the lesson, and he surprisingly said, "Like sharing with Joshie" (his then four-year-old brother).

I don't recall the lesson, but during an appointment with Ember, I remember hugging and kissing her and using that opportunity to remind her how much I love her and how proud I am of her. I can be such a tiger mom at times, focused on the few negative things about them, instead of the so many positives I love about them! In teacher-parent conferences that week, I was made a super proud mom of the people they're growing up to be, and I have no doubt who's behind the scenes assisting me in raising them:

"My help comes from the Lord, who made heaven and earth" (Psalm 121:2, NLT).

Dear God, may we never stop seeking Your guidance for our lives. Amen.

KEEP CALM—YOU'RE ROLLING WITH GOD

Day 92 — Live in God, Live in Love

WELCOME TO "THE SWEET LIFE"

I've stolen this line, and I'm making it mine!

I heard it from one of my favorite people, Oprah Winfrey, in her commencement speech to Spelman College. And, in case you haven't realized it yet, this is what I'm writing about every day: *this life with God is the sweetest!* Where you have so much joy, despite all your problems and challenges, knowing that you don't handle them alone, and you know the Creator of the entire universe goes with you and before you wherever you go. You're confident that whatever He wants for you is best for you, open to everything and attached to nothing.

It's the sweet life when you maximize every moment, unceasingly thanking God for everything—*the good, the bad, and the ugly*—knowing they all work together for your good.

You wake up knowing that anything's possible and all you should do is advance confidently in the direction of your dreams, where there is no such thing as failure, only loads of lessons. You know that not everyone will like you or understand you, but you keep going anyway. You've become a professional ignorer (kindly and respectfully, of course) and if someone says ten thousand words against you, you either improve from it or turn a deaf ear to it.

You're focused on constant and never-ending improvement "and do not take upon yourself useless cares." You do good, knowing everything is between you and God, and that the good you do will follow you. "How may I serve?" is the question you constantly ask God, with Him seeming to ask you, *How may I serve you?*

You've left the past in the past and realized it was only practice to become the person God would have you to be, anyway. You're not so hard on yourself or others, realizing that you may not get it right all the time. However, when you fall off the wagon, you simply get right back up, dust yourself off and keep going, committed to doing better the next time.

Welcome to the sweet life, baby!

Our Father, may our lives only get sweeter as we learn to keep our focus on You and not this world. Amen.

KEEP CALM—YOU'RE ROLLING WITH GOD

Day 93 — Live in God, Live in Love

A GOD WINK FROM JOEL OSTEEN... AGAIN!

He's been my messenger from God, lately. In thinking about what to write for one of my posts, the words, "In this life you will have trouble," kept coming to mind. I debated about not writing about this because I've probably written about it so many times before, but the feeling stayed with me the entire day, so I rolled with it.

Fast forward to today, of all verses, Joel and Victoria Osteen based their daily devotional on the same one. I'm totally taking this as a God wink and reminder that He is my constant Companion, with everything lining up perfectly. So enough from me; here's their spin on encountering trials:

"TODAY'S SCRIPTURE

"I have told you these things, so that in me you may have peace. In this world you will have trouble. But take heart! I have overcome the world" (John 16:33, NIV).

TODAY'S WORD from Joel and Victoria

It's easy to be positive and encouraging when everything is going your way, isn't it? But everyone is going to have obstacles to overcome in life. Problems have a purpose, and part of God's purpose for allowing you to face obstacles is to test your attitude. That's why you need to be positive, even in negative situations. Remember, God wants you to live life to the fullest. And He has provided a way for you to enjoy your life, even when you're going through hard times. Look closely again at John 16:33. Jesus has just told you that you will face tribulation. But then He says, "Take heart!" That's the secret. One translation puts it this way: "When you have trouble, cheer up." What God is saying is that you can choose to be joyful and positive no matter what happens. The reason you can do that is because Jesus has already won your battle, whatever it may be!

A PRAYER FOR TODAY

Lord, thank You for the trials that strengthen my faith. I know that all I need to do is look up to You when troubles come, and claim Your victory over them. In Jesus' name.
Amen." — Joel & Victoria Osteen

Sign up to receive their **FREE** daily devotional email: https://www.joelosteen.com

KEEP CALM—YOU'RE ROLLING WITH GOD

"IN ALL YOUR WAYS ACKNOWLEDGE HIM"

I'm in love with these Bible verses:

"Lean on, trust in, and be confident in the Lord with all your heart and mind and do not rely on your own insight or understanding. In all your ways know, recognize, and acknowledge Him, and He will direct and make straight and plain your paths" (Proverbs 3:5-6).

Here's the deal: pause and listen for God's input in everything you do, everything you say, and everywhere you go because He guides you on the path to the best life with Him. My life has become a wonderful adventure, and I'm having the most enjoyable conversation with God. In the 1,000 decisions you make every day, run to Him for His input, and you'll make great decisions. When I say, *God, I don't want to hear from you on this matter,* is when my *crazy self* shows up.

And, the more you practice listening to Him, the better you get at it. It's becoming like instinct to me, and automatically, I know what God would have me to do. The lesson lately from Him has been to practice genuine love, not pretend love. If anyone has anything against me, honestly, it's their issue to deal with because I'm going to be my most genuinely loving self with them. Going into any conversation with anyone from the standpoint of genuine love for the person has made me so much happier. Everything is between God and me, not between me and anyone else. I've learned that no one is perfect and that when I turn into a crazy lady is when I'm not my most loving self, so does everyone else. *We're all insane when we do not love genuinely.*

"I will listen to what God the Lord says; he promises peace to his people..." (Psalm 85:8).

I've made the best decisions listening to God, and that's trusting my internal guidance, my spirit, a deep knowing inside of me that I've learned is God's voice. When I follow His leading, God takes me on magnificent paths with Him, but, boy oh boy, when I go against His directions, it ain't pretty! "In all your ways acknowledge Him..."

Our Loving Father, teach us Your voice and direction for our lives and to lean on and be confident in You always. Amen.

KEEP CALM—YOU'RE ROLLING WITH GOD

Day 95 — Live in God, Live in Love

"YOU'RE LUCKY!"

Was what a customer said to me when I told her how I have the peace that surpasses all understanding because of my extraordinary faith in God. I shared with her the whole story of living in the U.S., and despite all the comforts in the world, I was miserable. It took coming to Nigeria, where I learned to trust God and to KNOW He's my constant Companion, Friend, Adviser, Strategist, Counselor, Helper, and Partner who's always with me.

We're not going by the ordinary rules of man because when we listen to God, going to Him in those 1,000 decisions every day, He guides us on what to do, where to go and even what to say to help us make the utmost best decisions for our lives. One day, I got the feeling from Him that we should call a particular customer who owed us some money. I told my assistant to remind my husband ten times if she had to call this customer, and less than two hours later, a check for payment arrived. Another day, the feeling was to call a different client on some business we had done the previous week, and he was happy to hear from me and wanted to find out about some new work we could help him with. "We're not going by the ordinary rules of man!" We're rolling with God, *and He knows everything!*

So, whatever you're going through, pray about it asking God for His assistance. Then pay attention to His direction on what to do. It could be a strong feeling, a slight nudge, a thought that pops to your mind, or a book that He uses to point you in the right direction. He used a calendar on the wrong date to direct me to move to Nigeria, and that has been one of the best decisions I've ever made. God's always communicating with us, but it's up to us to slow down, calm down, and listen. *Are you sticking to your appointments with Him?* My best days are when I stay close to God.

"My sheep listen to my voice; I know them, and they follow me" (John 10:27. NIV).

Dear God, may we all come to learn Your voice clearer and clearer every day. Amen.

KEEP CALM—YOU'RE ROLLING WITH GOD

"I WILL BE JOYFUL IN GOD MY SAVIOR"

Was what I read in my meditation book, *Jesus Calling*, and I'm taking that as a God wink because I was thinking how fantastic this is that, in a middle of a challenge, I'm happy. I went to my favorite Tumblr.com site again for a pep talk from God, and He never disappoints with me finding the perfect message: "There's nothing that you can't overcome with God on your side." Amen! That did the trick to get my mind focused back on what I needed to get done, but KNOWING I had lots of help backing me up.

We can live life without God, or we can live life with God giving us all the advice, solutions, and best directions. *He knows everything!* One morning, I came across a problem, and I wondered how I'd resolve it. As I took my shower, another of those God thoughts (solutions to my problems) came to mind, and I smiled with God for a little bit for *His answer*. I knew the answer was from Him because I'm not that smart!

I figured out why He didn't want me to stop writing while going through a challenge. It's so that I can share these unbelievably great lessons I'm learning. A big one has been not to stress the next ten steps. He shows me what to do one step at a time. And when I'm done with that one, the direction for the next step comes to mind. I've learned when I'm stuck on something that I should let it go, staying calm and somehow someway, a solution or direction will mysteriously come to mind.

I can already see a new me evolving through dealing with this situation. I'm feeling confident, strong, ready to take on anything and open to whatever may come my way.

"Within you is the power to rise above any situation or struggle, and transform into the brightest, strongest version of you EVER!" - Lorraine Cohen

Dear God, may every day be a good day, despite our challenges, knowing You're on our side. Amen.

KEEP CALM—YOU'RE ROLLING WITH GOD

Day 97 — Live in God, Live in Love

"GOD, I DO NEED YOU EVERY MOMENT!"

That's what my life is boiling down to, going to God in as many moments as possible, where He directs me on the path to the best life. I can't get over His love for me and His deep involvement in every aspect. For example, one morning, while having a snuggling session in bed with Emmie, he said to me, "I want to get all As next semester!" This made me so happy because last term he made the honor roll with only As and Bs.

But God's such a big part of this story, about two years or so ago He helped me to make the difficult decision to move Emmie back a grade from his kindergarten class back to prekindergarten. I feel God had me to attend a teacher/parent conference early one morning, when the invited speaker asked, "Why are we rushing our children out of school?" That was such a light bulb moment because that very week my son had cried at the table because he couldn't complete his homework by himself when I was told the other children in the class could. After hearing the speaker say this, I rushed to the school's vice principal asking her to please move him back a grade. Now, instead of crying over homework, he makes me proud showing me the best homework that he thrillingly completes by himself!

The other day I got upset with my hubby, and when I opened my meditation book a few minutes later, I found the perfect message from God: "Don't look to human relationships for perfection."

Thanks, God! Instantaneously, I felt better.

Guys, don't miss out on the most important relationship, the one you have with God. *Are you spending alone time with Him?* Join me in my appointments where I read anything spiritual that helps me to learn and grow more in my faith in Him, and I'm learning His voice more and more every day. I want you here with me, enjoying the best life with God!

Dear God, may we always pay attention to Your guidance in every aspect of our lives. Amen.

KEEP CALM—YOU'RE ROLLING WITH GOD

"LET'S HAVE A NEW BEGINNING"

I wrote to my longtime friend, Kira.

I met her in the fifth grade, and she has been another angel in my life. I'll never forget a summer with her in New Jersey with her uncle and his family. Growing up in a single-parent home with my mom, that entire summer was like a new world opening to me, watching her uncle so involved with his kids and us. One Friday evening had extra significance when her uncle barbecued outside their back yard. I said to myself, *This is the life I want.*

Astonishingly, God has granted my heart's desire, even down to the husband who loves to barbecue. I see my kids growing up so beautifully, and I know a big part of that is their dad's intensive involvement in their lives, including a family dinner together most evenings. I now call them my super kids and future world leaders.

But getting back to this new beginning, I wrote to my *Eat to Live* group this morning: "In areas where we've been weak, let's pray and ask God for His help and strength to be stronger." Leaving the past in the past and beginning again has been one my biggest lessons. God is my wonderful burden carrier, and I place them all with Him. The past only exists in my mind, and I again must constantly, constantly, constantly talk to myself and say, *Nik, you're not going there!* And instead focus on moving forward, living my best life with God.

I got a nudge from Him one day to read a little bit from a book by my bedside, where a quote from Mother Teresa greatly encouraged me:

"Each person's mission is a mission of love, and the work of love should begin in our own homes. You must have time for your own first, and only after that should you work for others. We should make our homes centers of compassion and FORGIVE ENDLESSLY. Let no one ever come to you without coming away better and happier. Let us begin then in the place where we are, with people with whom we are the closest and then spread out."

"Those who look to him (God) are radiant; their faces are never covered with shame" (Psalm 34:5).

Dear God, may we release everything that has happened in the past over to You and begin again, knowing You can use it all for our good. Amen.

KEEP CALM—YOU'RE ROLLING WITH GOD

"REMEMBER, WE ROLL WITH GOD"

Was what I wrote to someone who reads my posts regularly.

I was so happy when he told me, "I'm not anxious anymore. I just take life one day at a time." I told him that I take life one moment at a time and this, "We roll with God," has become my new life motto. Whenever I'm tempted to get down, stressed out or worried in any situation, I'm reminded that I don't go through life alone. I'm amazed how it instantly calms my mind knowing that all things are possible with God and I don't have to handle life's dramas alone and without His help. Everything seems to work out and even when they don't work out the way I would like, I still believe that it's all still so perfect. You're welcome to use it anytime: "We roll with God!" All these issues/problems/situations are there just to grow us up to be the people He would have us to be anyway.

"I'm in a constant conversation with God," was what President Barack Obama responded to a question from Oprah Winfrey, in O Magazine, and is also one of my favorite quotes. She asked him, "Do you involve God in your decisions in your presidency and if so, in what way?" His complete answer, which I loved was, "I'm in a constant conversation with God and that voice that is true about doing the right thing. And sometimes just giving strength when you're feeling low. There are going to be ups and downs in this job, like any job. The interesting thing is, the questions I deal with are big and have worldwide impact."

After reading this, I felt that I wasn't so crazy after all and I'm with good company. The President of the United States is also having conversations with God. We have the spirit of God dwelling within us. And I don't make a move without consulting with Him first. I pay attention to those feelings, and I go with the decision that brings me peace. I know this is something I repeat a lot, but once you get it that you don't have to go through life alone and that God is constantly with you and directing you, you begin living life on a completely different level.

"I can do all things through Him who strengthens me" (Philippians 4:13), and knowing this like President Obama said, you're "just given strength when you're feeling low." I always say, "*This life is not for weaklings!*" and I'm convinced that there's always going to be some issue/problem/situation that we must deal with, but we don't have to handle them alone.

"REMEMBER, WE ROLL WITH GOD"

A new smart friend I have wrote this to me in an email: "It's difficult sometimes, but I always try to wait a moment and reflect before I react to situations." This is so where I am. I take that moment to ask God,

"Where would You have me go? What would You have me do? What would You have me say and to whom?"

And I'm going to stick with my constant conversations with God because they *ARE* working for me.

Dear God, may we worry about nothing, pray about everything, and unceasingly thank You for Your faithfulness to us. Amen.

KEEP CALM—YOU'RE ROLLING WITH GOD

Day 100 — Live in God, Live in Love

"SEE HOW FAR YOU STILL ARE FROM TRUE CHARITY AND HUMILITY...

...which knows not how to feel anger or indignation against anyone but oneself."

This sentence has been on my mind since I quoted it from our meditation book the other day. Can you imagine getting to a place where you do not feel anger, insulted, offended or annoyed by anyone for what you believe is unfair treatment by them and having such feelings only against yourself? *Wow,* what a wonderful life that would be, but is that even possible humanly speaking?!?

I see myself getting closer and closer to this as I remember going for months being upset over something someone might have said or done to me. Now I try to take things in from the point of view of, "what can I take from this to improve" or I simply can turn a deaf ear to it and focus on positive things leaving people where they are in God's hands.

I have someone helping me get there quicker—my wonderful hubby and boss, who is assisting me tremendously in becoming the best version of myself. Whatever he has on his mind, he's quick to let me know and not always in the nicest way. I've found, though, that after days of being upset and being honest with myself, he's right in most cases.

It turns out this has been a good thing because he's helped me to grow in many areas. Now when he says something, forgetting excuses, I look to see what I can take from what he's saying to improve, humble myself, and apologize when appropriate. If there's nothing, that's where the professional ignorer comes in, and I focus on his other characteristics that I love and adore, freely telling him, respectfully of course, that I disagree with him.

"Many times it is very useful, for keeping you in greater humility, that others know and reprimand your faults." *The Imitation of Christ*

These are the people that help us grow and become our best selves.

So, the next time someone says or does something you may not like, think about it from the standpoint of how can I improve or learn from this or simply ignore them, kindly and respectfully, allowing no one to steal your peace and joy. *Got that?*

Dear God, may we learn "true charity and humility which knows not how to feel anger or indignation against anyone but oneself." Amen.

KEEP CALM—YOU'RE ROLLING WITH GOD

Day 101 — Live in God, Live in Love

"TAKE NOTHING FOR GRANTED!"

That's the message I came home with one day, starting when my then ten-year-old daughter, Julie, didn't come out to see me when I arrived from work like she usually does. I told her, "A time will come when you'll wish you had your mommy around for one more hug!" Then Joshie called me to help him in the restroom in the middle of my dinner. While wiping his little bum, I reminded myself that even that was an incredible blessing. *Nik, take nothing for granted! Your son can walk, speak, go to the restroom on his own... you're blessed!*

Living in Nigeria has changed me. I believe one of the reasons God wanted me there was to learn the lesson of being grateful and content, no matter the circumstance, and pass that message on to you. Somehow living in the U.S., sipping on my Starbucks' lattes, I was miserable, even though I had all the comforts of the world.

I have constant reminders in Nigeria that I have no reason to complain about anything. A man crawling in the dirt like an insect with deformed legs impacted me one day. I did a U-turn so that I could go back and give him some money. I had to get out of my car to go after him, and when I gave him the money, he said, "God bless you." I told him how much I admired his bravery. It was a huge wake-up call that I have no reason to complain.

Now I can watch my kids sleep and listen to them breathe, and I'm happy. I remind myself often to take nothing for granted. We can have one foot in heaven and one foot on earth when we're grateful and content.

"I would maintain that thanks are the highest form of thought; and that gratitude is happiness doubled by wonder." — G.K. Chesterton, A Short History of England

Dear God, may we be extremely grateful for everything, not taking anything or anyone for granted. Amen.

KEEP CALM—YOU'RE ROLLING WITH GOD

Day 102 — Live in God, Live in Love

STOP GETTING OVERWHELMED

This seems to be my constant reminder to myself lately. From now meeting a kitchen filled with plates for my Sunday's kitchen duty, to laundry, to organizing storerooms, thinking of my long business' work to do list and I can go on and on. It's been an important reminder, as I'm learning to maximize every moment, constantly talking to God about what is the work of today and the work of another day focused on doing my best and trusting God to guide my path, taking life one step at a time. And I have such peace! I'm also not dwelling on the past, but moving forward focused on constant and never-ending improvement. I love the following from Marianne Williamson's book, *A Return to Love*:

"The past is over. It doesn't matter who we are, where we came from, what Mommy said, what Daddy did, what mistakes we made, what diseases we have, or how depressed we feel. The future can be reprogrammed in this moment. We don't need another seminar, another degree, another lifetime, or anyone's approval in order for this to happen. All we have to do is ask for a miracle and allow it to happen, not resist it. There can be a new beginning, a life unlike the past. Our relationships shall be made new. Our careers shall be made new. Our bodies shall be made new. So shall the will of God be done, on earth as it is in Heaven. Not later, but now. Not elsewhere, but here.

Not through pain, but through peace. So be it. Amen."

KEEP CALM—YOU'RE ROLLING WITH GOD

"I'VE BEEN EXPERIENCING A VERY DIFFICULT TIME FINANCIALLY"

Someone wrote the above message to me when I asked them how their appointments with God were going. I certainly wasn't expecting this response:

"I started becoming anxious, my days became more and more consumed with panic attacks. By now, I knew that God provided all our needs, but He didn't provide for our lifestyle, and we had to part with some things. The road to the high life is difficult enough, but falling from it is much harder. I became bitter with God for allowing this to happen to us.

When you suggested appointments with God, my focus shifted from lack to gratitude. I started having peace that passes all understanding, joy instead of sadness, I returned to my first-love in Christ. And every appointment with God is an appointment with the Love of my life, my provider of gifts that money can't give. I have confidence in God's provision for my family, and I have no fear. There's no time for panic attacks; I'm too busy enjoying my life. And since my having regular appointments with God, I realize that I've lost nothing at all.

These appointments give me a fresh burst of energy and wisdom, after each appointment with God, I have everything I need to go through the day fearlessly. We're not living the high-life anymore, we've gone higher to living and enjoying the heavenly life."

And there you have it, folks, another testimony about the benefits of getting God more involved with every aspect of our lives through these powerful appointments (alone times) with Him. How He keeps up with each and every one of us is so beyond my brain capabilities, but somehow, He does.

My Julie and I had fun seeing who could come up with the most lessons learned from me accidentally breaking and spilling a big jug of water. My favorite one is that life is messy; sometimes and you must clean it up, knowing that whatever God wants for us is best for us, even financial messes. God is our faithful Helper who says, "Come on, it's clean up time!"

Dear God, thank You for being there to help us clean up all the messes we get into. May we lean on You and Your wisdom, making space in our lives for those important appointments with You. Amen.

KEEP CALM—YOU'RE ROLLING WITH GOD

Day 104 — Live in God, Live in Love

'NIK, WHY ARE YOU SO HAPPY CLEANING THE TOILET?'

I wondered to myself, smiling sweetly as I scrubbed the potty. Me and housework are *not* good friends, but in trying to teach my kids the value of hard work, we had no house help and surprisingly I was incredibly happy the entire day, despite all the cleaning, cooking, washing, grocery shopping and all the other household duties I normally despise. *"From where does my joy come from? It comes from the Lord."*

What else can I say? Trusting in God fills you with joy like no other, knowing I'm never alone and that I have the best Adviser, Helper, Friend, and Companion makes me extremely happy. I don't have to figure out life's challenges on my own and when I have constant conversations with God, paying attention to those feelings, as to what He would have me to do, where He would have me to go and what He would have me to say, from moment to moment. He leads me on this path to the best life, one step at a time.

And even with everything going on in my life right now, I *KNOW* God's helping me with them. I have no fear of bad news, as I *KNOW* the solutions, the people and everything else I might need are already in the future waiting for me to resolve any problem like they have so many times in the past. *God, I'm profoundly grateful!*

I was telling a friend about how stressful I was feeling about an upcoming situation and she brilliantly reminded me to trust God and that He would help me. When she said that, I began to relax, not worrying so much. Fast forward a month later, and the situation seems to be working out so much better than I expected. *Ain't worried 'bout nothing!*

"You (God) make known to me the path of life; you will fill me with joy in your presence..." "Whatever you do, do it enthusiastically, as something done for the Lord and not for men" - (Colossians 3:23, HCSB).

Dear God, may we all experience the joy of a life lived close to You. Amen.

KEEP CALM—YOU'RE ROLLING WITH GOD

"EVERY MEAL IS SACRED"

I said to my hubby, having a late-night supper together.

We had shortly returned home from a beautiful day of hanging with some extra special friends. The day started out with golf lessons for the kids, and I ended up having my golfing date with my then four-year-old, and a sweet then two-year-old on our private mini golf course, and I enjoyed every sacred moment of it. I'm learning with God that every moment is sacred and there is always so much going on. *PAY ATTENTION!*

"You really have to be a professional ignorer," I said to a new Facebook friend chatting. In a conversation with God, the feeling that day was not to go to church, and I ended instead having a sacred conversation with her that I felt was all planned out by God. When I told my Julie that God knew I needed her in my life, she asked why, and I replied, "Because He knew how much I would love you."

Every moment is sacred, and I don't want to waste any more of them. I'm a professional ignorer—kindly and respectfully, loving extravagantly, extending grace (clemency) and forgiving endlessly remembering that everything is between God and me. My prayer I learned from my friend Karen has made such a difference in my life, and I've printed it and have copies in my office and home that remind me that I shall be a happy being! We're repeating it nine times a day for nine days, and already I'm feeling like a new person.

"O God! Refresh and gladden my spirit. Purify my heart. Illumine my powers. I lay all my affairs in Thy hand. Thou art my Guide and my Refuge. I will no longer be sorrowful and grieved; I will be a happy and joyful being. O God! I will no longer be full of anxiety, nor will I let trouble harass me. I will not dwell on the unpleasant things of life.

O God! Thou art more friend to me than I am to myself. I dedicate myself to Thee, O Lord." – 'Abdu'l-Bahá (Bahai Prayers)

KEEP CALM—YOU'RE ROLLING WITH GOD

Day 106 — Live in God, Live in Love

STAY CALM

That's the simple, but very important message for you today.

I laughed with someone recently that I don't have much drama anymore to write about. My life is pretty drama free now, and I've learned to stay calm no matter what comes my way. Problems/situations/challenges are a part of life, and it seems as you resolve one, another pops up. Recently, in the months of dealing with a problem, I'm so proud that throughout it I remained calm. I didn't let it determine my happiness. I did what I could do to resolve the situation, and I left the rest to God. Whenever thoughts of worry came to mind, I kept reminding myself to *trust God always*, and everything worked out way better than I expected. I stayed calm and allowed God to direct me one step at a time, paying attention to my feelings and going with the decisions that brought me peace when I thought about them. Talking to someone about this he said to me, "Nikki, I like your strategy." I wanted to say to him, *I have the best Adviser in the business: God!*

I've not only learned to stay calm when dealing with problems but in staying calm in everyday interactions with others. When I first started my blog, there was someone who helped me to learn this lesson big time, as when they said anything offensive to me I would get so upset and I would spend days there. I've grown up a lot since then, and I was proud that in seeing them recently, the comments they made were still offensive, but I didn't allow them to upset me the way they did in the past. I examined the statements to see if there was anything I could learn from, but I realized that some people, no matter what you do, will find something to complain about. You can do so many things right, but they'll focus on what they think you're doing wrong. I'm learning to run my race and not be so concerned about the opinion of others. *I do my best and forget the rest.* I still plan to die exhausted, knowing I took on life and I lived it well! I just need more coffee please (lol)! I forgive quickly, I live kindly, I love extravagantly, I ask, *How may I serve?* and I do good knowing that it's all between God and me.

"Inner peace begins when *YOU CHOOSE* not to allow another person or event to control your emotions!" *Stay calm!*

Dear God, may we come to know true peace and joy that comes through having a relationship with You. Amen.

KEEP CALM—YOU'RE ROLLING WITH GOD

Day 107 — Live in God, Live in Love

"I FORGOT TO TELL YOU I MADE IT FOR YOU"

Ember casually said to me after I discovered a beautiful salad in our refrigerator.

"Where are you from?!?" I asked her. I love her spirit as she seems to continuously ask how she can serve without expecting anything in return. *She has inspired me, again!*

"On a spiritual level, I believe whatever you put out there, comes back to you!" is what I wrote and as I opened up Dr. Wayne Dyer's book, *Change Your Thoughts—Change Your Life*, this morning, I read: "Lao-tzu advises you to give without keeping an account or expecting something in return, for this is the nature of the Tao (God), and you are of the Tao. Giving is synonymous with receiving when you live by this illumination."

Be a giver, as every little bit counts! I'm blessed because of all the good my mom has done for others in her life. Going from the Bahamas to New York without any trouble finding jobs or paying my tuition, room, and board is something I'll never forget. I was always taken care of. I've watched my mom give all of my life. It reminds me of Psalm 37:25-26:

> "I was young and now I am old,
> yet I have never seen the righteous forsaken
> or their children begging bread.
> They are always generous and lend freely;
> their children will be a blessing."

And for me to see my oldest daughter giving freely and asking, "How may I serve?" makes me extremely happy. *This is the way to a blessed life!*

"And still, after all this time, the Sun has never said to the Earth, "You owe me." Look what happens with love like that. It lights up the sky." - Rumi

Our Father, open our hearts to be the people You would have us to be, remembering everything is between You and us, not between us and anyone else. Amen.

KEEP CALM—YOU'RE ROLLING WITH GOD

"THE 2ND MOST BRILLIANT POST: DUMP HIM!"

Was the Facebook comment I received, referring to my husband's remarks to me one day. Here's the deal: Only God's perfect and I'm learning to love and suck the enjoyment out of all the imperfect people in my life. The faster you learn this, the faster you hit the sweet spot of living and enjoying the *BETTER* life with God. Here's an excerpt from an old blog post I wrote:

"And enjoying the sweet life with God is what these posts are about! *'Because I'm happy'* is the chorus of a song I can't seem to get out of my mind. So even when so many people and circumstances around me try to steal my joy, I keep my focus on God and what He would have me to do from moment to moment. I'm learning to choose my battles very wisely, becoming a professional ignorer—kindly and respectfully—in lots of cases, and to *LIGHTEN UP* and enjoy life.

My *Jesus Calling* had the best advice for me one day: "Don't let the impact of the world shatter your thinking or draw you away from focusing on Me. The ultimate challenge is to keep fixing your eyes on Me, no matter what is going on around you. When I am central in your thinking, you are able to view circumstances from My perspective."

Getting here, with my focus always on God, has been the reason why I'm feeling so happy. *I'm finally learning to relax and enjoy our adventure together.* So even with all the challenges ahead of me right now, I'm trusting God that there's nothing He and I can't handle together. I feel completely safe and secure and I'm not worried about the future, or the past, but I'm learning to enjoy all life's moments.

Dear God, thank You for standing beside us as we journey through the difficult and good times. Amen.

KEEP CALM—YOU'RE ROLLING WITH GOD

Day 109 — Live in God, Live in Love

"THIS TIME LAST YEAR WAS THE WORST PERIOD OF MY PROFESSIONAL LIFE"

Was Oprah Winfrey giving the commencement speech to the graduating class of Harvard 2013. Glad I wasn't the only one who had a rough year that year! "I was stressed and frustrated and quite frankly, I was embarrassed," is how she described it and she felt as if she was stuck in a hole. Her network that she had recently started was considered a flop and a failure. She recalled taking a long shower and the words of a hymn came to her. "Trouble don't last always. This too shall pass." And it was then that she said, "I am going to turn this thing around, and I will be better for it." She then proudly proclaimed to the graduates: "I have turned that network around!" *That's my Oprah!*

See what I tell you, we're always going to have challenges, problems, situations to deal with, but we're always going to be better off for them. Like I tell my kids, "This life is not for weaklings!" You must be tough and hang in there knowing God wants you going through it for a reason. They're valuable experiences He would have you to learn from. My challenges last year taught me so many lessons, like trusting God always, doing what I could do and leaving the rest for Him, to have constant conversations with God that have become more consistent than ever. My entire life now is becoming a very enjoyable and peaceful conversation with Him.

And speaking of peace, my sister, Kelly, sent me this quote that I love: "PEACE, it does not mean to be in a place where there is no noise, trouble or hard work. It means, to be in the midst of all those things, still, quiet and calm inside."

This is where I want all of us. We're building our house on rock, "then it is sturdy and strong and the storms can't destroy it. We are not so vulnerable to life's passing dramas. Our stability rests on something more enduring than the current weather, something permanent and strong. We're depending on God." - Marianne Williamson

Our Father, may we always depend on You no matter the challenges we face. Amen.

KEEP CALM—YOU'RE ROLLING WITH GOD

Day 110 — Live in God, Live in Love

"I QUIT!"

I wanted to tell my hubby this when he didn't agree to do things *my way*. I completely lost my peace and was so upset I didn't even want to speak to him anymore. That was until I asked, *Okay, God, what do YOU say about this situation?* and I'm still bewildered how He perfectly answered me reading *The Imitation of Christ*. I opened directly to this:

"All seek peace, but very few find it, because many do not know and do not follow the right way to attain it. Some seek it in creatures; *others in having things go according to their will*. This peace can only be found in God, by doing all to please him, by gratefully accepting from his hand the good and the evil that befalls us.

My peace is with the humble and meek of heart. Your peace shall be in the exercising of much patience. If you will listen to and follow my voice you will enjoy much peace.

What then shall I do, Lord?

In everything you do consider well what you do and what you say; and direct your whole intention to this: that you please only me and neither desire or seek anything outside of me. Do not judge rashly the sayings or doings of others; neither busy yourself with things not committed to your care; thus it will happen that you will be little or seldom disturbed."

New Nik to hubby, seeking to please God instead of being upset of things not going my way: *Hon, how best may I help you?*

"Whatever you do, do it enthusiastically, as something done for the Lord and not for men" (Colossians 3:23, HCSB).

Dear God, may our lives bring glory to You. Amen.

KEEP CALM—YOU'RE ROLLING WITH GOD

Day 111 — Live in God, Live in Love

"ONE WHO TRULY TRUSTS IN GOD...

... has no right to be anxious about anything." *That's what I'm talking about!* I'm trusting God for and with everything. I feel divinely protected and that He goes before me and everything and everyone I need will be provided. This is truly a blessed life and that's where I want you with me, living your best and blessed lives trusting that God is with us every step of the way. Here's the deal:

I stay in the present. I don't start conjuring up the worst-case scenarios in my minds. I take life one moment at a time and I trust those feelings as God directs me one step at a time. I don't have to figure out five years or even five minutes from now. I only ask, *What can I do in this moment?* I do my best and leave the rest for God! "Therefore do not worry about tomorrow, for tomorrow will worry about itself. Each day has enough trouble of its own" (Mathew 6:34).

I thank God for everything and I've realized whatever the situation is I'm going through that it could always be a lot worse and there is always so much to be grateful for.

Trust God that everything happens to evolve us forward and to grow us to become stronger and wiser individuals. I've learned that everything happens for my good! The universe is growing me up in areas I need to improve in. "And we know that for those who love God ALL things work together for good" (Roman 8:28).

I remind myself that *ALL things are possible with God.* We're not going by the ordinary rules of man; We're living *supernaturally*. It's not my business how God does what He does.

I worry about nothing, I pray about everything and I thank God for all He has done. The times when I've said, *God, I need your help with this,* is when I've seen Him turn things around for me big time. God loves when we get Him involved in our lives.

Remember the 80/20 rule in your relationships and life! "Finally, brothers, whatever is true, whatever is noble, whatever is right, whatever is pure, whatever is lovely, whatever is admirable-if anything is excellent or praiseworthy--think about such things" (Philippians 4:8). *I focus on the positives!*

Dear God, help us to truly trust You always, knowing You are helping us to fight our battles. Amen.

KEEP CALM—YOU'RE ROLLING WITH GOD

Day 112 — Live in God, Live in Love

"GOD IS THE CENTER...

...The life, and delight of our heart, and our heart will never find peace and happiness unless it rests in Him."

I finally get a story I was told years ago, when I attended a church in Florida and a pastor by the name of Dan Hall started me on this love affair with God. He asked me to come every Sunday and I did. The story was about a time he went on a missionary trip and he visited the sick ward of an awful prison. He described it as one of the worst places you could possibly imagine. It smelled horrible and I will save you the other terrible details, but as he spoke to a prisoner who laid on his dying bed with his eyes closed, telling him how much God loved him, the prisoner surprisingly opened his eyes and looked at Pastor Dan, smiled, and responded, "I know."

This prisoner, even though he was in one of the worst places, had found that peace that passes all understanding, knowing that even there, God loved and cared for Him. No matter where life may take you, you're never alone. Sometimes I have to imagine God is holding my hands super tight to get through some fires, but that comfort in knowing He's with me is the best feeling. With Him, I'm strong. I can go through any situation with *Godfidence!*

And that's when we find real peace and happiness and hit the sweet spot of life, you can go through the toughest trials and have peace knowing God is with you, even if that's in a prison, hospital or anywhere for that matter.

One of my other favorite Pastor Dan moments was when he brought out an apple during one of his sermons. He told a story of a guy having a debate with some atheists, who gave so many reasons why we should not believe in God. After which, the man calmly took a bite of the apple and then asked the atheist, "Is this apple sweet or sour?" The atheist replied, "How would I know if I haven't tasted it?" The guy then replies, "That's the same with my God, until you've tasted the sweetness, you'll never know."

Our Father, we choose to believe You are working behind the scenes of our lives. May our hearts rest in You. Amen.

KEEP CALM—YOU'RE ROLLING WITH GOD

'GOD, WHAT ARE YOU UP TO NOW?'

I got a funny suspicion He was up to something when I was told I had to wait a bit at Starbucks for my coffee. I decided to use that time waiting to download some music, and after a few minutes a friendly person showed up behind me and asked if it was me playing it. The fact that I was listening to rap music surprised her and we laughed about it as she is a rap fan as well. I finally got to place my order and she says, "I'll have the same thing she's having!" I decided to pay for her and she says, "I wanted to pay for you!"

She then tells me a story when she was in a Starbucks drive-thru one morning and the car in front of her paid for her coffee and the cashier told her she could pay for the person behind her if she liked and that they were curious to see how far the chain of the customer paying for each other would continue. *She gave me goosebumps!*

I told her about my blog posts and that every day I end it with "Live kindly," so I loved her story. I got the inclination to ask her if I could include her on my email list and she gave me her address. We've even agreed to meet up sometime with our kids for a play date. As I was leaving I heard her telling the next person in line that she would pay for their drink. I don't believe it was a coincidence we met up that afternoon, wanting the same drink and each wanting to pay for each other's. *God was behind this connection for sure!*

Here's the deal: Lisa and I never got a chance to have that playdate, but we did meet up again at Starbucks. She complained that her life was very hectic at the time and she wasn't taking time for God. I ran down to the book department and purchased my meditation book, *Jesus Calling*, and gave it to her, encouraging her to have appointments with God. And she inspired me because I didn't recognize her because she had lost so much weight and looked so good and so much younger, and we both were the same age. *My exercise and eating healthy were back on!*

Dear God, may You be our top priority. Amen.

KEEP CALM—YOU'RE ROLLING WITH GOD

I'M LOVING MY APPOINTMENTS WITH GOD

One day in passing, I noticed our security guard on his knees praying.

He explained to me that he prays early in the mornings, 12 p.m. and 5 p.m. every day. "I want to join you!" I exclaimed! From that day on, he began reminding me of our prayer time. I don't want to make God another chore on your to-do list, but I just want to share what these appointments have done for me.

I love my *iPhone,* but I hate the short battery life. Well, just like the phone needs charging, so do I. My charger, though, is the world's best super charger: God! These appointments recharge me to take on whatever that may come my way.

Like my 5 p.m. appointment one day was after a stressful two-hour meeting. I slowly walked to that alone time with Him feeling down, but I came out feeling totally recharged. God is constantly talking to us and in these meetings with Him I'm learning His important voice and what He would have me to do from moment to moment.

God seems to point me to the perfect messages to read in these appointments with Him. It was reading a blog from a terrific God connect, who reminded me in all things to give thanks. It was incredible the way he told a story telling me that compared to the challenges others face, I should be grateful. *Nik, so what? You had a rough meeting, no big deal!* That blog was perfectly timed for me. *Thanks, Vince!*

Another day's 5 p.m. appointment was extra sweet, after sitting with a customer who shared her belief that once you walk uprightly in God, He will be our shield. Twenty minutes later was my appointment time with God and this time my intuition led me to read Pastor Joel Osteen's devotional, and I just randomly opened to the following, confirming her statement:

"But You, O Lord, are a shield for me, my glory and the lifter of my head."

Winkǃ Winkǃ

Dear God, may we never forget Your Presence in our lives, refusing to worry about anything! Amen.

KEEP CALM—YOU'RE ROLLING WITH GOD

Day 115 — Live in God, Live in Love

"WHEN I'M FOCUSED ON HIM, NOTHING EVER GOES WRONG...

...When I lose focus, that's that's when it starts to get crazy!"

I said to a new friend. And it's so true! When I'm trusting in God, remembering that He's my constant Companion, slowing down, calming down, taking life one step at a time and allowing Him to guide me, everything goes incredibly smooth. But, boy or boy, when I stop trusting everything gets out of control! I'm worried, I'm thinking of all the worst-case scenarios that could come up in the future. I'm questioning whether God will be there for me and my poor little heart starts pounding and life is overwhelming and crazy.

Learning to trust God is what these posts are mainly about and I know it gets difficult sometimes, but that's where that practice, practice and more practice comes in. I was so happy when someone commented to me, "Fall off the wagon and get right back on!" Trust me, I know this life can get overwhelming at times, but I want us bravely walking with God KNOWING we don't go it alone. *WE ROLL WITH GOD!*

My hubby and I are self-employed, no regular pay checks coming in for us and all these years we've always been taken care of. Customers seem to show up. And even when they didn't come as much during the recession a few years ago, we were still okay. That was all a part of our journey learning to trust God, whether we had lots of customers or not many customers. Thanks to that experience, we trust Him more than ever. *Is there anything too difficult for God?*

Let's keep our hearts, eyes and minds focused on God, no matter what is going on in our lives. Imagine that He's with you and holding your hands every step of the way. Don't make a move without having a constant conversation with Him as to where to go and what to do! I'm loving my three daily appointments with Him. It's a closer and sweeter walk with God that I'm after and this is helping a lot. My appointment in the evening was a few minutes looking at the plants in my yard and thinking, *God, I love You,* and that was enough.

"So long as we just keep putting one foot in front of the other, and do our best, that is all the universe expects of us." Some days, they are very small steps!

Our Father, help us to never take our focus away from You. Amen.

KEEP CALM—YOU'RE ROLLING WITH GOD

"HE IS MY WONDERFUL COUNSELOR"

This relationship with God is the best!

"Anything you're going through, He wants to help you with it," I told someone recently. This person is having very terrible mood swings and I suggested having appointments (alone times) with God, reading two of my go to meditation books, *A Year of Miracles* and *Jesus Calling*. It's amazing how God has used these two books to help me grow closer to Him, where I've learn to collaborate and get Him involved with every aspect of my life. *God's an expert in everything,* so if you're not seeking His help, you're definitely missing out on the best wisdom and insights.

Pastor Joel Osteen is also one of my messengers from God and I've signed up to receive his daily emails at joelosteen.com and its amazing how God would use his messages to speak directly to me. For example, one Thursday I'm having all these fearful thoughts (I'm still very much human!) and the email from Pastor Osteen that day began with 1 John 4:18: "There is no fear in love. But perfect love drives out fear..." He spoke of God's perfect love for us that never changes: "Today, open your heart to receive His perfect love. Let love drive fear out of your life and make you new!"

I felt instantly better, *Nik, what do you have to fear? God is with you, for you and He's taking care of you. Fear nothing and no one! Is there anything that can come your way that you and God can't handle together?* He knew I needed to read that message that day! See why He's my wonderful counselor?

I stay in my appointments with God until I feel as if I've gotten a high five from Him, reading from one of my meditation books or some free podcasts on iTunes.com that have inspired me. During these quiet times, I've developed my trust muscles and most importantly, I've learned God's crucial voice so that when I'm back out in the world, I can more clearly discern what God would have me to do on a moment by moment basis. I got my high five reading only one sentence in *A Year of Miracles* yesterday:

"Confident in God, I am confident as a person."

Heads high, my fellow superhumans.

Dear God, thank You for Your wisdom that leads us on the path to the best life with You. Amen.

KEEP CALM—YOU'RE ROLLING WITH GOD

SUPERHUMANS WE SHALL BE

I had the worst, yet best dream one night that my husband left me. In the dream, I saw him with another woman and I was left there standing, frantically watching them walk away together. I thought about the dream and remembered how the person he ran off with looked a lot like me. I'm not a dream interpreter of any sorts, but I felt it was God calling me to leave the old Nikki—neurotic, dramatic, insecure, emotional, and fearful—and become the Nikki He has created me to be—confident, secure, calm, wiser, and worried about nothing.

I feel He even confirmed my interpretation when the very screen I opened to in Marianne Williamson's brilliant book, *A Year of Miracles,* had this perfect message:

"A moment of crisis can be a moment of growth, as the wounded self prepares to transform. From the chrysalis of my pain I will forge my healing-THE WINGS OF MY NEWBORN SELF. Dear God, I am preparing to be a better me, facing ways in which I have not been the person You would have me to be. Be with me as I endure the pain of my own humiliation and emerge forgiven by You and by me. Amen."

Honestly, I get so embarrassed when I think about some of the things I do and I ask myself why I do those things (like checking my husband's phone). And the simple answer is that I'm human. But watching a movie with my kids recently and thinking about everything, I believe that it's time for me to accept God's challenge from that dream and leave my old self behind and move to a higher level of living and thinking, pass those lower-level thoughts, such as insecurity, fear and jealousy.

Dear God, may we become the people You have created us to be. In every moment, please guide our thoughts and actions as we slow down, calm down and seek You. Amen.

KEEP CALM—YOU'RE ROLLING WITH GOD

Day 118 — Live in God, Live in Love

"I AM HAPPY TO LIVE THIS LIFE FOR GOD. AMEN"

This Facebook comment blew me away.

I'm with her and I'm totally thrilled to live this life all for the glory of God. "Lord, what makes YOU happy?" is the question I wrote I want to continually ask God and a few hours later, at my noon appointment with Him, He told me something I'm quite guilty of that He is not so happy about:

When you are anxious or fearful, it is as if you are doubting My promises to supply all you need. My followers tend to think of worry as natural, even inevitable. At worst, they consider it their personal problem or quirk-harming no one but themselves. But the truth is, your tendency to be anxious grieves Me. Awareness of My pain can help motivate you to break free from this hurtful habit. Seek to bring Me Joy by walking trustingly with Me along the path of Peace. - *Jesus Lives* by Sarah Young

Now knowing my worry and anxious thoughts make God sad, I plan to catch myself in those moments and instead talk to Him, *God, I trust You. You haven't let me down yet and I know You're not about to start now.* He has been my constant Back-up when any problem in any aspect of my life has come my way. I truly have no reason to doubt that He will supply all my needs. From people showing up to help me, ideas magically popping in my head, directions from Him as to what to do one step at a time, no matter how overwhelming the problem may seem.

He's gotten me through so many challenges that I can say with absolute confidence: *Keep calm, you're rolling with God.* On Monday, having a conversation with Him about my to-do list for the day, it was a small item He told me to follow up on. Turns out this little item has proved to be huge and I'm thanking Him once again for His constant direction. I may slip, but I will not fall. I'm learning to pay attention to my Spirit (God's voice within me). It could be a quiet whisper as to something to do and now I *PAY ATTENTION.*

Dear God, may the way we live our lives bring happiness to You. Amen.

KEEP CALM—YOU'RE ROLLING WITH GOD

Day 119 — Live in God, Live in Love

STAY DISCIPLINED!

That's my reminder to all of us today. And don't let the word discipline scare you. It's a Greek concept which simply means "to train," and I want us teaching ourselves to develop positive, healthy habits. I wrote that God wants us to live life to the fullest, but to get there we must do our part, too. I thought to share a few areas in my life where I've incorporated some discipline, and I'm extremely happy I did:

- Exercise is on, baby! This has been a difficult one to keep going, but when I fall off the wagon, I get right back on and like I was telling someone the other day I feel more fit now than 20 years ago. "Take care of your body, and it will take care of you!"

- Veggie smoothie whether I feel like it or not! It's my breakfast every morning, made with lots of blended fruits and vegetables with water. The benefits such as a healthier immune system and no doctor visits outweigh the bad taste any day.

- Appointments with God are the best! In the mornings, noon, and at 5 p.m. are my alone times with Him and I stay with them until I feel I've touched base with my ultimate Boss. One morning, right after I discussed with my hubby that I'm still trying to learn balance, I randomly opened a book, and it said, "There is always the invitation to balance your life. That's the great interior struggle we all share." Just the reminder from God I needed not to be so hard on myself and more importantly that He's intimately involved in all my moments. I, therefore, refuse to worry about anything! The appointments have brought me closer to God, and I've realized the closer we are to Him the better and happier our lives. *What time are your appointments?*

- Staying away from Facebook after my postings are done! "Let us strip off anything that slows us down or holds us back." So many times during the day, I'm tempted to go and check back in, but I'm amazed how I now have so much time to do other things. I love life on another level without the constant distraction. *Are you with me?*

Dear God, help us to be the disciplined, balanced, superhumans you have created us to be. Amen.

KEEP CALM—YOU'RE ROLLING
WITH GOD

Day 120 — Live in God, Live in Love

FORTY-TWO YEARS TO GET THIS LESSON

In working on my book again, I came across a post from Tumblr.com that has opened my eyes:

"For two years I longed for a close friend, for intimacy, for love. For two years I wondered why God had left me alone. For the same amount of time God was teaching me how to stop depending on people emotionally, and to depend on Him alone. He's enough."

I depend on other people emotionally for their love, intimacy, and approval. *I was starving for love and didn't know it!* And for 42 years God has been trying to teach me that *His love is more than enough!* Any additional is merely icing on the cake or if you're eating healthy, extra grapes and strawberries in an already delicious fruit salad. This doesn't mean I won't give my best to my relationships, but I'm simply not going to be so attached to the results anymore of whether they return it back to me.

A good example is my daughter, Ember. *She's a sweetheart!* In fact, I just left her making pancakes for her little brother. But when Ms. Ember doesn't get her way, she turns on me! But that doesn't stop me from giving her my best as a mom. Whether she returns the love or not, is not my business. My job from God is to be the best mother I can be, holding her tightly, loving her extravagantly and holding her loosely (with open hands) at the same time, knowing she has her own path to follow.

And this is how we should be with all our relationships, acknowledging God in all our ways, seeking His direction as what He would have us to do from moment to moment, but not needing the love, intimacy, and approval from anyone to complete us. We're 1000% loved and complete, exactly as we are, imperfections and all.

God doesn't look at our past and say He doesn't love us because of something we did five years ago. God sees us as we are now and who we're capable of becoming and He has the best plans for us. But it's sad the way we spend so much of our lives seeking the love and approval of other people and are disappointed when we don't receive it.

In every moment of our lives, let's focus on God's unconditional love of us. We're never starved of God's perfect love.

Dear God, may we come to know that You are truly all we need. Amen.

KEEP CALM—YOU'RE ROLLING WITH GOD

Day 121 — Live in God, Live in Love

"YOU ARE AMAZING GOD"

I cried so much listening to this song play on the radio by Kierra Sheard:

> "Who imagined the sun and gave source to its light
> Yet conceals it to bring us the coolness of night
> None can fathom
> Incomparable, unchangeable,
> You've seen the depths of our hearts and You love
> Us the same, You are amazing God
> You are amazing God"

Wow! God has been such an incredible Father to me, and it's my pleasure every day to write this post and remind you how awesome He is and how much He loves each and every one of us. Incomprehensible, when I think about it! You guys know all the stories, from someone calling my husband from Africa while we were in the U.S. to tell me not to worry on the most worrisome day of my life, to shoes showing up for me in a London park with a stranger while I walked home barefoot one summer and me moving to Nigeria and finding the bestest and wisest friend ever, out of 170 million people living here, who has helped me become a better wife, mother and person through her shining example.

Someone reminded me of the time my daughter took my makeup out of my purse, unknowingly to me, right before we left on vacation. Then my mom showed up the next day to our hotel room, after I told her what had happened, with brand new makeup that she had purchased the day before, which was perfect for me.

I was so happy with Ember, who, as we sat eating pizza in Target, left us to go to Starbucks saying, "I'm going to check on Grandma to see if she's okay!" as my mom sat drinking a cup of coffee alone there.

> "Incomparable, unchangeable,
> You've seen the depths of our hearts and You
> love us the same, You are amazing God You
> are amazing God"

No matter where you are or what's happened in the past, forget what anyone else may think, you can hold your head high because God loves you! We've all made mistakes, but He knows the depths of our hearts and He loves us the same. *Keep up!*

Our Father, thank You for Your unconditional, perfect, and everlasting love. Amen.

KEEP CALM—YOU'RE ROLLING WITH GOD

Day 122 — Live in God, Live in Love

I LOVE MY ENEMIES!

I opened to an excellent quote from the Dalai Lama one morning: "The enemy is a very good teacher." That got me thinking about all my so-called "enemies." Looking back on my life and past experiences, I realized that all those enemies have been ultimately the best people for me. I even wondered if God intentionally sent them my way, just to grow me up.

I have so many examples, like the person who got me going to church every Sunday. After I had gone through such an awful experience with them, I ran to church thanking God for saving me from people like them all my life. There I met Pastor Dan Hall, who started me on this love affair with God. So many times, a neighbor had invited me out to that very church before, but I never went. It took that person to get me there!

Then it was the person who got me to Nigeria, fighting for my family. The simple life here, with no electricity most of the time and not being able to drive myself, offered me the perfect opportunity to begin writing these daily posts for Facebook. Forget about anyone else; these blog posts have me bouncing around with such joy, gratitude, and peace, rolling with God, forgiving quickly, relaxed, and enjoying my adventure with Him.

Like Pastor Joel Osteen would say, "these people didn't happen to me, they happened for me. "God said He would be my vindicator. God said he would pay me back double for every injustice. So I will not drag around defeated. I will stay in faith knowing that hard times [and I'll add in "difficult people"] just qualified me for double blessings." – Pastor Joel Osteen

Dear God, thank You for all our "enemies" who push us to be the people You would have us to be. May we come to love them the way Jesus taught us. Amen.

KEEP CALM—YOU'RE ROLLING WITH GOD

Day 123 — Live in God, Live in Love

WE SHALL BE HAPPY BEINGS

I had a conversation with someone who was pretty stressed out and unhappy over her relationship with her husband. I once heard a joke that married people wish they were single and single people wished they were married! My marriage was turned around recently when I realized that there are almost ten thousand things I love about my hubby and about three things I'm not so happy with. When I focus on those ten thousand things I love and become a professional ignorer, kindly and respectfully, of those three negatives, I'm happy. But when I focus on those three things I dislike, and my mind gets stuck there, boy oh boy, *I'm miserable!*

Here's the deal: that's not only for my husband—it's for all my relationships. I'm refusing to dwell on the negatives. I'm trusting God is in complete and total control of my life, and I will listen to Him, what He would have me to do, seeking to please Him in more and more of my moments. *Would this make Papa (God) happy?* Those three things in regards to my hubby that I'm not happy about, I pray about them leaving them in God's capable hands to fix. Whether or not God corrects them and when He does is not my business. God has given me the 10,000 things to be happy about and happy shall I be, sucking the enjoyment out of every moment of my life—whether it's spending time with my family, friends, customers, employees, strangers, working on my book, writing my posts, helping my son, Emmie, with his homework, or cleaning my bathroom. Every moment of life is sacred, so let's not spend it worrying about things that are not our business, and not in our control to fix.

To my friend, be the best wife, mother, and person you can be and leave the rest with God. I'm talking *spiritual ninja* here, holding your peace and allowing God to fight for you.

> *"O God! Refresh and gladden my spirit. Purify my heart. Illumine my powers. I lay all my affairs in Thy hand. Thou art my Guide and my Refuge. I will no longer be sorrowful and grieved; I will be a happy and joyful being. O God! I will no longer be full of anxiety, nor will I let trouble harass me. I will not dwell on the unpleasant things of life.*
>
> *"O God! Thou art more friend to me than I am to myself. I dedicate myself to Thee, O Lord."* – 'Abdu'l-Bahá (Bahai Prayers)

KEEP CALM—YOU'RE ROLLING WITH GOD

Day 124 — Live in God, Live in Love

WORRY ABOUT NOTHING, PRAY ABOUT EVERYTHING

It's where I am at this very moment. "Instead of desperately striving to maintain order and control in your little world, *relax* and remember that circumstances cannot touch My (God's) Peace." Unbelievably, that's exactly where I was, worried about how I was going to take care of the situations going on in my life, instead of trusting God, who has shown me that He's always so far ahead of me and always provides the people, things, and solutions to everything I may need. How God does what He does is none of our business, but our job is to relax and trust that whatever He wants for us is best for us, even when He takes us on those treacherous paths.

Here's the deal: we're not going by the ordinary rules of man. Calm down, take life one step at a time and know we have the Creator of the entire universe as our faithful Back-up. Our attitude should be, Our Father runs the universe. Don't mess with me!" Just go out every day, advancing confidently in the direction of your dreams, being your best self, forgiving endlessly, loving extravagantly, and doing your best with whatever God has called you to do. Remember, everything is between God and us, and whenever you give your best, He will give you His best.

I had a great appointment with Him at 5 p.m., when I joined two other people to read a message from the same meditation book: "I desire each of My followers to be a Light-bearer. The Holy Spirit who lives in you can shine from your face, making Me visible to people around you, as you wind your way through this day. Hold My hand in joyful trust, for I never leave your side. The Light of My Presence is shining upon you. Brighten up the world by reflecting who I AM."

Let's go out there and brighten the world with God's love!

Dear God, thank You for having our backs. Help us to walk calmly, confidently, trustfully, and lovingly with You by our sides. Amen.

KEEP CALM—YOU'RE ROLLING WITH GOD

"GOD SAID I SHOULD BE PATIENT WITH YOU"

I said to my wonderful hubby. "I need to be patient with you," he replied. It turns out we both need to be patient with each other; this is my latest and biggest lesson in marriage. And speaking of lessons, I have some that a new friend and I came up with on Saturday that not only apply to marriages, but most great relationships, as well:

- Make God the center. Acknowledge and please Him in all your ways. He's our ultimate Boss!

- Respect one another and always refer to rule 1.

- Forgive and forget endlessly; nobody's perfect! Become a professional ignorer—kindly and respectfully, of course!

- Remember the 80/20 rule. Focus on the 80% positives and be happy or concentrate on the 20% negative and be miserable!

- Live kindly and love extravagantly! Love covers many faults. Practice being patient and bearing with each other.

- Ask, *How may I serve?* and *What can I give?* not *What's in this for me?*

- Commit to sticking with it and battling it out through the tough times, as it only gets better after you go through those rough spots together.

- Don't worry about whether they'll be there tomorrow; savor every moment together instead. *Love fearlessly!*

- Leave the past in the past, but remember the lessons it taught you. See the innocence in your spouse and not their guilt, forgetting past hurts and failures.

- No digging through your spouse's phone. Give them privacy, space and respect. The battle and unnecessary policing belongs to God. Focus on doing your best to be the spouse God would have you to be and leave the rest with Him. "You shall hold your peace and the Lord will fight for you" (Exodus 14:14).

Dear God, may we learn to seek Your guidance in all our decisions regarding all our relationships. Amen.

KEEP CALM—YOU'RE ROLLING WITH GOD

"NIKKI, YOU'RE SUCH A NERD"

Some great friends wished me the best for the upcoming year and Nikki the Nerd said, "My wish for the year is for a closer walk with God." *Nik, who talks like that? I want a closer walk with God!* Good thing my friends already knew that I'm such a nerd! That was until Pope Francis gave his Christmas day message and included this excellent message:

"My hope is that everyone will feel God's closeness, live in His presence, love Him and adore Him. May each of us give glory to God above all by our lives, by lives spent for love of him and of all our brothers and sisters."

I pray for a closer walk with God for all of us each and every year.

"Lord, make me an instrument of your peace,
Where there is hatred, let me sow love;
where there is injury, pardon;
where there is doubt, faith;
where there is despair, hope;
where there is darkness, light;
where there is sadness, joy;
O Divine Master, grant that I may not so much seek to be consoled as to console;
to be understood as to understand;
to be loved as to love.
For it is in giving that we receive;
it is in pardoning that we are pardoned;
and it is in dying that we are born to eternal life." - St. Francis of Asisi

KEEP CALM—YOU'RE ROLLING WITH GOD

Day 127 — Live in God, Live in Love

WOW! A CHALLENGE FROM GOD

One Monday evening, I was asked, "Do you ever regret being kind to people who are ungrateful?"

I quickly responded, "Never! I regret when I'm not kind."

Fast forward to Wednesday morning in my appointment with God, reading a devotional of over 700 pages from the Catholic Church, I got a challenge for us from God in regards to those ungrateful people we all have in our lives:

"The Passage of today refers to God by name: 'The Most High.' There are certain obligations assigned to this name, which must be fulfilled in order to be worthy of being called Children of the Most High God. These include: love our enemies, do good, and lending without expecting repayment. These may seem easy, but in reality they are hard to fulfill. To achieve them will be to push ourselves to a heroic degree of extreme and go against all our natural inclinations. There is no natural motive for loving our enemies, only a supernatural one. This supernatural motive is to imitate God, for the 'Most High' is good to the ungrateful and the wicked. It is tough enough being kind to the ungrateful; those who never show any form of appreciation. It is even more difficult being kind towards the wicked. They are not only ungrateful, but repay good with evil to the one who is kind to them. As children of the 'Most High' we are challenged to go the extra mile in doing good."

Moral: "Everything is between God and us, it was never between us and anyone else." Every good thing in our lives is a blessing from God. What anyone else is doing is none of our business. Our business is to be the people God has called us to be. I offer my entire life to Him, not expecting anything in return from anyone because God is so astonishingly good to me. Today, I accept His challenge to go the extra mile and be my kindest self, knowing the repayment from God is always the best. *Are you in with me?*

God, help us to imitate You, being kind to everyone and going the extra mile in doing good, all for Your glory. Amen.

KEEP CALM—YOU'RE ROLLING WITH GOD

Day 128 — Live in God, Live in Love

A SHAKE UP TO WAKE HER UP

After a conversation with a friend who was going through some stuff in her marriage, I shared the following lessons I'd learned after 12 years with my hubby (BTW: most apply to all relationships):

Lesson 1- Keep your marriage fresh and exciting, working on constant and never-ending improvement and not taking your partner for granted. Don't settle for a good marriage and not work towards having a great one.

Lesson 2 - *Toughen up!* Every couple goes through stuff, but in my experience, those issues have always brought my hubby and me closer together. *Stick with it and don't give up!* We always come through with a deeper appreciation for one another, but you don't appreciate it when you're going through it, though.

Lesson 3 - Leave the past in the past. Whenever your mind is tempted to think about the past, catch yourself and say, *No, I'm not going there!* The past only exists in our minds. Instead, focus on believing and trusting God for the best marriage.

Lesson 4 - Worry about nothing, pray about everything! Be the best spouse you can be and leave the rest with God. He is in control and nothing's impossible for Him!

Lesson 5 - *Calm down!* Don't argue when both of you are upset. Find the right time to have meaningful discussions.

Lesson 6 - Become a professional ignorer (kindly and respectfully, of course). *Only God's perfect!* Choose your battles very carefully remembering not every battle is yours to fight!

Lesson 7- Practice the 80/20 rule. Focus on the 80% positives you love about your spouse and be incredibly happy, instead of making yourself miserable by focusing on the 20% negatives.

Lesson 8 - Accept the apologies you never get. Lighten up sometimes. Life and your marriage will become lots easier.

Lesson 9 - Love extravagantly, *be extremely patient*, and forgive quickly and endlessly. Life is too short to be anything but happy.

Lesson 10 - *Run* to God in every decision, seeking to please Him always. Everything is between God and us.

Dear God, may Your love shine through us in all our relationships. Amen.

KEEP CALM—YOU'RE ROLLING WITH GOD

Day 129 — Live in God, Live in Love

"WORRY ABOUT EVERYTHING AND PRAY ABOUT NOTHING!"

Was what I accidently said to my beautiful and cool daughter, Ember, one Sunday. I asked her to decide the topic for my daily post that day from three options, and she picked this one, the very one I didn't want to write about, but I have a feeling God wants me to share it:

This story begins almost exactly four years ago, on the very morning I was to go into the hospital to give birth to Joshie. The phone starting ringing at around 3 a.m. with the voice of a lady laughing in the background. She kept calling and hanging up that morning and about every other morning for a couple of weeks. These calls were literally and figuratively my wake-up calls to fight for my marriage and a big reason why I decided to move to Nigeria. In my husband's defense, he had a business relationship with this person, but apparently, she wanted me out of the picture. Whatever the case, she surely got my attention!

A lot has happened since then, and I thank God for a very good friend who taught me the valuable lesson to leave the past in the past. Whenever I'm tempted to bring up old hurts, I only remind myself to not go there. Instead, I kept hope alive and I worried about nothing and I prayed about everything I was concerned about. Now my hubby wakes me up to attend church with him Sunday mornings. I enjoy our work together and coming home in the evenings to have dinner with him, and the kids is something I cherish. I am a super proud wife of the man my husband has become, and I have so much love and respect for him. Our marriage is still a work in progress, but I'm happy and excited about our future together.

God doesn't promise us lives without challenges, but when we stay on the high road with Him, not only will He bring us out of those challenges, He will bring us better off than we were before them. *This is my testimony.*

Dear God, May we live our lives on the high road with You, forgiving endlessly, loving extravagantly and leaving the past in the past.

KEEP CALM—YOU'RE ROLLING WITH GOD

"... AND WHEN YOU'RE CLOSEST TO GOD, YOUR LIFE IS RICHEST!"

God's so incredible.

Everything and everyone I seem to need or want always shows up for me. I'm so spoiled that I just expect everything to go in my favor and when it doesn't I say, *Okay, God, what's going on here?* But I still know that what doesn't show up is still all a part of His perfection and His will for me. I feel so blessed and like Nene from Housewives of Atlanta might say, "I'm rich!" And I'm not talking just about financial riches (for some reason this isn't a concern anymore as I trust God will always provide me with all that I need in that department) but in regards to my happiness, peace, joy, health, relationships, and contentment...*I'M RICH!*

How do you get close to God and experience this abundant life? Start by watching your thoughts. Thoughts such as fear, unforgiveness, revenge, limits, jealousy, anger, worry, and hatred all take us away from God and only make us miserable. Whereas thoughts of love, kindness, joy, hope, gratitude, no limits, trust, faith, forgiveness, patience, and peace bring us closer to God and there we're happy. Thank you, Dr. Wayne Dyer, for teaching me this! What am I thinking about, am I getting closer to God or away from God? Ask yourself the following questions:

- How kind am I?
- How loving am I?
- How forgiving am I?
- How grateful am I?
- How trusting in God am I?

In areas where you're not doing well, keep practicing because that's what it's all about. *Practice, practice, practice and more practice.* We may not get it right all the time, but God sees our hearts, and He knows when we're trying to do better and become the people He would have us to be.

As St. Paul said, "God is able to provide you with every blessing in abundance." Get close to God, "and you will know it beyond any and all doubt."

Dear God, may we go out every day being our most loving, kind, forgiving, joyful, and grateful selves, trusting You always. Amen.

KEEP CALM—YOU'RE ROLLING WITH GOD

"WHAT KIND THING DID YOU DO FOR SOMEONE TODAY?"

I asked my kids.

It's so important to be kind, and I want them to get this. I'm constantly blown away when everything and everyone I need always shows up for me. Like the time my three kids and I walked from our house to one of our favorite stores, Target. *It was a Sunday morning we'll never forget!* Target turned out to be a lot further than we had anticipated by foot and they kept asking if we were almost there. By the time we made it, we were all exhausted. We ended up hanging out in Starbucks and met some new friends, sharing our little adventure there. After resting a bit, we did our shopping, but we were dreading the long walk back home. After paying for our groceries, we looked behind us and next in line to pay was our next-door neighbor, Scott, who piled us all in his car, stroller and all, and gave us a ride home. *Phew!*

Just like this neighbor showed up, anything and everyone I need seems always to be there when I need them, as if right on cue. That's why I repeat often, everything is between you and God, not between you and anyone else. Whatever you do for another is repaid by God, and His repayments are the best. The healthy, happy, and wonderful kids I have, the best husband in the world, the kindest mom, the most terrific and best family and friends are only some of the blessings He's thrown my way. And, I don't take that for granted. I joked with my hubby, as we ate some dinner he cooked, "'Hon, this is what I don't like about you. You prepare the most delicious foods, and I end up eating too much!"

Moral: I'm convinced that anything you do, no matter how small, is personally returned to you by God. Don't worry what anyone else is doing. Be the kindest person you know and God's blessings will chase you down. I ask God how I can serve, and it's like He turns around and says, *Nik, your wish is my command.*

"Don't get tired of doing what is good. Don't get discouraged and give up, for you will reap a harvest of blessings at the appropriate time" (Galatians 6:9).

Dear God, may we never tire of doing Your will. Amen.

KEEP CALM—YOU'RE ROLLING WITH GOD

Day 132 — Live in God, Live in Love

"SUPER WIFE, MOM, AND PERSON IS BACK, BABY, ALL FOR THE GLORY OF GOD"

That was the last sentence of a post that has motivated me to give my all for God.

"God gives you everything, but God asks everything of you because that is what real relationship is." As I often write, everything is between God and us, not between us and anyone else. Regardless of what my husband is doing or not doing, I'm going to be the best possible wife because I know that's what God has called me to do. And doing my best goes not only for my great hubby but for everyone in my life. Real relationships are not about getting, but about giving, and I want a genuine relationship with God where I'm not only praying to Him asking Him to do for me, but I'm constantly thinking about how I can do all that I can do for Him. Like Shaun T says in my ab work out, "Attack your life!" The attack is on for me to be who God would have me to be in every moment, every example, and every experience.

And speaking of God giving me everything, we saw the conclusion of a challenge we went through recently and as usual, God showed up and showed off, like He was saying, *Hey, don't mess with my people!* This situation was such a learning experience from day one to the end, with God showing me that He goes before me and beside me and together we can handle *anything* that may come my way.

The big lesson was to trust Him, and my faith muscles grew big time with everything and everyone we needed showing up to help us get through, one step at a time. We didn't need to know the next ten steps, only one at a time. I was quite astonished how I would get through one stage, and the next step would casually pop into my mind as to what to do. I came through it with more love and respect for God, which gives me even more reason to give everything for Him, who is always giving everything to me.

"May the days be gone when I took for granted all the blessings in my life." —Marianne Williamson, *A Year of Miracles: Daily Devotions and Reflections*

God, I'm grateful. Fear no one...

Dear God, may everything we do bring glory to You. Amen.

KEEP CALM—YOU'RE ROLLING WITH GOD

Day 133 — Live in God, Live in Love

"I HAVE A FATHER WHO'LL NEVER EVER FAIL ME"

That's the attitude I want us to have, knowing God, our Father, will never ever fail us.

I'm thinking about a disappointment that He has used for my good. No joke, instead of complaining about the lemon in my life, I've made lemonade. Instead of becoming bitter, I've become better. God gives us challenges, problems, tribulations to help us become the people He would have us to be. We can use any situation to grow and learn and become better. *Complaining is not what we super humans do!*

God wants us living our lives to the fullest and by looking at any situation from a perspective of *how can I be better from this*, you can turn a "negative" experience into a "positive" one. I love what Dr. Wayne Dyer wrote on this topic:

"Creative aliveness means looking around any setting where you find yourself and asking, "How can I make this into a terrific experience? What can I say, think, feel or do that will bring about learning and fulfillment for me?" This kind of an attitude is yours to have if you decide to want it, and to stop allowing yourself to be victimized by yourself or those around you.

Your capacity to be creatively alive in virtually all life circumstances will depend in large part upon the kind of attitude you choose for yourself. The most crucial test of your attitude development will be in the face of adversity, rather than while things are running smoothly."

Lately, I've been dealing with a challenge that came up. I felt God saying that I should use it to trust Him more. And from the beginning of it coming up, I've been getting winks from Him that He will help me. I've been constantly blown away with how He has been helping me with step by step instructions and guidance, people to assist me, the miraculous disappearance of a glitch in my computer that made my work tons easier. *It has been fun watching God work on my behalf.*

Moral: We all have a Father who'll never fail us, and He can incredibly use everything for our good. By keeping our eyes fixed on Him and what He would have us to do, and who He would have us to be, no matter the hurt, disappointments, or adversities that come our way, God will never fail us.

"Then you will know that I am the Lord; those who hope in me will not be disappointed." - Isaiah 49:23

Father, thank You for Your faithfulness. Amen.
KEEP CALM—YOU'RE ROLLING WITH GOD

"DEAR LORD, LET US BE A GENERATION THAT SEEKS YOUR FACE" (via letters-tothelord), Tumblr

This quote got me excited, and I want to do as much as I possibly can to make this a reality. Julie, at 10 p.m. one night, asked me if she could have an appointment with God before going to bed. Then, returning from school the next day, she asked me to join her in another one. That appointment was a total God wink at me, as I took some time to talk to a new young friend that afternoon and I encouraged her to get God involved in her life by listening for His direction. I quoted one of the most important verses in the Bible for me to her: "My sheep listen to my voice" (John 10:27, NIV). And less than two hours, having that appointment with Julie, I asked if I could pick what to read from her devotional for girls and I randomly opened to a scripture that read, "I AM your good shepherd... Try to depend on the help of the Spirit as you go through this day of life. Pause briefly from time to time, so you can consult this Holy One inside you. He will not force you to do His bidding, but He will guide you as you give Him space in your life."

I spent a good part of my day with an important customer. I wrote a post about him months ago, when I got a nudge from God to follow him when my hubby took him to one of our employees to do something pretty simple. My spirit told me to get involved, asking him if he would wait for an introductory letter from us to take to his firm. He did and based on our conversation and that letter, he has been back many times with lots of business for us.

Get God involved with everything, seeking his face in those 1,000 decisions you make every day, trusting your intuition/gut/feelings to guide you, doing as much as you possibly can and leaving the rest with God.

"As you seek God, you will find Him—His solutions, His comfort, His direction, His endurance, His wisdom, His love." — Maria Fontane, *Mottos For Success*

> Dear Lord, let us be a generation that seeks Your face. Amen.

KEEP CALM—YOU'RE ROLLING WITH GOD

Day 135 — Live in God, Live in Love

"ENJOY THEM!"

This was a needed reminder in regards to spending the summer with my kids from Carlos, another one of our God hook-ups. Ever since he wrote that in an email, I've changed my perspective from that I have to take care of them myself this summer, to *I get* to take care of them.

We had the best day together, pretty much in our kitchen waiting for an appliance technician to show up. We cooked, made smoothies, cleaned, played, and laughed. After the tech left, I then took them swimming and by the time I gave them dinner and cleaned up I was super tired. Emmie came and lied next to me in bed, and it was the sweetest thing because I always tell him he only comes to see me when he wants something.

And speaking of enjoying them, I especially enjoy my little, then three-year-old, Joshie! "Why can't everyone be like you?" is what I asked him one day taking out the trash together. *He's my little sweetie pie!* If everyone in my life were like Joshie, life would be super great! He always wants to help, always asking, "How may I serve?" in his little three-year-old way. If he ever does anything that I have to correct him about, no arguments, he says, "Sorry, mommy!" He's always happy and he's forever kissing me and hugging me. And he's also so grateful. While driving one day, out of the blue, like a little man, he said, "Thank you, mom!"

How do people experience being around you? Are you a happy person to be around, humble (quick to admit when you're wrong), grateful, asking "How may I serve?" instead of, "What's in it for me?" *Just asking!* The world needs more Joshies, don't you think?

Let's learn to enjoy everyone in our lives. I spoke to my mother-in-law for the longest over the phone, and I couldn't believe when she told me that I've been the perfect mother! Is this from the same person I've had so many arguments with in regards to how I was raising my kids? In all my years of life, I can say I've learned that nobody's perfect.

Dear God, may we lighten up, be quick to forgive and enjoy everyone in our lives. Amen.

KEEP CALM—YOU'RE ROLLING WITH GOD

Day 136 — Live in God, Live in Love

"YOU DROPPED THE BOMB ON ME, BABY...

...you dropped the bomb on me!" *Sing it with me!* I had the best time watching the BET Music Awards with my kids. Watching first name Charlie, last name Wilson, perform this song was one of the best moments and especially when he was joined on stage by Justin Timberlake, Pharrell, and Snoop Dogg/Lion. My then three and five-year-old sons danced with A$AP Rocky, during his performance, and the reggae artists were also some of my favorite entertainers of the night. Seeing Charlie Wilson totally reinvent himself at age 60 made me feel so good, and he rocked it! I'm hitting 40 and running on a treadmill, I said to myself that I refuse to get old. Seeing him on stage was the added inspiration I needed.

"Don't ask what the world needs, ask what makes you come alive and do that, because what the world needs is more people that have come alive!" Seeing all those performers last night reminded me of this quote from Howard Thurman, because they've all done that. I'm talking about actors, singers, athletes, and rappers to people such as doctors, firefighters, nurses, teachers, authors, social workers, and entrepreneurs, who have all followed their hearts and pursued their dreams.

And that's what I want to inspire us to be about. I love how God has designed everything so perfectly. This life is filled with such adventures and challenges, if we choose to see it that way. Yes, we all have some stuff that doesn't work out sometimes, but that's all a part of the perfection. *Really, though, what is there to complain about?* We should wake up every day excited, pursuing our dreams and focused on living the best lives. I know people probably think I'm crazy, but talking, writing, and learning about God makes me come alive, along with being super mommy, super wife and super person.

"Don't ask what the world needs. Ask what makes you come alive and do that, because what the world needs is more people who have come alive."

Dear God, may we all find our passions and do that which makes us come alive and makes You happy. Amen.

KEEP CALM—YOU'RE ROLLING WITH GOD

"WRITE ABOUT NOT COMPLAINING"

It was the suggestion of my brilliant then ten-year-old daughter, Julie, when I asked for ideas for my blog post.

She reminded me of the time we tried going consecutively for 21 days without complaining, but we never made it past one day. Every complaint meant starting all over again, but that experience was so good for us. We now catch each other whenever we complain, and even when she's not around, I remind myself to stop complaining and focus on all the positives in every situation instead.

Here's the deal: God took me all the way to Nigeria to teach me this all-important life lesson: *Really, what is there to complain about?* We have so much to be thankful for, and when we complain, we do not appreciate our many blessings from God. In every moment, there's so much to be thankful for.

One day driving the kids home from school brought this lesson home to me. I stopped at a traffic signal and freaked out when I saw a young man with deformed legs crawling in the dirt. I was so horrified that I screamed when it looked as if a reversing car was about to roll over him. I immediately did a U-turn so that I could go back and give him some money. I had to get out of my car to track him down, but I'll never forget seeing his legs up close. He said to me, "God bless you," and I replied, "You're so brave."

I was thinking I was doing him a favor by giving him that money, but he gave me so much more. A Nikki who complained about everything was now bubbling over with gratitude, instead. He opened my eyes to a world of blessings that I took for granted. I'm now focused on the 10,000 things I'm grateful for. Even for a smile, I'm thankful to God.

Gratitude is the way to the most beautiful life with God. I challenge you to go the 21 consecutive days without complaining. That experience will change your life, I promise you. Consistently catch yourself complaining and practice replacing those thoughts about anyone or anything with positive ones.

Our Father, in every situation, may we always remember that we have so much to be thankful for. Amen.

KEEP CALM—YOU'RE ROLLING WITH GOD

Day 138 — Live in God, Live in Love

... ENJOY THE DAY

Were the words that gave me happy chills yesterday, in an appointment with God, reading this Tumblr.com post:

"Morning is God's way of saying one more time, go make a difference, touch a heart, encourage a mind, inspire a soul and enjoy the day."

And enjoying my days I've been doing a little bit more of these days. This morning was a morning of sucking the enjoyment out of each moment kissing my hubby and our kids, especially my first son, Emmie. Yesterday in going to check up on him at school, I noticed he started racking up lots of "dots" again for misbehaving, so this morning was a kissing session to encourage him to improve on that – *nobody's perfect.*

With God's constant reminders that He's with me every step of the way, I can refuse to worry about anything, and I can relax and enjoy my life's adventure with Him. Like yesterday I was amazed when that morning I complained to my "Eat To Live" group that I had gained weight and I wrote to them, "We keep moving forward, *NOT BITTER, BETTER.*" Then, fast forward to my five-pm appointment with God, I got the feeling to read of all pages, page 80 of my unpublished book and unbelievably it was entitled, "NOT BITTER, BETTER." *Wink, Wink!*

I sent a message to that person I wrote about yesterday who I feel has been giving me the cold treatment lately, and they replied, "I love you and I will always love you, but that message is too long for me to read. LOL" I replied, "LOL," because that message was too long! I've decided not to take myself or the situation too serious, I will always love them too. God has filled my life with such beauty, and I'm not going to take any of it for granted. As I kissed my hubby, I also thanked him for everything he does for us to have this beautiful life. I know without a doubt I was born destined to marry him. Of all names in the world, my dad gave me the name "Oneka" meaning African Princess. Being born in the Bahamas, and to end up marrying an African and living and enjoying the best life in Nigeria, was no coincident. *God had everything all planned long before I was even born!*

Dear God, help us to relax, walk joyously with You and enjoy the day. Amen.

KEEP CALM—YOU'RE ROLLING WITH GOD

THAT WAS THE PERFECT MESSAGE FOR CRAZY LADY OVER HERE:

"BAD NEWS IS: you cannot make people like, love, understand, validate, accept, or be nice to you. You can't control them, either. GOOD NEWS IS: it doesn't matter." —Unknown

Wow! So true! It doesn't matter whether people like, love, understand, validate, accept, or are nice to you, it's much more important how God feels about us. One of the underlying reasons why I've been so crazy lately is because I'm trying to figure out what I could have possibly done to some people in my life who seem to dislike me, then this quote shows up right on time to say, *Nik, it doesn't matter.*

Here's the deal: I've seen people go from loving me one day and hating me the next, but that's life. I love how God is transforming me to be the person He has created me to be, where I stay on the high road with Him, doing the excellent and right thing I feel He would have me to do from moment to moment, regardless of how anyone may feel about me. God's love is constant and everlasting, and He never disappoints. He even uses the evil and turns it into my good.

I've asked God to use me however He likes, and I'm offering my life as a sacrifice to Him, and whether someone appreciates me or not is not my business, as long as I know I'm doing what I feel God would have me to do. I have a calendar I go to hear from Him that says: "It's much better to have the attitude of, 'Am I doing enough? What more can I do?' rather than the attitude of 'I'm doing so much, I'm giving so much. Others should be grateful.'"

"If you ever wonder if anyone cares and sees the effort you make, always know that God does." —Maria Fontane, Mottos For Success

"For God is not unjust to forget your work and labor of love" (Hebrews 6:10, NKJV).

I'll never get over how God reveals Himself to me to let me know He's with me, like reading through posts on tumblr.com and I saw one that read: "HE MUST INCREASE I MUST DECREASE"

I loved it so much I saved it, and fast forward about an hour or so later I had my 12 p.m. appointment with God and out of all the books I could've opened to, the very book and the very page I opened to said: "You must decrease so He can increase." *Wink! Wink!*

Dear God, may we come to know that Your love for us is enough. Amen.

KEEP CALM—YOU'RE ROLLING WITH GOD

WORKING TO BE THE MOST AWESOME VERSION OF ME

This is the thing to shoot for! Not competing with anyone else, only trying every day to be better than we were the day before.

I posted a picture on Facebook with the caption, "The belly is going down!" I had made up my mind that I would finally work on my big tummy, and I committed to my T25 workouts from beachbody.com six days a week, even when I didn't feel like it. Next areas to be worked on include procrastination, maximizing every moment, being more merciful, patient, less complaining, and practicing love in action every minute, example, and experience.

I love what my meditation book, *The Imitation of Christ,* had to say to get us motivated to accomplish our goals, which we can begin again at any moment *(hint: like right now!)*:

"Each day we ought to renew our resolutions and arouse ourselves to fervor as though it were the first day of our religious life. We ought to say, "Help me, O Lord God, in my resolution and in Your holy service. Grant me now, this very day, to begin perfectly, for thus far I have done nothing.

As our intention is, so will be our progress; and he who desires perfection must be diligent. If the strong willed man fails frequently, what of the man who makes up his mind seldom or halfheartedly? Many are the ways of failing in our resolutions...

Much as we try, we still fail too easily in many things. Yet we must always have some fixed purpose, especially against things that beset us the most.

If you cannot recollect yourself continuously, do so at least once a day at least, in the morning or in the evening. In the morning make a resolution and in the evening examine yourself on what you have said this day, what you have done and thought..."

I've only talked about this book for years, but excuse after excuse, it never happens. Fall off the wagon and get right back on. I'm a halfhearted creature for sure, but I'm pulling out major backup this time:

"Help me, O Lord God, in my resolution and in Your holy service. Grant me now, this very day, to begin perfectly, for thus far I have done nothing."

KEEP CALM—YOU'RE ROLLING WITH GOD

Day 141 — Live in God, Live in Love

"HAPPY"

I sang this song over and over again, by one of my fav people lately, Pharrell Williams, hanging out at the beach with the kids. Joshie kept pulling me in the water with him to catch all the big waves, jumping and screaming, "Big one! Big one!"

I was singing *Because I'm Happy* and I meant it because I know I handle nothing alone and God is astoundingly helping me in every aspect of my life. I can, therefore, relax and enjoy my life's adventure with Him, refusing to worry about anything. And even stuff that may be a little off, I am not worried about them because I know God is helping me piece by piece and little by little to get them on the right track again. He is always teaching us lessons, and each experience, if we're open, has so much to teach. Not everything will always run smoothly and go exactly how we want them, but the worst challenges have taught me a valuable lesson of being filled with hope, despite how everything might seem in my human mind, knowing everything is not only by my power but by God's power. I love how Pastor Joel Osteen puts this:

"A lot of times, we have our own ideas about how things should work out in life. But God's ways are not our ways. In scripture, God brought water out of a rock. Jesus told Peter to go catch a fish, open its mouth, and there was the money he needed for taxes. Another time, God caused a young lady named Mary to have a baby without knowing a man. He is God. He can use things we would expect, or He can make things happen another way."

In fact, God never ceases to amaze me with the perfect people, things (like the perfect sized walking shoes that showed up in a London park with a stranger as I walked home barefoot) and solutions to complicated problems (when I know I'm not that smart!). Again, we're not going by the ordinary rules of man. Let's take life one quarter mile at a time, listening to God by trusting our intuition/gut/spirit to guide us. Where our lives are a little something like this:

God, what do we do here? God, what do we do here? God, what do we do here?

And when we solve one set of problems together...*God, I'm exceedingly grateful!*

Dear God, may we never forget that we are not going by the ordinary rules and that nothing is impossible for You. Amen.

KEEP CALM—YOU'RE ROLLING WITH GOD

Day 142 — Live in God, Live in Love

"THE SUMMER OF OPRAH!"

That's what I called one summer with my kids.

She's been like a big sister whom I've never met, and I wanted to pass on to my children some of the important lessons I've learned from her over the years. They might hate me for it at the end of this summer, but even if I only engrained a little of the following into them, I'll feel like I've accomplished something great:

- Oprah's secret to success: Doing the right and excellent thing in every moment, every example, and every experience. God is our Ultimate Boss, and when we do everything pleasing to Him, He has our backs. "Many are the afflictions of the righteous, but the Lord delivers him out of all of them" (Psalm 34:19, KJV). *Wink, wink!* God, I love You!

- LISTEN! Don't make a move without first hearing from God as to what to do, where to go, or even what to say. This is the key to making the best decisions. A decision where I paid attention to those feelings turned out to be more valuable than I could've even imagined. "My sheep listen to my voice; I know them, and they follow me" (John 10:27, NIV).

- "There's no such thing as luck. Success happens when opportunity and preparation meet!" Every day I'm having my older kids summarize a New York Times' article and write the definition and sentences of two new vocabulary handwriting, and grammar.

- Work hard! I've come to realize life is lots of work and it's my job to prepare my kids for whatever may come their way. Like they say in Nigeria, "No food for lazy man!" And that means no housekeeper and lots of chores! One morning, I started helping my daughter with her kitchen duty, thinking it was a lot for her and she calmly said, "Mom, I don't need your help. This isn't much." *Thank You, God!*

- "When you do well, people notice." My mom was the person who taught me that you can take an entire day to clean a kitchen. When you take this same philosophy of going beyond the minimum of what's required of you throughout your life and doing everything exceedingly well, people notice, but more importantly God notices, and all our blessings are from Him.

Dear God, thank You for all teachers. Amen.
KEEP CALM—YOU'RE ROLLING WITH GOD

"THE BIG LESSON IN LIFE, BABY...

... Is never be scared of anyone or anything." – Frank Sinatra

"I take it this guy has lived a pretty charmed life...either that, or he's either delusional or profoundly stupid," was a comment I received after posting this quote on Facebook. Well, I guess I must be included as delusional because I 1000% agree with Mr. Sinatra on this. This is the big, big, big lesson. We can go through life having NO FEAR, no matter who or what comes our way, KNOWING we have major Backup: *God!*

Here's the deal: Whatever God wants for us is best for us. We're like his personal projects and every problem, challenge, difficulty, obstacle, or supposedly "bad" person that comes our way goes through His hands first, and they're all for our good to get us to be the people He would have us to be. They've all grown me up and trained me to trust God. UNFLINCHING is the word I love and where I always want to be, knowing I roll with God, who goes before me and is beside me always, guiding and directing my life. This gives me more reasons to suck up to Him and stay as close to Him as possible.

Let's not let the future spook us. Turn those fears about the future into confident trust. Whenever thoughts of fear come, remind yourself, "I'm trusting God here!" Do what you have to do and leave the rest to God. Honestly, He hasn't let me down yet!

I'm getting this lesson, Mr. Sinatra: Never be scared of anyone or anything. Slow down, calm down, and maintain those endless conversations with God. Even in dealing with people, while you're talking to them, talk to God as well. He'll give you the right words to say or, like He often does to me, tells you when to shut up, as well as what decisions to make based on those conversations.

I love a cartoon depicting a little girl walking along a path with a huge hand holding her little hand with the caption: "If God is for us, who can be against us?" (Romans 8:31, NIV).

Dear Lord, may we be FEARLESS, trusting You always. Amen.

KEEP CALM—YOU'RE ROLLING WITH GOD

Day 144 — Live in God, Live in Love

"WHAT'S THE NEXT RIGHT MOVE?"

My husband called me from Nigeria, and he suggested that we shouldn't return there immediately after he saw a terrible news report on TV. The whole day I spent thinking about what to do, and I even said to my hubby, "I know God will direct us. He has never let us down before. He told us the first time that we should move to Nigeria and I don't regret that decision, and I'm positive He'll direct us again."

Fast forward a few hours later, I'm having the best conversation with an old friend, and she tells me a God story. She confessed to being a worrier and one day as she worried about having an accident and not wearing her seatbelt, she incredibly heard the Holy Spirit say, "I am your protection," calling her by her name in a loud, clear voice. I got goose bumps all over when I heard that. I've heard the same voice before so to hear someone else hear it too got the God maniac a little excited.

I didn't get it at the time, but the next morning I realized that was also God's message to me through her. There I was debating all day concerning God's direction, worried about our safety in Nigeria and that story answered me—*Nik, I am your protection! Whether you're in the US or Nigeria, I am with you!*

I love that we're never alone and God's always with us, guiding and directing us. But we must PAY ATTENTION. He's always communicating with us, and His answers can come from anywhere. In this case, it came from my good friend, Brigitte! *Thanks, my girl!*

"God is our refuge and strength, an ever-present help in trouble. Therefore, we will not fear, though the earth give way and the mountains fall into the heart of the sea" (Psalm 46:1-2).

Dear God, thank You for love and guidance. Amen.

KEEP CALM—YOU'RE ROLLING WITH GOD

MY MESSENGERS FROM GOD LATELY: JOEL AND VICTORIA OSTEEN

God's always speaking to us, and lately, He's had the perfect messages for me from this couple. The devotional they shared has meant so much to me that I want to share it with you. It just reminded me to trust God and His timing. Not everything is in my control, but in God's control, and I have to stay on the high road with Him—forgiving endlessly, loving extravagantly, doing my best in what He has asked me to do, and leaving the rest with Him. Enough from me, though, here's what my messengers had to say:

The Time Has Already Been Set

TODAY'S SCRIPTURE: "My times are in your hands..." - (Psalm 31:15, NIV)

TODAY'S WORD: In life, oftentimes we are waiting for something; waiting for a dream to come to pass, waiting to meet the right person, waiting for a problem to turn around. When things aren't happening as fast as we would like, it's easy to get frustrated. But you have to realize, the moment you prayed, God established a set time to bring the promise to pass.

God has a set time for your opportunity. There is a set time for that problem to turn around, a set time for your healing, your promotion, your breakthrough. It may be tomorrow, next week or five years from now, but when you understand the time has already been set, it takes all the pressure off. You won't live worried, wondering when this is ever going to happen. You'll relax and enjoy your life knowing that the promise has already been scheduled.

Father, I choose to trust in Your timing. I trust that You have my best in mind. I believe that You are working behind the scenes on my behalf. Thank You for ordering my steps and leading me in the way!"
— Joel & Victoria Osteen

KEEP CALM—YOU'RE ROLLING WITH GOD

Day 146 — Live in God, Live in Love

PAY ATTENTION TO THOSE FEELINGS

For the most part, that's how God communicates with us - through our feelings and emotions.

Call it gut, intuition, spirit, or Sponge Bob, if you like, just pay attention to it! Living in Nigeria has been off the chain with lessons, and this has certainly been a huge one. I have lots of stories I could share with you, but here's one that happened recently.

I had to let go of a housekeeper who was with me for only about a month and a half. The funniest thing happened. Out of the blue one morning, a thought came to mind, *Pay attention to this.* It was something in my bedroom that my gut/spirit told me to pay attention to. Usually, I'm unconcerned about stuff, and I don't have expensive jewelry or anything because I don't want to spend my life worrying about or taking care of material things. Fast forward two days later, half of the items, what my spirit told me to watch, were all of a sudden, gone! This was just confirmation to my feelings, as the whole time she was there, I was just not comfortable with her around, and I felt she was someone I couldn't trust. I've learned now that you have to be careful who you allow in your space, especially around your family.

My spirit tells me who I should have around me and who I shouldn't have around. It tells me who to keep close and who to keep at a distance, and it hasn't led me wrong yet. I paid attention to those uncomfortable feelings with this lady in my house. Now that she is gone, the house has a completely different vibe, even with a new housekeeper. I'm not watching anything, and I feel good about this new person. I'm thanking God for the heads up.

Dear God, help us to pay attention to those feelings, promptings, impressions, and cues from You, always going with the decisions that bring us peace when we think about them. Amen.

KEEP CALM—YOU'RE ROLLING WITH GOD

I GOT KICKED OUT OF ANOTHER GROUP! LOL!

Members of the group told me over and over to leave, making comments like, "Go with God!"

Even though I tried my hardest to ignore the comments, I'm very sensitive and it was upsetting to me. *(I'm still a work in progress!)* It was so upsetting that another group that I was in, after I started receiving negative comments there too, and I removed myself! I eventually went back, and I'm now connecting with the members on an entirely different level. It's been good therapy for me, and I loved the following comment from one of the members:

"Nikki, thank you again for sharing. That post you made about "who am I carrying" helped me more than I expressed yesterday. I am so glad you decided to stay and share what you learned. I told my husband all about the story, and we went over a list of who I've been carrying around with me.

Sensitive (and not knowing it most my life) left me holed up inside myself, and as I try to open myself, I am exposed to hurts, most unintentional, but some intentional as well. I cannot hamper myself by carrying those people around like a big burden. This is going to be a long, slow journey, but I do look forward to each day.

"Come to Me, all you who labor and are heavy laden, and I will give you rest. Take My yoke upon you and learn from Me, for I am gentle and lowly in heart, and you will find rest for your souls. For My yoke is easy and My burden is light" (Matthew 11:28-30).""

One reason I'm so thankful for all these groups that are kicking me out is that in life we should be open to everything and attached to nothing. I'm learning that lesson so well now. No one will be in our lives forever. At some point, we must say goodbye to everyone. I love everyone as much as I can now and try not to waste time on trivial matters because tomorrow they may not be there.

Dear God, thank You for all the experiences that help to grow us up so that we're mature, not lacking anything. Amen.

KEEP CALM—YOU'RE ROLLING WITH GOD

Day 148 — Live in God, Live in Love

IT'S COMPLICATED

That's not my relationship status. That's the situation of my life right now! But it's all good! Challenges in life are gifts in disguise and every time one presents itself, I become a better person because of it. And the great part is that now I know I don't deal with them alone and I feel as if God is right next to me holding my hand through them all. I'm leaving the past in the past and taking life one moment at a time. *Keep moving forward, people!* "When the going gets tough, the tough get going!" I have so many balls in the air right now, but taking one down at a time and asking God, who's my constant Companion, *What do we do here?*

It's all a part of walking bravely with God, open to everything that may come our way. "I need not, I must not trouble myself about anything except the task of this moment." I still live, says the Lord; ready to help you and console you more than before, if you put your trust in me and devoutly call upon me." – *The Imitation of Christ*

I have some big projects ahead of me, but Dr. Wayne Dyer gave me some good advice by putting it all in proper perspective: Don't look at the bigness of them, take it piece by piece and step by step. He wrote the book I was reading one chapter at a time, not looking at the entire book at once.

God's the best strategist, as well. With all the balls in the air, He tells me which ones are the task of each day and which ones to leave up there. It's a lot of balls going up and down as I examine each one. He directs on what to do with it that day and maybe I won't pull it down for weeks or months, depending on what my spirit tells me each time I think about it. The constant conversations with God continue: *Does this feel right to work on today? God, what should I do here?* I'm always amazed when the perfect answers come to mind. God's ways are the best!

> **Dear God, may we remember You in every moment, paying attention to what You would have us do. Amen.**

KEEP CALM—YOU'RE ROLLING WITH GOD

Day 149 — Live in God, Live in Love

SUPERHUMANS HAVE INTEGRITY

I was again thrilled by the principal of my kids' school at their Friday's assembly.

The topic was about persevering, but he took advantage of an opportunity to discuss integrity when an example came up of someone who had great perseverance but was later discovered lacked integrity. I'll never forget the day at a school event when this principal said to me that you don't go far in life without discipline. I would now add integrity in here.

There was a day in my office in Nigeria when I counted money with a customer that came up short. He said he knew it was his driver that stole the money, but he wasn't going to say anything to him about it; he just wasn't going to give him any opportunity for advancement within the company. With the little money that was stolen, this driver blocked his chances of promotion, without even realizing it. Like I always write, everything is between God and us, not between us and anyone else. God incomprehensibly knows every thought we think and everything we do! I don't know about you guys, but I'm going to do my best to please God in all my ways. He's my ultimate Boss and when I do everything pleasing to Him, I've discovered this is how He guides me on the path to my best life. The best people show up here, the best adventures and He's continually leading me to greater and greater levels of peace, joy, and happiness. *God, I'm grateful.*

You can go the opposite direction if you want to, but I'm sucking up to God, going to Him in the 1,000 decisions I make every day: *God, what do we do here? And here? And here? And here?* Always going with the choices that bring me peace when I think about it. "And don't neglect DOING GOOD and sharing, for with such sacrifices God is pleased" (Hebrews 13:16).

"Lean on, trust in, and be confident in the Lord with all your heart and mind and do not rely on your own insight or understanding. In all your ways know, recognize, and acknowledge Him, and He will direct and make straight and plain your paths" (Proverbs 3:5-6).

Dear God, help us to be people of good character and integrity, as we represent You in the world. Amen.

KEEP CALM—YOU'RE ROLLING WITH GOD

'WHY AM I SO HAPPY?'

I thought to myself, wondering why I found myself smiling for no apparent reason.

Is it because my hubby finally appreciates everything I do as his wife, mother to four kids, and work partner? No, he's still telling me I don't help him enough. Is it because I finally got my to-do list down to a comfortable level? No, I don't think that will happen anytime soon! Is it because I'm finally getting proper sleep? No, my sons are still following me wherever I go to sleep with me. Is it because I finally got my belly down? No, it's still big! Is it because the person who was irritating me has stopped? No, they're still irritating me, but I'm praying lots and learning to ignore most of it. Is it because I've finally learned balance? No, I'm still a huge work in progress there!

Well, why are you so happy then? I have this overwhelming sense of peace that God is with me as my constant Companion. *Thank You, God* is the prayer I repeat to myself all day. I'm not stressing life. I'm taking everything one step at a time, doing my best and leaving the rest with God. I'm not beating myself up about the past, and I love me as I am right now (big belly and all!), working on constant and never-ending improvement. I know God is my Helper and He goes before me to make my paths straight. I have no fear because I roll with God! I'm content, but still advancing confidently in the direction of my dreams. And I'm trying to be my most loving and forgiving self in every moment, every example and every experience knowing, in the final analysis, everything's between God and me.

Dear God, may we all come to know You and love You. Amen.

KEEP CALM—YOU'RE ROLLING WITH GOD

"REMIND THEM TO MAKE GOD A PARTNER IN EVERYTHING"

Was the comment from my fellow God maniac and friend. I proudly told him that I had finally finished my manuscript and I had included the three big lessons I've learned from him:

- *to be extremely grateful for every little thing,*
- *to remember God in every moment,*
- *and to know that God loves the humble.*

But in thinking about God being a Partner in everything, I'm again blown away by God having a book show up at my house shortly before Christmas. Julie, my daughter, was asked to exchange gifts with a classmate and with so much on my plate, I remember thinking, *Why are they doing this to me?* because that meant me going out and looking for a gift with Julie to give. But the gift Julie received is one I now cherish. It's a book called, *VeggieTales 365: Very Veggie Devos for Girls*. We use it in our appointments with God. The writers have a remarkable way of putting significant life lessons in a way kids can understand, from the all-important God perspective.

In discussing with Julie how school went, she proclaimed, "No dots, Mommy!" which she receives when she misbehaves in class. It was during an appointment with God reading this book that she learned about self-control and she happily told me, "I don't talk in class anymore when I'm not supposed to."

While going to pick up the kids, I went a little early and got to see my then four-year-old getting special homework assistance. It was an idea that popped in my head *(a God suggestion!)* when his teacher complained that his homework was not being completed correctly. To see this teacher so lovingly helping him made me very happy.

One morning, upon waking up, my older daughter, Ember, came and laid next to me in bed, resting her head on my chest. This was a treat because Ember has been going through a phase where she wants *nothing* to do with me. Another suggestion I got from God was to calm down with her and not be so focused on what she's doing wrong because she's doing so much that's right.

Day 151 — Live in God, Live in Love

"REMIND THEM TO MAKE GOD A PARTNER IN EVERYTHING"

I went to our kitchen last night and found it surprisingly clean. Ember did such a great job with it without any nagging from Mom. *I love you, my First Place Daughter!* In fact, just call me Nikki so Proud because I have the best kids in the world!

Here's the deal: God is our incredible Partner in *everything*, including parenting. Pause before making any decision and seek His direction.

Dear God, thank You for sharing Your wisdom in every aspect of our lives. May we get You involved in everything. Amen.

KEEP CALM—YOU'RE ROLLING WITH GOD

"MOMMY, GOD IS SO GOOD TO US"

Said my little son, Joshie, before leaving for school. I asked him why he said that and he replied, "God helped us to find my shoe lacing." We've been missing one lime green shoelace for his sneakers for the longest time, and it showed up suddenly one night. I read that there are two ways to look at life: as if nothing is a miracle or as if everything is a miracle.

I'm picking door number two with Joshie—*everything is a miracle.* Before finding it, I seriously wondered where I could find lime green shoe lacing in Nigeria.

Another miracle happened right after I wrote a post about God reminding me again that He's on my side when I read one sentence in my meditation book, "You have Me (God) on your side, so what are you worried about?"

Out of the blue, I then found a notebook that belongs to my then eleven-year-old daughter, Julie, and I decided to open it up. It was a few months ago after she complained and complained and complained that I told her to write 100 things that she was grateful for instead. Astonishingly, number six on that list was:

"GOD IS ALWAYS ON MY SIDE."

Wink! Wink! And once again everything lined up a little bit too perfectly with God confirming He *is* on my side! What 11-year-old thinks like that, though? *My Julie!* That made my entire day extra special as I thought about how God goes overboard in showing me how much He loves me with her words confirming His earlier message to me. For me to open up that book and read those words from Julie written months ago, had me in awe of God. I sat thinking about God, then opened my same meditation book, *Jesus Calling*, and read the following:

"As you go through this day, look for tiny treasures strategically placed along the way. I lovingly go before you and plant little pleasures to brighten your day. Look carefully for them, and pluck them one by one. When you reach the end of the day, you will have gathered a lovely bouquet."

Dear God, thank You for the endless ways in which you show Your love for us. Amen.

KEEP CALM—YOU'RE ROLLING WITH GOD

Day 153 — Live in God, Live in Love

"THERE IS SO MUCH THAT'S RIGHT!"

I can't get over how changing my attitude to thoughts of gratitude has made such a difference. *I'm bouncing off walls with gratitude!* I'm grateful to God for everything and everyone in my life. There is so much that's right, but I spent so much time focused on what was wrong. "Our preoccupation with what is wrong with us, is exactly what keeps us from seeing and enjoying what is right with us and life. There is so much that's right – if we are willing to see it." – Alan Cohen, *I Had It All The Time*

My hubby made me cry when he said to me, "Nikki, you're irreplaceable. I see everything you do, and I appreciate having you as my wife." The reason I cried is that I've been feeling so insecure lately about myself, thinking of everything that's wrong with me. From today forth, I want us all to be more focused on what's right with us and others in our lives. Yes, let's keep trying to improve, but also give yourself and others some credit for where you are right now at this moment. *Got that?* "Anyone can find the dirt in someone. Be the one who finds the gold" (Proverbs 11:27).

Speaking of Alan Cohen, I love this quote from him: "But there is a Source that can give you a guarantee, and that is Spirit. God's guarantee is that if you trust, follow your heart, live your truth, and love, you will be taken care of. You will be led to the right people and the right circumstances at the right time. You will not be comfortless."

When I think of everything that went on behind the scenes to make sure I had shoes to wear on that walk home from that London Park barefooted, I'm dumbfounded! The lady who loaned me the shoes had planned to come on Sunday, but ended up coming on Monday, exactly when I needed those shoes. And compared to everything that God has done and continues to do for me, believe me, the shoes are nothing.

Dear God, may we turn over all disappointments, despair and guilt over to You, with our eyes focused on You and Your unconditional love for us. May our hope remain in You. Amen.

KEEP CALM—YOU'RE ROLLING WITH GOD

NIK, WHO WAS THAT BEAUTIFUL LADY HANGING WITH YOUR HUBBY?

The other day a very attractive woman came to meet with my hubby at our office.

In fact, everyone stopped what they were doing to admire her. My hubby took her to his office for a private meeting and shortly called me in to introduce us. Honestly, I was so happy with the Nik that stepped into that office that day. Not at all intimated by this gorgeous lady sitting with my hubby, not feeling the slightest bit territorial, but happy and confident with simply being me—the wife, mother, and person God has called me to be.

It's about time! It's only taken me 41 years to get there, happy in my skin. There will always be more attractive, smarter, charming, captivating women, but I love this space where I am right now, content and filled with gratitude for who I am. We even talked about cosmetic surgery, but I'm not at all interested. There are enough pretty women in the world. I'm here with a different assignment; *to bring you closer to God!* However, I do believe in constant improvement and working on becoming the most fantastic version of myself. I'm proud that for the last couple of weeks I've been back on my exercise and eating healthy wagon. And I love my naturally curly hair, no more relaxers to straighten it, and most importantly I'm enjoying doing me. The night before this I was sick for a few hours, and that was enough to remind me not to take my health for granted. I got up the next morning to exercise and enjoy my veggie smoothie. *God, I'm abundantly grateful!*

Dear God, may we all learn to love and accept ourselves exactly as we are, as we strive to be the best people we can be. Amen.

KEEP CALM—YOU'RE ROLLING WITH GOD

Day 155 — Live in God, Live in Love

EVERYONE, REMAIN CALM

I called a friend to tell her how much she has changed me for the better. Following her advice to leave the past in the past, her next best advice to me is simply, *Calm down!* I think about all the times I've called her freaking out and she always has the right words to say to help me to *relax*. I still can't get over how God connected me with her. She's another reason why every day is my birthday. I'm surrounded by the best! I can't figure out how she's gotten so wise, though, when we're the same age!

Calm down! is some valuable advice. So much trouble we can avoid for ourselves when we do this. I got an email that was a little disturbing one day. I first told myself, *Nik, calm down and take it one step at a time.* I did calm down after a few minutes, and after having some conversations with God as to what to do next, I got the feeling to call the person sending the email to tell my side of the story and to ask what he would recommend. He turned out to be a cool guy. He told me exactly what to do and not to worry that once I did what he was asking, the problem would be resolved. A few hours later...problem resolved! Walking bravely with God 101: *slow down, calm down and listen to God, always going with the decision that brings you peace taking life one step at a time.* I don't make a move without this!

And want to know one of my secrets to a peaceful marriage or any relationship? Don't discuss stuff when you're upset with each other! If my hubby's upset, I let him vent. When he calms down, I find the right time to discuss issues with him. *There's more than one way to skin a cat!* I do my best to be the sweetest, most loving wife, and in return, I have the best husband! I'm telling you guys all my secrets here! And don't forget—become a professional ignorer (kindly and respectfully, of course!).

Dear God, may we remain calm and seek You, no matter the situation we face. Amen.

KEEP CALM—YOU'RE ROLLING WITH GOD

"GUIDED BY GOD"

Were the words on a license plate/tag frame of a car I walked by at the mall. Those three words got me so excited, perfectly summing up what these posts are about—*allowing God to guide our lives.* I still can't get over God's humility. The Creator of the entire universe loves and cares for each one of us and He's involved with every aspect of our lives, wanting the best for us. *Incomprehensible!* How He keeps track of us all is far beyond my brain capabilities, but I have this unbelievable confidence that I know I'm never alone and God's always with me. I can therefore *relax* and *enjoy* our adventure together.

Every day is special, is my new reminder to myself. I'm learning to be present fully in all my moments sucking the most out of each one of them. "Be joyful," was a beautiful reminder I saw on the back of another car while driving one day. Even though this life is not easy sometimes, if we cleave close to God in all our moments, we can live life filled with joy. I'm in a cleaning mood and I snuck away to write this, leaving my kids with some more work to complete. But as I cleaned, I was happy and cheerful, filled with gratitude and hope with positive expectations in every area of my life, knowing I have the best Helper, Friend, Companion, Adviser and Strategist with me always, as I move forward moment by moment. *God, I'm abundantly grateful!*

I ain't worried 'bout nothing, with God showing me over and over again that there's nothing that will come my way that He and I can't handle together. I still can't over the bags that I needed to be strapped on to the top of our car and God led me to the perfect people to assist me, a former truck driver who was a professional with tying down loads. *Miraculous!*

So, let's be joyful, knowing we're never alone and we rest in God, as He directs us through our feelings, nudges, insights, impressions and promptings as to what we should pay attention to. I do my best to take care of what I need to take care of, but the things that are out of my control, I pray about them and leave them in God's hands. *Surrender, baby!* And He hasn't disappointed me yet! I, therefore, can go through life light and unburdened taking care of only what I need to take care of, *always guided by God.*

Dear God, thank You for Your guidance. May we all come to know Your voice and follow You always. Amen.

KEEP CALM—YOU'RE ROLLING WITH GOD

Day 157 — Live in God, Live in Love

"ANOTHER DAY IN THE LIFE OF A SUPER MOMMY...

... SUPER WIFE AND SUPER PERSON!" was me to my aunt, finally returning home from a hectic day of running errands.

I often quoted from Rumi, with my daughters and romping about in our exercise clothes and no make-up: "I want to sing like the birds sing, not worrying about who hears and what they think." Getting home and chatting with my mom and aunt about some current family issues, I kept repeating what I wrote before that whatever God wants for us is best for us, and as confirmation of this I got a beautiful God wink when already opened up on my computer screen was this from Pastor Joel Osteen: "It may be difficult, but God will not allow a challenge to come into our lives unless He has a divine purpose for it. I've found that nothing happens to us; it happens for us. If we keep the right attitude, God will always use it for our good."

Repeatedly, God amazes me when I think that the worse things that can happen, happens and He uses them all for my good. I had the best time with God one morning getting dressed for work, dancing and singing to myself. I was so incredibly happy. But for the last few weeks before that, I was in a period of mourning, but now I've bounced out of the sad period, and a whole new world has opened to me. I woke up at 5:30 am to exercise, and I had a little pep talk with my daughters when waking them up to say I'm raising them to be superhumans for God. I've changed my attitude from one of fear to such love, focused on being the best wife, mother, and person I could be.

My husband and I also had an appointment with God that encouraged both of us. That we're training our children to be great people of God in the world and that will help build a stronger society. Then, when we have grandchildren, our children will pass on what we have taught them and so on throughout generations and generations. This gave me extra motivation to keep fighting for my family with God as my major Backup. I'm simply to stay calm and He will fight for me.

And God's divine purpose for my mourning: To tell you an important message: *fight for your family, too.* Future generations are counting on us. It's our important work for God. *Love never gives up.*

Dear God, thank You for our good times and our bad times that You use to teach us important lessons You would have us to learn. Amen.

KEEP CALM—YOU'RE ROLLING WITH GOD

GOD, WHO WOULD YOU HAVE FOR ME TO MEET WITH TODAY?

After exercising one morning, I thought of two items I needed from the store.

Should I stop now or after I dress for work? I asked God, and I got the feeling to stop right then. After I had taken care of one of the items, I went to get a can of beans. I met Robert, a store clerk, unpacking boxes and restocking the shelves. He gave me an extra friendly, "Good morning!"

I said, "Wow, you're happy today!"

He replied, "Yes, I'm happy every day!"

We started a conversation about God and the tornadoes and how God certainly knows how to get our attention. He then says to me, "You should write." I smiled to myself because I knew God had me to meet Robert with that special message.

Driving home from work, I remembered I wanted a book from Wal-Mart that a Facebook friend had told me about. I got the feeling that now was the time to go and get it. I found the book and went to pay for it. I met a cashier standing in front of her aisle and asked her if I could pay her for the book. I joked with her because that was one of the very few times I've ever gone to Wal-Mart and didn't have to wait on a very long line. She said it was because people didn't realize that her lane was open. I purchased my book, and she then asked, "What is it about?" I told her that it was about God and I read her some of it:

"I, the Creator of the Universe, am with you and for you. What more could you need! When you feel some lack, it is because you are not connected with me at a deep level. I offer abundant Life; your part is to trust Me, refusing to worry about anything."— *Jesus Calling*

She shared with me that she had drifted away from God, but wanted Him back in her life because of some difficulties she was facing. I told her she might have drifted from God, but He hasn't strayed from her and that He's her true best friend forever and would never leave her or forsake her. I gave her that copy of the book and purchased another one for myself. *I got a feeling God wanted her to have it!*

Dear God, may we be Your mouth, hands and feet in the world, spreading Your love wherever we go. Amen.

KEEP CALM—YOU'RE ROLLING WITH GOD

Day 159 — Live in God, Live in Love

"I'M LIKE ENOUGH LESSONS, ALREADY!"

I commented to my Facebook friend, Christie. She's been my little messenger from God, lately. She posted, "The only thing I need to do is keep my Faith up and do what I can a little at a time..." This was exactly what I've been thinking all day, as I'm trying to complete a project I'm working on. She commented, "I've been frazzled and overwhelmed. He is up to something... Lol ... Strengthening us... Sandpaper ... The wilderness... 40 years it took the Israelites. Only 11-day journey. Lol" *Well, that makes two of us, my girl!*

I needed the laugh after an afternoon of watching Oprah Winfrey in her new show, *Where Are They Now?* The stories of what people go through in this life are unbelievable. God is constantly trying to strengthen us with the constant lessons. But here's the deal: They're all for our good. Like my new friend, Randy, wrote:

"... progress only stops when you give up, so keep your head up and your heart in it, and never give up. It took me awhile, but it took progress, not perfection, 2 become the person I am 2day...never give up on progress! One day at a time."

I want to challenge us today to make ourselves proud. Let's live the best lives ever, despite our difficulties, problems, and struggles. They're only God trying to grow us up to be the people He would have us to be, anyway.

Dear God, may we walk with our heads held high, never forgetting that You are always with us. Amen.

KEEP CALM—YOU'RE ROLLING WITH GOD

"MY HELP COMES FROM THE LORD...

"... Who made heaven and earth" (Psalm 121:2).

I sent an email to a person who was a part of a big challenge in my life over a few months, thanking them for the excellent learning experience. And the biggest lesson of all is now knowing God is our Helper. The entire experience was so astonishing from solutions magically popping in my head, people showing up to assist me, and an unexpected vacation trip to the U.S. from Nigeria after my hubby insisted we weren't travelling that Christmas. It turned out to be an important business trip in sorting key issues out and a visit to a friend's house and hearing one comment from her that helped me make some urgent decisions. Down to God letting me know He was with me as I worked alone at 4 a.m. and that He even knows computer software—*It was all inspired by Him!*

Remember the shoe story in that huge London park when I walked barefoot, and a stranger just so happened to have the perfect-sized walking shoes in her bag that she was returning to a store? The store told her to mail the shoes in since she lived a distance away, but she insisted that she wanted to bring them back personally and she happened to stop and meet us at the park that afternoon. My daughter had popped her sandals and being the super mom that I am, I gave her my shoes, and I walked back home without shoes. Well, dealing with this situation, was the same. Everything and everyone I needed were provided every step of the way.

"My help comes from the Lord, Who made heaven and earth."

Dear God, You are our faithful Partner. May we face each day with confidence knowing our help comes from You. Amen.

KEEP CALM—YOU'RE ROLLING WITH GOD

NIK, WE'RE TRUSTING GOD HERE

That's my constant reminder to self whenever I'm tempted to worry.

Here's the deal: We can spend our lives worried and fearful, or we can spend it trusting our constant Companion - God. I admit, it has taken lots of practice for me to get to this point, where I have such faith in God, but it's thanks to all the experience I've gotten from dealing with so many problems and challenges over the years. *Go figure!* The bigger the problems, the greater God has shown up for me and He hasn't let me down yet. I love this quote from my meditation book, *The Imitation of Christ*, which I'm finding so true:

"To God, 'therefore, must you run in every decision, and not depend on your own judgment. For the just will not be troubled whatever comes to them from God. And if any unjust charge be pronounced against them, they will not care much.'"

I simply hold my peace and God fights for me. Everything and everyone I need seem to always show up. I'm focused on constant and never-ending improvement, trying as much as possible to do the right, excellent, and most loving thing in every moment, example, and experience. And I'm advancing confidently in the direction of my dreams.

Let's build our faith muscles through practice, practice and more practice. When you catch yourself feeling worried about anything, replace those thoughts with ones of trust and faith, *God, I trust You.*

And don't forget about our constant conversations with God, running to Him in every decision. Relax *(not in a lazy or careless manner)* and let's enjoy the sweet life with God.

"When I am afraid, I put my trust in you.

In God, whose word I praise—in God I trust and am not afraid.

What can mere mortals do to me?" (Psalm 56:3-4, NIV).

Dear God, help us to trust You no matter the challenges we face, doing our best and leaving the rest with You. Amen.

KEEP CALM—YOU'RE ROLLING WITH GOD

Day 162 — Live in God, Live in Love

A BEAUTIFUL MORNING WITH GOD

Looking for a book for my son, Emmie, I ended up pulling out one for me, *The Happiness Digest,* and I had the best morning with God reading it. The set-up to a God wink started from the day before. I had some time with Him looking up at some birds in a tree saying, *You even take care of the birds!*

I thought of this Bible verse: "Look at the birds of the air; they do not sow or reap or store away in barns, and yet your heavenly Father feeds them" Matthew 6:26 (NIV). And I watched those birds, smiling, in total awe of God.

The next morning, I randomly opened the *Happiness Digest,* and of all stories, the same story about the birds shows up: "... Christ taught His disciples precious lessons in regard to the necessity of trusting God... The Saviour pointed his followers to the birds of the air... for "they sow not, neither do they reap."

God had my full attention and I then locked myself in the bathroom to see what else He had to say to me in this book. For some weeks up to this morning, I was having serious doubts about writing my book: *Is this the right time? Am I a good enough writer? What will people say or think? They're only silly stories about my life.* And the list went on and on. Well, God answered me in that very book:

"You are not to wait for great occasions or to expect extraordinary abilities before you go to work for God. You need not have a thought of what the world will think of you. If your daily life is a testimony to the purity and sincerity of your faith, and others are convinced that you desire to benefit them, your efforts will not be wholly lost.

The humblest and poorest of the disciples of Jesus can be a blessing to others. They may not realize that they are doing any special good, but by their unconscious influence they may start waves of blessing that will widen and deepen, and the blessed results they may never know until the day of final reward. They do not feel or know that they are doing anything great. They are not required to weary themselves with anxiety about success. They only have to go forward quietly, doing faithfully the work that God's providence assigns, and their life will not be in vain."

Dear God, may our lives become a beautiful conversation with our Beloved. Amen.

KEEP CALM—YOU'RE ROLLING WITH GOD

Day 163 — Live in God, Live in Love

GOD WANTS US TO PROSPER

But don't get it twisted!
I'm not saying that means only having financial prosperity. He wants us to be blessed with the best relationships, the best children, the best health, lots of peace, joy, and for us to live incredibly fulfilling lives. I saw some friends and the little time I was with them, I sucked every moment of enjoyment out of it. Julie, got me all excited when she said, "Mommy, I followed my intuition, and I got a star." My Joshie sat down next to me to eat and ended up eating most of my dinner, as we both ate some delicious Nigerian soup made with okra with our hands. He was saying something and because he thought I wasn't listening he asked me, "What did I say?" At that time, he was only three, going on four, yet so smart – *another blessing!*

Don't miss out on the better life with God. Some people are so poor because they focus on what they don't have and what's missing from their lives. I'm so rich because I'm always thanking God for all my blessings. I can't even count everything God does for me in one second. *God, I'm grateful!*

It was an important life lesson we learned from Julie that week. She was announced star of the month for her class, after months of trying, but she never gave up. The important lesson here is Julie lived by faith, not by sight. Pretty much for seven consecutive months, she lost, but she kept believing and having faith that she could do it. Sadly, so many of us give up without having faith that anything's possible with God.

I've had to deal with lots of challenges in my life and without my faith and trust in God, I don't know where I would be. *We're never alone.* We truly have an awesome Father who's always with us and for us. I got a beautiful message from Him recently from my meditation book, *Jesus Calling,* written as if God is speaking: "... you have access to as much of Me as you have faith to receive. Rejoice in My abundance- living by faith, not by sight."

I don't know about you, but I believe for the best of everything. *No good thing shall we lack! Amen!*

Our Beloved, thank You for all our blessings, especially the ones that money cannot buy. May we not take any of them for granted. Amen.

KEEP CALM—YOU'RE ROLLING WITH GOD

Day 164 — Live in God, Live in Love

LIFE LESSONS FROM NIGERIA

Today is Nigeria's Independence Day.

Here are some valuable lessons I've learned from this beautiful country:

- *I have nothing to complain about.* One day I went for a walk with my son and in front of us was a lady carrying a baby on her back, a bucket of water in each hand, and another bucket of water on top of her head. I thought to myself, *Nikki, you have nothing in life to ever complain about again!*

- *Manage what you have.* My favorite Nigerian term is the word *manage;* in other words, use what you have. One morning, for example, my son needed a green and yellow crayon to complete his homework, which we didn't have. Julie came up with the perfect solution: use highlighter markers instead, and since we didn't have green, she remembered blue and yellow together made green. *Mission homework completed!*

- *Cook at home with organic ingredients.* I've turned into my mother-in-law! She cooks all the time, and now I get why; it's the healthiest way to eat. We rarely eat out because we now enjoy our home-cooked food so much more. We buy 90% of what we eat from local farmers, so it's real food, not processed foods with added chemicals, made in factories.

- *Be happy and content with what you have.* Nigerians, on average, make less than $2 a day, yet are some of the world's happiest people. Being around them has taught us to be happy and content with what we have.

- *For the first time in my life, I've realized I need friends.* It was a bit of a transition period for me, and I even started drinking a lot, but I'll never forget a friend who was always there for me. In all my crazy moments, she always had the right words to say.

- *ALL THINGS are possible with God.* It was in Nigeria where I felt God started to speak to me and why I felt I had a message to share with the world.

Our God, thank You for the never-ending lessons that help us live our best lives. Amen.

KEEP CALM—YOU'RE ROLLING WITH GOD

Day 165 — Live in God, Live in Love

'HE WHO SERVES THE MOST REAPS THE MOST'

The Monk Who Sold His Ferrari by Robin Sharma is so wonderful.

At the time I started my blog, I thought I was a pretty happy person and that I would write something to encourage others to live happier lives too. Boy or boy, I had no idea that the Nikki I was then was such a miserable soul compared to the Nikki I am today. The main reason for this major transformation in my life is because I asked, *How may I serve?* and asking that question has changed my life so much for the better.

My mission to make the world a happier, healthier, and more loving place has also made me happier and it seems as if God turns around and asks me, *Nik, how may I serve you?"* And anything or anyone I need seem to show up for me right on cue. I'm still convinced that God told the owners to build the school my kids attend because He knew my family was relocating to Nigeria. It's the perfect school for us and opened the first year we were here on my eldest daughter's birthday. *Wink! Wink!* Here's the full quote from the book:

"Basically, the sages of the Himalayas guided their lives by a simple rule: he who serves the most, reaps the most emotionally, physically, mentally and spiritually. This is the way to inner peace and outer fulfillment...Yet another ancient principle for enlightened living: the purpose of life is a life of purpose. The real source of happiness can be stated in a word: achievement. Lasting happiness comes from steadily working to accomplish your goals and advancing confidently in the direction of your life's purpose. This is the secret to kindling the inner fire that lurks within you....

Every one of us has a heroic mission while we walk this Earth. We have all been granted a unique set of gifts and talents that will readily allow us to realize this lifework. The key is to discover them, and in doing so, discover the main objective of your life."

My mission is to bring one billion people closer to God. *How may you serve?*

Dear God, assist us in focusing, working hard and advancing confidently in the direction of Your purpose for us. Amen.

KEEP CALM—YOU'RE ROLLING WITH GOD

Day 166 — Live in God, Live in Love

THERE ARE NO MISTAKES IN LIFE

I wrote that I felt that I've wasted the last 38 years of my life, but it all has brought me to this moment where I can confidently tell you that there are no mistakes in life. The darkest periods are where I found God. Not only did I come through those times stronger and wiser, I came out with greater love and trust in Him.

The person I wrote about recently, who called me for some information, can you believe, I hated that person? You always hear that everyone is in your life for a reason. Well, this person taught me it's possible to love anyone because I've turned that hate to love. I now know it's a burden carrying around someone by being unforgiving and unloving. I'm free and happy when I forgive. When I spoke to them, I didn't mention that I've called them several times and they didn't take my calls. I didn't say that they left a terrible message on my voicemail, but now they're calling me for help. No, I now realize all of that is a complete waste of time. I just want to be my most loving self because that's where I'm happiest. They asked me for help and I helped. And through that experience, I can teach you to do the same. I now get what Jesus said when he told us to love our enemies, as your life is so much better when you do.

If you have any regrets or wish you had done things differently—forget about it. Those decisions have brought you exactly where you are. The only way to get experienced in life is through having experiences. There were no wrong choices as each step was for your personal growth and unfoldment. There are NO mistakes in life, only loads of research and development.

Let's be the kindest and most loving people we know, leaving the past in the past.

"Everything that happens fits into a pattern of good for those who love Me. Instead of trying to analyze the intricacies of the pattern, focus your energy on trusting Me and thanking Me at all times. Nothing is wasted when you walk close to Me. Even your mistakes and sins can be recycled into something good through My transforming grace. Beloved, remember that when I "recycled" your mistakes and sin into something good. I won't let anything be wasted if you live close to Me- trusting and thanking Me at all times."
— *Jesus Calling*

Dear God, may we trust that our dark times are all our good. Amen.
KEEP CALM—YOU'RE ROLLING WITH GOD

Day 167 — Live in God, Live in Love

"MOMMY, GO AND READ YOUR MEDITATION BOOK"

Said my super smart, little sweetie pie, Julie.

She saw that I was fuming over the fact that the technician forgot to reconnect my refrigerator back to its power supply after he had worked on it, and I had to throw out lots of food after they told me they couldn't come back out for few days. I got someone else to come from another company, who quickly discovered that was the problem, but at that time it was too late. Julie heard me saying I had planned to call his office and speak to his supervisor and have them refund the service charge I paid. *That was the maddest I've been in a long time!*

Then I remembered my post from about Paula Deen and what was being done to her in the media. What happened from just a few hours ago, when I wrote, "so I may never pardon myself, but will always pardon others." There I was ready to file a complaint against someone who made a little mistake of forgetting to plug in my appliance. You're so smart, my Julie, because the minute I thought about what I had learned from my meditation book, I was happy again. I forgave quickly, and when she asked if I would still call his company to complain, I proudly said, "No, I've pardoned him completely!" I thought about all the mistakes I've made on the job and my hubby/boss would only say, "Take care of it."

We're not perfect, and that's why these posts are our daily reminders to practice being our best selves. We may not get it right all the time, but let's keep practicing, practicing and practicing some more. When we fall, like I did that day, let's get right back up, accept God's grace and forgiveness, dust ourselves off and keep going.

Dear God, may we represent You, reflecting to a watching world Your mercy, love and kindness. Amen.

KEEP CALM—YOU'RE ROLLING WITH GOD

"DID YOU ASK GOD IF THAT'S THE PLACE WHERE HE WANTS YOU?"

I asked this of a customer and new friend, Eno. He believes he has found a new home, and I said to him, "Don't make any move until you get the okay from God. If it doesn't feel right, that's God telling you that's not the place for you!" He's a smart, young guy who has impressed me, and I'm thrilled he's reading my blog posts. I got goosebumps when he told me about his God winks and how he's waking up earlier in the mornings to have appointments with God. *Sweet! Way to go, Eno!* I promise you won't go wrong with God.

Here's the deal: get God involved with everything you do, everywhere you go, and everything you even say. My life is an enjoyable conversation with God because He always gives me the best advice when I listen and obey Him. *Does this feel right?* is the constant question, and I pay attention to those feelings I get in response. I wrote the day before that I'm still struggling with my Facebook distraction, and in my 5 p.m. appointment with God, I opened *Talking to God* by Peter Bakka. I got the feeling to buy this book the day before, and there's an entire chapter dedicated to distractions. I'm so encouraged by the advice given in a practical application there:

"So I at once turn to those distractions and calmly present them to God. I deal with them fully; and where there are solutions needed in these distractions, I look for those answers from God... This strategy can be used with any issue you're dealing with. Catch yourself in whatever it is you're struggling with and calmly turn to God and ask for His assistance."

No matter how small or how big the issue, I'm learning to talk to God about it. When I needed help with a major challenge, I prayed and God delivered, with me doing my best and God doing the rest.

Dear God, who are we that You care so much about us? Help us always to listen and obey, getting You involved in all our decisions and to strip off anything that holds us back from living the best life with You. Amen.

KEEP CALM—YOU'RE ROLLING WITH GOD

Live in God, Live in Love

"I LOVE YOU... EVEN THOUGH YOU'RE MY PAIN IN THE ***"

Is what I jokingly tell my hubby sometimes.

He calls me his pain-in-the-*** wife and he's my pain-in- ***/wonderful/handsome/incredible/confident/hardworking/fearless/determined hubby. I was shocked that in a Facebook group I'm in, the members were so quick to advise one member to leave her husband after she complained of having some problems with him.

Life is pretty much about relationships, and "the right relationship is everything," says a bank's ad. I want to encourage you not to give up so easily on any relationship. Every time my hubby and I have a big blow up, it ends up bringing us closer together. The new me has calmed down a lot. And the smarter me has learned to choose my battles wisely. I've learned that sometimes in life, it is more profitable to follow another, forgive and forget quickly, be a professional ignorer (kindly and respectfully, of course), love extravagantly, follow the 80/20 rule (focusing on the positives of others and not their negatives), as no one is perfect and to enjoy all my relationships. I surprised my friends one night by showing up, and we shared a delicious dinner together. I was so happy, even for the little time we had. *Let's love each other the way God would have us to.*

Our Father, give us the love, commitment, wisdom, strength and endurance to fight for our families, our important work from You. Amen.

KEEP CALM—YOU'RE ROLLING WITH GOD

"IT'S STILL BIG"

My hubby said to me after I proudly showed him that my tummy is finally going down.

Gotta appreciate his honesty (lol). But I've realized what's keeping me from the flat belly of my dreams and all my other aspirations such as writing my book and it's called, *"resistance"* that I'm learning all about in an excellent book called, The War of Art, by Steven Pressfield. He describes resistance as anything that's in between the life we're living and the life we've imagined for ourselves and "when we fight it, we are in a war to the death."

Today I've conquered resistance! is what I say to myself after completing my T25 workouts, especially the ones where I must go to the floor and focus on my core area. I'm fighting it and that's what I want from you. Don't let resistance stop you from going to a higher level in any area of your life.

"Procrastination is the most common manifestation of resistance because it's the easiest to rationalize. We don't tell ourselves, "I'm never going to write my symphony." Instead we say, "I'm going to write my symphony; I'm just going to start tomorrow...Never forget: This very moment we can change our lives. There never was a moment, and never will be, when we are without power to alter our destiny. This second, we can turn the tables on Resistance. This second, we can sit down and do our work."

Dig deep! Resistance...I declare war!

Dear God, may we live the lives You intended for us. Amen.

KEEP CALM—YOU'RE ROLLING WITH GOD

Day 171 — Live in God, Live in Love

GOD'S DEEPLY INVOLVED IN OUR LIVES

I met a Catholic priest at work one Friday, and I was all excited discussing God with Him.

I told him that I want to publish a book and he promised to give me ten books of his that he has written and published so that I can be inspired to go ahead with getting my book done, too. By Tuesday of the following week, I got the books and decided to share them with my staff so we can take turns reading them. The one I selected to read, Fatimah, one of my assistants, grabbed it from me asking to please let her have that one first, and I quickly picked another one.

Fast forward to Wednesday and I was having one of the worst days in my 12 years of marriage. I told you guys, love can get messy at times. Still upset with my hubby, I went to bed early, and I began reading the book I selected from the ten books. I started at the beginning and on page 31 was a prayer for the family:

"Heavenly Father.

Please shine your light upon my family.

Give us strength to overcome all of the difficulties that we are dealing with now and protect us against any future problems we may encounter in the future.

O Lord, bring us together as we are meant to be, May the love that binds us only grow stronger as we fulfill the destiny you have laid out for us.

Grant my family forgiveness for any sins we have committed. May we also forgive one another Lord, as it is sometimes difficult to do.

Bless us Lord, as we humbly and confidently pray in your name. Amen." - *Oremus: He Lives Well Who Prays Well* by John Ifeanyi Okoro

The fight for my family continues, but with major Back Up—*God.*

"I have told you these things, so that in Me you may have [perfect] peace and confidence. In the world you have tribulation and trials and distress and frustration; but be of good cheer [take courage; be confident, certain, undaunted]! For I have overcome the world. [I have deprived it of power to harm you and have conquered it for you.]" - John 16:33

KEEP CALM—YOU'RE ROLLING WITH GOD

Day 172 — Live in God, Live in Love

"BECAUSE OF MY MOM'S KINDNESS I AM WHERE I AM"

I said to my family.

They tell me I'm too kind, but it was the kindness of my mom to a foreigner and stranger about 35 years ago in the Bahamas that changed the trajectory of my life.

I was walking across campus when a fellow classmate approached me asking if I was interested in a job with the firm he worked with. I said yes, as I was about to graduate from this two-year college. Going home and telling my mom about it, she smiled and said she had known the owner for many years. At the very end of my interview, I snuck in that my mom, Mabel, told me to say hello.

He hired me, and in the eight years I worked with him, he set my life on a new path. My mom told me that I had to work because she could no longer pay for me to finish college. I'll never forget the afternoon this gentleman came to my desk saying that he wanted me to finish my education, but not just at any university, but the same one his son attended in New York.

One summer, my mom told me the story of how they met. She said she had no dealings with him, but my mom just has a kind nature. So, she would offer him tea, make him comfortable, and chit chat with him whenever he came to her office to work. And they developed a friendship over the years. Years later, he took me in under his wings and much of the foundation of everything I know work wise came from the experience of working with him, along with my job and school experiences in New York.

My family may not get it yet as to why I try to be so kind, but I get that everything is between God and me, not between me and anyone else. *Saying I'm blessed is an understatement.*

I'm so focused on the 10,000 positives in my life that I have no more time to think about the negatives anymore. We're not going by the ordinary rules, and I know that God Himself personally repays my kindness.

Dear God, may we spread Your kindness and love in the world. Amen.

KEEP CALM—YOU'RE ROLLING WITH GOD

"I ACCEPTED THAT SOME PEOPLE WOULD NEVER COME AROUND...

...to the wonder of me! So, I became a professional ignorer, and I must say, I'm very good at it. I'm all for treating every person with respect, kindness, and consideration. But I no longer try to appease or please my critics." – Pastor Joel Osteen

I'm not there yet! I was so upset with myself that I took criticism to heart this week. It showed me that I still have lots of growing up to do in this area of becoming a professional ignorer.

A reporter asked Bill Cosby the secret of success. He said, "I don't know the secret of success, but I do know the secret of failure, and that is to try to please everybody."

"You have to accept that not everybody will support you. Not everyone will like you. Not everybody will understand you. That's Okay. Be the best that you can be, and God will take care of your critics. Stay focused on the main goals God has put in your heart. He will do amazing things. Ignore the distractions, and you will accomplish your goals all the quicker." - Pastor Joel Osteen.

My meditation book, *The Imitation of Christ,* had the perfect words for this: "Many things also must you pass by with a deaf ear, and think instead of those things which are for your peace."

Our God, help us learn to truly become professional ignorers – kindly and respectfully, focused only on what truly matters. Amen.

KEEP CALM—YOU'RE ROLLING WITH GOD

HE'S TURNING US INTO SUPERHUMANS

My life has totally turned around since I allowed myself to become so upset and emotional over some harsh words thrown my way.

It was in an appointment with God when the verse came to mind that said, "Have I not commanded you? Be strong and courageous" (Joshua 1:9, NIV). They were the tough words I needed from God to say to myself, *No, no, no! Who was that weak, crazy person? Nik, you can do better than that!*

Here's the deal: God uses all these experiences, the good, the bad, and the ugly, to help us become the people He has created us to be. And He has created us to be SUPERHUMANS! No matter what comes our way, we should be calm, strong, and courageous knowing we have God on our side. The harsh words will still come and can we look to see what we can take from them to improve, becoming the best versions of ourselves.

Expect disappointment! I said to Julie's (my daughter's) classmate when she told me about something she was promised. "Disappointments are a part of life. You should expect them so that when they come up, you can shrug them off immediately, handing them over to God to correct, and happily keep going."

The challenges and difficulties will always be there, too, but we deal with them one step at a time and piece by piece, getting God involved through regular conversations with Him, doing our best with whatever He would have us to do and we leave the rest to Him. This formula has successfully gotten me through so many challenges that have come my way. *Relax*, we roll with God. *FEAR NOTHING AND NO ONE.*

Every superhuman should have a super mission as to why they're here on earth. My mission is to bring humanity closer to God, one person at a time, to live the best life close to Him. I say to God, *Use me!* I wake up every day excited about my work in the world. *What's your life's mission?* A life lived only for self is an empty life. We're here to serve each other and through this serving is when our lives light up.

Dear God, help us to become superhumans, strong and courageous, no matter what comes our way, knowing that You will never leave us or forsake us. Amen.

KEEP CALM—YOU'RE ROLLING WITH GOD

Day 175 — Live in God, Live in Love

AND HOW OLD ARE YOU?

I thought to myself as my then ten-year-old daughter, Julie, spoke to me one night about a beautiful art project she had completed of a butterfly.

She said, "Mom, the reason this work is so good is because I humbled myself. The art teacher gave me ways that I could improve, and I listened and made the corrections." *Wow!* Our entire lives, I believe, is a lesson in learning how to be humble, so for her to get this at age ten is quite impressive.

How are you doing in this lesson of humility? This has been a tough one for me, but a good one, because when you get it, life's great, as it leads to much peace and harmony with others. Humility for me is learning to think nothing of myself. No more "How dare they say or do that to me?" and forgetting what others may or may not think, as what anyone thinks of me doesn't make me any better or any worse than who I am. Someone says 10,000 words against me, I see what I can take from it and correct myself, like Julie did, or I simply ignore it. I used to spend days upset with my hubby over things he would say to me. Now, I see what's in it that I can take to improve myself and I run with it, quick to say, "I'm sorry" when I'm wrong.

And always asking God, *How I may serve others?* has turned my life around, as I feel God has asked me, *Nik, how may I serve you?* God's behind the scenes of my life arranging for everything and everyone to be there when I need them. I'm no longer concerned about other's opinion of me, but I'm more concerned with God's opinion. "Being your best at what God wants you to be doing-that's the thing to shoot for." - Priscilla Shirer, *The Resolution for Women*

"Our God, make us humble and grateful. Amen"

KEEP CALM—YOU'RE ROLLING WITH GOD

"THAT DOESN'T SOUND LIKE LOVE TO ME"

That was my reminder to my kids and now to you.

I want us to be the observer of ourselves, and when we're talking to that co-worker that irritates us or talking to our spouse or our kids or that person who cuts us off in traffic, I want us asking, *Am I sounding and behaving like love?*

It only took me almost a year of writing these posts, years of reading and studying, years of asking God what is the secret to the universe. I finally get it: *Love is the answer!* I now understand why when I'm my most loving self, I'm also my happiest self. These are the times I experience God in my life. "Love is the shortest and swiftest way to God." When I love, it is as if I've entered the VIP section of life, where I enter a most wonderful place and the universe seems to ask me constantly, *Nikki, how may I serve you?* How God does what He does is so far beyond my brain capabilities. Want God to show up in your life and truly live this blessed life I write about blissfully happy and God favored? *LOVE!*

I had a good laugh with a friend one day as we both thought we were such good people until I quoted some Jesus to her, "If you love only those who love you, what reward is there for that? Even corrupt tax collectors do that much." I think Jesus was saying that the real reward in life comes when we learn to extend that love outside of the people who love us, those that are not easy to love. I had some important phone calls to make after that discussion.

"Masters who have walked the planet are those who have discovered the secret... Masters are those who have chosen only love. In every instance. In every moment. In every circumstance. Even as they were being killed, they loved their murderers. Even as they were being persecuted, they loved their oppressors."

"Am I sounding and behaving like love?"

"Whoever lives in love lives in God and God in them" (1 John 4:16).

Dear God, may we put Your love into action in the world. Amen.

KEEP CALM—YOU'RE ROLLING WITH GOD

Day 177 — Live in God, Live in Love

"'WE GO WITH GOD' TURNED ONE TODAY"

Was the email from Tumblr.com.

It was my nephew, Justin, who wrote saying he would like to help me get more exposure for my posts and he did all the setup work. But the beautiful part about this is that I didn't get so much exposure for the posts, but like I always write, I go there to hear from God and time after time I get the perfect messages where I feel I did a high five with Him.

From only one day, here are three posts I loved from simply searching for "God":

"Worry ends when FAITH IN GOD begins" (via elijahramos).

"Give to God the remaining years of your life. Beg God to use them in the kind of life that is pleasing to Him" - St. Padre Pio (via confessionsofsomeoneanonymous).

"For two years, I longed for a close friend, for intimacy, for love. For two years, I wondered why God had left me alone. For the same amount of time God was teaching me how to stop depending on people emotionally, and to depend on Him alone. He's enough."

On a day that I officially moved forward with my book with a publisher, they were just the high fives I needed from God. What I especially like about this website is I get to hear from people from so many different religions, and that's exactly what I would love to see more of in the world, us all fellowshipping together and learning from each other about our love of God.

A post from the Seventh Day Adventists inspired me with sharing that that weekend in their church was about teaching kids about kindness that I wanted to spend time with my children, too, sharing that message that we should be God's mouth and hands in the world to love and encourage each other.

Dear God, thank You for Your constant communications with us that can show up anywhere. Amen.

KEEP CALM—YOU'RE ROLLING WITH GOD

Day 178 — Live in God, Live in Love

"FRIENDS MAY COME AND GO...

…But a true friend sticks closer than a brother," was my little wink from God, reading my children's daily devotional.

It's been bothering me for the last week or so about how I seem to be getting the cold shoulder from someone, and God, knowing every thought I think had me open to the perfect Bible verse. Thanks, God! But speaking of real friends, I'm blessed to have one. She called me last night to say, "I just called because I didn't hear your voice all day." I called her one day to get all mushy. I told her how God sent me to her for training and the Nikki that's about to have her book published would not be this person if not for her. She has taught me such important lessons like leaving the past in the past, *CALMING DOWN,* and keeping my focus on God. Every time I'm around her, I leave a better person, more committed to being a better wife, a better mother and better person. In fact, my husband has seen such a difference in me from hanging out with her that he too is thanking God for her.

We're such on the same page in our lives, and we even talked about having appointments with God whenever we get together with the kids, as a daily devotional for kids has such good, practical advice written in a way for children to understand. Having a God-appointment with my girls, the messages of self-control and kindness kept coming up, telling them to be slow to speak and act and be about doing good in the world for God.

Out of 170 million Nigerians, God has connected me with her. *Unbelievable!* Nobody pays me to write these blog posts, but I KNOW God is behind the scenes of my life connecting me with everyone and everything I need to live my best life with Him. *Ain't worried 'bout nothing...*

Dear God, Your plans for us are more than we can ever imagine. May we trust Your direction and guidance for our lives. Amen.

KEEP CALM—YOU'RE ROLLING WITH GOD

Day 179 — Live in God, Live in Love

I HAVE THE SWEETEST MOM IN THE WORLD

We got a chance to talk for the longest one night.

She told me that she was telling a friend my hubby joke and about when I met him, that if God Himself had said, *Nik, this is not the husband I picked for you,* I would've argued back, *God, you're wrong. This is my husband!*

Well, let's say I'm in Heaven and God and I are discussing my life and says, *I think I could've found you a better mother."* I would say, *God, no disrespect, I know you created the sun, the moon, and the stars, but Your finest creation was indeed my mother. And I know anything is possible with You, but finding a better mom for me, I don't know about that one!*

I must get writing my books, so that my mom's legacy can live on forever, as so much of who I am and the Nikki that comes through in these posts, is because of my mom, Mabel. I write them asking God, *How may I serve in making the world a better place?* because my mom is the original *How May I Serve?* person, as my entire life I've watched her give her all to all! She puts the "K" in kindness! Every day, she puts her best out for everyone, and at age 81, she goes to help a friend who owns a restaurant, offering customers drinks.

I remember growing up, we had some neighbors who thought we were their grocery store, but there was never a time my mom didn't give them if we had it. But on the other hand, she taught us that what we didn't have, we should do without and be content.

And that explains so much of my happiness today. Even cooking with my kids and we only had one more small onion, and I said to them, "What you don't have, you do without!" and we enjoyed our meal with extra red peppers. I can go on and on with lessons from my mom, but I just want her to know how much I love and appreciate everything she has done for me.

Dear God, may we Partner with You in making the world a better place for everyone. Amen.

KEEP CALM—YOU'RE ROLLING WITH GOD

"I TOLD YOU... WE ROLL WITH GOD"

I said to my kids one night in their school parking lot for their Christmas concert.

We were late, as usual, and by the time we got there they told us at the gate that there were no more available spaces inside for parking. But because I feel I'm special (LOL), I thought for sure they would find room for us. I drove up to someone and asked very nicely, "You don't have any more parking?" and unbelievably he said, "I'm going to move my car so that you can park in my spot." And he did! *I told you. We roll with God!*

Shhh! This is my latest constant reminder to myself. Honestly, the meditation book was right when my nephew asked the question, "Do I talk too much like aunty says I do?" and he randomly opened to the following quote: "Of avoiding Useless Words ... I often wish that I had kept silence, and that I had not been in company."

This is now an important lesson for him and his aunt. Let's be careful about what we say. I told my kids this morning, "If you don't have something nice to say, don't say it. And if you feel that's it's something that should be said, find a kinder and gentler way to put it." The smarter and wiser Nikki is slowly learning to know when to keep silent, calm down and keep herself out of trouble. Constant conversations with God again, *Should I say this?* and many times the answer is coming back, *Shhh!*

"Let everything you say be good and helpful, so that your words will be an encouragement to those who hear them" (Ephesians 4:29, NLT).

Dear God, before we speak, may we calm down, refer to You and say only what we feel You would have us to say? Amen.

KEEP CALM—YOU'RE ROLLING WITH GOD

MY HUBBY IS LEAVING ME FOR A YOUNGER WOMAN

And that thought kept going!

Before I knew it, we were divorced living in separate countries with the kids going back and forth between the two of us. Here's the deal: *You must watch what you think about.* Don't let thoughts of worry and fear get the best of you. Crazy ideas come to mind, and you should make the decision not to dwell on them.

Instead, I've decided to turn the negative thoughts into positive ones. *How can I improve my marriage? How can I be the best wife I can be?* It doesn't matter what hubby is or is not doing. I do my best and leave the rest to God. *Everything is between God and me!* I've noticed unbelievable things go my way when I turn my worries over to Him. Even if hubby was to leave me, I'd be okay no matter where I land because I know God will never leave me or forsake me.

Turning 40 in a few months is already playing tricks on my mind, but I'm not going to let it get to me. I'm going for fabulous at forty and some friends, and I are doing 'the biggest loser' to see who can lose the most weight over the summer.

And to my wonderful and brilliant hubby, I love you, and I thank God for you! I'm still a super proud wife, and I pray God continues to bless our family.

Dear God, help us not to dwell on the negative things of life, with our minds focused on You and all that which is pure, excellent and praise worthy. Amen.

KEEP CALM—YOU'RE ROLLING WITH GOD

Day 182 — Live in God, Live in Love

"I KNOW YOU GET TIRED OF ME!"

I said to an extra special friend.

I thought of calling her to share some good news, but decided not to and a few minutes later, out of the blue, she called me. *Wink! Wink!* I shared how her advice of keeping my focus on God has been so good for me. I opened to another famous verse in my children's daily devotional: "The righteous live by faith." And that's exactly what I'm doing. In any area of my life, I know it's not me handling everything alone. God is my Helper, Friend, Adviser, Comforter, Strategist, Companion Partner, and Protector who's always with me, ahead of me and most importantly for me. I trust Him and listen for His direction on a moment-by-moment basis. I can't explain how He does what He does, but if He can create the sun that weighs 333,000 times the weight of planet Earth, then I can certainly trust Him to handle my little issues. And repeatedly He has demonstrated to me that I can trust Him. "Be strong and courageous for the LORD your God will be with you wherever you go" (Joshua 1:9). *Believe this!*

God didn't create us and leave us saying, "Good luck with this life thing!" When we acknowledge Him in all our ways, He directs us. I constantly seek his advice one step at a time. I don't have to know the next ten steps, only one at a time and this strategy of listening to Him and seeking His counsel has helped me through many challenges.

"Walk by faith, not by sight. As you take steps of faith, depending on Me (God), I will show you how much I can do for you. When I gave you my spirit, I empowered you to live beyond your natural ability and strength. That's why it is so wrong to measure your energy level against the challenges ahead of you. This issue is not your strength but Mine, which is limitless. By walking close to Me, you can accomplish My purposes in My strength." - *Jesus Calling* by Sarah Young

Dear God, thank You for Your help in every aspect of our lives. May we not lean on our own understanding, but instead, trust You always. Amen.

KEEP CALM—YOU'RE ROLLING WITH GOD

Day 183 — Live in God, Live in Love

"I THINK I'M BIPOLAR TOO SOMETIMES!"

I jokingly commented to a friend. That's probably why I love the following quote:

"What I learned from *A Course in Miracles* is that the change we're looking for is inside our heads. Events are always in flux. One day people love you; the next day you're their target. One day a situation is running smoothly; the next chaos reigns. One day you feel like you're an okay person; the next day you feel like you're an utter failure. These changes in life are always going to happen because they're part of the human experience. What we can change, however, is how we perceive them.

There's a biblical story where Jesus says we can build our house on sand or we can build it on rock. Our house is our emotional stability. When it is built on sand, the winds and rain can tear it down. One disappointing phone call and we crumble; one storm and the house falls down.

When our house is built on rock, it is sturdy and strong and the storms can't destroy it. We are not so vulnerable to life's passing dramas. Our stability rests on something more enduring than the current weather, something permanent and strong. We're depending on God (*A Return to Love* by Marianne Williamson).

"You gain confidence through knowing that I (God) am with you – that you face nothing alone. Anxiety stems from asking the wrong question: "If such and such happens, can I handle it?" The true question is not whether you can cope with whatever happens, but whether you and I together can handle anything that occurs. It is this you-and-I together factor that gives you confidence to face your day cheerfully (*Jesus Calling* by Sarah Young)."

God is our constant Companion, and our life is all about a journey with Him. *Don't forget this!* Have those *endless conversations* with Him and trust those feelings, always going with the decisions that brings you peace.

Our Father, with You on our side and by our side, there is nothing that We can't handle together. Amen.

KEEP CALM—YOU'RE ROLLING WITH GOD

"I LOVE YOUR POSTS, THEY HAVE BECOME SO IMPORTANT TO ME"

I thanked the person sending me this message for reminding me why I write them, having no idea of their influence. She admitted that she was a recovering alcoholic and her drinking had caused a lot of damage to her family. I didn't know what to say, but I responded, "God has a way of turning all the bad to such good!"

Fast forward about an hour later. God had some more to say. In one of those 1,000 daily decisions, I asked Him if I should stop to pick up more copies of *Jesus Calling* and I got the feeling of peace to go ahead. I was so excited to see that they stocked a new bigger and nicer copy, and as I randomly opened it, written in italics on that very page, written as if it was God speaking, unbelievably, was the following:

"Everything that happens fits into a pattern of good for those who love Me. Instead of trying to analyze the intricacies of the pattern, focus your energy on trusting Me and thanking Me at all times. Nothing is wasted when you walk close to Me. Even your mistakes and sins can be recycled into something good through My transforming grace.

Beloved, remember that when I "recycled" your mistakes and sin into something good. I won't let anything be wasted if you live close to Me-trusting and thanking Me at all times."

Even a challenge, a result of a "mistake" has turned out to be so good for me. *In this life you will have trouble!* It has brought me so much closer to God, with Him directing me each step of the way on what to do. Brilliant ideas flowed. At one point I remember thinking, *Wow, God, You're so smart! You know everything!* I constantly felt His Presence, and I can boldly and confidently say, *God is with us! We're never alone!* The big, big lesson has simply been to go to Him in my 1,000 daily decisions.

Our Lord, You take away the sins of the world. Thank You for Your mercies that are new every morning. Amen.

KEEP CALM—YOU'RE ROLLING WITH GOD

Day 185 — Live in God, Live in Love

"IS THAT SO?"

Here's a story that from Eckhart Tolle's book, *A New Earth,* that reminds us to stay at peace, no matter what comes our way in life:

"The Zen Master Hakuin lived in a town in Japan. He was held in high regard and many people came to him for spiritual teaching. Then it happened that the teenage daughter of his next-door neighbor became pregnant. When being questioned by her angry and scolding parents as to the identity of the father, she finally told them that he was Hakuin, the Zen Master. In great anger, the parents rushed over to Hakuin and told him with much shouting and accusing that their daughter had confessed that he was the father. All he replied was, "Is that so?" News of the scandal spread throughout the town and beyond. The Master lost his reputation. This did not trouble him. Nobody came to see him anymore. He remained unmoved. When the child was born, the parents brought the baby to Hakuin. "You are the father, so you look after him." The Master took loving care of the child. A year later, the mother remorsefully confessed to her parents that the real father was the young man who worked at the butcher shop. In great distress they went to see Hakuin to apologize and ask for forgiveness. "We are sorry. We have come to take the baby back. Our daughter confessed that you are not the father." "Is that so?" is all he would say as he handed the baby over to them. The Master responds to falsehood and truth, bad news and good news, in exactly the same way: "Is that so?""

Imagine all the drama we can avoid in life by accepting events as they come, without judging them. Staying at peace no matter what comes our way and not let the passing dramas of life determine our happiness. I love in the story it says, his reputation was lost, but this did not trouble him. Nobody came to see him anymore and he remained unmoved. He took loving care of the baby, although it was not his. I think what Tolle is teaching us is that we should stay in the present moment and calmly deal with everything that comes our way. Someone may say something we don't like, but we can still maintain our peace. We may lose our job, but we can stay at peace. We may get sick, but we stay at peace. Whatever comes, we welcome it and stay at peace, importantly remembering that God is with us!

Dear God, You give peace not like the world gives. May we always have Your peace. Amen.

KEEP CALM—YOU'RE ROLLING WITH GOD

THIS GREATLY INSPIRED ME

A guest writer today, beautiful words from Joyce Meyer:

"For years, I have pondered what being "more than a conqueror" means. I'm sure other people have other perspectives, but I have come to the conclusion that being more than a conqueror means having such confidence that no matter what comes up in your life, you know that through Christ (God) you can handle it. You know before you are ever faced with a problem that you're going to have victory over it. Therefore, you don't dread things, nor do you fear the unknown or live in anxiety about what's going to happen in uncertain situations. It doesn't really matter what the specifics of the situation are; you know you can handle it through Christ. For you, defeat isn't an option!

Begin to think every day, I can handle whatever life hands me. I can do whatever I need to do in life. I am more than a conqueror. I am equal to anything through Him who infuses inner strength into me. Even before you get out of bed in the mornings, let these thoughts roll over and over in your mind, and your confidence will skyrocket and you will find that indeed, you can do whatever you need to do in life.

Right thinking is the first step toward a better life. Wishing won't work. Being jealous of someone who has what you desire does no good. Self-pity is a waste of time and energy. Discovering God's will through an accurate knowledge of His Word and beginning to think as He thinks is the beginning of a new life for anyone who desires one.

Trust in Him: In what specific situation do you need to believe you are more than a conqueror? Trust that through Christ (God), you are equal to anything."

Dear God, may we be more than conquerors in every aspect of our lives. Amen.

KEEP CALM—YOU'RE ROLLING WITH GOD

Day 187 — Live in God, Live in Love

GOD HAS ME SO SPOILT!

"Give me the number to call!" I said.

That was me to my nephew, Duro, after he seemed to be getting nowhere in getting accepted into a college in the U.S. he had applied to. I called and explained the situation to the lady who answered and she gave me two other numbers to try. My feeling (pay attention to those feelings!) was to call the second number. Immediately a woman answered and after a few words from me, she quickly interrupted and said, "You have the wrong number." She didn't hang up, though, and she said, "I wish I could help you, but I can't. Let me see if I could get you connected with the right person who can assist you." She placed me on hold for a while and came back saying she found someone, gave me their name and number, and then transferred me to them. The lady she forwarded me to was also super friendly and was incredibly helpful and bent over backwards to answer all my questions and volunteered herself to personally assist my nephew through the admissions process. And believe or not, she did stick with us all the way, directing us on every step of a complicated process because my nephew was coming from a high school in Nigeria. Just call me "Nikki So Spoilt" because God always finds a way to get me connected with the right people!

Then recently travelling and with so many bags to check in, we noticed that the person checking us in was not paying attention to the weight of our bags, which has become such a big deal with airlines these days. When we questioned him as to whether we needed to take some stuff out of one that was overweight, he calmly said, "I'm not worried about the weight. I just want to get you checked in." We even had a few extra bags that technically he should have charged us for, and he didn't even mention it. *Say what?* I'm telling you, I'm pretty spoilt!

Talking to someone who was frustrated over a problem with their vehicle that delayed their travel plans for about three hours, I asked, "Didn't you say there were armed robbers that robbed some people right before you got to a certain location? The car problem was the delay God used to protect you from them." She didn't think about it that way. Her face lit up, and she quoted one of my favorite Bible verses, Psalm 8: 3, 4:

"When I consider your heavens,

the work of your fingers,

the moon and the stars,

which you have set in place,

GOD HAS ME SO SPOILT!

what is mankind that you are mindful of them,
human beings that you care for them?"

Dear God, what shall we render onto You? May our lives reflect our gratitude for all Your kindness towards us. Amen.

KEEP CALM—YOU'RE ROLLING WITH GOD

Day 188 — Live in God, Live in Love

THANKS, GOD

I was complaining to someone how my wonderful hubby never has anything nice to say to me, and he would always let me know things he's not happy with, repeatedly. We have the biggest fights about it. "You never have anything good to say to me!" I complain to him all the time.

But since my 5 p.m. appointment with God one day, all of that has all stopped. "Hon, you never have to say another nice thing to me again in life," I told him on our drive home. I got a feeling to read Dr. Wayne Dyer's book *Wisdom of the Ages* during that time with God and there I read the perfect words:

"For me, the measure of greatness and happiness is the ability to subjugate ego to the point of needing no credit for accomplishments, to be beyond needing gratitude or applause, to be independent of the good opinion of others, to just be doing what I do, because it is my purpose to do so. The spirit of what it truly means to be impeccable or magnificent, to learn to give anonymously and resist the temptation to be praised...to just be doing what I do, because it is my purpose to do so."

Wow, I'm free! From now on, I'm going to do everything I do because it is solely my purpose from God to do so, without needing any applause from anyone. It reminds me of a time a friend bragged about his wife: "If I ask her to make tea for me at 2 a.m. in the morning, she would without any complaint." She casually responded, "Why wouldn't I make tea for my husband?" I'm getting there!

I had an extra special mommy moment with Joshie while getting him ready for school. I said to him, as I carried him on my back, "Thank You, God, for this son!" and he responded, "Thank You, God, for this momma!"

Bottom line: everything's between God and me! Super wife, super mommy, and super person!

Dear God, everything we have is from You! May we always remember that You are our Boss, doing everything pleasing to You! Amen.

KEEP CALM—YOU'RE ROLLING WITH GOD

"GIVE YOUR MOMMA A KISS GOODNIGHT"

I said to my daughter, Ember.

She came over, and I kissed her all over her head telling her how grateful I am for her. I was again in awe of God speaking to a family friend in Nigeria. They almost named their oldest daughter "Ember" because it means "I'm grateful," but changed it to "Seember" because it means "We're grateful." And silly me thought I was giving my daughter the name Ember only because it started with the letter "E" after her dad's first name Emmanuel. Only to come to Nigeria and find out it means "I'm grateful" in their Nigerian language when gratitude has been one of my most valuable lessons from living here. This was a sweet God wink, when out of the blue everything, again, lined up a little bit too perfectly.

Moral: Somehow living in the US, with all the comforts in the world, I was miserable because I had yet to learn this life-changing lesson of gratitude. Now I'm bouncing around with it, seeing everything as a miracle from God. *God, I'm grateful* has become my favorite prayer, before even learning that this was the meaning of my first child's name. *I now take nothing for granted.*

But this is also an important reminder of how God's always so far ahead of us. It's fascinating how when we look back and connect the dots of our lives that we see God's hands in everything. There I was, out of all the names in the world, giving my daughter a name simply because it was cute and began with the letter "E," only to relocate to Nigeria to find out that name has such a deep meaning, not only in the largest local Nigerian language, but to me personally and my walk with God twelve years later. Another dot connected. *God, I'm grateful!*

I loved the message from my meditation book, *Jesus Calling*, as if God was speaking to me: "I am perpetually taking care of you. That is the most important fact of your existence. I am not limited by time or space; My Presence with you is a forever promise. You need not fear the future, for I am already there. Your future is in My hands; I release it to you day by day, moment by moment. Therefore, do not worry about tomorrow."

Dear God, may looking back on our lives and everything you have done for us, only gives us more confidence in You. Amen.

KEEP CALM—YOU'RE ROLLING WITH GOD

"HI NIKKI, STARTED ROLLING BESIDE YOU WITH ALMIGHTY SUPERMAN OF THE UNIVERSE"

Was a Facebook comment I received.

In a conversation with a new friend, I told her that we're not going by the ordinary rules of man. The old Nikki used to try and figure out how she alone would control the issues in her life. But now I know I have the Superman of the Universe rolling with me and there is NOTHING I can face, that He and I can't handle together.

The sun is 864,400 miles (1,391,000 kilometers) across. This is about 109 times the diameter of Earth. The sun weighs about 333,000 times as much as Earth. So, someone, please tell me what is impossible for God?

I have tasted and seen that the Lord is good and I have something to tell:

"Trust in the Lord with all your heart, and lean not on your own understanding: in all your ways acknowledge Him, and He shall direct your paths" (Proverbs 3:5-6, NIV).

We don't have to have everything in our lives figured out, in fact, I've stop trying to find stuff that happen and why people do what they do; that's not my business. I simply trust God and that He has everything under control. I can, therefore, RELAX and go out every day enjoying my life's adventure with Him. Like a smart customer and friend taught me, *I try to remember God every moment.* When a situation came up, I asked Him what I should do, and my spirit/gut and His answer was simple, *Stay out of it!* I did and the situation resolved on its own.

Our human minds can conjure up the worst-case scenarios, but let's remember to include Superman in on those scenarios. *His plans for us are real good!*

"'Not by might nor by power, but by my Spirit,' says the Lord Almighty" (Zechariah 4:6).

Our Superman of the Universe, may we never forget that there's nothing that's too difficult for You. Amen.

KEEP CALM—YOU'RE ROLLING WITH GOD

"DO NOT LEAN ON YOUR OWN UNDERSTANDING"

This is my incredible lesson lately. I drove to work feeling down, uncertain about a decision I needed to make. I had no idea of which way to go with it. Just as I was about to get out of my car, it was time for my 12 p.m. appointment with God, so I continued reading from where I had last left off from in my last meeting with Him in Oprah Winfrey's book, *What I Know For Sure*. I still can't get over the perfect message God had there for me:

"Those years of becoming focused taught me a powerful lesson about letting go of the outside pressures and distractions and instead tuning in to my gut-that inkling that says, hold on. Something's not right here. Please pause and make an adjustment. For me, doubt often means don't. Don't move. Don't answer. Don't rush forward. When I'm mired in uncertainty about what the next step should be, when I'm asked to do something for which I feel little enthusiasm, that's my sign to stop—to get still until my instincts give me the go-ahead. I believe that uncertainty is my spirit's way of whispering, I'm in flux. I can't decide for you. Something is off balance here. I take that as a cue to re-center myself before making a decision. When the universe compels me toward the best path to take, it never leaves me with 'Maybe,' 'Should I?' or even 'Perhaps.' I always know for sure when it's telling me to proceed—because everything inside me rises up to reverberate 'Yes!'"

Moral: the fact that I couldn't decide was God telling me not to move forward with that decision. Oprah is so right, when God's directing me with something, I have no doubt about it; it's always a big YES! I didn't go ahead with that move because I didn't feel the excitement and peace from God that I was looking for. God knows what I do not know and His direction has always been the best. "Do not lean on your own understanding." Listen to God's directions!

Dear God, may we seek You in all our decisions, always paying attention to where You are directing us through our feelings. Amen.

KEEP CALM—YOU'RE ROLLING WITH GOD

"SOMETIMES YOU TAKE TWO OR THREE STEPS BACKWARDS"

Was my very surprising God wink! I tried downloading the latest *RobCast* by Rob Bell from iTunes.com, when for some reason, it refused to download and the last episode I started listening to maybe a week or so before kept playing instead. When these glitches happen now, I pay attention because they usually mean God is up to something. I paused and said to Him, *Ok, whatever You want!*

When Rob said, "Sometimes you take two or three steps backwards," I freaked out and played that portion again a few times because that's exactly how I'd been feeling. I go forward in an area and then next thing I know I feel as if I've moved a few steps backwards. But God had the perfect reminders for me in that podcast and when I was done listening, I honestly felt like celebrating.

He said that when this happen we just have to dust ourselves off and get back on the path and that it's like a journey of 1,000 steps and sometimes you feel you may have taken some steps backwards, but when you look at how far you've come, you should celebrate all the progress you have made instead of being upset about the few backward steps. *Wow!* That made me so happy because I see the huge improvement in this area and there was plenty for me to celebrate. It was as if God Himself was saying to me, *Nik, hold your head high, you have come so far, and you have so much to be proud of.*

I went home and had the best evening with my family. I told them we should celebrate because God has been good to us. We started our family prayer again with my husband and my two other Emmanuels praying. *To God be the glory! Great things He has done!*

We have to be patient with ourselves and others. We may not be where we want to be, and others may not be where we want them to be, but let's celebrate the victory in how far we've all come. Constant and never ending improvement. I've surrendered this entire area over to God and in His perfect timing it'll all work out.

Dear God, the battle is Yours, not ours. May we do our best with what You would have us to do and leave the rest with You. Amen.

KEEP CALM—YOU'RE ROLLING WITH GOD

"LEAVE ME ALONE, I'M MAXIMIZING THIS MOMENT!"

I said jokingly to my kids driving back home from Target.

We went there to shop for Spiderman bed sheets and comforters to encourage my sons – then three and five-year-olds – to sleep in their room. It sort of worked as my older son slept half way through the night and my three year old said to me in the sweetest voice before going to bed, "Mommy, wanna sleep you!"

"All we have is this moment!" is what a customer said to us. She's an amazingly smart lady, and I'm so happy I stayed late and got a chance to talk with her. These words are really life changing if we can learn to maximize and enjoy every moment of life. No more spending time thinking about past regrets, being angry or unforgiving towards anyone or worried about the future. If we could be fully alive in every moment, being our most loving, most kind, most forgiving, most trusting in God selves, we really could take our lives to a whole new level of living. "All we have is this moment!"

This lady so impressed me as she talked openly about the fact that she and her husband had separated for the past three years, but they're now back together. "Looking back on it, was it the best thing that could have happened?" I asked her. "Yes!" she replied enthusiastically, as it brought her closer to God. She now has lots of conversations with Him, and she's opened to everything, attached to nothing, as she has learned what it feels like to lose everything, but still have everything with God. *God plus nothing equals everything.*

Dear God, may we rejoice and trust You always, live kindly, love extravagantly, forgive quickly and remember that all we have is this moment! Amen.

KEEP CALM—YOU'RE ROLLING WITH GOD

Day 194 — Live in God, Live in Love

"HUMAN LOVE SUCKS, I RATHER HAVE THE GOD KIND OF LOVE."

I'll never get over how God seems to constantly remind me of His love for me.

From the problems and challenges that He guides me through, to my sad moments with Him finding ways to let me know He's right there with me. Like recently I've been getting the cold shoulder lately from someone I love very much, feeling a little bit rejected by them. Roughly an hour before having an appointment with God, I had sent them a message, as it perfectly described how I've been feeling:

"It's hard to comprehend how much God loves us because we are all used to human love, we had to behave properly, and we had to do certain things to keep our relationships with people going. People blow you off when you don't do things to please them as we know that conditional love, it lets you down... With God kind of love, it's totally different it's awe-inspiring...May I be lifted above the pain of rejection, as I remember that who I really am cannot be rejected. May God's acceptance mean more to me that the acceptance of any person, for it is based on my true worth. – *A Year of Miracles*

I felt as if God was wrapping His arms around me and comforting me, saying, *Nik, I know this situation has been painful for you, but never forget how much I love you. The real you, My child, can never be rejected.*

Another nonessential we need to drop from our lives: *feelings of rejection.*

Our Father, may we always remember that the real us, Your child, can never be rejected. Amen.

KEEP CALM—YOU'RE ROLLING WITH GOD

"MOMENT BY MOMENT"

Has been my God wink for the last few days. I pray for you to feel this closeness with God the way I do, where I know exactly what He is saying to me on a moment-by-moment basis. I love this quote from Rumi:

"Make everything in you an ear, each atom of your being, and you will hear at every moment what the Source is whispering to you, just to you and for you, without any need for my words or anyone else's. You are —we all are—the beloved of the Beloved, and in every moment, in every event of your life, the Beloved is whispering to you exactly what you need to hear and know. Who can ever explain this miracle? It simply is. Listen and you will discover it every passing moment. Listen, and your whole life will become a conversation in thought and act between you and Him, directly, wordlessly, now and always. It was to enjoy this conversation that you and I were created."— Rumi

Case in point: My husband had an argument with a staff, and he had decided to let them go. I agreed and supported him until I started getting the feeling from God that this was not what He wanted. I thought about a song I taught my daughter, Julie, the night before that she and I sang repeatedly together:

"And they'll know we are Christians by our love, by our love. Yes, they'll know we are Christians by our love. We will walk with each other; we will walk hand in hand. And together we'll spread the news that God is in our land. And they'll know we are Christians by our love, by our love. Yes, they'll know we are Christians by our love."

Then there was this email from Pastor Joel Osteen that I expected the previous day, but it showed up that day: "We are called to be different. We are called to rise higher. We are called to be examples of God's grace, mercy and forgiveness. It may not make sense to others but that's okay. God will promote you to a new level of blessing and victory when you commit yourself fully to Him. Don't live a life of mediocrity, live a life of excellence for God. Live a life pleasing to Him and don't be afraid to be different!"

"Anyone can find the dirt in someone. Be the one who finds the gold" (Proverbs 11:27).

Dear God, may our lights shine brightly in the world, reflecting Your mercy, love and grace. Amen.

KEEP CALM—YOU'RE ROLLING WITH GOD

Day 196 — Live in God, Live in Love

"I WILL LIE DOWN AND SLEEP IN PEACE FOR YOU ALONE...

...O Lord, make me dwell in safety."

My God wink from Tumblr.com.

I had a big meeting, and one of the people that were present asked if I had slept well, thinking I would be all stressed out about it. I responded, "I slept like a baby! In fact, it was one of the best night's sleep I've had in a long time. I even commented to my family when I woke up just how great I had slept!"

I then thought of this verse that it's because of my trust in God that I'm able to have such sound sleep despite my challenges. And when the meeting was over, I went back to my Tumblr.com site, continuing from where I last left off, to see this verse posted there: "I will lie down and sleep in peace for you alone, O Lord, make me dwell in safety." God knows every thought we think and every moment of our lives He's a part of. *Relax. We totally roll with God.*

In fact, on the drive to the meeting that morning, I was happy. I sang a song on the radio to God: "Your love pours down on me, surrounds me like a waterfall. And there's no stopping us right now, I feel so close to you right now." – Calvin Harris, *Feel So Close*

And again, I want you here with me, feeling close to God, which is the best place to be. I loved what I read in my meditation book recently in that if you must say it 1,000 times a day, say it, *God, I trust You*. Don't sweat life, do as much as you can and leave the rest with Him. This challenge again has shown me how great God is and how deeply He's involved in our lives. He's been directing me one step at a time on exactly how to resolve it. I had to do my part: calm down, pay attention, listen to His direction and most importantly, trust Him.

"Faith Redefines Fear!" - Mark Jarvinen

Dear God, may we all feel so close to You. Amen.

KEEP CALM—YOU'RE ROLLING WITH GOD

"THIS IS NOT THE WORK OF A DAY"

Was my important reminder from my meditation book, *The Imitation of Christ*.

I went looking for it after my hubby/boss brutally criticized a project that I was so proud of. I thought I was over the lesson of getting hurt by him, whose tongue I describe as a razor, as he says anything he wants with total disregard to my feelings. After then 12 years of marriage, and working with him in our businesses, I thought I had this lesson conquered, but the book reminded me that this spiritual life is not a day's work:

"It is easy to converse with the good and the meek. For this is naturally appealing to all. And everyone prefers to live in peace with those who agree with them and love them best. But to know how to live peacefully with those that are stubborn and perverse, or undisciplined and opposed to us, is a great grace, worthy of much praise, and a sign of great strength."

I'm much better than I used to be in this area, though. I remember a time crying bitterly one Sunday, in front of my two young daughters, after my husband called me fat. A few days later, one of them came to ask me, "Mommy, why did Daddy make you cry?" That was a needed wake-up call, as I didn't want my daughters growing up seeing their mom play the role of a victim. Instead, I wanted them to see a strong, tough and confident woman, not crying because someone said something hurtful to her. It was the beginning of me learning to get my self-esteem back.

I thank God for this meditation book, even though it was written almost over 600 years ago, as it offered the perfect advice, teaching me the important lesson of humility and if someone says 10,000 words against me, I look at it to see what I can take from it to improve myself and go about making those improvements, ignoring the rest (kindly and respectfully, of course!).

I now know my husband may not be a smooth, sweet talker like some men, but he shows me every day through his actions his love and commitment to our family. I honestly need is toughness because he's helping me to become the superhuman God has created me to be. *Love you, my monkey!*

Our Father, thank you for all the people that help us to grow. Amen.

KEEP CALM—YOU'RE ROLLING WITH GOD

Day 198 — Live in God, Live in Love

"NIKKI, I PICKED UP A BOOK TO READ FROM THE LIBRARY TODAY..."

...in Glasgow, Bonnie Scotland and upon opening it I immediately thought of you.

I read:

"Blessed are those who trust in The Lord... They are like trees planted along a riverbank, with roots that reach deep into the water. Such trees are not bothered by the heat or worried by the long months of drought. Their leaves stay green, and they go right on producing delicious fruit" (Jeremiah 17:7-8, NLT).

I received this message a while ago, but it's one of my favorites. To know this person was all the way in Scotland and thought of me when she read this verse was so sweet. I love this: "Blessed are those who trust in The Lord." *Are you guys here with me, trusting God?* This life will throw all sorts of stuff at us, but when we're trusting in God, we know He has a plan for it all—*the good, the bad and the ugly!* I've learned to have those constant conversations with Him, taking life one step at a time, doing what I can do and leave the rest to God, KNOWING He has everything under control. I'm like that tree planted along a riverbank, not bothered by whatever comes my way. When thoughts of doubt or worry come, I just remind myself of who I roll with.

It's all a part of walking *bravely* with God, open to everything that may come our way! And one lesson I'm learning lately is patience. Sometimes stuff lingers for years, but God's timing is the best! "I need not, I must not trouble myself about anything except the task of this moment." "I still live, says the Lord; ready to help you and console you more than before, if you put your trust in me and devoutly call upon me."

"So long as we believe in our heart of hearts that our capacity is limited and we grow anxious and unhappy, we are lacking in faith. One who truly trusts in God has no right to be anxious about anything." – Paramahansa Yogananda

Dear God, may we all become soldiers for You, bravely being the fathers, mothers, husbands, wives, sons, daughters and people You have called us to be. Amen.

KEEP CALM—YOU'RE ROLLING WITH GOD

RELAX

This is my constant reminder to myself and it's working.

I feel loads lighter in that I've stopped trying to control everything. I just KNOW all things are possible with God and how He does what He does is none of my business. I simply relax and enjoy our adventure together. I do my best every day by staying close to Him as to the day's agenda, taking life one step at a time, collaborating with Him about everything. No issue can come up that He and I can't handle together like we've done so magnificently in the past. I love the following from a calendar:

"There are many factors outside your control, but they are all under God's control. And when you're going by His timetable He's able to take care of those things for you." – *Mottos For Success*

"Get God involved with everything!" has been the message of the week and I even got Him involved with my facial cleanser. I'm in Nigeria now and I ran out of the skin cleanser that I usually purchase from the U.S. I have very sensitive skin, and I've found this one to be good for me. I freaked out one morning until reminded myself to *relax*.

That Saturday I went to a store I usually shop at looking at every facial cleanser they had stocked, but after having some conversations with God and I didn't get the feeling from Him to get any. On Sunday, we stopped at a new store in our neighborhood to pick up something quickly, and I ran in to see if there was anything there. This time, I got the feeling to purchase one of their cleansers and remarkably, after only using it for a few days, I love it more than the original one. Over a year later, I'm still using it!

I'm talking constant conversations with God here about everything! Pay attention to those feelings from moment to moment going with the decision that brings you peace when you think about it. You don't go wrong with God. Slow down, calm down, and run to Him in every decision, even facial soap choices.

"The Lord is my strength and my shield;

My heart trusted in Him, and I am helped." – Psalm 28:7

Our Father, thank You for Your help in every aspect of our lives. Amen.

KEEP CALM—YOU'RE ROLLING WITH GOD

Day 200 — Live in God, Live in Love

NO HE DIDN'T TELL ME TO SHUT-UP!

Yup...he did! This was my wonderful hubby of then 12 years. We had an important discussion and what did I do? I went to God, as this was one of those 1,000 daily decisions I certainly needed His help with. Funnily enough, before this conversation with my hubby, I had finished a talk with another person who told me how much he's improved in becoming a much calmer person. So, what did I do? *I calmed down, shut up, and listened to what my hubby had to say.*

This situation offers the perfect example to back up my belief that we can use the valuable time that we'd otherwise spend judging people and situations to have constant conversations with God instead. Looking at everything from God's perspective, I realized that I have the best hubby in the world. Is he perfect? No! Am I perfect? No, but close!? LOL! I'm so getting the hang of accepting these apologies I'll never get, and I accepted one in that moment, instead of getting all upset and dramatic, and I was the better-off for it. Instead of spending hours or even days upset, I loved extravagantly, covered some faults and forgave quickly. *Life is too short to be anything but happy.* I listened to hubby, he then listened to me, and we came up with a plan to move *happily* forward.

Dear God, thank You for guiding us with Your counsel. May we tell of all your deeds. Amen.

KEEP CALM—YOU'RE ROLLING WITH GOD

"I PROBABLY BE GETTING ON GOD'S NERVES I TALK TO HIM SO MUCH! LOL!"

This cracked me up from a Facebook friend, Tassica.

"Like if you're having constant conversations with God," was the post she responded to. What about you? *Are you having constant conversations with God?* I've been lately asking Him, *What about this prayer thing? I don't get it! You'll do what you want to do, anyway, so what's the point?* And He answered me! I've only been reading Marianne Williamson's book, *A Return to Love* for the past two years or so, but I said I must finish it, and as I continued reading from again, where I had last left off, and there was my answer:

"Once we truly understand that God's will is that we be happy, we no longer feel the need to ask for anything other than God's will be done."

That's exactly where I am! I'm trusting God that He knows what's best for me. Even my sickness the other day was all good. I'm eating healthy and exercising again. I don't want to get sick! This was only after two days of sickness, and it was enough for me. *God, I learned that lesson!*

Don't stress life! God wants us to be happy, and sometimes He teaches us some important lessons by taking us sometimes through some *treacherous paths* that we need to help us get there.

Our eyes must stay fixed on Him, which is extremely difficult at times. When our minds want to get stuck in a negative fog, we have to beat it with a stick and focus instead on trusting and thanking God. I immediately take time to talk to Him and remind myself that I have nothing to complain or be anxious about. I lay all my affairs in God's *sovereign* hands and go on my joyful way. Again, I do my best and I leave the rest for God. *How He does what He does is none of my business!*

Dear God, may Your will be done in our lives. Amen.

KEEP CALM—YOU'RE ROLLING WITH GOD

Day 202 — Live in God, Live in Love

"GOOD TO GREAT"

Were the words printed on a Nike T-shirt I walked by at the mall, hanging out with my kids and mom. It was the inspiration I needed, as sometimes I feel like such a failure in trying to be a super wife, super mommy, and super person that maybe I spread myself too thin and I'm a super nobody.

Here's the deal: every moment we're alive we have a new opportunity to begin again. Constant and never-ending improvement is my life's motto. *Never stop improving.* In every area, I want to go from good to great, becoming the most magnificent version of myself. In turn, I hope to inspire you to live your best life rolling with God, leaving the past in the past and to keep moving forward, maximizing every moment. And helping us in that is the Creator of the entire universe, who is guiding us every second.

And now a word from my meditation book, *The Imitation of Christ*:

"Why will you put off your resolutions from day to day? Arise, and begin this very instant, and say: now is the time to do, now is the time to fight; now is the proper time to amend my life. When you are troubled and afflicted, that is the time to gain merit."

This will take lots of discipline, but we can do it. *God, help me,* is my go to prayer when I have trouble being the person I know God has called me to be in any moment. *No excuses! Let us strip off anything that's holding us back.*

But he said to me, 'My grace is sufficient for you, for my power is made perfect in weakness.' Therefore I will boast all the more gladly about my weaknesses, so that Christ's power may rest on me" (2 Corinthians, 12:7–9, NIV).

Dear God, we accept your grace. Give us the strength and courage to now pick ourselves up, dust ourselves off and continue our life's adventure with You, determined to do and be better than we were in the past, going from good to great, all for Your glory. Amen.

KEEP CALM—YOU'RE ROLLING WITH GOD

"PRAYER IS YOU TALKING TO GOD. INTUITION IS GOD TALKING TO YOU"

I got this quote from Dr. Wayne Dyer, someone I will always cherish in my heart of hearts for what he has taught me. Strangely, the day Dr. Dyer died, I found myself drawn to listen to him read his audio book, *Change Your Thoughts, Change Your Life*. He gave me such peace that evening, reminding me to let go of trying to control events and to stay in God's flow for my life. I was shocked to learn of his death minutes later from a Facebook post.

Moral: we're never alone, and I believe our intuition/gut/spirit is God talking to us. The closer we get to Him, the better we hear and know His voice. The thoughts we think are so important because either they're taking us closer to God or away from Him. Dr. Dyer taught me that thoughts such as *love, kindness, forgiveness, gratitude and feelings of trust, joy, and peace* all take us closer to God. Unloving thoughts, *anger, revenge, unforgiveness, fear, and worry* lead us away from Him.

It's like when I get mad at my hubby, and I refuse to call a friend because I don't want any of her stinking positive advice. That's what happens when we go away from God with those negative thoughts; we're missing out on His positive direction. In the end, I'm the one usually apologizing to my hubby for my crazy behavior, but sometimes wrong decisions leave us in terrible predicaments.

When we think those thoughts that take us closer to God is when we're able to understand His direction more clearly and He guides us to the best path. When we're upset, frustrated, angry, fearful, or worried, we're not in the right frame of mind to understand clearly what God would have us to do.

I've found, though, that I've had to calm down and slow down to pay attention to what God is telling me. He incredibly knows everything, and His plans for us are real good. In any given moment, He knows the best decisions we should make. Trust His wisdom and insights always to guide you by paying attention to your intuition/gut/spirit, which is God speaking to you.

"Love is my gift to the world. I fill myself with love, and I send that love into the world. How others treat me is their path; how I react is mine." - Dr. Wayne Dyer

Dear God, may we all know Your voice and the work You have called each of us to do in the world that Your will be done on earth as it is in heaven. Amen.

KEEP CALM—YOU'RE ROLLING WITH GOD

"WHY DIDN'T YOU COME TO ME?"

I felt God was asking when I spent a few hours a little agitated.

I'd just heard my then three-year-old son, crying over the phone. It was especially difficult because he was so far away from me. He was in Nigeria, and I was in the U.S. After feeling sad for quite a bit, I remembered to open my new meditation book, *Jesus Calling*, and here's what God had to say to me:

"Look to Me continually for help, comfort, and companionship. Because I am always by your side, the briefest glance can connect you with Me. When you look to Me for help, it flows freely from my Presence. No matter what losses you experience in your life, no one can take away this glorious gift."

I then prayed, *God, thank You for always being there for us. I know my family is in Your perfect care and protection.* I slept peacefully, reminded that God is always with us. *I have absolutely no doubt about this now.* Even at 4 a.m. working, I felt His Presence there with me. I've learned so many lessons from this challenge, and I'm forever changed. I want to encourage you guys to have a sweeter and closer walk with God. Here are some of my latest lessons:

- "Look to God continually for help, comfort and companionship." Make Him a part of the 1,000 decisions you make every day.

- Don't dwell on what's going to happen in the future, *just trust God one day/step at a time.*

- Stay on God's path for your life. Do the excellent and most loving thing in every moment, every example, and every experience. Don't let anyone take you off track by making wrong decisions.

- Don't worry about anything and trust God with everything. How God does what He does is none of our business. Have NO FEAR! Do your best and leave the rest to God.

- Never give up. God's strength will help you through moment by moment. *This too shall pass.*

Dear God, thank You for Your help, comfort, companionship and Your constant and everlasting love. Amen.

KEEP CALM—YOU'RE ROLLING WITH GOD

"BE HAPPY"

This was my God wink watching a Nigerian film with my family. I had just written the message, "Be happy," to a friend and seeing these words flash across the screen was another reminder from God that He's intimately involved in all my moments. I was in our bedroom all alone when I got the feeling I should go and watch TV with everyone. There I felt I was where God wanted me, and we ended up having such a fantastic day together watching movies. We laughed and cried and had the best Sunday.

One thing I love about Nigeria is that we live a very simple and happy life. Our Sunday brunch was tuna sandwiches. Hubby bought my favorites of mangoes, grapes, and sugar cane from the market, and I had the best time enjoying them. Our youngest son, Joshie, was participating in their school's assembly the next day and we all practiced repeating his lines with him and the next morning, I overheard my husband practicing with him again before he left for school.

Every moment is sacred and even when we have stuff that don't work out sometimes, it's still a great life. We have God on our side guiding us with His counsel and when we stick with Him, little by little, He will help us get things on the right track again.

"Whether you turn to the right or to the left, your ears will hear a voice behind you, saying, 'This is the way; walk in it'" (Isaiah 30:21).

Our Father, may we calm down, slow down, and listen for Your direction in more and more of our moments, as we live happily with You as our Guide. Amen.

KEEP CALM—YOU'RE ROLLING WITH GOD

GET GOD INVOLVED WITH EVERYTHING

That's the important message for today.

I love a comment I read: "I trust God in every aspect of my daily walk." I want all of us there. We can live the most beautiful and incredible lives in alliance with God. I'm learning to go to Him from moment to moment with everything. Even one Saturday, I had the make the difficult decision to let go a house staff that I suspected of stealing. It was tough when I always want to do the right, excellent and most loving thing in every moment, example and experience, but after having lots of conversations with this person and with God, I went with the decision that brought me peace. I thought of the Bible story where Abraham said to his nephew, Lot, "Let us go our separate ways," realizing everyone is on their own path with God.

I also decided to get God involved after being fussed out by my hubby/boss. I humbled myself, apologized to him for my error and promised to be more careful next time. I could've easily gotten upset like I've done in the past. *And stayed there for days!* But turning to God, I was reminded of the amazing hubby I have, who has truly earned my respect. Instead of getting annoyed, I turned the situation around and invited him out on a date night. Focused on God, I looked at the situation from His perspective and hearing a few harsh words from my hubby/boss is nothing to get upset about.

Even the decision to go to a hot yoga class was something I got God involved in. I remember strangely getting the feeling to go, even though I hated yoga! After the class, I thanked this beautiful (inside and out) person for the time with her, which I enjoyed much more than the actual class, trading notes on our journeys with God.

Dear God, we need Your involvement in everything we do from moment to moment! May we KNOW, without a doubt, that there's nothing we can't handle in collaborating with You, learning to relax and enjoy our adventure together. Amen.

KEEP CALM—YOU'RE ROLLING WITH GOD

"LEAN NOT ON YOUR OWN UNDERSTANDING"

So many times in my life, I've seen God show up and show off!

This was a big part of the reason why I got so excited by that message from Tiffany when she said God told her to say to me: "And time and time again will I deliver you. Keep your hope in me steadfast and watch as I turn things around to bless you beyond what you dream and ask of me." *This is exactly what He has done, repeatedly!*

A customer said to me one day, "90% of what goes on in the world is spiritual and only 10% is material and what we can actually see," and I truly believe him. I'll never forget the most worrisome day of my life when someone called my husband from Africa, while we were in the US telling him to tell me to stop worrying. I didn't tell anyone how I was feeling, so I knew that the only way this person could known I was so worried that day was from God.

In the years that followed in dealing with this problem, I kept my *focus on God*, trusting Him and not worrying. I did what I felt God was directing me to do from *moment to moment* and things worked out better than I could've possibly imagined. I have no doubt it was God working behind the scenes of our lives. God, I'm grateful!

"Though they stumble, they will never fall, for the LORD holds them by the hand." I'm now convinced that we'll always have trouble. As one challenge goes away, another takes its place, but when we trust God, do our best in what He asks us to do, and leave the rest with Him, He will direct our paths, and no matter what comes our way, God will guide and help us get through.

"Trust in the Lord with all your heart; and lean not on your own understanding. In all your ways acknowledge Him, and He shall direct your paths" (Proverbs 3:5-6, NIV).

Dear God, give us the courage to hold our heads high and hold Your hands super tight, no matter the challenges that comes our way. Amen.

KEEP CALM—YOU'RE ROLLING WITH GOD

Day 208 — Live in God, Live in Love

I'M SO HAPPY

I love how Pastor Joel Osteen described God: "Notice He's not just any kind of counselor. He is the Wonderful Counselor. He's the very best counselor you could have because He knows all things!" And, He certainly has been my Wonderful Counselor. I remember feeling sad and hurt months ago, talking to God about it an appointment with Him. The feeling I got indicated that He was saying to me repeatedly was that I should thank Him. *God, how can I possibly thank You for this?* I asked, but at the end of the appointment, I half-heartedly and under my breath, thanked Him.

Months later, I'm really thanking Him, though. The insecure, anxious Nikki has been replaced with a confident, *WORRIED ABOUT NOTHING* Nikki. The entire experience taught me to keep my eyes fixed on God, staying on the high road with Him. People will disappoint us. It's a part of life. But God never disappoints and whatever He allows to happen to us is ultimately best for us, even though we can't see it when we're going through life's storms.

Anything you're going through, talk to God about it. His ways are higher than our ways, and He will always lead us down the path to the best life. I'm happy and loving my life, despite the hurts, challenges, problems, and frustrations that may come my way. God is transforming me (slowly, but surely) into the person He would have me to be and to love others the way He loves me. Apostle Paul perfectly describes this love:

"Love endures long and is patient and kind; love never is envious nor boils over with jealousy, is not boastful or vainglorious, does not display itself haughtily. It is not conceited (arrogant and inflated with pride); it is not rude (unmannerly) and does not act unbecomingly. Love (God's love in us) does not insist on its own rights or its own way, for it is not self-seeking; it is not touchy or fretful or resentful; it takes no account of the evil done to it (it pays no attention to suffered wrong). Love bears up under anything and everything that comes, is ever ready to believe the best in every person, its hopes are fadeless under all circumstances, and it endures everything (without weakening). Love never fails (never fades out or becomes obsolete or comes to an end)" (I Corinthians 13: 4-8, AMP).

Dear God, help us become the people You would have us to be. May we always seek Your guidance and direction. Amen.

KEEP CALM—YOU'RE ROLLING WITH GOD

AND WHAT IF HE DOES LEAVE YOU?

I was asked this after writing that I had a dream that my husband left me for another woman.

Here's the deal: A friend encouraged me when she asked me to look down to see what's right beneath my nose, without looking in a mirror. I said that I couldn't see anything. She explained that this is how life is; we can't see beyond this moment. Since then I keep going back to what she said, and it has had a profound influence on me. I can't see what's right below my nose, but I can trust God that He knows and He's the one guiding and taking care of me. I can't predict the future, and I'm simply taking life only a quarter mile at a time dealing with everything as it comes. I'm not looking back too often, and I'm not going too far ahead trying to predict the future either, I'm practicing staying in the present moment, focused on God, following His leading, and taking life one step at a time.

Proverbs 3:5-6 (NIV) tells us to "Trust in the Lord with all your heart, and lean not on your own understanding: in all your ways acknowledge Him, and He shall direct your paths." I'm learning to seek God in every moment and listen to Him through my spirit. Like in a discussion with my husband, His advice was simple, "Shut up and listen." A big lesson I'm learning is that my husband and I can't both be angry at the same time. But when I seek God in every moment He gives me the wisdom and the insight as to when to discuss important matters.

God has these unimaginable plans for our lives when we stick close to Him, not leaning on our own understanding. Is this hard listening to God and following his nudges and cues as to what He would have us to do? Yes, in fact, it takes supernatural strength at times. I love a cartoon picture with a little girl walking along a path with a huge hand holding her little hand with the caption:

"If God is for us, who can be against us?" (Romans 8:31).

"Even though I walk through the valley of the shadow of death, I fear no evil. I shall not lack companionship - why? You are with me."

God, I'm sticking with You and the best husband in the world. I plan to enjoy every day of the rest of my life with him living our best lives together.

Dear God, this life is not always easy. May we follow Your direction, being our most loving and forgiving and merciful selves, even when we go through difficult times. May our families bring glory to You. Amen.

KEEP CALM—YOU'RE ROLLING WITH GOD

Day 210 — Live in God, Live in Love

"I LOVE YOUR HOUSE"

The comment was from a charming, 11-year-old visitor to my home one Sunday afternoon. "Thank you, I love my house, too," I replied. Even though I'd then lived in this house for about five years, I never really liked it and didn't put much effort into it, thinking there were so many things I disliked that I wanted to move somewhere else. I compared it with other people's homes and wanted my home to be the same as theirs. But another miracle happened reading *A Year of Miracles* late one night. God had me reread the introduction of the book *(another nudge from Him!)* after a *whole* day of complaining about my house:

"What are my thoughts about this chair, or this table, or this wall? That they're not good enough, or nice enough? Or do I never really think about them all, taking them for granted?

Now try a simple shift: Wow, how lucky I am to have a chair. Billions of people do not. How fortunate I am to have a table. Billions of people do not. And how lucky I am to have walls around me. Billions of people do not. Think something isn't good enough, and it never will be. Think something is wonderful, and it will only get better. So thoughts like this are miraculous thoughts: I give thanks for this chair, for this table, for this wall.

I remember with compassion those who do not have such amenities, and I pray they will receive what they need. I surrender myself, that I might be used in bringing the end of suffering to all the world."

Moral: I took my house for granted, big time. And not that my house is perfect. I took someone to the guests' restroom and there was a hole in the wall and the lights didn't all work, but I was grateful to God for blessing me with a home that I could enjoy with my family and friends. *My house is wonderful!*

What are you taking for granted in your life? It could be your spouse, your children, your job. Remember billions of people are wishing they had what we do.

The miracles continue...

Dear God, thank You for all our blessings. May we not take any of them for granted. Amen.

KEEP CALM—YOU'RE ROLLING WITH GOD

Day 211 — Live in God, Live in Love

WHERE MY SUPERHUMANS AT?

I had an appointment with God where He beautifully reminded me to let go of the past and other meaningless and unimportant thoughts reading again from Marianne Williamson's extraordinary book, *A Year of Miracles*:

"Wherever I stay stuck in the past, I keep the present from unfolding miraculously. Wherever I see myself as having been victimized, I tie myself to the experience of victimization.

The part of me that can be offended, or victimized in any way, is not the real me. The real me lives in triumph and spiritual victory regardless of what I have been through or what has been done to me. Only my holding on to grievances can keep the universe from providing me with the miracle of a new beginning."

So, we're not victims, we're superhumans and anything you feel someone has done wrongly to you in the past, let it go and hand it over to God to pay you back any wrong done, staying on the high road with Him. Like Pastor Joel Osteen says, "Nothing happens to us, it all happens for us," as God uses all these experiences to grow us up so that we're mature not lacking anything. I felt so silly after reading these words from Ms. Williamson about all my grievances that I seem to dwell on a little too much lately. All such thoughts only keep us burdened from the *joy* filled lives God intends for us. *We can be joyful knowing He is with us in every moment and nothing can separate us from His love.*

Now anytime I catch myself going there, I intend to pray and ask God to help me replace those thoughts with superhuman thoughts such as love, mercy, and forgiveness and to refocus on more significant areas of my life like the pursuing of important goals.

Every moment we can begin again and areas where we've been weak we can become strong. As Rumi stated, "If all you can do is crawl, start crawling." Let's not let the past rob us of great lives, moving confidently forward with God as our Partner, Friend, Counselor, and Strategist, striving to become the best superhumans possible. Heads held high, everyone. *No victims here!*

"Dear God, I surrender to You my grievances, the people I cannot forgive, the place where I hold on and cannot let go, the darkness in my own heart. Please remove the sickness of unforgiveness from my soul. And so it is. Amen." - Marianne Williamson

KEEP CALM—YOU'RE ROLLING WITH GOD

Day 212 — Live in God, Live in Love

"I HAVE NOTHING TO BE SAD ABOUT"

This life will throw all kind of stuff our way!

But I want us leaning on, trusting, and confident that God is with us and for us. I love a prayer I have posted on my bathroom door:

"O God! Refresh and gladden my spirit. Purify my heart. Illumine my powers. I lay all my affairs in Thy hand. Thou art my Guide and my Refuge. I will no longer be sorrowful and grieved; I will be a happy and joyful being. O God! I will no longer be full of anxiety, nor will I let trouble harass me. I will not dwell on the unpleasant things of life.

O God! Thou art more friend to me than I am to myself. I dedicate myself to Thee, O Lord." – 'Abdu'l-Bahá (Bahai Prayers)

"I will not dwell on the unpleasant things of life," is the part I need to work on continually. It seems as if God is doing 10,000 positive things in my life, yet I will dwell on the three negatives I want out. But I feel Him constantly reminding me to lay those negatives in His hands and go about enjoying the beautiful life He has blessed me with.

I'm again blown away by His intimate involvement in our lives. We've been terribly upset about a matter over the last few months, and although I did my best to help resolve it, the problem wasn't going away. Can you believe it turned out that this troublesome situation was God's way of protecting us from making a very big mistake? I'm looking back now and laughing about it. *We may stumble, but we will not fall, for You, God, are upholding us.* He sees and knows what we don't know and what's best for us in any given moment. *Incredible.*

With all of this happening behind the scenes, I'm feeling even more *relaxed* than ever, and KNOWING God is indeed my major Back-up. *What can mere mortals do to us?*

"O God! Thou art more friend to me than I am to myself. I dedicate myself to Thee, O Lord." Amen.

KEEP CALM—YOU'RE ROLLING WITH GOD

Day 213 — Live in God, Live in Love

GOD IS OUR HELPER

I wrote in a post:

"God is our faithful Helper who says, 'Come on, it's clean up time!'"

Shortly after writing this, I opened a book, but closed it because I felt that wasn't the one God wanted me to read in an appointment/alone time with Him. I instead got a feeling to read a book I hadn't read in a while, *Jesus Lives* by Sarah Young. The very page I randomly opened to read said, "You need only to ask the Holy Spirit to help you in this way. He delights in being your *helper*." Wink! Wink!

Just the God wink I needed, when out of the blue everything lined up a little bit too perfectly, with God reminding me that His invisible presence is always with me. And how great is this, *He delights in being our Helper,* as He has demonstrated repeatedly to me, no matter what I'm faced with. In every aspect of my life, He's always there to give me the best advice, only asking that I stay on the high road with Him, as He leads me on the best path. The people, things, brilliant solutions and directions I need always show up right on time. But, we must be alert to His voice: "My sheep listen to my voice; I know them, and they follow me" (John 10:27).

I know we're good at talking to God and telling Him what we want, but I encourage you to listen more to what He has to say to you. Sometimes He's telling us exactly what we don't want to hear and staying on the high road is not always easy. *Why do I have to be loving, kind and forgiving?* I vent sometimes, eventually realizing that I'm happier and more at peace when I do, and I turn into crazy lady when I'm not.

The appointments I have with Him are so important in learning His voice. Just a few minutes in the mornings, 12 p.m. and 5 p.m. I read from my meditation books, again listening to God for direction on what He would have me to read in that moment and I don't leave until I feel I've touched base with Him. This gives me the confidence and wisdom I need to face anything that may come my way. In the 1,000 decisions I make every day, I know intuitively (mostly through my feelings, nudges and impressions) exactly what God would have me to do.

"Have I not commanded you? Be strong and courageous."

"Lord, intersect my life with Your grace and give me wisdom to make choices that honor You." - Leah DiPascal, First5.org
Amen.

KEEP CALM—YOU'R ROLLING WITH GOD

"THIS IS MY SISTER"

Said a lady breastfeeding her baby at the wedding I previously wrote about, but never actually attended. I gave her sister one of the calendars, as well, where I hear from God. I asked her to open it randomly and see what God had to say to her. She opened to January 1, which read:

"This year there will be new knowledge to gain, new concepts to take in, new skills to learn, new people to meet, new friends to enjoy, new sights to see, new thrills to experience! You crown the year with Your goodness, And Your paths drip with abundance (Psalm 65:11)."

I rattled on with my favorite God stories to her, and I noticed she was very quiet the whole time. Thinking I was going on too much, I stopped talking. About twenty minutes later, she opened up to me and said (I paraphrase here), "You've changed my life today. I was about to make a very bad decision thinking God wasn't answering my prayers. I've been depressed for the last two years, but I feel God did speak to me in that calendar and today is a new beginning for me. My friends say I'm stupid because I'm pretty and I can have money, but today I will follow God, going wherever He leads me. I just graduated, and I'm about to be placed on a new job and I'm excited to see where God takes me." I got goosebumps all over! God did want me there with them.

"And Your paths drip with abundance," is how I would describe this life with God, too. I told her all about my surprise vacation with my family. Five hours before I was to leave on a flight, my hubby decided that he and our kids would join me on that trip, calling our travel agent at the very last minute, and it was such a bonding experience for us, as I felt we came back closer than ever. For the first time, I gained weight, and I wasn't upset about it because I enjoyed my hubby cooking for us almost every day. On the flight back home, he says to me, "I will never do anything to mess up my life with you and the kids." I replied, "I believe you."

This is the best life with God! Seek Him first in every decision going with the ones that feel right and give you peace when you think about them, and He will lead you on the path He has designed for you.

God, let us not forget that You are the Boss of our lives. May we always do what is pleasing to You, following Your lead in every aspect, as You direct us on the path to the abundant life in Your kingdom. Amen.

KEEP CALM—YOU'RE ROLLING WITH GOD

"ALAS! WHAT SORT OF LIFE IS THIS...

... from which troubles and miseries are never absent, where all things are full of snares and enemies? For when one trouble or temptation leaves, another comes. Indeed, even while the first conflict is still raging, many others begin unexpectedly. And yet, it is loved, and many seek delight in it."

This made me laugh reading it in my meditation book, *The Imitation of Christ*. Shockingly, this book was written about six hundred years ago, but yet it describes my life today. I now realize that we're always going to have problems and challenges to deal with, but they're all part of God's master plan to stretch us to become our best selves, so that when anything comes our way, we're able to handle them.

But then the book goes on to describe the sweetness of God. For me this is knowing that I have God as my constant Companion in dealing with all the issues that may come up, where I've learned to take life one step at a time, trusting God to guide me every step of the way.

"Nikki, that type of person is going to be hard to find?" is what my new manager said to me when I told him of the person I would like to hire to help us. "I disagree with you! *Is there anything too hard for God?* Was it hard for me to find you?" is what I replied to him. The very next day, a customer came and was happy to take the position and has already started working!

This is the sweetness of God in action, where I know He's my constant Companion, and nothing is too difficult for Him. That's not to say I don't have my moments, like in the produce aisle of the food store, feeling a little bit overwhelmed. But right then and there, I took a few minutes to talk to God. Afterwards, I was okay again. *We're human,* and we all will get down sometimes, but I want us to keep practicing, trusting God always, knowing that whatever He wants for us is best for us. Let's continue to walk *bravely* with God. *We're never alone!*

Dear God, whenever we have our weak, human moments, may we go to you immediately for comfort, support and guidance on what You would have us to do. Amen.

KEEP CALM—YOU'RE ROLLING WITH GOD

Day 216 — Live in God, Live in Love

"SO MY GIRL, WE CAN HOLD OUR HEADS HIGH"

Was my message to my friend, Danny, late one night.

The next morning, in an appointment with God, I decided to read another meditation book, *Jesus Lives,* where God reminded me again that He's intimately involved in all my moments. I incredibly opened right up to read the following:

"Now you can walk upright—*with your head held high*-rejoicing in Me (God).*"

Wink! Wink! This friend and I have been having some pretty sacred conversations, and its amazing how God connected us. It was like He was saying, *You two need to talk.* We both have had some people show up in our lives lately that we're not thrilled about, but in watching *Super Soul Sunday* on The Oprah Winfrey Network, in between cleaning, I had a light bulb moment that these same people that we're not happy about have been gifts from God sent our way. I believe they came to wake us up and look at everything from completely different perspectives.

God is such a complete and total set-up in that He knows exactly who and what we need to put/push us on the path to the best life with Him. My party crashers have pushed me to get my book completed, to suck the enjoyment out of my loved ones, and to be extremely grateful for every little thing, focusing on the 10,000 things I should be happy about and not the three things I want to complain about. And I'm learning to be content *(not that I've given up hope on everything getting better).*

"Blessed are those who mourn" (Matthew 5:4), because once you get through that mourning period, you wake up to a new life. Those problems, challenges, difficulties are all there to grow us up, helping us to become wiser, stronger, better, happier, more at peace and closer to God.

A big part of rolling with God is holding our heads high no matter what we're going through or have been through. As *Jesus Lives* went on to say: "It is utterly impossible for Me (God) to stop loving you." And that alone gives us every reason to hold our heads high, knowing we're loved with an everlasting and unconditional love by the Creator of the universe Himself.

Dear God, may the difficult people and situations that come our way challenge us to be better, more loving, wiser, happier and closer to You. Amen.

KEEP CALM—YOU'RE ROLLING WITH GOD

"WHENEVER YOU LOOK FOR ME (GOD)... YOU WILL FIND ME..."

… My promise to be with you always ensures you never have to face anything alone. However, to reap the benefits of this amazing blessing, you must look for Me in the midst of your moments. This sounds like an easy thing to do, but it goes against the grain of the world…" - Sarah Young

I loved this reminder in my morning's appointment time with God. That was enough to bring me back to my *calm center,* where I rest in God and trust Him, leaving all my burdens, knowing I face nothing alone and that we don't go by the ordinary rules of man. *But it isn't an easy thing.* Case in point: "You didn't tell me you love me," my hubby said to me at about 1 am. We had just talked on the phone about 20 minutes before this (he was in Nigeria, and I was in the U.S.), but he was calling back again, sensing something was wrong. To be honest, I was upset with him about something, but in that moment and wanting to give him a piece of my mind, I *paused*, and I went to God. The feelings were to *calm down* and be my most loving self, instead of losing it and saying something I might regret later.

I still haven't told him why I was upset with him, but in thinking about it, I believe this experience with my hubby was a lesson for me from God to trust Him. *Not every battle is for me to fight.* I feel I have the best hubby in the world, and in our years of marriage, he has earned my love and respect, so much so that I can overlook a fault every now and again-*nobody's perfect.* I see him doing his best at being a husband, father and person and I'm a super proud wife.

Going to God at that moment was the best solution, and I'm happy I did. I'm learning not to discuss things with anyone when I'm upset, but to wait until I'm calm and can discuss things sensibly like this time, *or not at all.*

Dear God, in the difficult moments, may me learn to pause and seek You and what You would have us to do, being the super loving, patient and forgiving people You have created us to be. Amen.

KEEP CALM—YOU'RE ROLLING WITH GOD

Day 218 — Live in God, Live in Love

MY MOST IMPORTANT MESSAGE: LISTEN TO GOD

I write all the time about listening to God and seeking His direction in those 1,000 decisions we make every day.

One day, that advice probably saved our lives. *Exactly how do I seek God in every decision?* I pay attention to my gut/feelings/spirit (my inner voice). I've learned to slow down and listen to Him before making any move. If I get a peaceful feeling deep down, that's my cue to go ahead, but no peace means no move.

Case in point: Having so much on my plate to accomplish for my daughter's graduation, I prayed, *God, please help me.* I had no idea how I would be able to accomplish it all, as we still needed to pick up her dress from our tailor, buy shoes, and get her hair done, all in that planned order.

When we got to the tailor shop, the dress wasn't ready. As we waited, I remembered that there was a hairdresser right next door, and I debated as to whether to get my girls' hair done there. I walked into the salon to inquire whether they would be able to help us, but before deciding, I remember standing at the door for a moment and going to God for help with that decision. The cue – THE FEELINGS OF PEACE – was to go ahead and have their hair done there, instead of going to our regular hairdresser.

Shortly after this, still at the salon, a friend called to say there was a bomb blast at the exact shopping center we had planned to buy her shoes. It was maybe a week before this that my daughter's teacher told me it would be a good place to look for them, as I rarely shopped for stuff like that in Nigeria. If the dress had been ready on time, and if I hadn't stopped and listened to God as to what He would have me to do, we would have been at that plaza around the same time of the bombing.

"My sheep listen to my voice; I know them, and they follow me" (John 10:27, NIV).

My condolences to all the families and friends who lost loved ones.

Dear God, living a frenzied life distracts us from You. May we learn to pause, slow down and listen to You before doing anything. Help us keep all our plans tentative, going to You from moment to moment. Amen.

KEEP CALM—YOU'RE ROLLING WITH GOD

A GOD WINK AT DISNEY WORLD!

I was enjoying our God planned vacation one summer.

Just after watching the fireworks and acting like a nerd when we were asked to make a wish out loud, and I told my friend who I was with that I wish we could be friends forever *(nerdy, right?)*. I was also thinking about how I didn't speak to my hubby that entire day, and I was feeling guilty that I didn't call to check on him. We're having fun, and he's working hard, as usual. And as I held my phone in my hand, debating if to call him in Nigeria, about 3 a.m. his time, I decided not to wake him. About one minute later, still holding the phone in my hand, it rings, and astonishingly it's my hubby calling to tell me he loves me and that I'm the best wife in the world.

God's in complete and total control! He can even wake my hubby up at three in the morning to say nice things to me, which otherwise I only get once every blue moon. *Wow, anything is possible with God (lol)! I refuse to worry about anything!*

And about my friend who I made that nerdy statement to, I know that out of the 170 million people in Nigeria, God knew I needed her and He sent me to her for training to do this important work in the world with Him. Her humility, calmness, love, and closeness to God have rubbed off on me every time I'm around her, and she inspires me to be the best wife, mother, and person possible. She was born in the same city as my husband and the fact that her mom was named "Mabel," just like my mom, is no coincidence. *She's my hand-picked sister by God.*

Dear God, thank You for Your intimate involvement in our lives and all Your Divine connections. Amen.

KEEP CALM—YOU'RE ROLLING WITH GOD

Day 220 — Live in God, Live in Love

"MAKE SURE YOU GET THE BIGGEST CUP"

Was the remark from the friendly Publix Supermarket's deli staff who prepared our dinner—the most delicious sandwiches.

I was there out of the blue, as I would guess the last time I had a sub from there was probably a year prior, but suddenly, I had a craving for one. I had no idea, though, that there was a very special message from God tailored especially for me.

All day, I had had anxious thoughts about lots of stuff going on and every time I was tempted to worry, I would remind myself, *Nik, relax. We roll with God!* Over and over, I did that throughout the day. I kept telling myself to relax. *Nik, has God ever let you down?*

I reread early that morning, in my appointment with God, my message that my friend, Tiffany, shared that God wanted her to tell me: "My beloved, I am ever with you. Do not be afraid and do not panic. For I am that I am; I walk with you. I guide you. I understand you. I am with you. And I truly love you more than you could ever understand. Be not afraid of overwhelming troubles that rise up against you. I am your peace of mind. I will cause you to be still when you are stressed and afraid. And time and time again will I deliver you. Keep your hope in Me steadfast and watch as I turn things around to bless you beyond what you dream and ask of Me. It is the Lord's will that you be glad and satisfied in my house and in Me. Amen."

I also reread another post I shared recently: "Focus on Me (God)! In other words, Nik: 'Trust God from the bottom of your heart; don't try to figure out everything on your own. Listen for God's voice in everything you do, everywhere you go; He's the one who will keep you on track.'"

They all helped tremendously in setting the tone for the day of not worrying and relaxing. So what was the special message from God that night, in the Publix Deli department? Printed on the biggest cup, just like the lady suggested, one very important word: *relax*.

Dear God, thank You for Your everlasting and unconditional love and all the little miracles and love notes that remind us that Your Presence is always with us. Amen.

KEEP CALM—YOU'RE ROLLING WITH GOD

AND THE CRAZY LADY RETURNED

I'm so onto God! He knows exactly the experiences we need to grow us up to become stronger, wiser, braver, and bring us closer to Him. A small thing happened that got me thinking all sorts of craziness. And, it was in my appointment with God that got me back to my senses. After reading *A Year of Miracles,* I surrendered the entire situation to God:

"I give my life to God today. Today I will not burden myself by thinking I need to run the universe. I needn't control anyone or anything. I need only to show up fully with my heart and in my excellence. I surrender everything to God, who lives within me. Every burden and decision I place in his hands. I know as I do so I will be led to divine right thought and action. The universe will arrange itself on my behalf. How wonderful it is to relax at last and fall back into the arms of God. It is not a stiff neck but a soft heart that will guide my course of action. I will not forget to trust God today."

It was if the author wrote this specifically for me at that moment. I immediately handed that burden over to God. My sanity returned, and I was happy again. *I remembered that I was trusting God.*

Here's the deal: we can truly *relax* with God, but we must trust Him. So many things are not within our control, and we can turn those things over to God to handle for us. *He's great at that!* We only need to go out every day being our excellent selves, doing our best with whatever we feel He's asking us to do and leaving the rest with Him. "Often it's said we can be bitter or we can be better" *(A Year of Miracles).*

"The LORD will fight for you; you need only to be still" (Exodus 14:14, NIV).

"While we do this, we should not allow the weeds that prop up from time to time to overshadow the wheat."

There have been lots of bombings in Nigeria lately, and I'm even turning that over to God, knowing He's our protection. The economy is not as strong as it used to be, but I'm trusting God that He's taking care of us. We're not going by the ordinary rules of man, we're living supernaturally with God as our faithful Back-up.

Our Father, may we not forget to trust You today and every day. Amen.

KEEP CALM—YOU'RE ROLLING WITH GOD

Day 222 — Live in God, Live in Love

"LIFE WITH GOD IS A WONDERFUL ADVENTURE"

I'm having such a great time reading through all my old posts for the last three years.

I pay close attention to my feelings as to the ones God would have me to include in my book of daily reminders that I'm currently compiling. Like the time I found that note from Ember that read: "Remember to ignore mommy, too. She will mess up my life." And that Sunday I called Joshie, and he came saying, "Yes, Mommy? Are you calling me to tell me a God wink?" *Guys, am I that bad with the God winks?* Then there was my summer vacation in London for the 2012 Olympics and another summer with my mom teaching the girls to gamble (lol), which all brought back such great memories.

Then there were all the challenges that I've gone through in the past few years, with me describing 2013 as my worst year ever. But learning to be brave about everything, I came through the difficulties the confident person I am today with the best message ever: FEAR NO ONE! That was also the message of a stranger who sat with my hubby and me for three hours for free and helped us through a big challenge we needed to deal with. God is indeed our constant Companion/major Back-up, who's always with us and before us, our Tour Guide on this beautiful life's adventure.

I've lived in the Bahamas. I left there to finish university in New York. I then moved back to the Bahamas. My husband came there to meet me and on the second day of our meeting, he got on his knees and prayed: "God, thank you for helping me find my wife!" I then moved to Florida with him, and we're now loving living between Florida and Nigeria. "Live the dream!" he said to me earlier that day, as I'm about to embark on a totally different adventure in finally publishing my book with his full support.

Dear God, may we enjoy every day as a wonderful adventure with You as our Guide and Partner. Amen.

KEEP CALM—YOU'RE ROLLING WITH GOD

"WHY DO YOU DO THIS?!"

Fisayomi, a young lady we've come to know and love in Nigeria, asked me.

She didn't get why I open my life on my blog and even going as far as publishing the posts in a book. The answer is this: I want you to feel this love that I feel from God. *He makes me feel as if I'm the only person in the world with all His love and attention towards me.* I know these writings are my calling, my assignment that He has personally given to me. To encourage you and spread the fragrance of Him everywhere.

And because He's so faithful to me, I ask Him: "What shall I render to You for all Your benefits towards me?" I'm determined to do as much good as I can, for as many as I can, as often as I can, for as long as I can. I feel so blessed by Him that I'm bursting with happiness, despite the challenges, trials, hurts, frustrations, and difficulties that may come against me. He shows me repeatedly that He is on my side and no challenge is too big for He and I to handle together. I've seen God connect me with the perfect people to assist me, no matter what comes my way. I don't fight battles alone. I simply keep calm and follow His direction.

I would be a bad human if I was to keep all this knowledge to myself. Sal, my friend, shared something that was written in 1965 and now every blog post for each day in my book, I ask if I've accomplished this:

""He writes with the sole thought of reaching the hearts of people, giving them something of vital value, something that will broaden, sweeten, enrich, and beautify their lives; that will lead them to the finding of the higher life and with it the higher powers and the higher joys."— Ralph Waldo Trine, *In Tune with the Infinite: Fullness of Peace, Power, and Plenty*

That's my prayer, that I may assist God in taking you to this higher life, power and joy through a relationship with Him. I no longer react to situations. I ask Him, through my spirit, what strategy we should implement to handle anything in any aspect of my life. Nothing is hidden from Him. And let me tell ya, *His ways are the best!*

Dear God, "What shall I render to You for all Your benefits towards me?" Amen.

KEEP CALM—YOU'RE ROLLING WITH GOD

Day 224 — Live in God, Live in Love

"I AM NO LONGER THEIR FIRST LOVE"

That was all I needed to read in an appointment with God.

I've been encouraging someone lately and I've said to them so many times, "You've forgotten, God should be our First Love." I'll never get over how much God loves each one of us and how intimately He's involved in every tiny detail of our lives. Upset with my hubby, I go to my unpublished book, asking God for His input before I turned into crazy lady again, and out of 366 old posts, God funnily led me directly to this one:

"And I'm feeling extra in love with my hubby these days. I realize every relationship has its ups and down, but we always seem to come through rocky times closer, with more love and respect for each other. I sent him a text message: "Today and always, I promise that I will love and cherish you to be my lawful husband and soulmate. I will stand by you through sickness and health, through richness and poorness, through happy times and bad times, 'til death do us part."

Laughing, I said to God, *Of all the posts, You have me to read this one!* The crazy lady went away with Him reminding me to stay on the high road and practice being a professional ignorer, kindly and respectfully, of course.

God should be our first love, no one else. Right where you are right now, believe and know you are incredibly loved by the Creator of the entire universe; no other love required. People will disappoint us, but God never disappoints.

"No matter what I am doing, it is so wonderful to know that He is with me. In difficult situations, He reminds me, "I am holding you by your right hand —I, the Lord your God. And I say to you, 'Do not be afraid, I am here to help you'" (Isaiah 41:13). When the pressures are great and the problems are overwhelming, I thank my faithful Lord and Savior for His never-ending commitment: "Be strong and courageous! Do not be afraid of them! The Lord your God will go ahead of you. He will neither fail you nor forsake you" (Deuteronomy 31:6). - *The Joy of Intimacy with God: Rekindling Your First Love,* by Dr. Bill Bright

Dear God, may You be our first love and priority. Help us in our weak moments to keep our focus on You. Amen.

KEEP CALM—YOU'RE ROLLING WITH GOD

Day 225 — Live in God, Live in Love

"I'M ACCEPTING THE APOLOGY I'LL NEVER GET!"

Like from someone I was upset with who came to my house and acted a complete hot mess, despite everything I do to help them. In the final analysis, everything is between us and God. *And His blessings are off the chain!* He's always doing like 10,000 things for us that we probably only take for granted. Like driving into work one morning and meeting a container with a shipment from the U.S. that made it all the way to Nigeria without any problems, like they had so many times in the past. *God, I'm grateful!*

My kids topped the cake, though! Joshie was so happy to have me home with them that he must have kissed me about 50 times, never leaving my side. At one point, I lied down in bed for a few minutes and he came and snuggled next to me. Ember showed me her report card filled with such beautiful comments from all her teachers that I said to her, "This Ember that they're talking about, can you please bring HER home instead and leave this one at school?"

I'm enjoying my life with God and I'll never get over how he arranged for us to meet that gentleman in Miami who sat down with my hubby and I for free for three hours and gave us the best advice to help us resolve a tough problem we were going through. When I skip my conversations with God, I end up upset and miserable. When I truly live in my God space of peace, joy, and love, forgiving quickly, however, I'm bouncing around with gratitude, super happy knowing He's with me, for me, and way ahead of me helping me to fight my battles.

As St. Paul said, "God is able to provide you with every blessing in abundance. Tune in to God's frequency, and you will know it beyond any and all doubt!" - Dr. Wayne Dyer

Dear God, may we all live in Your flow for our lives. Amen.

KEEP CALM—YOU'RE ROLLING WITH GOD

Day 226 — Live in God, Live in Love

"HAPPY WE SHALL BE!"

Was the text message I sent to a friend.

I was feeling a little depressed *(I'm only human)* and during an appointment with God, I got a nudge to call her and tell her how I was feeling. As usual, she had the perfect words for me, again as if she was expecting my call. She told me about the Nigerian who didn't win the last season of the TV reality show *Big Brother Africa*, despite a huge number of supporters. In an interview, he said that he refuses to be sad about not winning because he has so much to be grateful for such as a new baby, a beautiful girlfriend, the experience of being on the show, and so many other things. I thanked her and said, "Me too, I have nothing to be sad about!" *God, I'm grateful for such a wise friend!*

After hanging up, I opened to the perfect message in my meditation book, *Jesus Calling*, written as if God is speaking to me:

"TRUST ME ONE DAY AT A TIME. This keeps you close to Me, responsive to my will. My Spirit within you is your resident Tutor helping you in this supernatural endeavor. Yield to His gentle touch; be sensitive to His prompting. Exert your will to trust Me in all circumstances. Don't let your need to understand distract you from My Presence. I will equip you to get through this day victoriously, as you live in deep dependence on Me. Tomorrow is busy worrying about itself; don't get tangled up in worry-webs. Trust Me one day at a time."

And watching TV with the kids for a few minutes, even the actress, Cameron Diaz, had some good advice for me. She said that she doesn't look back and she doesn't look forward too far ahead; she simply tries to keep herself in the present moments of life. We should all have this as our goal, trusting God one day at a time, leaving the past in the past, refusing to worry about the future, and sucking the enjoyment out of every present moment. We have nothing to be sad about. *Happy we shall be!*

"It's only later you learn to lean your head in the lap of God, and rest in love" (Maggie Cassidy).

Our Father, may we all come to rest in Your lap, trusting You one moment and one day at a time. Amen.

KEEP CALM—YOU'RE ROLLING WITH GOD

Day 227 — Live in God, Live in Love

THE SWEET LIFE CONTINUES

We can truly have heaven on earth experiences when we ask God to take the *lead role in* every aspect of our lives, acknowledging Him in all our ways where:

- Our cups are overflowing with blessings because we're so focused on the 10,000 things God's constantly doing for us, not the three things that we feel are missing.
- We feel so loved by God that no other human love or approval is required. We live not to please man, but to please God, doing what He would have us to from moment to moment.
- We accept that there will be disappointments and hurts, but we immediately shake them off and hand them over to God, knowing He will correct them in His timing.
- We're *relaxed*, knowing God is in complete and total control of everything and His ultimate plans for us are good. He's not only with us, but He's also for us.
- We cherish every moment, thanking God and savoring and sucking the enjoyment out of everyone and everything. We're content trusting whatever God wants for us is best for us, while still *advancing confidently* in the direction of our dreams.
- We know that the challenges, problems and frustrations will always be there, but we've learned to pray and let God worry how they'll be handled, allowing His spirit to guide us on what to do one step at a time, doing our best at what He would have us to do, leaving the rest with Him.
- We tightly hold on to loved ones, loving them extravagantly, practicing endless mercy and forgiveness, focused on their innocence and who they're capable of becoming, not on their faults and guilt, accepting that no one is perfect. But we also hold them loosely with open hands knowing that each has their own paths to follow and no one is in our lives forever.
- We accept that there will be some treacherous paths on the journey as well, but we've learned how to hold on to God's hands super tight to make it bravely and courageously through them.
- We love and appreciate God so much that we now ask Him, *God, what can I do for You?* asking Him to use us to partner with Him to co-create a better world for everyone. Every day you wake up excited about your own personal mission, as your *sweet life* with God continues...

KEEP CALM—YOU'RE ROLLING WITH GOD

Day 228 — Live in God, Live in Love

"STAY ON THE HIGH ROAD"

Was the great advice I got from my mediation book, *Jesus Calling*.

This is what I'm learning from God, to stay on the high road with Him, as He leads me on the path to the best life. I remember complaining to Him in an appointment one day and the feeling I got was to give thanks for my circumstances. Although I didn't get it at the time why I should be giving thanks, I can see now that the whole experience turned out to be so good for me. A new, confident, happy, loving God with all my heart, soul, mind and strength Nikki emerged. I'm learning to live above my life's circumstances, as I enjoy my life's adventure with God, trusting Him with every fiber of my being.

And how exactly do I stay on the high road with God? I leave the past in the past, forgive endlessly, practice being patient, love extravagantly, give my best always by trying to do the intuitively right and excellent thing, and I work on constant and never ending improvement. I've humbled myself and if 10,000 words are said against me, I try to take whatever I can from it to improve and ignore the rest, constantly seeking God's advice on what He would have me do in every experience. And honestly, I'm the happiest as I've ever been. *Everything's between me and God!*

"My friends, fear not. Be still (relax, let go, cease strife) and know that you will live to see the LORD's goodness in this present season. Trust and have faith in the LORD," was what my friend, Sal, shared and I'm sticking with this, too, confident that I will see the goodness of God in the land of the living. *Thanks, Sal!*

Our God, may we learn to live above our circumstances, trusting that You know what is best for us in any given moment. Amen.

KEEP CALM—YOU'RE ROLLING WITH GOD

I FORGOT

I'm the God Maniac here, but can you believe I started stressing about all the balls I have in the air right now and I forgot that I'm trusting God to help me handle every single one of them? It was this line from another post that brought it to my attention:

"When you FORGET I (God) am with you, you may experience loneliness or fear." This was exactly what happened, I forgot about God and I started looking ahead to the future and thinking how I (Nikki) was going to handle everything, not how God and I were going to handle everything together. And that's what these posts are about, learning to trust God one step at a time:

> "Trust in the Lord with all your heart,
> And lean not on your own understanding;
> In all your ways acknowledge Him,
> And He shall direct your paths" (Proverbs 3:5-6, NIV).

Slow down, calm down, and listen to God, going to Him in those 1,000 decisions you make every day, and He will guide you and help you make the best ones. I love the words of a calendar that was given to me by a wonderful friend:

When things get to be too much for you, you can automatically know that your part is becoming too big and God's part is becoming too small. You're holding too much of it in your tiny hands, when His huge hands are right there waiting to bear the load for you." - Maria Fontane, *Mottos For Success*

"You are the God of great wonders! You demonstrate your awesome power among the nations" (Psalm 77:13, NLT).

"So long as we believe in our heart of hearts that our capacity is limited and we grow anxious and unhappy, we are lacking in faith. One who truly trusts in God has no right to be anxious about anything." – Paramahansa Yogananda

Dear God, may we never lack in faith. Amen.

KEEP CALM—YOU'RE ROLLING WITH GOD

Day 230 — Live in God, Live in Love

"MAY GOD BLESS YOU AND GRANT YOU YOUR HEART'S DESIRE"

Was the special blessing I received on Facebook.

And I do feel God is behind the scenes of my life, granting me those heart desires. I decided to give my daughters and myself hot oil treatments, and as I took my time doing Ember's hair, I've realized how God has helped me, even with my relationship with her, which seemed to be going way off track a few months ago. I'll never get over how God is so intimately involved in our lives. He's on our side guiding us with His counsel and when we stick with Him, little by little, He will help us get things on the right track again. No matter the challenge area, *He's an expert in everything, including parenting.*

I have a feeling God was even behind us going with this natural hair, using no chemicals to straighten it for about a year now. It's a lot more work, but it has brought my daughters and me closer together. It forces us to spend time with each other with mommy being the official hairdresser.

The lessons from God with Ember, who was then 12, have been to be more gentle, calm down as a tiger mom, focus on her positives, be her biggest encourager, inspire her to be her best self, be patient with her when she messes up, and most importantly, show and tell her how much I love her and how proud I am of her.

Here's the deal: when we stay in touch with God, I'm talking constant conversations with Him, He can help fix any problem area in our life—little by little. And in this case, He has helped me get closer to my daughter. My appointments with Him have made me a better parent as I'm filling myself with God's wisdom each time I have an alone time with Him.

"Prayer is when you talk to God. Meditation is when God talks to you." —Yogi Bhajan.

Sometimes only for two minutes or less, I open my meditation books and I'm astonished how God seems to speak directly to what is going on in my head, or I'll pick up some other piece of excellent wisdom to use in a future decision. *These appointments are the bomb!*

Dear God, may our lives not distract us from developing a relationship with You. Amen.

KEEP CALM—YOU'RE ROLLING WITH GOD

NIK, HOW DO YOU GET OVER STUFF?

A recent hurt was miraculously healed when I read only two sentences in Marianne Williamson's book, *A Year of Miracles*: "Those who have shown me mercy have been angels in my life, creating a space for me to rise when I have fallen down. May I be that to others, and pass the mercy that has been shown at times to me."

I then saw a hurtful situation from a totally new perspective. I recalled all the times this person had forgiven me when I had messed up, not to even mention all the other people who had been angels in my life. *Who am I to withhold forgiveness from anyone? Every day I mess up!* I began looking at this person's innocence, not their guilt, and of all the things I love about them. Instead of focusing on what they did wrong, I focused on what they're doing right and there were lots. "Anyone can find the dirt in someone. Be the one that finds the gold" (Proverbs 11:27).

I also saw who they're capable of becoming, not who they are right now. I felt God was telling me that my job was to love and endlessly forgive and leave the rest with Him. I, therefore, don't have to figure out how to control them to prevent what happened from happening again, that wasn't my job. My job was to do my best, focus on what God would have me to do from moment to moment following His will.

We're not going by the ordinary rules of man that say forgiveness and love are weak and that we need to punish the guilty. The superhumans opt for mercy, handing over disappointments to God, while being our most loving selves and trusting *God will correct whatever wrongs in His timing.*

"Love endures long and is patient and kind; love never is envious nor boils over with jealousy, is not boastful or vainglorious, does not display itself haughtily. It is not conceited (arrogant and inflated with pride); it is not rude (unmannerly) and does not act unbecomingly. Love (God's love in us) does not insist on its own rights or its own way, for it is not self-seeking; it is not touchy or fretful or resentful; it takes no account of the evil done to it (it pays no attention to suffered wrong). Love bears up under anything and everything that comes, is ever ready to believe the best in every person, its hopes are fadeless under all circumstances, and it endures everything (without weakening). Love never fails (never fades out or becomes obsolete or comes to an end)" (I Corinthians 13: 4-8, AMP).

KEEP CALM—YOU'RE ROLLING WITH GOD

"IT'S ALL GOOD!"

This was from Helen, another marvelous person I've gotten to know here in Nigeria. She told me about a challenge that's she's facing, but in the end, she said, "It's all good!" That's where I am, too, not questioning anything anymore because I now know whether it's the good, the bad or the ugly, God has His way of turning it all to my good. Even my sickness the other day has me thinking more about taking better care of myself. I'm now eating more veggies again.

I want us getting to the point that we don't even see whatever comes up as good or bad, but just all experiences, which we can learn and grow from. I'm rereading *The Monk Who Sold His Ferrari* by Robin Sharma and here's what he wrote:

"There are no mistakes in life, only lessons. There is no such thing as a negative experience, only opportunities to grow, learn and advance along the road of self-mastery. From struggle comes strength. Even pain can be a wonderful teacher. But I suggest that you stop judging events as either positive or negative. Rather simply experience them, celebrate them and learn from them. Every event offers you lessons. These little lessons fuel your inner and outer growth. Just think about it in your own life. Most people have grown the most from their most challenging experiences."

I know I certainly have! And my meditation book, *The Imitation of Christ*, says this:

"Do not think yourself wholly forsaken, though for a while I have sent you some tribulation; for this is the road to the kingdom of heaven. And without doubt it is more useful for you, and for the rest of my servants, that you be tried by adversities, than that you should have all things go according to your desire."

It's all good!

Dear God, may all our experiences, the good and the bad, help us grow to be the people You have created us to be. Amen.

KEEP CALM—YOU'RE ROLLING WITH GOD

Day 233 — Live in God, Live in Love

I GOT MY SWAGGA BACK!

Going through a difficult challenge for some weeks, I wasn't exercising or eating healthy, but I'm happy to report my swagga is back, baby! *Can't keep a good woman down*, at least not for long.

God is so funny, though, it's like He's said to me, So, Ms. Nikki, you want to write books and teach people how to handle problems and trials of life. Well, here's some stuff for you to go through and let's see how you handle yourself. Honestly, everything that I write has been right on point:

- Take life one step at a time.
- Calm down.
- Slow down.
- Listen to God before making any move.
- Keep moving forward.
- Do your best and leave the rest to God.
- Trust radically.
- Maintain constant conversations with God.
- Do the right thing and excellent thing in every moment, every example, and every experience.

They've all worked for me in dealing with this challenge. I'm now THANKING God for the experience. It's grown me up so much to new levels of confidently trusting Him. He's been with me every step of the way, *truly my Partner and Strategist!* Solutions, as to handle situations, came right to mind and all the people I needed to help me also showed up. *In this world, you will have trouble,* but my new attitude is, "If my God is with me, whom then shall I fear?"

"... but we also glory in our sufferings, because we know that suffering produces perseverance; perseverance, character; and character, hope. And hope does not put us to shame, because God's love has been poured out into our hearts through the Holy Spirit, who has been given to us" (Romans 5:3-5, NIV).

Dancing through the fires, baby!

Dear God, may we all come to know Your love for us! Thank You for helping us carry all our burdens. Amen.

KEEP CALM—YOU'RE ROLLING WITH GOD

Day 234 — Live in God, Live in Love

"STRIVE TO PLEASE ME (GOD) IN EVERYTHING, NOT JUST IN MAJOR DECISIONS"

This was the one sentence I needed to get my mind focused back on God.

In life, there will always be stuff coming at us from one moment to the next and I was guilty of feeling annoyed and frustrated, until I asked God what was the lesson. This one sentence did the trick, reminding me that everything was between me and God, not between me and anyone else. I then did what I felt was pleasing to God in that moment. I forgave and I was grateful. *I truly have nothing to complain about!*

How do we stay close to God? *Watch our thoughts.* Thoughts such as fear, unforgiveness, revenge, limits, jealousy, anger, worry, and hatred all take us away from God, and we're miserable. Whereas thoughts of love, kindness, joy, hope, compassion, gratitude, no limits, trust, faith, forgiveness, patience, and peace bring us closer to God and we're happy. *We must catch ourselves constantly!* What am I thinking about? Am I getting closer to God or away from God? And having that appointment with Him saved me from lots of aggravation. Taking a moment to hear from Him, opening a meditation book and reading only that one sentence was enough.

The appointments are me touching base with God, and I don't leave them until I feel I've done exactly that. I go to Him with all my worries, fears, frustrations and concerns and I feel constantly reminded that I'm never alone and He's my Helper in every aspect of my life and therefore I have nothing to worry about. I simply do my best with what He has for me to do, as He guides me from moment to moment, and I leave the rest with Him.

"I will bless the Lord who guides me; even at night my heart instructs me. I know the Lord is always with me. I will not be shaken, for he is right beside me" (Psalm 16:7–8, NLT).

Dear God, may everything we do bring glory to You. Amen.

KEEP CALM—YOU'RE ROLLING WITH GOD

TALK ABOUT GOD COMMUNICATING WITH US

I got a Facebook message one day asking if I would like to contribute to a project called, *Creating Abundance God's Way*.

The project was said to comprise of the publication of four books within the next year or so. I joked with the lady asking, since my latest post was about working hard, that she was giving me more work, but I'll think about it. She sent me some more information and it sounded like something I wanted to be involved with, but I didn't want another distraction from getting my book done. As I thought about it, it, asking God His opinion, I opened my meditation book, *Jesus Calling*, and it randomly opened to the following: "As you sit quietly in My (God's) Presence, remember that I am a God of *ABUNDANCE*, I will never run out of resources; My capacity to bless you is unlimited."

And if that's not enough for you, a friend on Facebook commented on a picture of the kids that we took last summer while on vacation. I went to read his comment and right above his comment was a remark from another friend which read, "A family based on GOD'S WAY is a happy one." This all happened within an hour and a half of getting the initial message from her! The first book was to be called *Creating Relationships God's Way*, and I thought of the post I wrote recently where I told my hubby that God asked me to be patient with him and about having great relationships. I shared the post with her thinking I would only have to expand on the 10 points, and she wrote back:

"That is perfect! I knew He connected us for a reason. That's a beautiful message! I love it." God's always communicating with us, but we simply should PAY ATTENTION to His messages.

Dear God, may Your voice of what You would have us to do become clearer every day. Amen.

KEEP CALM—YOU'RE ROLLING WITH GOD

"DO NOT FEAR I (GOD) WILL HELP YOU"

I can't get over how God, the Creator of the entire universe, is so deeply involved in our lives. *And He wants to help us in every aspect of it!* Sounds crazy, right? But, it's the truth! The most important verse in the Bible, and I'm going officially on record with this, is: "My sheep listen to my voice; I know them, and they follow me" (John 10:27).

For example, one Sunday, a friend contacted me about starting a group or page on Facebook and she asked me what we should name it. A small subtle thought came to mind that said we should name it *Hearing from God* and I typed it in a message to her and she agreed. In another conversation with her on Thursday of that week, I admitted that I didn't think it was me, but God who picked the name. That Saturday I'm at work (and I usually don't work on Saturdays) when a customer showed up, and incredibly says to me, "I want to bring you a book called *Hearing from God*, and he came by with it the following week. The actual title was, *How to Hear from God* by LaFAMCALL (Endtime) Ministries. I took some time to read it, and it confirmed some of my beliefs. Like me getting to the point of knowing my thoughts from God's thoughts. Another example happened the other day when I needed to handle something at work. I was headed the wrong way with it, when another God prompting subtly again popped in my mind saying, *Do it this way.* I listened, and I followed, and I still can't get over how I was about to make a major mistake, but God saved me.

So, when I saw this verse in an appointment with God, "Do not fear I (God) will help you," I believed it, because He has over and over and over again, when I slow down, PAY ATTENTION, listen and follow His directions. He'll tell us what to do now and what to do next.

And how do you hear from God? I've heard an actual verbal voice about three times, but I get the God thoughts, impressions, promptings and nudges more often and I get messages from Him from all over the place, like the calendar that said I should relocate to Nigeria and I love it here. But mostly through my feelings (His inaudible voice) I hear from Him all day long. Like the feelings that told me to marry my husband after only knowing him for five months. I wrote a message to him after only one week saying, "I know and I know, and I know we were meant to be together!"

Dear God, may our lives be awesome adventures with the best people and where we hear lots from You! Amen.

KEEP CALM—YOU'RE ROLLING WITH GOD

"I DON'T UNDERSTAND...

... How it's possible for God to love and care about each one of us so much!" was from a stranger one day. I met him at the bookstore where I buy one of my meditation books, as I promised someone that I would get it for them. This was so astonishing hearing him say this out of nowhere to me, as only two days before I wrote, "just can't get over how much God loves and cares about every single one of us!" Then later that day I get an email from my friend Angela, who started again writing positive emails to her friends about God, and that day she wrote:

"Can a woman forget her nursing child, and not have compassion on the son of her womb? Surely they may forget, Yet I will not forget you. See, I have engraved you on the palms of my hands; your walls are ever before me (Isaiah 49:15-16).

Our God has not forgotten us. He knows our needs, our struggles, our shortcomings, our desires & most of all our hearts. He is concerned about everything that we are concerned about; remember He's always waiting to hear our heart's prayer. Lord, help us to know that You are always available to hear our prayers. Thank You for being a God who cares about us. We ask for Your grace, mercy & love. Keep us safe & guide our footsteps. Thank You for being a God who cares about us."

Maybe we all needed this reminder. I sure did. *Thanks, my Angela!* Wherever you are and whatever you may be going through, God has not forgotten about you. "You are loved to the max right this second. There is not one thing you can do to make God love you less and not one more thing you can do to make God love you more. That's the essence of grace, amazing grace. You're supposed to dance this unconditional love." - Rev. Ed Bacon

Our Father, may we all come to know Your love and may that love transform every decision we make to one that pleases You. Amen.

KEEP CALM—YOU'RE ROLLING WITH GOD

Day 238 — Live in God, Live in Love

I'M SUCKING UP TO GOD AS MUCH AS I CAN!

I have this unbelievable calmness and confidence in knowing God is with me.

In every moment, every example and every experience, I'm doing my best to have constant conversations with Him. *God, what do I do here?* and marvelously everything seems to fall into place when I follow His leading. Even in difficulties with my hubby. An employee and I were both feeling frustrated that every time we have ideas and suggestions, it seems as if my hubby doesn't want to listen to anything we have to say. *He wants everything his way!* It got so bad that I didn't even want to go to work because I felt like what's the point, as my hubby acts like he knows it all and doesn't need any input from me. That was until God put it in my heart, *Nikki, your job is to help!* Oh my goodness, that turned everything around! I told this staff, and he too is on board with me. We're excited to go to work now asking, "What can we do to assist in making the company better and to help our boss?" When he looks good, we look good! This mindset is now catching on with other employees, and I'm thrilled. *How can you help your boss/company more?*

"Just handle it," is what my hubby said when I took a task from his plate to help him with. It was something super important that we needed to locate for some special customers. An idea came to mind, and I asked my assistant to help me with the phone call to a stranger asking if there was any possible way for them to help us and shockingly they agreed. I was in Nigeria with this urgent matter to attend to, and out of nowhere that idea came *(a God solution!)* to me to give these people a call. They had no other reason to help us other than to be kind.

See why I'm sucking up to God?

Dear God, may we treat our jobs as assignments from You, where we give our best knowing You are our ultimate Boss. Amen.

KEEP CALM—YOU'RE ROLLING WITH GOD

"I'M SO RICH...

...that I'm always thanking God for all my blessings! I can't even count everything God does for me in one second. God, I'm grateful!" was what I had written in my last post. Fast forward a few hours later, I got a beautiful God wink. I met up with, someone who said she had thoroughly read and enjoyed a book I had given her months ago. I decided I wanted to give her another one, and deep down I felt to give her a book that I was currently reading and enjoying. I tried to ignore the feeling, wanting to hold on to that one, trying to think of another book I could give her instead. But the feeling wouldn't go away, so I decided that God must want her to have it, and thought I'll download another copy for myself. I got the book and headed off to work, but first needed to buy gas for my car. While waiting for the gas, I decided to read a little bit more from the book before giving it away and on the very page I opened to, it said:

"You are far richer than you realize." *Wink! Wink!*

That's the great message I want to share with you. We're all far richer than we realize. We have a Creator who loves us so much. He didn't create us and leave us saying, *Good luck with this life thing!* No, He's constantly with us and for us! I also wrote that *God wants us to be blessed with the best relationships, the best children, the best health, lots of peace and joy and for us to live incredibly fulfilling lives.*

And that doesn't mean we won't have challenges and dark moments, but the rich part comes in when these challenges and dark moments bring us closer to God than we could possibly get without them. Every challenge has done exactly that for me, they've brought me closer to God, enjoying the sweet life with Him, refusing to worry about anything. I now KNOW I'm never alone and no matter what I'm going through I KNOW God's with me. I only try to do what is pleasing to God in every moment, example and experience, sucking up to Him as much as possible, acknowledging Him in all my ways and He's directing me to a much better life.

Dear God, may we do as Romans 12:12 taught us: "Rejoice in hope, be patient in tribulation, be constant in prayer." Amen.

KEEP CALM—YOU'RE ROLLING WITH GOD

Day 240 — Live in God, Live in Love

"YOU LEFT US?"

I asked all hurt and teary-eyed, my hubby early one Sunday morning, realizing that even though we had planned to go to church with him, he went without us. I had a new dress to wear, the kids went to bed early, all so that we can make it out with him to church. Without telling us anything, he left. My then three-year-old woke up, "Mommy, where's Daddy?" Next my then eleven-year-old, "Mommy, where's Daddy?" *Mommy was not happy at all!* By the time he got back home, I was not speaking to him. I was so hurt and upset that he didn't want to attend church with us.

That was until I remembered what I had written a few hours before in a blog post about why I was so happy lately: "And I'm trying to be my most loving self in every moment, every example and every experience knowing, in the final analysis, everything's between me and God!"

I told myself to get over it and forgive him. Here I have a hubby that does so much right *(80/20 rule: focus on the positive 80%)* that when he does something that falls into that 20% category, I should practice being a professional ignorer. *No one is perfect.* In his defense, getting five kids out to church for 6:30 a.m. service is not easy!

And because I decided to be my most loving self, we ended up having a beautiful Sunday together. This life is so short, let's be about forgiving quickly and endlessly, being merciful, extending grace *(pardoning without punishment)* and loving extravagantly, remembering everything is between us and God.

Our Father, may we all come to know and experience Your love and may Your love shine through us onto others. Amen.

KEEP CALM—YOU'RE ROLLING WITH GOD

"GOD IS BUT A WORD IN MY DICTIONARY"

Was a comment I received on Facebook.

I responded, "You're missing out on the best and most significant relationship."

Take this latest challenge I faced; I had to work extremely hard, but I felt God's direction every step of the way. I didn't have to worry about the next ten steps and how it all would come together. Just as I was about to finish one step, the next step would miraculously come to mind without any stress. It was surprising how everything fell into place. Even when I was headed down the wrong path with it, a small, gentle voice said, *Do it this way,* and without that one piece of advice from God, I would've been in big trouble! *With God, we can work smarter, not harder!*

Knowing I was not handling this situation alone, but with God's help, was such a major lift off my shoulders. It was like God was constantly saying to me, *Nik, just do as much as you possibly can and leave the rest with me!* I had peace during the storm. I kept that reminder on my phone that said, "There's nothing that you can't overcome with God on your side." And I'll never forget my moment of doubt, when I thought that perhaps I was overconfident. I opened a few minutes later, in my meditation book, *Jesus Calling*, to the perfect reminder from God: "You have every reason to be confident, because My Presence accompanies you all the days of your life and onward into eternity."

I called one of our favorite customers to thank him for thinking to send me lots of fruits this week. No one pays me to write these posts, but I know God is behind the scenes of my life sending us customers like him. He's been one of our biggest supporters here in Nigeria. He's another God Maniac who has taught me some important lessons like remembering God in every moment, the importance of being grateful and that God loves the humble. *God, I'm extremely grateful!*

O God! Thank You for Your intimate Presence in our lives and helping us to fight our battles with the confidence that You are on our side. Amen.

KEEP CALM—YOU'RE ROLLING WITH GOD

MY BIGGEST REGRET OF THE SUMMER

I had a wonderful summer with my kids, but with one major regret: *not enough appointments with God.*

The kids took possession of my cell phone, which would normally alert me to my appointments with Him, when I would find a quiet spot to read one of my electronic meditation books. These precious times with God remind me that I'm never alone and that He is always with me. *Sweet.*

In an early morning appointment when I was feeling pretty hurt about a certain situation, the perfect message showed up in *A Year of Miracles*. I feel as if Marianne Williamson wrote this book especially for me because it felt as if God was wrapping His arms around me through her words:

"If I choose to see guilt, then it will be there; but if I choose to see innocence, it will be there and I will not see guilt. I accept that every perception is a choice and today I choose to see love. May my mind be disciplined today to see past guilt to the love that lies beyond it...

Let my heart be guided by mercy today. Today, I remember that all people make mistakes. Let me not be harsh but magnanimous. May I show mercy to others as God has shown to me. All of us live in fear at times. May I be kinder today than I have been before, that all those around me - those who rise, as well as those who fall, may feel from me the love of a friend. Those who have shown me mercy have been angels in my life, creating a space for me to rise when I have fallen down. May I be that to others, and pass the mercy that has been shown at times to me."

Love is pretty messy. We're going to get hurt sometimes, and sometimes by the very people we love the most, but going through this experience has been so good because it taught me that I have a choice to either focus on someone's guilt or their innocence. *Wow, I didn't know I had a choice!* And, I can also choose to show mercy like I have been shown so many times in my life and never speak of the offense again.

Our Father, may we not to look to human relationships for perfection. Fill us with Your love so that we may love others the way You love us. Amen.

KEEP CALM—YOU'RE ROLLING WITH GOD

Day 243 — Live in God, Live in Love

"LISTEN TO THE LOVE SONG THAT I'M CONTINUALLY SINGING TO YOU"

Was my message from God when I played my love song to Him repeatedly in my car, anytime I drove anywhere.

And honestly, since then, I've paid attention to the love song that God is singing to me, taking absolutely nothing for granted and I must say, it's so beautiful. For example, earlier this week, I posted a Bible verse on Facebook with a side note, "this explains why I love clouds so much lately!" The verse was Psalm 19:1: "The heavens declare the glory of God; the skies proclaim the work of his hands." Fast forward a few days later, not having my meditation book handy and feeling in a dull mood, I decided to read a Bible that we leave open in our bedroom that I hardly ever read. Debating on whether to read forward a page or backward a page, the feeling was to go backwards. Guess the verse I first read on those pages: "The heavens declare the glory of God; the skies proclaim the work of his hands." Once again everything lined up a little bit too perfectly! This was the God wink I needed to get myself up and at it, with God again reminding me that His "unseen Presence is a constant" in my life.

I'm now calling the God winks my continual love song from God. *Are you listening to the love song He's singing to you?* PAY ATTENTION and take nothing for granted.

"Make everything in you an ear, each atom of your being, and you will hear at every moment what the Source is whispering to you, just to you and for you, without any need for my words or anyone else's. You are—we all are—the beloved of the Beloved, and in every moment, in every event of your life, the Beloved is whispering to you exactly what you need to hear and know. Who can ever explain this miracle? It simply is. Listen and you will discover it every passing moment. Listen, and your whole life will become a conversation in thought and act between you and Him, directly, wordlessly, now and always. It was to enjoy this conversation that you and I were created."—Rumi

Our Father, thank You for your goodness everywhere and Your concern about every detail of our lives. May we all know and listen to the love song You are continually singing to us. Amen.

KEEP CALM—YOU'RE ROLLING WITH GOD

"IN ALL YOUR WAYS ACKNOWLEDGE HIM...

...And He shall direct your path... That's your testimony," said my friend, Funmi. *She's right!* That pretty much sums up my message—that in everything you do, from moment to moment, focus on God. Seek His guidance as to what to do, where to go, and even what to say, and you can live the best life, as God directs you on the path that He has designed for you.

Here's the deal: as a baby, born on a small little island in the Bahamas and of all names, my dad gave me the name "Oneka," which means African Princess. I hated that name and even my mom thought it was stupid, but now we understand, that it was all a part of God's plan/destiny for me. I love living in Africa and the lessons I'm learning here are fantastic. My latest one is knowing that every moment counts. Those 1,000 decisions we make every day, they're important! I'm learning to suck as much enjoyment and fulfillment from every single one of those moments and to pay attention, because God has something going on in every one of them.

For example, it was during a play date with Funmi and her kids that I paused for a moment and suggested to her that she begin writing a blog every day, too. It was another friend who happened to tell me one day that Funmi loves to write, but stores everything on her computer. Now, she is writing every day and bringing so many people closer to God, with someone telling her the other day, "I wait for your email." *I'm so proud of her!* See what I'm saying? There's something going on in every moment. God has a plan and purpose for each one of us, and when we tap into His plan for our lives, *BAM!* We're living the best and most unimaginable lives.

Call it instincts, gut, Holy Spirit, intuition, a sixth sense or Sponge Bob, but I now know that it's God directing us from moment to moment on the path He has for us. He's with us and for every single one of us and it's never too late to tap in. I always go with the decision that brings me peace when I think about it, and I love my life with God. *I roll like that!*

Dear God, may we all fulfill the unimaginable plans You have for us, doing what You would have us to do from moment to moment. Amen.

KEEP CALM—YOU'RE ROLLING WITH GOD

Day 245 — Live in God, Live in Love

"IF YOU DON'T TAKE THE TIME TO THINK ABOUT...

...and analyze your life; you'll never realize all the dots that are all connected."

This is a quote from Beyoncé that I've been thinking about. After watching her interviewed by Oprah Winfrey, I have a totally new respect and admiration for her.

In my life, I thought about the break I took when I graduated high school before rushing off to college. Just so I would have something to do, my mom paid for me to go to a computer school that my brother ran. Those few months in that school has made such a difference in my life. Everywhere I've worked, having that computer knowledge was and still is an asset to me.

At one point, I made the crazy decision to go to New York to a university with only enough money to complete one semester, and I needed about five semesters to graduate. That meant I had to work while also going to school. Miraculously, I never had a problem finding a job in New York, thanks to that computer and work experience I had from the Bahamas. I had such confidence that I quit some great jobs in search of more experiences. And, it all fit perfectly with the business I married into, my degree, and all my experiences from working in New York and the Bahamas. *It is all perfect!*

What's my point? That God has a plan and purpose for everything. Follow that *KNOWING* that you have as to where to go and what to do, taking life one step at a time. The decision to go to university was "crazy," but I had this *KNOWING* that I should go. Getting married to my hubby after only knowing him for five months was another *crazy* decision, but again I had a *KNOWING* deep inside of me that I was making the right decision. Moving to Nigeria was another *crazy* decision, but again I followed that *KNOWING*, and that's where I began writing these *crazy* posts. I've learned to follow and trust that *KNOWING*, as I *KNOW* that's God directing us.

Dear God, thank You for Your constant love, guidance and direction. May we all tap into Your voice and Your purpose for us. Amen.

KEEP CALM—YOU'RE ROLLING WITH GOD

A SMALL STORY WITH A BIG MEANING

I'm still thinking about a morning when I sat reading through posts on the Tumblr.com website where I go to hear from God.

I stopped at one that read, "I have decided to follow Jesus," and I started singing the song with these exact words to myself in my head. Maybe 20 minutes later, my hubby comes in and out of nowhere he started singing the very same song too, "I have decided to follow Jesus." I thought to myself, *Wasn't that the same song I was just singing to myself in my head?* I rushed back to the Tumblr.com site and indeed it was the very song I was singing. *Now, what are the chances of that happening?*

The BIG meaning I'm taking from this story is that God is in total control. We want to control our little worlds, including people and circumstances, but God was saying to me, *Nik, I'm the one in control of everything!* In quietness and confident trust is our strength. We're not going by the ordinary rules of man. God is working behind the scenes of our lives, and when we trust Him, He works everything out on our behalf. We don't need to stress ourselves worrying how we will control things, but instead, we can let go, handing situations over to God. We then follow God's will for us in every moment, trusting our spirit/gut to guide us.

I'm so on to God! He knows exactly what and who we need to get us/push us where He would have us to be. He sent someone in my life that got me to relocate with my family all the way to Nigeria from the U.S., and I'm now looking back and laughing at it, even though I wasn't finding it funny at the time. He helps us to make important decisions to keep us on the path He has for us to live the best life with Him. I'm now thanking Him for that person because I love my life in Nigeria!

"If the LORD delights in a man's way, he makes his steps firm; though he stumbles, he will not fall, for the LORD upholds him with his hand."

RELAX...

Dear God, may our faith and confidence in You grow stronger every day. Amen.

KEEP CALM—YOU'RE ROLLING WITH GOD

"I GOT THE EYE OF THE TIGER...

…A fighter, dancing through the fire

'Cause I am a champion and you're gonna hear me roar

Louder, louder than a lion 'Cause I am a champion and you're gonna hear me roar."

I love these words from Katy Perry's song, *Roar,* and this is where I want us whenever any problems, challenges, or adversities come our way. We gotta be fighters, dancing through the fire, ready to tackle anything, KNOWING we roll with God, who is always fighting with us. "The LORD himself will fight for you. Just stay calm" (Exodus 14:14, NLT).

Easier said than done, right? This is from the same person who woke up feeling overwhelmed, but when I reminded myself who I roll with, I was back roaring again. This life will get you down sometimes, but you must keep fighting. *WARNING: this life is not for weaklings!* You must be tough and confident. As the song says, "You held me down, but I got up, already brushing off the dust."

I love what Pastor Joel Osteen said, "You have to be unflinching!" No matter what comes up, you can say, "Bring it on! I know my God is with me!"

"You gain confidence through knowing that I am with you – that you face nothing alone. Anxiety stems from asking the wrong question: 'If such and such happens, can I handle it?' The true question is not whether you can cope with whatever happens, but whether you and I together can handle anything that occurs. It is this you-and-I together factor that gives you confidence to face your day cheerfully." - *Jesus Calling*

Dear God, may we have the confidence (no doubts!) to dance through all the fires knowing You are always with us. Amen.

KEEP CALM—YOU'RE ROLLING WITH GOD

Day 248 — Live in God, Live in Love

A TEST FROM GOD... I LOVE IT!

One Saturday, after writing my post for that day, I thought about everything that I had going on with me. Feeling a bit overwhelmed by it all, I had a conversation with God about giving up the daily posts for a little while until things settled down. As I posted, I kept thinking to include a note that my readers probably wouldn't see me for a couple of weeks, but the feeling was to keep thinking about it. While posting to one of the groups, I saw the top of a message saying, "The greatest test." I was quite curious what that test was and scrolled down to continuing reading. It said:

"The greatest test is to be a blessing to others while you go through your own storm."

Sounded like a challenge from God to me and I said, *Okay, God we can do this! The posts go on!* On Thursday of that week, and feeling a bit anxious because someone disappointed me in some help they were to give me, I got a feeling to read through some of my old posts. I came to the one where I purchased *Jesus Calling*, for the very first time at Walmart, meeting a cashier there who asked me what the book was about. Strangely, we were alone for some time (Walmart is usually extremely packed with people), so I opened to a random page and read aloud to her:

"I, the Creator of the Universe, am with you and for you. What more could you need! When you feel some lack, it is because you are not connected with me at a deep level. I offer abundant Life; your part is to trust Me, refusing to worry about anything."

I cried as I read this, because that day I needed that message. God was saying that person might have disappointed you, but I'm here with you and for you; *Nik, what more could you need?*

Wanting to hear more from God, I went again to our fav Tumblr website where I usually get messages from Him, and I came across the perfect one: "Be strong and courageous for the LORD your God will be with you wherever you go" (Joshua 1:9).

"My sheep listen to my voice; I know them, and they follow me" (John 10:27, NIV).

Dear God, we will pass all the tests and challenges that come our way, with Your help, of course!!! Amen.

KEEP CALM—YOU'RE ROLLING WITH GOD

Day 249 — Live in God, Live in Love

"IT'S ABOUT INSTINCTS AND INTELLECT!"

Is what I said to someone who has an opportunity to get a very important job here in Nigeria. I told him all about our secret weapon—*God!* Here's the deal: instincts (those inner feelings/nudges you get throughout the day on what to do) are God directing us, moment by moment, from what to say, what to do and where to go. You pay attention to it, and when combined with your intellect, you have an unbeatable combination for success.

One day, I saw my hubby taking some people to meet with our assistant. My instincts told me to follow them, so I did! It turns out they were representing a big organization, and they needed a quote from us. I asked them if they would give me a few minutes to draft an introductory letter to their firm and they happily agreed to wait. Early the next morning, they were back saying that their boss was impressed with our letter and decided to give us the job.

I used my instincts when it told me to follow them and then my intellect to ask if I should prepare a formal letter of introduction. You use both – instincts and intellect! Also, while the representatives were there, I spoke to them, telling them what my instincts led me to say based on what my understanding has been picking up about conducting business in an entirely different environment than I'm accustomed to. So, all day long now, this is what I do. I pay attention to my instincts, and I allow God to guide my actions.

I will always have a very long to-do list, but I'm learning to work smarter, not harder. All day, God is my important Helper, as He guides me to what's important on that list and what I need to pay attention to, moment by moment. God knows everything that we don't know including everything that's going on behind the scenes of our lives that we have no clue about. Therefore, I'm using my instincts and my intellect, *running to God in every moment,* going with those decisions that bring me peace when I think about them.

Our Beloved, may we use our instincts and intellect in every aspect of our lives: parenting, marriage, friendships, all aspects, and ALL problems. Always trusting Your wisdom and guidance. Amen.

KEEP CALM—YOU'RE ROLLING WITH GOD

Day 250 — Live in God, Live in Love

STOP GETTING OFFENDED!

I've noticed that we spend so much of our lives getting offended by what others say and do and this only takes us away from God. I believe we can all learn something from my then four-year-old son, Joshie, who told me, "Mommy, I just ignore them!" I learned a big lesson about getting offended when someone spoke rudely to my husband on a three-way call. For two days, I carried that lady around with me in my head always attacking her every time I thought of her. *How dare she talk to us the way she did? Does she know we pay her salary?*

Looking back on it, I laugh at myself for how crazy I got! I wasted two days of my life thinking about that lady when I could have ignored her like my son said and not taken the whole thing so seriously. I could have joked with my hubby about it that maybe she forgot to take her anxiety pills that day, instead of letting her ruin two entire days of my life!

Dr. Wayne Dyer in his book, *The Power of Intention,* wrote, "That which offends you only weakens you. If you're looking for occasions to be offended, you'll find them at every turn. As *A Course in Miracles* reminds us: "Peace is of God, you who are a part of God are not at home except in his peace." Stay close to God and stop getting offended all the time as every time you're offended by something you move away from God. When you're able to respond with love and kindness, instead of getting offended, you get closer to God. Remember, "It's not between you and anyone else; everything is between you and God!" As St. Paul said, "God is able to provide you with every blessing in abundance." Tune in to God's frequency, and you will know it beyond any and all doubt!"

Dear God, help us to constantly catch ourselves when we're moving away from Your peace and ask, "How can I respond to this in a more loving and kind way?" seeking to always please You. Amen.

KEEP CALM—YOU'RE ROLLING WITH GOD

"I'M COMING BACK"

Was my response to a sweet friend, who asked if we're coming back to Nigeria, with all the bombings that were going on.

I even got a special God wink that confirmed my feelings that it was okay to return. The kids and I were out spending the day at a park in the U.S. when we heard the news that there was another bombing, and my mind immediately started racing, questioning whether we were making the best decision to go back there. God, incredibly knowing all my thoughts, spoke to me in *Jesus Today,* which funnily enough, I'd been carrying around with me in my purse. I took a few minutes to open it and spend with God after hearing this terrible news, and I opened right up to the perfect words from Him:

"I AM THE ONE WHO KEEPS YOU SAFE. YOU TEND to rely heavily on your thinking and planning, as if that is where your security lies. When you start to feel anxious about something, your mind goes into overdrive —searching for solutions, searching for security. All the while I am with you, holding you by your right hand."

Guys, I am so about keeping all plans tentative, paying attention to where God is directing me on a moment-by-moment basis, because this is where I get the best direction from Him. My kids and I had planned to go to another park, which was about 45 minutes away from where we were, and in pulling in somewhere to turn around, there was, hidden behind lots of trees, a beautiful park. The lady at the gate even waived the entrance fee for us and we ended up having such a great day there that I didn't want to leave.

"The steps of a good man are ordered by the Lord" (Psalm 37:23, KJV). When we stop and pay attention to our feelings and what God would have us do, He leads us on the path to the best life. I still make plans, but I keep them tentative, trusting God's guidance more than all my thinking and planning. *God, what should we do here?* I'm talking constant conversations with Him, always going with the decisions that bring me peace when I think about them.

Dear God, may we not live a rushed and frenzied life. Help us to slow down, calm down, and listen to Your moment by moment instructions. Amen.

KEEP CALM—YOU'RE ROLLING WITH GOD

Day 252 — Live in God, Live in Love

"WHEN I THINK IT CAN'T GET ANY BETTER, IT DOES"

Is what I said to my friend, Sal, in South Africa. God, once again, took a negative and hurtful experience and turned it into my good. It's like a whole new and better world opened to me. The last few weeks have been an emotional roller-coaster ride, but I'm happy to report the biggest miracle: *God has healed my heart and replaced sadness and pain with such love, peace, and joy.* Instead of focusing on petty matters, I'm focused on important things like *finally finishing* this book. *What is too difficult for God?* He's used this experience to turn me into the superhuman He has created me to be and in areas where I've been weak, He's helping me to become stronger, especially in the mental department *(those darn thoughts will keep you down if you let them! You must beat your mind with a stick! No time for negativity!)*

I placed an important prayer on my bathroom door and reading it several times a day helped me tremendously: "O God! Refresh and gladden my spirit. Purify my heart. Illumine my powers. I lay all my affairs in Thy hand. Thou art my Guide and my Refuge. I will no longer be sorrowful and grieved; I will be a happy and joyful being. O God! I will no longer be full of anxiety, nor will I let trouble harass me. I will not dwell on the unpleasant things of life. Amen." – 'Abdu'l-Bahá (Bahai Prayers)

Here's the deal: honestly, I'm *not* dwelling on the unpleasant things of life. Life will get messy at times. I'm *calm*, laying all my affairs in God's hands, trusting that *He will fight my battles* for me. I follow His leading, and let me warn you, it's not easy staying on the high road with God, where He has called us to be our best selves, striving to please Him in every moment, and not worried about what anyone else is doing. I want us to get to the point that we know without a doubt where God is leading us and in this situation, He asked me to be my most loving and forgiving self and a new Nikki has emerged: happy, focused, confident, and stronger than ever before. "Anyone can find the dirt in someone. Be the one who finds the gold" (Proverbs 11:27).

Super wife, super mom, and super person is back, all for the glory of God!

Dear God, thank You for Your peace that passes all understanding. Help us to be super loving and forgiving, especially in our homes, radiating Your love to others. Amen.
KEEP CALM—YOU'RE ROLLING WITH GOD

A LOVE NOTE FROM GOD

One Sunday, I fell in love with a magazine article and since then I've been carrying it around with me in my handbag. Reading it gave me goosebumps all over as the writer described her love note from God that showed up in the form of a smiley face on a towel drying outside in a town she drove through. I shared a portion of it in my post for that day:

"I've been learning to enjoy life more and savor its many pleasures, big and small. I'm noticing God's loving presence more, how He helps me, guides me, and sprinkles my life with His blessings, like little love notes to remind me how much He cares." – *Activated Magazine*

This smiley face has also become my little love note from God whenever I see one. On a particularly stressful day, it showed up for like half a second on a huge TV screen and I took that as *my cue from God not to worry* and everything unbelievably went better than expected.

Fast forward to the next day, when my assistant helped me with obtaining a new SIM card for my phone and she noticed that my phone case was old and needed replacing, so she purchased a new case for me without me asking her to. She then gives me a gift from the owner of the phone shop. *Can you believe it was a yellow phone case filled with smiley faces?*

"I've been learning to enjoy life more and savor its many pleasures, big and small. I'm noticing God's loving presence more, how He helps me, guides me, and sprinkles my life with His blessings, like little love notes to remind me how much He cares."

I'm enjoying my summer holiday with the kids. They're enrolled in *Camp Nikki* with lots of cooking, cleaning, and appointments with God.

Dear God, may nothing separate us from Your love! Amen.

KEEP CALM—YOU'RE ROLLING WITH GOD

"LIFE'S MOST PERSISTENT AND URGENT QUESTION IS...

...What are you doing for others?" - Martin Luther King, Jr.

Honestly, my life has come alive since I started my blog. I get to take all my *"negatives"* and reflect on all the huge positives that come about because of them. Like I told my mom, nothing bad happens to us; it's all for our growth and development to be the people God has created us to be. I started writing about my experiences with the intent of helping others, and in the process, I've helped myself to a new life. I now realize, to be truly happy, you must be doing something for others.

I would go as far as saying anything you do for another person, no matter how small, you're doing it for yourself, as well. I wake up every day excited about my life and my personal assignment from God to bring you closer to Him. I'm so much closer myself, and He has filled my life with happiness, peace, joy, gratitude, and contentment.

"Taking time to help others is one of the most important things that you can do in life. And in doing so, you make God want to help you more as well." – Maria Fontane, *Mottos For Success*

God has truly been my Helper in every area of my life! I feel as if I've hit an extraordinary level of living where I get extra special attention from Him. I experience such tremendous miracles and know they're all from Him. He's behind the scenes of my life, helping me. I'm blown away when perfect solutions pop into my head or when He organizes the best people to help me with my personal challenges. Even on the worst days, it is as if He comes and wraps His arms around me to let me know that He's there. He then stays with me and helps me to get through those sad periods. He sticks by my side, and I'm sticking with Him asking, *God, how may I serve You?*

"If another's heart can be made glad through your sacrifice, it's no longer a sacrifice but a privilege." - George Van Valkenburg

"No one has ever seen God; but if we love one another, God lives in us and his love is made complete in us." -1 John 4:12 (NIV)

"May your life be a living legacy to your God." - Joyce Rupp, *A New Year's Blessing*

Dear God, today, may we love others deeper, sharing Your love for us with the world, beginning in our homes and spreading out from there. Amen.

KEEP CALM—YOU'RE ROLLING WITH GOD

"THANKS, HON, FOR PUTTING UP WITH ME"

I said to my hubby on the drive back home from work. I finally finished working on my book *AGAIN*, and I was thanking him for his patience and support, knowing it's certainly *not easy* having a God Maniac for a wife.

He replied, "It's your work for God." I was extremely happy to hear this from him. It's a good lesson for all of us about being patient with each other.

"Are you married?" I asked a bank representative over the phone. He answered no, and I responded, "Lucky you!" I was only kidding, and I told him one of the best decisions I've ever made was marrying my husband. I love our life together, and like I said recently, I look forward to savoring every day of the rest of my life with him. It doesn't mean we won't have our issues and stuff we go through, but I've found that every time we go through something, we always seem to come away happier, with more love and respect for each other, committed to sticking together, no matter what.

I love two posts I found on Tumblr.com:

- "Sometimes marriage looks like this: going grocery shopping together and finding that your hubs snuck the prettiest cluster of baby's breath into your cart. long, honest, open talks that fill you up and make you feel safe and heard and cared for. spontaneous weekend trips to the ocean. sweet words. all the kisses all the time. trust. growth. hugs when you get home from work.

sometimes marriage looks like this: staying up til midnight arguing; tears, dark eyes, crossed arms. shaky communication skills. circular conversations that leave you drained. feeling betrayed. feeling distant. feeling alone. feeling misunderstood. selfishness. pride. Unmet expectations. unforeseen change. the challenge is to love, respect, and honor the other person in both scenarios: no more and no less. love should not be conditional. love shouldn't shift based on circumstances."

- "Life point: Paul says in Galatians 6:2 that we must learn to get along with each other. We are going to have to learn to put up with some things we do not like. All the people around us are not going to think and speak and act the way we want them to. But forgiving them is part of what we must do as members of the body of Christ. Not everyone is going to be or do what we want, but we can forgive them and love them anyway."

Dear God, give us the strength and courage to put up with the things we may not like, doing our best to be the people You would have us to be, and leave the rest with You. Amen.

KEEP CALM—YOU'RE ROLLING WITH GOD

Day 256 — Live in God, Live in Love

I CRIED LISTENING TO LUKE WHYTE

His podcast, *The Youth Workshop, on iTunes.com*, has changed me after listening to him interview so many people with such deep faith talk about their passionate work for God in the world. I cried listening to him interview Larry Acosta who described himself as a "kid from a jacked-up family." Larry grew up in a raged-filled home with a physically abusive father and one day after his father beat up the family, his mother said to him, "My son, someday God is going to use this to motivate you to help kids growing up in a similar situation with all this pain and brokenness."

That part got me crying because growing up in a single-parent home is something I've always questioned God about. I've wondered how different my life could have been growing up with a dad. I believe God is using that to motivate me, with one of the underlying message of these posts being to fight for your family. And most importantly, to remind you that God is our ultimate Father and Mother, and He's the one taking care of us.

Here's the deal: we're all children of The Most High God! Looking back on my life, I can now clearly see His hand in everything. He picked the most amazing mom ever for me. I don't know how she did what she did, but she was and still is the world's best super momma. Going to college, I didn't have a dad to call for money, yet the scholarships, loans, and jobs all came through to help me graduate. In my marriage, God's even teaching me how to be the best wife.

Be anxious for nothing! Our Father is with us wherever we go! He constantly communicates, directs, instructs, and advises us with His love and wisdom. He has the most unimaginable plans for our lives when we stick with Him. He gives us a choice, though. We can choose door number 1 and have absolutely nothing to do with Him, or we can choose door number 2 and live the most joyful, purpose-filled, delightful, and peaceful adventure, acknowledging Him in all our ways. *I highly recommend door number 2! Wink! Wink!*

Dear God, thanks for being the best Father ever! May we all come to know You as the world's number one Dad! Amen.

KEEP CALM—YOU'RE ROLLING WITH GOD

A BEAUTIFUL APPOINTMENT WITH GOD AND HUBBY

We didn't make it to church one Sunday, but hubby and I took some time with God reading through Rick Warren's book, *A Purpose Driven Life*. I write over and over about these appointments with God because they have changed me. With every quiet time I take to listen to Him, and what He has to say to me, I leave a new person. It's like a story I read about a poor, peasant girl going into a town and staring at a golden statue. I don't remember the exact details, but the next day, she came again to stare at the figure with her hair combed. The following day, she wore cleaner clothes, again coming to stare at the statue. This is what has happened to me. He's transformed and refined me little by little each time I seek Him.

One day it was reading one sentence that especially touched me from Pastor Warren's book: "You can become a best friend of God through constant conversations with Him and continual meditation on His word."

This is so me! I'm finally getting to the point of calming down and seeking God's wisdom and what He would have me to do in every moment. Like I always say, this life can be tough sometimes, but when I focus on God, He guides me through the most frustrating situations. The latest lessons He seems to be teaching me is endurance and patience. Not everything in our lives will be 100% perfect, and there are things we must endure. But if we stick to the high road with God, doing the supernatural tasks that He asks of us, He's the one to reward us. "... in quietness and trust shall be your strength..." (Isaiah 30:15, NIV).

Like Shaun T, my DVD exercise trainer, says, "You need endurance for your life." But I'm thanking God for these troublesome times because they're bringing me closer to Him. I feel like I'm His personal project and He's constantly whispering in my ears, *Okay, here's how we're going to handle this...* And, following His advice and direction gives me such peace. I'm not going by the ordinary rules of man anymore, merely reacting to situations. *No, no, no!* I'm going the supernatural route, doing the tough things God has called me to do and my life is happier, filled with joy and peace, knowing I handle NOTHING alone.

Dear God, thank You for Your love. May we all be best friends with You. Amen.

KEEP CALM—YOU'RE ROLLING WITH GOD

"FEAR NOT"

That was my God wink at my 12 p.m. appointment with Him. I was encouraging someone to have their appointments with God when she asked me how she would know what to read. I explained that she would go by her feelings, allowing God to lead her to what He would have her to do. I told her about my appointment with God one Sunday when I was feeling nervous and anxious about finally going ahead with publishing my book. My hubby and kids all agreed at our brunch together that on Monday I should begin talking to the publisher and go ahead with launching it. That afternoon, envisioning all the worst-case scenarios, I got a feeling to read Dr. Wayne Dyer's book *Wisdom of the Ages* and the book randomly opened to the chapter entitled, *Fear and Risk Taking,* where he quoted the famous lines:

"Tis better to have loved and lost Than never to have loved at all."

God led me to the perfect words with Dr. Dyer suggesting that the poet is telling us "to go on in life as if failure were not a consideration, and ignore our fears as we proceed. It is better to jump in and experience life than to stand on the sidelines fearing something might go wrong."

And on Monday, the day to call the publisher and again feeling anxious, my 12 p.m. appointment with God involved reading my manuscript. I felt led to the following words I had written:

"The next day I found myself constantly rereading this calming prayer and reminding myself that I shall be a happy being, even as I sat in a prayer room at a bookstore I visited. I entered and immediately felt God's presence with me there, reading the words arranged on the wall:

"FEAR NOT. I AM WITH YOU"

Our Father, confident risk takers we shall be, doing what You have called us to do, knowing You are with us and guiding us every step of the way! Amen.

KEEP CALM—YOU'RE ROLLING WITH GOD

Day 259 — Live in God, Live in Love

HE DID IT AGAIN

The principal at my kids' school that is!

He said to me, "You won't get too far without discipline." And let me tell you, to get to a superhuman level requires lots of discipline – mental, physical and spiritual. But let's not let this word "discipline" scare us, it simply means to train.

Like I've trained myself that as soon as I wake up, workout clothes are on and I exercise, even if only for five minutes. I've disciplined myself to stick with it. I've also trained myself to drink my awful tasting fruit and veggie smoothies because that's what's giving me the supernatural energy to be the person I want to be in the world. And I've disciplined myself to have my appointments with God. I was blown away in listening to a podcast in one of them for only four minutes, but it left me revved up to continue my partnership with God to make a difference in the world. The words of a profound rapper, Prince EA, asked us to open our minds to the possibility that we've been brainwashed, loyal to conditioned thoughts. He asked us to question thoughts like "love is weakness," going by what our culture and parents have taught us. He said this is the time we can make a difference by looking into ourselves and who we are in the deepest sense, as there will never be external peace until there's internal peace. He promises the entire world will transform once we figure out who we are.

"Mom, why did daddy make you cry?" This important question was asked by my daughter years ago, and it woke me up. I decided I was no longer going to play the weak woman victim role anymore. My hubby simply mentioned something about my weight, and I lost it! I committed for the sake of my daughters to not be that emotional, sad woman, and instead, I wanted them to see a strong, confident, brave person, capable of doing and achieving anything.

I now know I am a child of the Most High God and I'm loved unconditionally by Him, no other love and approval required. And as His child I can hold my head high and focus on being the best possible version of myself. There is nothing we lack; it's all within us — God's strength, wisdom, knowledge, power! *We're not going by the ordinary rules of man!*

Our Father, may we never feel starved for love, always remembering Your love for us in every moment of our lives. Amen.

KEEP CALM—YOU'RE ROLLING WITH GOD

Day 260 — Live in God, Live in Love

"I TALK TO GOD LIKE THAT BECAUSE WE'RE COOL LIKE THAT!"

Are you noticing my constant conversations with God? From the big decisions like hiring new staff to the little decisions about when to stop at the grocery store. I'm having regular conversations with Him (paying attention to those feelings), and my life is at peace, and I'm super happy. *I refuse to worry about anything.* Thoughts come up as to stuff I need to take care of and I do my part trusting God to do His part. "Pray then let God worry." *I'm talking radical trusting here!* Are you with me?

God makes me laugh! I told you He cleared my schedule so that I have time to focus on writing my book and guess what? I started to doubt myself thinking that I wasn't a good enough writer. And the very next day I listened to a podcast from Marianne Williamson. I couldn't believe what she said, "Sometimes we spend so many years preparing for something, so many years praying for something, but when it actually happens we're like, "ahhh, I don't know if I'm ready!" She said, "You are ready, whatever that dream is trying to be born within you! God has more faith in you than you have in yourself. You're afraid of what could happen. You're attached to results. Just ask for God's will to be done." She explained, "God knows how everything will turn out, we don't have to worry how it's all going to come together. When you say yes to the future God has for you, then all the capacities necessary to help you create and manifest that future are born within you. Say yes to God's will." This is why I smiled, too, when the grocery store clerk out of the blue said, "You should write!" *God, I got the message!*

Then I continued reading her book and I hit the nail on the head as to why I felt I wasn't ready. She wrote, "We're often afraid to do anything unless we can do it extremely well. But we get to Carnegie Hall by practicing...Bob Dylan's early songs weren't so wonderful."

Dear God, may we advance confidently and joyously in the direction of our dreams. Doing our best and leaving the details to You of how it's all going to work out. Amen.

KEEP CALM—YOU'RE ROLLING WITH GOD

Day 261 — Live in God, Live in Love

"I WILL PRAISE THE LORD NO MATTER WHAT HAPPENS...

...I will constantly speak of his glories and grace. I will boast of all his kindness to me. Let all who are discouraged take heart. Let us praise the Lord together and exalt his name."

I still can't get over that these verses from Psalm 34 were probably written some 3,000 years ago, yet resonate so much with my experiences today with God. *Incredible!* "Let all who are discouraged take heart," because I KNOW we roll with God and He's our constant Companion. I'm so onto God, and I think everything is from Him—the good, the bad, and the ugly—because He knows *exactly* what we need to get us where He would have us to be.

2013 was a terrible year for us. As we got rid of one problem, another one showed up and sometimes we were battling a few at a time! But we came through all those trials new people, with a new love and respect for God, who was with us every step of the way.

I was a little sad when someone said a post I wrote depressed them. I had said how happy I was, and they wanted to know why they weren't so happy. I explained that I didn't wake up one day and become this joyful person. It has taken lots of challenges to get me here, where I now KNOW I don't go through life alone because God truly is my Helper, and yours, too if you allow Him. Now I'm radically trusting, running to Him in every decision, going with the choice that excites me and brings me peace when I think about it, taking life one step *(sometimes very tiny steps)* at a time. I'm happy for all those trials in 2013, as I now have the peace that surpasses all understanding, in that I can let go and let God take control of so many issues that I've been carrying around with me.

Here's the deal: *practice, practice, and more practice.* It has taken lots and lots of practice to learn to trust God's guidance and faithfulness. When I catch myself worrying, I have to say constantly, *NO! I'm not going there. I'm trusting God here!*

"Happy is he that hath the God of Jacob for his help, whose hope is in the LORD his God" (Psalm 146:5, KJV).

Dear God, may we put our hope and trust in You always. We might not see a way, but let our hope be in you all day. Amen.

KEEP CALM—YOU'RE ROLLING WITH GOD

Day 262 — Live in God, Live in Love

"DON'T LET LIFE DISTRACT YOU FROM HAVING A RELATIONSHIP WITH GOD"

That's what I said to someone when they admitted that they don't make time for Him. "You have to *simplify* your life," I told him. When you have too much stuff going on, and you're living a frenzied/chaotic life, you're missing out on the best direction from God. I've learned to *slow down and pay attention* to what God would have me to do in those 1,000 decisions I make every day, allowing Him to set my agenda by following and trusting those feelings I always write about.

And even before I was this God Maniac, those same feelings have been directing me in helping to make some big decisions all my life. In my early twenties, I was dumped by an ex-boyfriend through a letter. I got the strong feeling after reading that letter to move on—no arguments, no drama, no craziness; I kept going and never looked back. I didn't know it was God at the time directing me, but there was a book that showed up in my life with the perfect message that said, "Living well is the best revenge," and reading that one quote brought me such peace that I knew that I was making the right decision. *Who wants to be with anyone who doesn't love them, anyway?* That was the best letter I ever read because God has since connected me with the best hubby in the world.

Now this God maniac has learned to get God involved in everything I do! I'm learning His voice more and more every day by having those important appointments with Him so that when I need to make critical decisions, I know exactly what He would have me to do. When challenges come up, I can stay at peace and have joy despite them knowing I have God directing me every step of the way.

Are you learning God's voice? It can take lots of practice, but it's worth it. Let's have a closer walk with God this year and every year!

Dear God, help us not to miss out on the real joy of life, a closer walk with You. Amen.

KEEP CALM—YOU'RE ROLLING WITH GOD

Day 263 — Live in God, Live in Love

"HOW DOES IT FEEL TO HAVE A GOD MANIAC FOR A MOMMA?"

I asked my older daughter, Ember, having a snuggling moment before she left me, saying that watching *CNN* was boring. She's upset because she feels that I hardly write about her, so this post is dedicated to her—my beautiful, smart, sweet, wonderful, caring, patient, polite, and terrific daughter, Ember. I thank God for you. As I always tell you, "God knew why He sent you to me first. Keep setting the positive example for everyone to follow."

I was upset with myself after I punished her when she went a little crazy on Julie for simply saying something she didn't like. *Then I thought about how she does so much that's right. You should not be so hard on her when she messes up.* I had a conversation with her the next morning, explaining the importance of calming down and not allowing herself to get so crazy, doing things you may later regret. At my age, I told her, I'm *still* learning this life changing lesson.

Here's the deal: one of my favorite meditation books, *The Imitation of Christ*, had this to say:

"Endeavour to be patient in the defects and infirmities of others, be they what they may; because you also have many things, which others must bear with. If you cannot make yourself what you would be, how can you expect another according to your liking? We would willingly have others perfect, and yet we do not amend our own faults. We would have others strictly corrected; but are not willing to be corrected ourselves. The large liberty that others take displeases us; and yet we do not want to be denied anything we ask for. Thus it is evident how seldom we weigh our neighbor in the same balance with ourselves.

But God has disposed things that we learn to bear one another's burdens; for there is no one without defects; no one without burdens; no one sufficient for himself; no one wise enough or himself; but we must support one another, comfort one another, assist, instruct and admonish one another. Therefore, we should treat others as we would like others to treat us."

Dear God, grant us humility and patience, reflecting Your love, mercy and kindness in everything we do. Amen.

KEEP CALM—YOU'RE ROLLING WITH GOD

"AHHH! WHERE DID THAT COME FROM?"

I screamed shockingly, looking at a jar of hair gel that showed up in my kitchen one morning.

I had debated for the longest time about buying it at Walmart the night before but decided not to because I had already spent way too much money on different hair care products on our new natural hair care journey. And although I felt drawn to buy it, for some reason, I said, *No! Nik, no more hair products!* And I walked away.

So how did it end up in my kitchen if I didn't buy it? My mom, who wanted to shop apart from the kids and me, accidentally purchased it thinking it was some type of hand cream (Hey, she's 82. Give her a break!). When Julie read that it was a gel for natural hair, my mom left it in the kitchen for me.

Walmart is a huge store, so how did my mom end up buying a product that I debated purchasing out of the thousands and thousands of products sold there? Remember my post earlier this week that whenever I see *"I am"* anywhere that this has been my personal reminder from God that He's with me? Well, you're not going to believe the brand name of that product my mom accidentally purchased: *"As I AM."*

A few minutes later I decided to read my meditation book, Jesus Calling, and I randomly opened to March 16 to read: "I love to reveal Myself to you, and your seeking heart opens you to receive more of my disclosure."

I played *Latch* by Sam Smith at least 50 times that week. Driving around, Ember says to me, "Mommy, play the song, Latch. I excitedly and accidentally blurted out, "This is my love song to God."

I had such a surprise when I read in the meditation book another message from God that day: "Listen to the love song that I'm continually singing to you. I take great delight in you...I rejoice over you with singing."

I had to send out some important paperwork in regards to a big ball I have in the air, one that gets me anxious at times, and there in line at the post office, I cried as I read another message from God: *"You have Me on your side, so what are you worried about?"*

Dear God, may we all relax, knowing You are intimately involved in every detail of our lives. Amen.

KEEP CALM—YOU'RE ROLLING WITH GOD

FIGHT FOR YOUR FAMILY

This is the title of my favorite Pastor Joel Osteen's sermon.

I listened to it years ago, and the message has always stuck with me. Believe it or not, this is even the reason why I'm in Nigeria! Lately, I've been enjoying picking up my kids up from school and spending time with them every afternoon. I say we only get one chance to raise them, so we better do it right. I was so happy to hear from a teacher that she thought my kids are the politest kids in the entire school. I'm trying to teach them to be respectful of everyone, and I'm such a proud momma with all of them doing so well. We can't take all the credit, though, as God is helping us to raise them and is guiding them in the right direction. I want them to grow up with the sense of wanting to make a difference in the world, to live kindly and to be grateful for what they have.

Some quotes I love from Mother Teresa:

"To parents: It is very important that children learn from their fathers and mothers how to love one another – not in school, not from the teacher, but from you. It is very important that you share with your children the joy of that smile."

"Everybody today seems to be in such a terrible rush, anxious for greater development and greater riches, so that children have very little time for their parents. And parents have very little time for their children and for each other. So the breakdown of peace in the world begins at home."

"There will be misunderstandings; every family has its cross, its suffering. Always be the first to forgive with a smile. Be cheerful, be happy!"

Love never gives up.

Dear God, may we make time for our family, knowing that fighting for them is our important work for and from You. Amen.

KEEP CALM—YOU'RE ROLLING WITH GOD

Day 266 — Live in God, Live in Love

YOU KNOW YOUR WIFE GETS CRAZY SOMETIMES

I'm completely stunned how God is behind the scenes of our lives, working everything out so perfectly. I don't stress life anymore. I instead constantly remind myself that wherever I go, I always go with God, my life Partner who promises never to leave me nor forsake me. *Nothing can separate us from His love!*

And, I want you here with me, having such faith and trust in God that your life is at *peace* and you're filled with *joy*. Here you know that everything that happens is only for your good. Even the people in our lives that drive us the craziest are the ones who are there to teach us the biggest and most valuable life lessons.

For example, someone who came to teach me many, many, many lessons is my wonderful hubby. It's now 11 years since we met and he has certainly driven me the craziest and has taught me the most. I had a lot of growing up to do over the years, and I'm still growing. I'm still laughing at myself that the other day I got mad at him about something and I fussed him out big time about it, but a few hours later, I was the one apologizing to him, "Please forgive me, Hon; You know your wife gets crazy sometimes!"

However, I learnt several lessons that day: to focus on the 80% positive stuff I love about him, be happy and grateful I have such a great hubby, to accept him for who he is and not compare him to anyone else, and that I can calmly and respectfully discuss that negative 20% that I feel we can improve on.

The same goes for all those life dramas; they're all there to teach us something! Ask yourself, *What would God have me to learn from this situation?*

Is it to be more loving without expecting anything in return?
To trust Him more to guide and direct me through those feelings, nudges, and cues?
To learn to stay at peace no matter what comes against me, knowing God is with me?
To teach me that people will hurt me until I decide they can hurt me no longer? Or, is the lesson this time about forgiveness?
Trust me, there's always a lesson or two or three somewhere in there.

Our Beloved, may we humble ourselves under Your loving hands of correction, learning everything You would have us to learn. Amen.

KEEP CALM—YOU'RE ROLLING WITH GOD

"THE GLORY OF GOD IS A HUMAN BEING FULLY ALIVE"

If this quote is true, then God must love me because I feel I'm living the life of two people!

A usual day for me is getting up at 5 to write and post, exercise, make breakfast and my veggie/fruit smoothie, cook lunch, go to work, back home to spend time with everyone, then off to bed exhausted. When an aunt who was visiting asked me how I do it all, I replied, "I wouldn't have it any other way. I'm enjoying trying to be super wife, super mommy and super person!"

Every day I wake up excited about life, and I love it! I'm learning to maximize every moment because soon we're not going to be here. I have my constant conversations with God, and all the plans for the day were put on hold when I got the feeling to go swimming with my kids, a cousin, and some friends. I also spent some time with my mom and lots of time house cleaning and packing lots of stuff to donate was therapeutic. *My home feels so much lighter!*

Yes, there are challenges/problems to deal with, but that's all a part of God's plan to have us live this full life. I'm on to God now, and anything that comes my way I say, *Bring it on!* because it's all for my good, as I'm learning to walk *bravely* with Him. J.C. Penney was asked the secret to his success and his reply was, "Adversity and Jesus Christ." Jesus was his guide and the adversities were what pushed him to become his best self! We roll with God, and He's our constant Companion for living our best lives, no matter what comes our way.

"The purpose of life is a life of purpose," is a quote I love. I'm still on my mission to make the world a happier and more loving place than I met it, to see my kids grow up to be the best people they can possibly be and enjoy every moment with my hubby, living out the dream of becoming the world's most perfect couple. When I meet God, I'd like to thank Him and say, *I enjoyed a full life! When can I do it again?*

Dear God, may our lives be happy, purpose filled adventures with You as our Guide. Amen.

KEEP CALM—YOU'RE ROLLING WITH GOD

Day 268 — Live in God, Live in Love

THIS WAS PRETTY FREAKY

Over a year ago, I wrote a chapter that was included in a published book called *Sources of Wisdom,* a compilation of life stories from several authors. And, I had a God wink-filled evening where He used my words from this very book, written over a year ago, to remind me to *RELAX*. His invisible Presence is always with me, and He mystifyingly knows every thought I think, every word I say, every word I write, even before I can think or say or write them. *Unbelievable!* Here's how one of those winks went:

"God built this school for us!" I said braggingly to someone about the most breathtaking school in Nigeria my kids attend. My girls were so worried when I told them we were relocating to Nigeria, as their school in the U.S. was a newly-built school that they loved *(and I did, too!).* I promised them repeatedly that I would find an excellent school. And we came to Nigeria and found the most impressive school, which we love. As proof that this school was built for us, it opened its doors for the very first time on my older daughter's birthday, during the first year we were here. The lady I bragged to asked, "Is there anything too difficult for God?"

Fast forward less than an hour after that conversation, I remembered that I didn't have an appointment with God that day. I quickly went to open my meditation book, but instead, I opened to the chapter in the book I wrote. I was bragging to someone else how I'm a published author now, and as I kept reading from where I last left off, my very words asked, *...is there anything too difficult for God to handle? Wink! Wink!*

Thinking about this, I'm in awe of God because I went to the doctor's office when I was pregnant with my daughter asking if I could have my labor induced so that I would have her before the September 1st school cutoff date in the U.S. to begin kindergarten, and the midwife told me a story that convinced me that God's timing was the best. *If she only knew how right she was!*

> *Dear God, who are we that You care so much for us? May we all come to know Your love for us. Amen.*

KEEP CALM—YOU'RE ROLLING WITH GOD

Day 269 — Live in God, Live in Love

"WE GO CALMLY, COOLY AND CONFIDENTLY WITH GOD"

Was the Facebook comment from David. Here's what that means to me:

- We're sticking super close, running to Him in every decision and everyone is filled with genuine joy, happiness, and contentment, despite their problems/challenges.

- We do not desire to please others, nor fear to displease them and we enjoy much peace.

- We're running our race, doing what we feel God would have us to do.

- We're not concerned about who's against us, as we know that God's for us.

- We constantly ask, *How may I serve?* as God seems to ask us, *How may I serve you?*

- We live kindly, love extravagantly and forgive quickly and endlessly, remembering everything is between God and us, not between us and anyone else.

- We advance confidently in the direction of our dreams.

- We live life fully, sucking the enjoyment out of every moment.

- We've left the past in the past, focused on going forward and living our best lives with the people who choose to be there and the people who choose not to be there, we simply wish them well.

- We've stopped with the excuses, but with God as our Partner; we make stuff happen.

- We love and respect everyone, no matter their race, sexual preference, financial status, religion, or gender.

- We've stopped getting offended and instead work on constant and never-ending improvement no matter what is thrown at us.

- Our "choice is in every way, in every example, in every experience is to do the right thing and the excellent thing" *seeking to please God in everything we do* (thanks Oprah Winfrey!).

- We *know* that whatever God wants for us is best for us and nothing comes to us without going through His hands first.

Our Father, help us make those tough, superhuman decisions, always doing what we believe You would have us to do in every moment. Amen.

KEEP CALM—YOU'RE ROLLING WITH GOD

Day 270 — Live in God, Live in Love

"PUT THAT BACK"

It was the feeling I got from God when I erased the last sentence of a post one day that said, "Never stop improving!" In listening to my spirit, I felt that God was saying He wanted it there, telling me to put it back, even though it didn't make sense to me. I even remembered arguing with Him a little bit, thinking of something more related to that post, but the feeling I got again was simply to *put it back*. I paid attention and did what I was told. *God, whatever you want!*

Fast forward a few hours, feeling somewhat anxious about some changes in my life, and I decided to have an unscheduled appointment with God. This time, I read from my book that I've finally sent back to the publisher, and the second post that I randomly scrolled to read:

"Life is about recalibrating (adjusting). About continually asking yourself: what do I have to do get where I need to be? How do I create the life I want? We have to make ourselves over daily, consistently, in order to keep moving forward. We are not meant to be stagnant." – Oprah Winfrey, *What I Know For Sure*

And recalibrating/adjusting is what I've seemed to be doing lots of. Instead of feeling overwhelmed or frustrated by the changes going on around me, Oprah simply reminded me that this is what life is about and every day I have the opportunity to bring all my valuable lessons from the past and make myself over daily to face whatever changes that may come my way. *NEVER STOP IMPROVING!"*

Seeing those words show up, which I had argued with God about, was just the high five from Him that I was looking for, when once again, out of the blue, everything lined up a little bit too perfectly. That's how I know it must be God behind it. I felt as if He was saying, *Yes, Nik, there are some changes going on right now, but My invisible Presence with you is a guarantee, and that will never change. Whatever changes, setbacks, and challenges come your way, remember I am with you in every moment, and there's nothing we can't handle together.*

With that boost from God, I jumped up from that appointment with all the *Godfidence* in the world knowing I have the best Backup, Helper, and Partner: *GOD!* I'm always astonished when He leads me to these perfect messages in my appointments with Him, even from my unpublished book.

KEEP CALM—YOU'RE ROLLING WITH GOD

"AND EVERYTHING IS POSSIBLE WITH GOD"

I love how these words are sprinkled throughout *I Can See Clearly Now* by Dr. Wayne Dyer, as I *too* can see clearly that there are no accidents or coincidences.

God has everything under full control. It was a calendar (on the wrong date) that He used to speak to me, giving me the go ahead with a move to Nigeria, despite all the negative reports on CNN about all the violence there, from my beautiful, gated community home in South Florida. After months of asking God, *Should we go or not go?* I suddenly felt a KNOWING that God spoke to me through that calendar that said: "You shall go to a land flowing with milk and honey." I was so sure that this was a message from God that I sent a text to my husband, who was in Nigeria at the time, telling him that this was our confirmation that our entire family should make the move there.

Before our move, my husband flew back and forth between the U.S. and Nigeria and it wasn't good for us as a family. And I'm positive that it's no coincidence that my favorite all-time favorite Pastor Joel Osteen sermon is the one entitled, *Fight for Your Family*. I loved this sermon so much that I ordered copies of it to share with married friends. And when I saw that my marriage was on shaky ground, I realized it was time for me to fight for my family. And going to Nigeria would be the first battle move. *Don't mess with my family!*

I'm sure it was all a part of God's plan to get me there. I can see clearly now that my simple life in Nigeria (not driving, no TV, no electricity 50% of the time) put me in the perfect space to begin writing. And about a year later, God did confirm that it was a message from Him in that calendar. I briefly listened to a TV announcer, putting on my sneakers before exercising, when he incredibly said, "Nigeria: The land flowing with milk and honey." *Wink! Wink!*

Dear God, we're confidently rolling with You! May we never lean on our own understanding knowing everything is possible with You, including the best marriages. Amen.

KEEP CALM—YOU'RE ROLLING WITH GOD

"GOD IS A TOTAL SETUP"

I said to a friend. I'm totally onto Him and how He unbelievably knows how to shake us up to wake us up. There is an incredibly deep verse in the Bible, Matthew 5:4, that says, "Blessed are those who mourn." I never understood that verse until someone explained that once you come through the mourning period, you wake up to a whole new world.

Like recently, everything I shared with you about the hurt and disappointment I was going through was the mourning part. But now I'm awake and I've come through it for the better, feeling so unbelievably blessed. I literally feel like a new person! I'm happier and I see such blessings in every aspect of my life—*I have nothing to complain about!* I wake up usually between 4 and 5 am, excited and looking forward to what God has planned for me that day—*every moment is sacred.* The best part of it is that I've come through feeling so immensely loved by God because in my worst moments, He revealed Himself to me as to say, *Nik, don't worry, I'm right here with you.* And, He kept saying, *Come to Me, I'm always here waiting for you.* He led me on the high road and helped me to make the best decisions. *God, I'm truly grateful!*

The lessons are never ending with God, and He takes us through all these life's challenges to continually teach us and grow us. This situation has taught me lots of lessons like forgiving endlessly, that no one is perfect, to work on constant and never ending improvement, to be a *prisoner of hope*, to trust in God's timing, to remember to focus on the positives in life and not the negatives, that God knows what's best for us and to trust Him, and to lighten up and laugh more. We all have our crosses to bear, but with God, the crosses can be light, as He's with us every joy-filled step of the way to help us carry them. We can, therefore, relax and enjoy life more, focused on God's continual Presence with us.

O God! In our most difficult moments, may we never take our eyes from You, being the tough, committed, faithful, loving, compassionate and merciful people You would have us to be. Amen.

KEEP CALM—YOU'RE ROLLING WITH GOD

AGAIN...I'M IN AWE OF GOD

God is too much, and in a conversation with one of my assistants, Sheba, I was reminded how deeply God's involved in our lives. It was a conversation with God one Saturday that led me to ask her friend if she was still looking for a job. I had interviewed her some months prior but didn't hire her at that time. I called her back for another interview, and she was there to meet me within an hour. That day, I told her that I wanted to see what she can do and gave her an assignment. She did so well that I invited her to spend a week with us this time.

Both my husband and I felt good about her, so we hired her permanently. That was over two years ago, and she has been such an asset to our company. She's very wise and gives us such good advice, and I appreciate her integrity and concern for our business. *God, I'm grateful!*

So, while I'm busy writing posts, God's behind the scenes of my life bringing the best people to assist us. There're so many things going on that I look back at them and say, *Wow, that's God working for us!* My new focus in life is simply to be about being the *best* person God would have me to be and to follow His will for my life without expecting any praise or applause.

In everything I do, I try to do what is pleasing to God in every moment, every example, and every experience. I want to be the best wife, the best mom, and the best person I can be because I realize that everything is between God and me. Forget about it being between me and anyone else. *God, what would You have me to do?* And when I give Him my best, He gives me His best! "The greater the sacrifice, the greater the reward," is how my fav calendar puts it and I'm feeling greatly rewarded.

Our Father, may we love others without expecting anything in return, knowing Your reward is always the best! Amen.

KEEP CALM—YOU'RE ROLLING WITH GOD

Day 274 — Live in God, Live in Love

"UNDAUNTED WE SHALL GO"

I commented to a Facebook friend. I hesitantly included the word *"undaunted"* in my post one day, and after much thought, I decided to go for it.

A friend commented back, "Yes, *undaunted* is an amazing word," as if she read my thoughts.

I came across the word "undaunted" in an appointment with God reading from John 16:33: "I have told you these things, so that in Me you may have [perfect] peace and confidence. In the world you have tribulation and trials and distress and frustration; but be of good cheer [take courage; be confident, certain, undaunted]! For I have overcome the world. [I have deprived it of power to harm you and have conquered it for you.]"

The word has stuck with me ever since, and this is where I want us: "Undaunted, unafraid, undismayed, unalarmed, unflinching, unshrinking, unabashed, unfaltering, unflagging, fearless, dauntless, intrepid, bold, valiant, brave, stout-hearted, lionhearted, courageous, heroic, gallant, gritty, steely, indomitable," no matter what comes our way knowing without a doubt that we roll with God, and He'll direct us one step at a time. "As you look to Me (God) I show you what to do now and next." – *Jesus Calling*

All that week I had been saying to my hubby, "God is our Partner!" He probably gets tired of me talking about God all the time to him! I even said it to one of my assistants, "God is our Partner!" and surprisingly that same week, out of the blue, my friend Sal in South Africa sends me an email: "I'm trusting my business Partner and Adviser, God."

Later that day, my alarm went off at 12 p.m. for my appointment with God as I was walking past someone and I asked them to join me in that appointment. We randomly opened to a date from my meditation book and read: "We are assured and know that [God being a partner in our labor] all things work together and are [fitting into a plan] for good to and for those who love God and are called according to [His] design and purpose" Romans 8:28 (AMP). I was extra thrilled when one of my other fav verses showed up, too: "My sheep listen to my voice; I know them, and they follow me" (John 10:27, NIV).

Dear God, thank You for being our Partner. May we look to You for guidance in all our decisions. Amen.

KEEP CALM—YOU'RE ROLLING WITH GOD

"HON, YOU'RE THE BEST DECISION I'VE EVER MADE"

I said to my hubby, while we enjoyed a bottle of champagne for Valentine's Day. Almost 14 years ago then, he flew to the Bahamas from the U.S. to meet me for the first time and the very next day, he got on his knees and prayed, "God, thank You for helping me find my wife."

One week later, I wrote him a note saying, "I know and I know, and I know that we were meant to be together and we'll be the world's most perfect couple!" How were we both so confident that we were right for each other? *God helped!* We both paid attention to those feelings that I so often write about, as that's how I believe God mostly communicate with us. We both had feelings of peace and excitement, which is God's way of telling us to *go for it.* Doubt and uneasiness, I've learned the hard way, means God is saying, *don't do that.*

I've made the most important decisions in my life by following these peaceful feelings, and they've always worked out. Time and time again, God has directed me. God knows what we do not know, and the unimaginable part is that He wants to guide us in making these important decisions as well as the minor ones. We must slow down, calm down, pay attention, and listen to Him before making any move, getting Him involved in every aspect of our lives.

Years ago, we hired a professional to assist us with a challenge we faced, and this person advised us to go a certain direction with it, but my hubby and I didn't feel we should follow his advice. So, we went the direction we felt God was leading us, based on feelings of peace when we thought about doing things our way. Turns out, years later, this was the perfect decision as everything worked out extremely well for us. God astonishingly turned things around in our favor. If we had instead listened to the professional, it could've been disastrous for us. *God is an expert in every matter!*

"Trust in the Lord with all your heart and lean not on your own understanding; in all your ways acknowledge Him, and He shall direct your path" (Proverbs 3:5-6, NIV).

"My sheep listen to my voice; I know them, and they follow me" (John 10:27, NIV).

Dear God, may we lead others to You so that the entire world may come to know Your voice and follow You. Amen.

KEEP CALM—YOU'RE ROLLING WITH GOD

Day 276 — Live in God, Live in Love

I WANT TO LOVE OTHERS THE WAY GOD LOVES ME

I know I will never come even close, but God has inspired me to do better. Everything is between Him and me, and I want to be about doing His will in every moment, every example, and every experience. He has constantly shown up for me! My favorite experience lately was in one of my darkest moments last year. God had another stranger to show up with a book, that as I read it, at that moment, I knew God was right there with me reminding me in a prayer to forgive: "May we also forgive one another Lord, as it is sometimes difficult to do." – *Oremus, He Lives Well Who Prays Well* And that was the perfect advice, as I'm learning not to look to human relationships for perfection.

I hope you're not missing out on the best relationship ever —*our relationship with God!* I joked one day with my hubby that I was cheating on him. He gave me a serious look until I admitted that it was with God, who inspires me to be an even better wife, mother, and person. He's the best Adviser for any problem we could ever face, telling me recently a better way to get some important work completed in time for a deadline. *God is too much!*

Let's live the best lives close to God, making Him a part of more and more of our moments to share in the difficult times, as we imagine He's right there with us holding our hands, to the happy moments. *Are you sticking to your appointments with Him?* I texted this to our customers recently:

"Learning to rest in God is forming a new habit—one that promises to change your entire life."

O God! We want more of You in our lives. May we never stop seeking You with our relationship with You growing stronger every day. Amen.

KEEP CALM—YOU'RE ROLLING WITH GOD

Day 277 — Live in God, Live in Love

"YOU'RE GOING TO MAKE ME CRY, TOO"

Said a close friend to me when she called and I was crying over the phone. That disappointment and hurt that I was crying about turned out to be so good for me. She gave me the best advice, "Keep your focus on God." I did, and now I'm thanking Him for the entire experience, which brought along with it loads of lessons, like staying on the high road and doing what He would have me to do from moment to moment.

After lots of practice, I'm good at discerning what God would have me to do and in this incident, He directed me to forgive endlessly and be the best person I could be because everything was between Him and me. My job was to do my best and leave the rest with Him. The entire experience has brought me so much closer to God. I now know not to look to human relationships for perfection, but to keep my focus on God and following His direction has brought me such peace and happiness.

And, this is where I want you guys, focusing on God no matter what you're going through. Every negative experience can be turned into positive when we use it as an opportunity to seek God's direction and get closer to Him. It doesn't matter how the situation may seem; *don't lean on your own understanding.* God is in complete and total control, and I've seen Him do some astonishing things. For example, in that last challenge I faced, I did exactly this, and God showed me what to do one step at a time, as I kept my focus on Him. The road ahead seemed rocky in my human mind, but knowing I was not going through it alone and that God was my wonderful Partner, Helper, and Adviser, gave me the Godfidence to face each day without fear or worry.

This friend, (AKA my Alien) I called has been such a blessing to me. The other day I called her complaining that someone doesn't like me and she even had the best advice then. She said, "So what they don't like you?" Again, the perfect words I needed to hear! Everyone doesn't have to like me, but I plan to continue being my best and most loving self because everything's between me and God.

Dear God, give us the courage to face each day confidently, holding Your hands super tight, being the people You would have us to be as we live supernaturally, close and intimately with You. Amen.

KEEP CALM—YOU'RE ROLLING WITH GOD

Day 278 — Live in God, Live in Love

"WE'RE NOT GOING BY THE ORDINARY RULES OF MAN"

Was me to everyone. With everything that was going on in Nigeria at that time - upcoming elections, bad economy, and what some may consider a civil war - everyone was a bit on edge and this was my reminder to put their trust in God, not man.

Listening to Pastor Joel Osteen talking about secret frustrations that we all have about some aspect of our lives, I've realized that they're simply a part of life. There's always something we wish was different or better in some way. He spoke of the Apostle Paul, who wrote half of the New Testament, but yet he too complained about a thorn in his side.

Here's the deal: I didn't get away, either, with my secret frustrations, but those, too, I'm leaving in God's hand because we're not going by ordinary rules. I believe He'll turn these situations around. I simply give my best and leave the rest with Him. But even if God doesn't, I've decided to be happy regardless. I trust God's timing is always best. Whatever God wants for me is best for me, and I can already see how having these problems has been extremely good for me. I have grown in ways I've never expected, learning not to look to the world, circumstances, or human relationships for peace. *My peace rests in God!*

I'm focused on the 10,000 positive things God's doing, not the three things I may unhappy with, going out every day with my head held high, determined to suck the most enjoyment out of every moment.

"I will be a happy and joyful being. O God! I will no longer be full of anxiety, nor will I let trouble harass me. I will not dwell on the unpleasant things of life." - Bahá'í Prayers

"I have told you these things, so that in Me you may have [perfect] peace and confidence. In the world you have tribulation and trials and distress and frustration; but be of good cheer [take courage; be confident, certain, undaunted]! For I have overcome the world. [I have deprived it of power to harm you and have conquered it for you.]" - John 16:33

Dear God, our hearts can never find rest until they rest in You. Help us to rest in only You always. Amen.
KEEP CALM—YOU'RE ROLLING WITH GOD

"WE'RE STRIPPING, BABY!"

I said to a friend one day. Iron sharpens iron, and we've been exceptionally good for each other, pushing ourselves to strip away anything that's stopping us from evolving into the best people God has created us to be. We're moving lightly forward with Him as our Partner, leaving behind all the nonessential junk we've been carrying around with us that include:

- Worry. We're refusing to worry about anything, trusting God to direct our lives one step at a time.

- Excuses. We roll with God and all things are possible with Him. Excuses be gone! *If all you we can do is crawl, let's start crawling!*

- A spirit of laziness and indiscipline. God honors hard work and we won't get too far in life without discipline.

- Procrastination and any form of resistance that's holding us back. No more, "I'll do it tomorrow."

- Guilty feelings about ourselves and others. We're leaving the past in the past focused on being our most loving, merciful and forgiving selves knowing God's repayment is best.

- Anxious thoughts about the future. Focused on God, we're not worried about the future because we know He is already there to help us with anything we may need.

- Disappointments, mistakes, and failures. We're surrendering them over to God who knows how to use them for our good.

- Crazy thoughts of lack and limitations that are told to us by the world, such as, "You're not good enough." We're rolling with Godfidence!

- Distractions that are keeping us back from doing what we know we should be doing. (My Facebook check-ins and my natural hair madness!) *God, help us!*

- Hurts and pains. All handed over to God who in time will heal all our wounds when we stay close to Him.

Dear God, may our entire lives bring glory to You. Amen.

KEEP CALM—YOU'RE ROLLING WITH GOD

Live in God, Live in Love

"NIK, YOU'RE NOT WORKING HARD ENOUGH"

Were the words from my hubby/boss recently. Helping to raise five kids, run two businesses on two different continents, as well as being a wife is not enough for him? I thought to myself—until I got the perfect message from God at the top of my newsfeed on Facebook, when my friend Stephen shared my post for that day, but included my favorite poem from Mother Teresa at the end: "Give the world the best you have, and it may never be enough. Give your best anyway. For you see, in the end, it is between you and God. It was never between you and them anyway."

I'm missing my meditation book that taught me that if someone says 10,000 words against me, to look at it to see what I can take to improve myself and if there is nothing, simply ignore. In this case, I decided to improve. And God confirmed that this was a good decision by way of the calendar that He often speaks to me through:

"It's much better to have the attitude of, 'Am I doing enough? What more can I do?' – Rather than the attitude of 'I'm doing so much, I'm giving so much. Others should be grateful.'"

"I'm loving these kisses, my Emmie," I said to my then seven-year-old son. Lately, he's gotten into the sweet habit of kissing me and hugging me out of the blue and then Joshie runs to join him in the kissing. *Talk about everything being between you and God.* I'm exceedingly grateful!

Our Father, any way we can please You, let us learn. Amen.

KEEP CALM—YOU'RE ROLLING WITH GOD

Day 281 — Live in God, Live in Love

MY BIGGEST GOD WINK EVER

One Christmas Day, we were visiting with my mother-in-law in her home in a city away from where we live in Nigeria, and we both were sitting at her dining table, and I shared with her my new focus as a mother was most importantly to teach my children about having a relationship with God. She said, "If you have God in your life, you have *all you need*. I'm living proof of this because my husband died 30 years ago, but I'm still alive because God's the one keeping me."

Fast forward to the next day, when my family and I left my mother-in-law to go to Dubai, and I kept asking them, "How did this happen that one minute we're in a small city in Nigeria and the next minute we're in Dubai?" I'm totally in awe of God, enjoying my life's adventure with Him.

We went to an attraction called *Ski Dubai* the first day we were there where me and my smaller bubba boys hung out together. At one point, we were trying to get on a little slide suitable for their age, but we ended up on another line accidentally. I couldn't figure out how to get out, so I decided to see if they would allow us to enter the chairlifts that would take us up to the top of the ski slopes. They did, and we enjoyed the view from high up as we watched people ski down the slopes beneath us. As we got to the top, there was this huge sign that covered the entire back wall of the place and written across were three words: *ALL YOU NEED*.

I still can't figure the significance of why those words were there, but I thought back to the words of my mother-in-law, "If you have God in your life, you have ALL YOU NEED."

This year, I've learned the lesson that even when hurts and disappointments come our way, we can shrug them off immediately and keep moving forward because even when humans disappoint, God never disappoints, as long as we stay on the high road with Him, again forgiving endlessly and loving extravagantly.

I don't know about you, but I'm rolling with God all the way because *He truly is all you need. God plus nothing equals everything.* I was starving for love most of my life until I realized how God's heart is overflowing with love for me. I no longer have to settle for the scraps of love others have to give me. *God's love is all I need.* I now love others with the love I receive from Him.

Our God, may we reject thoughts of loneliness, despair, sadness, rejection and lack, KNOWING You are all we need. Amen.

KEEP CALM—YOU'RE ROLLING WITH GOD

Day 282 — Live in God, Live in Love

"LORD, I'M AT YOUR SERVICE"

This statement from Pharrell Williams at the 2015 Grammy Awards blew me away. I changed my screensaver on my phone to say, "Whatever this year holds let me bring glory to You."

What are you here to do for God? He has a plan and a purpose for each of our lives. I feel He has given me the assignment to write daily blog posts to remind you and encourage you that we can live the best lives when we stick close to Him and asking, *How may I serve?* We can have heaven on earth experiences when we all join in and do our part for God.

I'm so impressed with the Muslims and seeing them pray during the day inspired me to have my appointments with God. I asked a Muslim customer about the core message of their faith and he said to me, "We believe in one God, and we want peace." That makes me extremely happy because I, too, believe there is only one God; and we're not the human race, we're the human family.

A Facebook friend, Tracey, inspired me, as well, when she commented the following: "I must go hug my neighbor and give them unconditional love! My light must shine! I must glow in the dark! I must be drawn to people! Glory to God! He is so Holy! He wants to make us whole and complete. Full of Love! Full of Passion! Father God, who is seated on the right hand of the Father! He is so Holy! He said 'Be Holy because I am Holy!' Hug! Love! Give! Listen! Change the world with Him who is in you! Not by power! Not by might but by His Spirit. Just your presence must change your surroundings! Be still and know that I am God! God of Power, Might and Authority! I am here to bring someone out of darkness into His marvelous light!"

I'm with you, Pharrell and Tracey; Lord, I'm at Your service, let's change the world together!

Dear God, "Whatever this year holds let me bring glory to You." Amen.

KEEP CALM—YOU'RE ROLLING WITH GOD

Day 283 — Live in God, Live in Love

GOD & HUBBY I GET IT

My message from God lately seems to be WORK HARD! This has been the biggest complaint from my hubby, that I need to work harder (I'll admit it, life in Nigeria has made me very lazy because of all the help I get). And now, God seems to be joining in with this message that has shown up all over the place.

It all began as I ironed some clothes for my hubby one Sunday and I thought to myself that life is hard work. Then I decided to write a blog post about it later that day. When I went out, I saw someone I hadn't seen in over two years. I told him that we're guaranteed to be winners if we go with God, and he responded, *"and work hard!"*

Later that same night, an email newsletter from Joel Osteen came in with the scripture verse quoted for the day: "*Work hard* and cheerfully at whatever you do, as though you were working for the Lord rather than for people" (Colossians 3:23, NLT).

The next day, we saw the movie *Annie* and again *"work hard"* was mentioned in a conversation between two of the characters. *It kept showing up!* The next night, we went out to dinner and met someone for the very first time, and she says to me: "You have to work hard!" Then the following morning, a post came up on Facebook: "Hard work opens the channel through which God releases His blessings to you!!! #WorkHard"

I love my God winks when He reminds me that He's intimately involved in all my moments. That day, I got more than enough. I surrendered. *Okay, God and hubby, I will work harder.* Like I always tell my mom, I'll rest when I die!

"Whatever you do, do it enthusiastically, as something done for the Lord and not for men" (Colossians 3:23, HCSB).

Dear God, help us not to get distracted, working hard and cheerfully at whatever you have called us to do. Amen.

KEEP CALM—YOU'RE ROLLING WITH GOD

"THANK YOU, GOD, I GET TO BE THE SON OF THIS MOMMA"

Was the cute response from my Joshie when I said, "Thank You, God, I get to be the mother of this sweet son!"

This overwhelming feeling of gratitude for everyone in my life started at work one day. I stopped what I was doing to send my hubby a text message: "I said a prayer thanking God that He picked me to be the wife of such an incredible husband! Love you, boo!" Despite everything, we may go through, *the good, bad and ugly*, I'm thankful that I get to be his wife. He has truly earned my love and respect over the last then 14 years we've been together, and I enjoy helping him in our businesses and being the mother of our four terrific kids God has blessed us with.

"Lord, what makes YOU happy?" is the question I want to continually ask. And doing my best to be the best wife, mother, daughter, sister, friend and person is how I intend to make God happy in every moment of my life. God gives me everything and I want to give Him everything because that's what real relationships are about.

Keep Calm—You're Rolling With God is the new name I'm considering for our book," I said to my friend, Sal, in South Africa. I'm also thankful to God for sending this more than great friend into my life. She has been my biggest supporter over the years of writing these God blog posts. This lesson of calming down has been huge for both of us, where we've stopped reacting to situations, but instead listen for God's wisdom and insight on whatever it is we're facing, on a moment by moment basis. We have another friend we both should thank for teaching us this valuable lesson - *Thank You, God, I get to be the friend of this shining example of a person!*

Despite everything, we all have so much to be thankful for! We get to live full lives with God as our Partner, Friend, Counselor, Teacher, Provider, Confidant, Adviser, Strategist and Father.

Lord, what makes YOU happy? Give us the courage to do that. Amen.

KEEP CALM—YOU'RE ROLLING WITH GOD

'CAUSE I GOTTA HAVE FAITH'

Was my God wink driving with my kids, running some errands.

My God winks are my constant reminders from Him that He's with me and He incredibly knows every thought I think. I had a hectic day, but for some reason I started singing George Michael's song in my head, a song I hadn't heard in years: "Gotta have faith, faith, faith!" As I'm driving home, a few hours later, I turned on the radio, and unbelievably, this was the second song played. Once again, out of the blue, everything lined up a little bit too perfectly. *Wink! Wink!*

And that's exactly what my writing is about—building our faith, faith, faith. Eventually, if I have anything do with it, we'll all learn to relax and enjoy our fantastic adventures with God. *We're never alone.* God's with us every moment of every day and there's always so much going on that every moment is sacred. *Pay attention,* as God's always communicating with us.

This song was the perfect example when I needed a reminder to relax and trust Him. Don't forget we're not going with the ordinary rules of man; we're rolling with God, the Creator of the entire universe, and with Him ALL things are possible. He's our Helper, Friend, Comforter, Protector, Healer, Strategist, Provider, and Adviser, and He'll never fail us. It's unbelievable how when we go to Him in those 1,000 decisions every day, He has perfect solutions to help us in every aspect of our lives. *God is too much!*

Are you going to give in to fear, worry, anger, revenge, unforgiveness, hate, unkindness or are you going to be *mentally strong and disciplined,* being your most loving self, forgiving quickly, trusting God completely, optimistic that there is *nothing* that will come your way that You and Him can't handle together? Every day I want to focus on becoming a better and more loving person, knowing God is helping me and guiding me every step of the way.

Heads held high, everyone! We're moving forward, and we're *leaving the past in the past.*

Dear God, may we stay on the sometimes-difficult high road with You, moving forward as if nothing has happened, trusting Your guidance for every decision we make. Amen.

KEEP CALM—YOU'RE ROLLING WITH GOD

Day 286 — Live in God, Live in Love

"EVERYTHING'S BETTER: WELCOME TO THE BETTER LIFE"

Life with God is better...

- Where you *refuse to worry* about anything. You instead *pray* about everything – "Pray then let God worry."
- You know all your troubles are only light and momentary compared to what they are doing for you—growing you up so that you're mature and not lacking anything.
- You're grateful for everything, bouncing around with gratitude, and you're content knowing whatever God wants for you is best for you.
- You wake up knowing that anything's possible and all you should do is advance *confidently* in the direction of your dreams, where there is no such thing as failure.
- You know that when you walk uprightly with God, you shall lack no good thing.
- You're focused on constant and never ending improvement "and do not take upon yourself *useless cares*" (The Imitation of Christ).
- You *run to God* in every decision knowing you have the best Adviser, who'll never let you down, always going with the choices that bring you peace when you think about it.
- You're not so hard on yourself realizing that you may not get it right all the time, but when you fall off the wagon, you simply get right back on and keep going, committed to doing better next time
- You love your critics! Someone says 10,000 words about you, you take from it what you can to improve yourself, and you run with it and professionally ignore the rest.
- You have the best relationships, forgiving quickly and loving extravagantly realizing only God's perfect.
- You suck the enjoyment out of everyone on your path knowing that no one will be there forever and if someone decided they don't want to be there with you, you're OK with that knowing you have God with you, who will never leave or forsake you.
- You've left the past in the past, and you're focused instead on enjoying and maximizing the present moment.
- You're filled with joy and peace that surpasses all understanding *KNOWING* that there is NOTHING that you and God can't handle together.
- You've stopped getting overwhelmed taking life one step at a time, focused on God, Who is with you in every moment.

O God, life with You is indeed the better life! May all come to know and love You. Amen.

KEEP CALM—YOU'RE ROLLING WITH GOD

Day 287 — Live in God, Live in Love

"SOMEONE THAT I TRUSTED BETRAYED ME...

... And is trying to do everything he can to destroy me," was a message I received from a fellow Facebooker.

In thinking about my deepest betrayals, they have been some of the best things that could have ever happened to me. God certainly knows how to shake us up to wake us up! One memorable one had me running to church every Sunday, and dragging my kids along, no matter how tired I felt. Those trips to church led me to a charismatic pastor, who through some brilliant sermons and his encouragement to read the Bible every day for myself, was the beginning of my love for God. A few years later and I'm a certifiable God maniac, as my daughter, Ember, calls me. *I could now kiss that person who betrayed me.*

In dealing with a betrayal now, this is where endless conversations with God would come in, as each situation is unique and God knows everything down to every thought we think before we even think it. Therefore, God would be the best Adviser. I've never met a perfect person, and you'll experience hurtful situations at some point in life.

My best advice is to shrug it off immediately, forgiving them quickly and take the high road with God, who will pay you back more than you could ever imagine, when you do this. This strategy has never failed me. Not that I've stayed best of friends with everyone who has betrayed me, and like a smart friend has taught me, some people you love from a distance, and you treat them with a very long handled spoon.

When we give our best in life, being our most loving and forgiving selves, God gives us his best. What people have meant for my harm, God has used it for my good. Stay on the high road with Him, running to Him in every decision, and going with the decisions that bring you peace when you think about them. I'm living my best life with God. I can't change anyone, I patiently leave them in God's hands and work on being the best person I can be for Him, and He hasn't let me down yet!

"A successful man is one who can lay a firm foundation with the bricks others have thrown at him." - David Brinkley

Dear God, Your ways are not our ways. May we always seek Your guidance and do what You would have us to do. Amen.

KEEP CALM—YOU'RE ROLLING WITH GOD

I'M SUCH A PROUD MAMA BEAR

Can I brag about my wonderful kids today? At their school's coffee morning meeting, I listened as other parents voiced their very minor complaints. As far as I was concerned, I'm happy. Between the job of what they're doing at school and what we're doing at home, my kids are terrific.

Honestly, we can't take all credit, though, as I believe God has His hands in there, too, helping us to train them the way they should go. Here are my top three parenting tips:

- *Teach them about God and including Him in all their decisions.* I asked my then four-year-old, Emmie, "How do you get closer to God?" His reply was, "When I'm kind to Joshie (his then two-year-old brother)." I believe if I can teach them to have a close relationship with God and to know that He is always with them and directing them wherever they go in this life and to pay attention to those feelings as God leads them in making the best decisions, I've done my job.

Teach your children to be independent of you as soon as possible. You would be surprised at how remarkably smart these kids are once given the opportunity to do stuff. One Sunday, my daughters, then ages 8 and 10, cooked breakfast for everyone, as I sat watching them. Teaching them initially will be messy, but stick with it. Don't do anything for them that they can do for themselves. You're not helping them when you do this. I always tell you this life is not for weaklings. Let's raise strong, responsible, and confident kids.

Teach them to love, be kind, and ask, How may I serve? After giving my then 8-year-old her allowance for the week, she "dashed it" (the Nigerian term meaning to give away) to a staff that helps us. She gave the lady a hug and said, "Thank you for all you do for us." Like I said, when you ask God, *How may I serve?* He turns around and asks you, *How may I serve you?* I want my kids in on this blessed life, too, and loving kindness is how to get there. As Lao-tzu said, "To the giver comes the fullness of life; to the taker, just an empty hand." Let's change the world and future generations by raising great kids.

Dear God, may every generation seek Your face. Amen.

KEEP CALM—YOU'RE ROLLING WITH GOD

"GO TO THE PLACE OF BLESSING"

Was the title of Joel and Victoria Osteen's inspirational emailed message. They wrote about the prophet Elijah who God told to leave a certain city and "go down to the brook Cherith," where God had commanded the ravens to feed him. And every morning, the ravens did show up with food for him. And like Elijah, they explained that there is a place, too, for us to be blessed—our favor from God and our abundance.

I believe this! It was a calendar on the wrong date that told me that I shall go to a land flowing with milk and honey. I knew beyond a doubt that it was God directing me to relocate to Nigeria with my kids, even though we were extremely comfortable living in the United States. That honestly was one of the best decisions I've ever made because I love our life here. I called a friend a little while ago and asked her, "Have I told you lately how much I love you?" Out of 170 million people, God had the perfect friend waiting for me. Now my girls get to grow up with her and learn from her, too. "Walk with the wise and become wise, for a companion of fools suffers harm" (Proverbs 13:20, NIV).

And, I'm feeling extra in love with my hubby these days! I realize every relationship has its ups and downs, but we always seem to come through rocky times closer, with more love and respect for each other. I sent him a text message:

"Today and always, I promise that I will love and cherish you to be my lawful husband and soul mate, I will stand by you through sickness and health, through richness and poorness, through happy times and bad times, 'til death do us part."

Again, I'm in awe of God when I think of the name my father gave me when I was born: "Oneka" which means African Princess. It was destiny for me to live in Nigeria. I found my place of blessing. Constant conversations with God continue, and He hasn't let me down yet.

Dear God, may we follow Your leading, as You guide us on the path to the best life with You. Amen.

KEEP CALM—YOU'RE ROLLING WITH GOD

Day 290 — Live in God, Live in Love

"PAPA (GOD) WANTS US CLOSE TO HIS HEART"

Was the message that blew the God maniac away from a special Facebook friend, Stefanie.

I have no doubt God was behind our sacred conversation. She had an important message for me from Him that I'm not to be concerned about the number of "likes" the posts receive because I have no idea of their influence and that she has even shared them. "See, you are international already!" she said. And God had me deliver a message to her, too: Stefanie, get to work!

At one point, she commented, "He (God) will complete what he has started!" This reminded me that I didn't have my 5 p.m. appointment with Him and I immediately went to my Tumblr.com website, where I often get messages from Him. I searched for "God," and I immediately got the high five from Him that I was looking for, when out of the blue everything lined up a little bit too perfectly, when a top post read: "What God begins, God completes," which was a special confirmation for me that day.

That morning, I woke up groggy from some allergy medicine and in opening my meditation book He reminded me that He was my strength when I'm weak. In getting a little frustrated, He reminded me to keep my eyes fixed on Him and the 10,000 things I'm grateful for. I have some important work I need to take care of and I'm amazed how once again the perfect person has shown up to help me. He came to support our business, and we ended up hiring him. He called me saying everything is on track. God seems always to be saying to me, *Nik, don't worry, I got you!* There is nothing that could come your way that you and I can't handle together.

God, may we live the rest of our lives close to Your heart. The difficulties we know will still come, but we can have peace knowing we can handle anything with You as our Partner. The hurts and disappointments will still be there, too, but You're the best heart healer. You even can weave our mistakes and failures into a beautiful pattern for our good. Amen.

KEEP CALM—YOU'RE ROLLING WITH GOD

"WHEN I FEEL WEAK, TIRED OR OUT OF SORTS..."

... you're right there to put your arms around me, to comfort me and tell me that everything is going to be okay. You reach out and soothe my ruffled nerves, melt away my worries and fears and blow away the confusion that seeks to surround me."

These are surprisingly the words from a meditation book a friend gave me, and they perfectly described my morning with God. I didn't sleep well, and I was feeling a bit tired after exercising and for no concrete reason I had some unexplainable anxiety. I decided to read through some old posts in an appointment with God. That almost always does the trick to get me back on track whenever I'm feeling that way. I did feel lots better after reading a few of them and decided to go back to my postings on Facebook. A friend messaged asking for prayers, and I commented back: "I'm praying. God's timing is the best!"

But, feeling like I didn't touch base with God in that last appointment, I decided to go back for another appointment with Him and read some more of my old posts. The very next post I read, less than eight minutes after I sent that message, was about the school I felt God had specially built for us, that my kids now attend that opened for the very first time on my eldest daughter's birthday the very first year we relocated to Nigeria. I wrote:

"Thinking about this I'm in awe of God because I went to the doctor's office when I was pregnant with my daughter asking if I could have my labor induced so that I would have her before the September 1st school cutoff date in the U.S. to begin kindergarten, and the midwife told me a story that convinced me that God's timing was the best. If she only knew how right she was!"

God's timing is indeed the best! Seeing those words show up was just the high five I needed from Him when once again everything lined up a little bit too perfectly, and God reminded me that He's intimately involved in every moment of my life, and therefore I had no reason to be anxious about anything. My mojo was instantaneously back! I jumped out of bed, and within no time I was at work!

Dear God, "thank You for Your touches of love that melt away the mountains of obstacles and problems." Amen.

KEEP CALM—YOU'RE ROLLING WITH GOD

Day 292 — Live in God, Live in Love

IT'S NOT EASY HUMANISTICALLY FOR SURE!

I commented to someone who shared that after 40 years, he and his wife have parted ways.

After I shared that my husband blasted me over a decision I had made, my terrific and wonderful friend, Star, wrote: "Sometimes I think your husband is too rough and authoritative over you..." So humanistically, I totally get it that this marriage/relationship thing is not easy, but that's why I believe God is calling us to be superhumans. God has been my wonderful Counselor, and He seems always to be calling me to leave the old Nikki—weak, neurotic, dramatic, insecure, emotional, and fearful—and become the superhuman Nikki He has created me to be—confident, secure, calm, wiser, mentally strong and disciplined, fearless and worried about nothing. *My eyes are to be fixed on God,* and not losing my cool over some words thrown my way. I either improve or I kindly and respectfully ignore them.

God is teaching me all about *messy love,* and I'm not happy with the husband who screams at me and has a bad temper at times, but I'm learning the importance of focusing on the 80% that I love about him and not the 20% that I'm not so thrilled about. I look at my marriage not as an obligation, but as an opportunity for us to live our best lives together. We're both extremely excited about some plans we're making. Every moment is sacred, even the terrible and tough ones because they're the times *God is sandpapering us to be stronger.*

My best marriage advice, though, is making God your first love and priority. Going to Him before making decisions has helped me to create a beautiful life filled with love, health, and happiness. God incomprehensibly knows how I should conduct myself in any and every situation that would work out in my highest possible best interest and I've learned to trust and depend on His wisdom and guidance. Like I always say, I don't want to be this happy all by myself, I want you guys here with me living incredible and fantastic lives with God, too. His plans for us are very good! Learning His inaudible voice clearly through my gut/spirit/feelings has brought me to this point to confidently say, a life lived close to God is the sweetest life.

Dear God. take away any weak, victim mentalities within us and replace them with attitudes of strength, courage and mental toughness. Amen.

KEEP CALM—YOU'RE ROLLING WITH GOD

"WHO AM I TO JUDGE"

I said to a friend about a controversial issue we've agreed to disagree about.

I then received this email from Joseph Prince's Ministry that reminded me that *"all of us have faults"* and "God's grace is bigger, deeper, wider and more powerful than all the world's sins put together":

"Sin cannot stop God's grace (Romans 5:20)! Moreover, the law entered that the offense might abound. But where sin abounded, grace abounded much more. When a top executive is charged for corruption or a church minister is caught in the very act of adultery, you will probably hear the phrase "fallen from grace" being used of them. We have come to believe that when someone falls into sin, he falls from grace.

But God wants us to know that when someone falls into sin, he does not fall from grace — he actually falls into grace! Thank God His grace is there to put the person back on his feet. The Bible tells of prostitutes and corrupt tax collectors — sinners — who fell into God's grace and got back on their feet. If the sin in their lives could stop God's grace, they would never have been able to receive His grace of healing, help and power to live right.

Now, it is important you understand that God hates sin because it destroys our lives, relationships and bodies. Sin is evil! But sin is not overcome by us talking about it and relying on our willpower to overcome it. It takes God's grace to destroy sin. In fact, it is when you are under His grace that sin has no dominion over you (Romans 6:14). It is when you see His grace in providing His Son to put away your sins and make you eternally righteous that sin will not dominate you.

The devil will say to you, "You think that you can still expect God's blessings after what you did this morning?" That is when you must remind yourself that Christ alone is your perfection and righteousness. All of us have faults. None of us deserve God's blessings. That is why we plead the grace of God, which is His unearned, unmerited and undeserved favor toward us.

"WHO AM I TO JUDGE"

My friend, God's grace is bigger, deeper, wider and more powerful than all the world's sins put together. Receive His grace right now to walk in total victory over that weakness or evil habit in your life!"

God, thank You for Your grace and may we extend that grace to ourselves and others. Amen.

KEEP CALM—YOU'RE ROLLING WITH GOD

BIG MAGIC

That's the name of the fantastic book I'm reading by Elizabeth Gilbert. She described exactly how I feel about my life with God and how He's always giving me clues as to what He would have me to do:

"It's a clue. It might seem like nothing, but it's a clue. Follow that clue. Trust it. See where curiosity will lead you next. Then follow the next clue and the next. Remember it doesn't have to be a voice in the desert; it's just a harmless little scavenger hunt. Following that scavenger hunt of curiosity can lead you to amazing, unexpected places."

Then when I was thinking of posting an old post that day, the number 22 came clearly to mind and talking of *BIG MAGIC*, here's what I had written on page 22 of my unpublished book out of 437 pages:

"... but Mr. Coelho perfectly articulated something in that interview that I watched the next day, which I've been feeling for a while. He explained that life is something like a scavenger hunt, and we pick up clues along the way as to where to go next. And this is exactly what I'm finding. The clues can come from all over the place. From songs on the radio, books, TV shows or even from a moving repair truck like it did recently for me."

And a big clue came on Saturday for me from a lady I met at a party. About two hours before meeting her, I purchased a book for my kids with Bible stories. There was a picture of Adam and Eve and I explained to my younger sons that they were the first people God created. I'm at this party and this lady's name, of all names, was Eve. She has already published eight books and I told her how I'm struggling to get one out and my sad story of sending my manuscript to the publisher then asking for it back because I felt it wasn't good enough. She had the perfect words for me (I paraphrase here): "The longer you keep the book from being published, you're keeping it away from the people who need your words. The book will never be perfect so stop striving for perfection. Let it go, then move on to the next one."

It wasn't a voice in the desert, but God, I got the message loud and clear.
The scavenger hunt continues.
"O Lord, Speak, Your servants are listening!" May our ordinary work, done with great love on Your behalf, become all that You would have it to be." Amen.

KEEP CALM—YOU'RE ROLLING WITH GOD

Day 295 — Live in God, Live in Love

"THOU SHALL NOT KILL!"

I said to my Emmie as he was about to roll over a *caterpillar* with his skateboard. Instead, we just took the *caterpillar* outside where it belonged. Fast forward a few hours, and I'm discussing with my friend a matter that had me so upset and I said to her, "I've *surrendered* everything to God." Hanging up from her, my alarm went off for my appointment with Him and I decided to go to my Tumblr.com site where I go to read the perfect messages. A post immediately caught my attention that read: "Just when the *CATERPILLAR* thought her life was over she began to fly."

God certainly got my attention with *"caterpillar"* showing up *(wink, wink)* and I continued reading the perfect message from Him to me at that moment:

"God is making all things new! Don't give up today or tomorrow, or next week or ever! God is doing something much more greater than we can see or think. God isn't just making a great thing for us in the Kingdom of God, but in the future. When we *surrender all* to God. Everything and everyone...God will bless it and cause us to triumph. Declaring victory in the name of Jesus hourly, and *keep God first!"*

Talk about a high five from God! I felt like I was God's special child the entire day. God promises to bless me and cause me to triumph because I decided to surrender and stay on the high road with Him. That's why I always write that *everything is between God and us, not between us and anyone else.* He is the one to cause us to triumph in every aspect of our lives. *We all have our crosses to carry, but with God, we can carry them joyfully, patiently and peacefully because He's helping us to carry them.*

"O Lord, if you are with me, who can be against me? If you help me, I will not fear what others can do to me. Grant me the grace to preserve the peace and tranquility of spirit in the midst of tribulations, contradictions and calumnies. I place all my trust in you, O Lord. I will patiently wait for the hour of liberation from the trials, which surround me. Infuse the virtue of patience in my heart, O God. Amen."

KEEP CALM—YOU'RE ROLLING WITH GOD

PAPA (GOD) DOESN'T LIKE IT WHEN WE'RE SAD

In all my sadness, God figured out a way to cheer me up.

It all started the day before with me counseling a friend through a terrible day she was having. She had turned into a crazy lady and that day it was my turn. We joked how our emotions from one day, or even sometimes within the same day, can go from one extreme to the other. We had a good laugh and about 20 minutes later I left to pick up my kids from school. On the way, though, still feeling like the crazy lady, I decided I needed to hear from God from one of my old favorite meditation books, *The Imitation of Christ*. I stopped by the bookstore, quickly purchased a copy, and unbelievably opened right to the perfect message from Papa:

"My child (I love when He calls me this!), trust not your affection of the moment, for it will soon be changed into another. As long as you live, you are subject to change, even against your own will; so that sometimes you are joyful, at other times sad; now at peace, then troubled; at one time devout, at other arid; sometimes fervent, at other times lazy; one day blue, another elated.

But if you are wise and well-instructed in spirit, you will be above all these changes: not minding what you feel in yourself, nor on what side of the wind of instability blows; but that the whole inclination of your soul may be directed towards the desired end. For then you may remain one and the selfsame, and unshaken, by unceasingly directing, through all this change of events, the single eye of your intention towards me.

Reflection

The flightiness and inconstancy of the human heart is inexpressible and incomprehensible. This is because the human heart seeks for peace and rest in creatures and, not finding it here or there, it keeps on trying elsewhere. Only those who are truly wise are constant and unchanging because they concentrate all their intentions and desires on God, who gives them special guidance through the Holy Spirit.

> *O Lord, do not permit my heart to be in constraint. Grant me the grace of a firm and constant love for you. Amen."*

God, I get it! I'm to keep my eyes fixed on You and not this world or anyone in it!

KEEP CALM—YOU'RE ROLLING WITH GOD

GREAT IS THY FAITHFULNESS

Is the hymn I couldn't seem to get out of my head.

I decided to snooze on an appointment with God the day before, thinking I would have one later reading some books I enjoy at a friend's house about the fruits of the spirit. After the week I had had fighting with my hubby, I needed a reminder of being *a faithful wife—constant, loyal, dependable, devoted and putting them all into consistent practice despite our circumstances.* This is not always easy, but God reminded me in that book that He's the one to reward my faithfulness.

"Whatever you do, do it enthusiastically, as something done for the Lord and not for men" (Colossians 3:23, HCSB).

And God's *faithfulness* is off the chain! He's constant, loyal, dependable, and devoted to us. His plans for us are always good, even when we can't see it, like with the terrible bombing that occurred in Paris. I feel it's all a part of His plan to remind us that we're not the human race, but we're the human family. And I believe if there were more faithfulness in the world, starting in our homes with less infidelity and divorce, our family units would become stronger, thereby creating stronger, more peaceful societies and a more peaceful world.

That appointment with God certainly did the trick, and I woke up this morning committed to being a more faithful wife, mother, daughter, family member, and person. *I was even the one to apologize to my hubby,* realizing his incredible faithfulness to our family and that sometimes I take it all for granted.

"Great is Thy faithfulness! Great is Thy Faithfulness!

Morning by morning new mercies I see;

All I have needed Thy hand hath provided—Great is Thy faithfulness," Lord, unto me!" Amen.

KEEP CALM—YOU'RE ROLLING WITH GOD

Day 298 — Live in God, Live in Love

LET'S HAVE A NEW BEGINNING, AGAIN

I love the idea of new beginnings!

In any moment, we can decide to leave the past in the past and begin again to make things even better than they were before. And when we add the God factor into these new beginnings, they get even sweeter.

One night, watching my girls on the *Housewives of Atlanta*, I was sad watching Cynthia all emotional over some bad choices her husband made that got caught on camera.

Here's the deal: *No relationship is perfect!* I would give her the same advice a friend told me years ago that forever changed me, "Leave the past in the past." I left her house that day light and free with a mission of beginning again, and I'm so much happier for it. It's as God gives us these fantastic lives to enjoy, but when we decide to carry around the hurts and pains from the past we say to Him, "God, thanks for all the beauty in my life, but I think I'm just going to sit here in this cesspit." And that's exactly what we do whenever we dwell on the negativity of the past. Every moment spent there is a moment spent not enjoying life! I don't know about you, but I want to suck the enjoyment out of every minute.

I had some important work to complete, and I had the best time doing it blasting my music in the background thinking how God has even given us music to make our lives even more wonderful. I love the message from Joseph Prince about extending grace (clemency, love, mercy, forgiveness) to ourselves and others, because when we do this, it frees us from so much pain. If Cynthia can say to her husband, "Peter, I forgive you," and let it go and move on to enjoy her life and her marriage, she would be so much better off for it. Or she can stay in the cesspit and be miserable!

The hurts and disappointments are a part of life. But the sooner we learn the lesson of handing them over to God, who will correct them in His perfect timing, the happier we will be. *Nobody's perfect!* Extend grace often and generously, let go of stuff and refuse to dwell in the cesspit (pool of negativity) of life. Say it with me, *"I refuse to dwell in the cesspit of my life."*

Dear God, may we live our lives on the high road with You, extending lots of grace to ourselves and others with the courage to begin again, as if nothing has happened, whenever necessary. Amen.

KEEP CALM—YOU'RE ROLLING WITH GOD

"NOT EVERYONE WANTS TO HEAR ABOUT GOD EVERY DAY"

I said to my *Helen Honey*, when we showed up at her house.

We had an unplanned belated birthday celebration for her, and she apologized for not following my blog. I'm still eating the delicious cake she insisted I take home. She said to me one day after I thanked her for giving my kids a ride home from school, "No need to thank me, we're family now." And coming to Nigeria and getting to be around this sweet family has been a huge blessing from God. I had to leave the party to head back to work, but the kids stayed and came back so happy telling me how fun their house is. It's no coincident that we relocated to Nigeria and their home is only a two-minute drive from our home. *God, I'm grateful!*

I'm also incredibly grateful to God for His constant reminders that He's always with me. Like driving back to work, I was thinking about a situation that has come up and God's message to me that morning from my meditation book was, "I'm training you in steadiness." I said to Him, "God, I get it, I'm to be steady, calm, confident and trusting You, no matter what comes up. As I'm about to turn into work, the bus for "*Steady* Flow Driving School" appears in front of me. *Wink! Wink!*

And the night before that, a "glitch" on Facebook, which I knew was God, surprisingly brought up a blog post from months before, with a message from my friend, Tiffany, of what God wanted her to tell me:

"My beloved, I am ever with you. Do not be afraid and do not panic. For I am that I am; I walk with you. I guide you. I understand you. I am with you. And I truly love you more than you could ever understand. Be not afraid of overwhelming troubles that rise up against you. I am your peace of mind. I will cause you to be still when you are stressed and afraid. And time and time again will I deliver you. Keep your hope in me steadfast and watch as I turn things around to bless you beyond what you dream and ask of me. It is the Lord's will that you be glad and satisfied in my house and in me. Amen."

Our God, thank You for all the training lessons in steadiness. May we never doubt You again! Amen.

KEEP CALM—YOU'RE ROLLING WITH GOD

WE'RE NOT GOING BY ORDINARY RULES

Some weird stuff seems to be going on.

I've been asking God about it because it was like too good to be true. It involves an issue that I've decided to pray about and let God worry how it was going to be resolved, but seeing God in action, has even caught the God Maniac a little bit off guard. I woke up again this morning, talking to God, still asking how all this happened, and as usual, He answered me in my children's daily devotional: "Live full lives, full in the fullness of God. God can do anything, you know-far more than you could ever imagine or guess or request in your wildest dreams! He does it not by pushing us around but by working within us, His Spirit deeply and gently within us" (Ephesians 3:10-20, MSG).

Let's do it! "Live full lives, full in the fullness of God." *What is too difficult for Him?* "Impossible is where God starts!" When we stick with God, seeking to please Him in all our ways, He leads us on the path to these unimaginable lives - I'm talking meaningful, joyful, peaceful and happy. And we don't have to worry about what anyone else is doing; God is in complete and total control. Everything is between God and us, not between us and anyone else. I'm sucking up to God, staying on the high road, acknowledging Him in all my ways – *God, what do we do here?* And watching Him show up and show off has been beautiful to witness.

"There's no storm that God won't carry you through. No bridge that God won't help you cross. No battle that God won't help you win. No heartache that God won't help you let go of. He is so much bigger than anything you will face. Leave everything in His hands confidently knowing that He will take care of you." — Unknown

Our Beloved, may we surrender every aspect of our lives over to You, doing our best with what You ask us to do and leaving the rest with You. Amen.

KEEP CALM—YOU'RE ROLLING WITH GOD

"SLOW DOWN, CALM DOWN AND LISTEN TO GOD"

Was the message to a friend early one morning.

These have been some valuable lessons I, too, had to learn. She's been going a little bit crazy on me lately, doing things she later regrets and I encouraged her to stay in touch with God before she makes any move by slowing down, calming down and having those constant conversations with Him as to what to do, where to go and even what to say.

I love my relationship with God, where I've learned to keep my eyes steadily fixed on Him and not this world. People will disappoint us, but God never disappoints! His plans for us are good, and He never leaves us or forsakes us. We can have positive attitudes and outlooks, despite all the dramas in our lives.

I'm telling you from lots of experience here that when I get God involved in every aspect of my life, things turn out more beautiful than I could even imagine. It was God who I felt was advising me not to push my son, Emmie, in a class that was too advanced for him. It was a big fight with my husband when I took him back a grade level, but years later, that was the best decision. As he was leaving for school today, he agreed that he's working towards all A's this semester. Now he's in the perfect grade for his age and maturity level. I gave him lots of kisses while waking him up and honestly, I must be the proudest mom in the world. He was even the student of the month last month, both him and my other son, Joshie.

Little by little, when I get God involved by listening to Him, things work out spectacularly. God knows what should fall into place and sometimes what needs to fall out of place, but when we get all crazy, we're not paying attention to where He is leading us. I want our entire lives to be intertwined completely with God. Always asking, *God, what would You have me to do here?* Seeking to be our best selves for Him. Don't make a move without talking to Him first. And the more you practice listening to Him, leaning on your spirit/gut/intuition to direct you, the better you'll begin hearing His moment by moment guidance.

Dear God, guide us with Your counsel. May we slow down, calm down and listen to You in our every decision. Amen.

KEEP CALM—YOU'RE ROLLING WITH GOD

Day 302 — Live in God, Live in Love

GOD HAS HEALED MY BROKEN HEART, AGAIN

Early one Sunday morning, my mom asked me to help her find the channel where she could find Pastor Joel Osteen's previously recorded TV program, as she normally watched him about 8 am on Sunday mornings in the Bahamas. I couldn't find it, so we agreed to watch his live stream service at 9:30 am on TV through the internet connection. I told her how I was depressed and I believe Joel would have a message for me from God.

Fast forward to us watching, Joel wasn't there, and another Pastor (Nick) replaced him to give the sermon. I was disappointed missing Joel and wanted to leave my mom to watch by herself, but I got a feeling (nudge) to stay. And I'm so happy I did because it was like he was speaking directly to me.

There I was, very upset at my husband and Pastor Nick started talking about not judging others and extending grace (forgiveness). He said we might want to judge other people based on only a glimpse of the story without knowing there are many chapters, but we focus on only one. And that was exactly what I was doing, looking at only a glimpse of something and imagining the worst-case scenarios, without looking at the complete story. And the full story is that in my marriage of then 14 years, 90% of the chapters are beautiful and that's what I needed to focus on, not the other 10%.

Pastor Nick then told a story of a time he got pulled over by the police and his soon to be father-in-law came to his rescue and defended him, even though he was wrong for not having his driver's license or insurance renewed. He didn't speak to him in a judgmental way or make him feel stupid or guilty for his mistakes. Hearing that story reminded me that this is how God wants me to be in my relationships. So happened that my husband called right after I had listened to that story. I apologized to him for the way I'd been acting. I asked him, "Do you know how much your crazy wife loves you?" He responded, "Infinity percent."

I went back on the high road with God, extending lots of grace (clemency without punishment). I want to be that father-in-law in the story, spreading God's love and mercy wherever I go. God not only healed my heart but looking at all the wonderful qualities of my husband, I now love him even more than before this whole incident came up. *God is too much!*

Dear God, may we push back all the darkness in the world by shining Your light everywhere. Amen.

KEEP CALM—YOU'RE ROLLING WITH GOD

Day 303 — Live in God, Live in Love

"PEACE IS NOT THE ABSENCE OF PROBLEMS, BUT THE PRESENCE OF GOD"

I got this from my Tumblr.com website in an appointment with God.

And that's exactly what I've discovered and why I write these posts every day, to tell you that we can truly have the peace that passes all understanding KNOWING God is with us every step of the way. I agree with Pastor Rick Warren who said in an interview, "Life is a series of problems: Either you are in one now, you're just coming out of one, or you're getting ready to go into another one."

The problems, challenges, disappointments, frustrations, hurts, pains, I promise you, will always be there in some form or the other, but once you keep your focus on God, there's nothing that can come your way that you can't handle together with God's moment-by-moment guidance and direction. For me, it's no more reacting to situations, but going within and having quiet conversations with God, then paying attention to the cues, nudges, whispers of my ultimate Adviser, Strategist, Counselor, and Partner. He's an *expert in everything*, and His guidance hasn't failed me yet, down to computer software, *He knows it!*

A big word I've been focused on lately is *discipline*. The principal of my kids' school is so right when he said, "You don't go too far without discipline." Discipline has gotten me out of my bed to exercise every day, to finish up my manuscript to send to the publisher, to eat healthy and most importantly to change my thinking.

Instead of allowing my mind to dwell on negativity, I mentally discipline myself *(beat my mind with a stick!)* to fill it up with thoughts of love, gratitude, contentment, hope, courage, mercy, forgiveness, trust and the higher things of life. When my mind starts to conjure up craziness, I regularly catch myself and tell it, *"Nope, I'm not going there!"* And honestly, I'm happiest here, at peace with everyone in my life, focused on their positives, granting everyone lots of grace (clemency) and endless forgiveness.

Our God, may we all come to know Your peace that passes all understanding. Amen.

KEEP CALM—YOU'RE ROLLING WITH GOD

I LOVE GOD!

What more can I say? Knowing me, lots! I had such a beautiful day with Him. I read a quote late the night before that said, "Keep your eyes open to the beauty that surrounds you. God has placed many blessings upon your path. Gather them with joy." - Maria Fontane, *Mottos For Success*

It was as if I woke up with new eyes, gathering my blessings, instead of complaining. Joshie gave me a hug and kiss goodbye as he left for school, and watching him (independently) leave, I gathered the blessings with joy, thanking God for him. And those gatherings continued the entire day. *God, I'm grateful for so many blessings You have placed on my path!*

But for some reason, I woke up with some anxious thoughts about a certain situation. This doesn't happen often, but that morning, I found myself a little worried. I decided for my appointment with God to read through some of my old posts, and I read one from about six months ago, where I was concerned about the same thing. Then I opened my meditation book, *Jesus Calling*, to the perfect message from God: "You have Me on your side, so what are you worried about?" That did the trick, with me feeling as if I did a high five with God because the anxious thoughts were gone. These appointments with God have brought me so much closer to Him, where I'm trusting that He is on my side and I have nothing to worry about. He goes before me and with me, and they remind me that I'm never alone and the Creator of the entire universe is always with me.

Are you sticking to your appointments with Him? Sometimes I can go to my *Tumblr.com* website and search "GOD" and a few words there could be an appointment. Or I love listening to podcasts on *iTunes* of people like Pastor Joel Osteen, Rev. Ed Bacon, and Rob Bell or the *Youth Workshop* podcast with Luke Whyte. Or listening to a song on my phone, but I stay until I feel I've touched base with God and I'm ready to go back into the world again.

Dear God, may every day lead us closer and closer to You. Amen.

KEEP CALM—YOU'RE ROLLING WITH GOD

Day 305 — Live in God, Live in Love

EVEN AT 4 AM, YOU'RE WITH ME

Was me to God.

I couldn't sleep for some reason, and at about 4 a.m., I got a feeling to listen again to a podcast I loved from the day before with Rob Bell interviewing one of my favorite people in the whole world, Oprah Winfrey. Almost at the very end, she quickly mentioned her favorite Bible verse: "In God we live and move and have our being."

I remember going to sleep and thinking about those words and that I need to write a post about us letting our entire lives be wrapped up in God. With those thoughts, I went fast asleep. Fast forward a few hours later, in posting my post to all my Facebook groups, I noticed a picture flash across the screen with a Bible verse as I left one of the groups. I rushed back in to search for it and unbelievably it said: "For in Him we live and move and have our being" (Acts 17:28). *Wink! Wink!*

And there you have it, folks, another God wink, when out of the blue everything lined up a little bit too perfectly that I know it's God behind the scenes of my life, constantly reminding me that His invisible Presence is always with me, even at 4 am. *He knows our every move and thought!*

Speaking of God winks, I had one on Sunday in a tough conversation with my husband. He was relaxing listening to his favorite podcast, Pastor Joel Osteen's, when I got the feeling to discuss something that was on my mind. I told him how I want a real marriage and not a PRETEND one, with us always working on improving our relationship, not letting our love become stagnant. As I'm saying this to him, Pastor Osteen is in the background as if he was right there with us, because of all words he kept repeating the word "PRETEND" repeatedly in his sermon. I said to my hubby, "See there, God is telling us that he agrees with me, no PRETEND marriage!" and we were able to have a good laugh about it.

But, this whole idea of living and moving and having our being in God is so where I want us. I now know that I'm never alone and God is always guiding me, whether in the sleepless moments, telling me to listen to Rob Bell or in the difficult conversations, directing me on the right words to say.

Our God, may our entire lives be a grand collaboration with You, enjoying the sweet life with You as our wonderful Guide. Amen.

KEEP CALM—YOU'RE ROLLING WITH GOD

"I'M JUST ONE BEGGAR TELLING ANOTHER BEGGAR WHERE TO FIND FOOD"

This quote made me cry listening again to the podcast on iTunes.com that has changed my life, *The Youth Workshop Presented by Luke Whyte*. Thank you, Luke, I'm now sleeping, not so distracted by Facebook, and I'm asking just about everyone I meet, "Are you having appointments with God?" *Sleep, guys, it's such a beautiful thing!*

And where I've found the best food is sticking close to God! He is our ultimate Guide who leads us on the path to the best life. In talking to someone, I came up with some pointers to stay on the path God has designed for us, where He does more than we could ever imagine possible:

- Go to God for moment by moment decisions. Trust your instincts/gut/spirit as to what God would have you to do. Feelings of peace and excitement are God telling you to go in that direction, whereas feelings of uneasiness and stress are God's way of saying, *Don't do that!*

- Work hard and be exceptional in everything you do! Work as if you're working for God, not for imperfect human masters. *God's our Boss!*

- Have those appointments with Him! I didn't go to work because of an issue in our house, and God used that opportunity to help me with some very critical decisions I needed to make. Amazingly, my daughter, Julie, brought the Bible for me to read at my 5 pm appointment, and there was my answer to one issue and another podcast asked a question as if they were talking directly to me!

- Love! "God is love, and whoever abides in love abides in God, and God abides in him" (1 John 4:16). This beggar has found that when I stay on the high road with Him, being my most loving self, extending lots of grace (clemency/forgiveness without punishment) to others, this leads me on the path to the best life where I'm super happy, at peace, content, and grateful. The problems, hurts, and disappointments will still be there, but you can relax as God seems to say, *Nik, don't worry, I will help you.*

Dear God, guide and protect us. Help us learn Your important voice as we seek Your wisdom to guide our lives. Amen.

KEEP CALM—YOU'RE ROLLING WITH GOD

Day 307 — Live in God, Live in Love

"IN THE MULTITUDES OF MY ANXIETIES WITHIN ME...

... your comfort delights my soul." - (Psalm 94:19)

I have the peace that surpasses all understanding knowing God is with me, despite all the problems/challenges/situations/frustrations I must deal with on a moment by moment basis. I have such confidence that God is my constant Companion and Partner and He's always with me and directing my every move. *And I want you here with me!*

God never ceases to amaze me. He designed everything so perfect. Perfect, I say! Who would have thought having problems would be a good thing? They're His way of growing us up. You live, and you learn. You get experienced in life through having experiences. I'm thrilled at the difference in myself from someone who got broken from problems to someone who can confidently say, *Bring it on! I know my God is with me to help me fight all my battles!*

This life is not for weaklings! I love this quote from Oprah Winfrey: "Transformation happens when you dare to be awakened to greater heights. When you stay open no matter what. Letting each experience, especially the tough ones, strengthen you and add depth and wisdom."

My strategy to problem solving is to simply take life one moment at a time. I don't dwell on the past and I don't worry about the future. I simply ask myself, *What can I take care of at this moment?* consulting God for direction, letting Him set the agenda for my days based on what I feel He is advising me to take care of. The decision that brings me peace when I think about it is the one I go with. I simply take one step at a time doing exactly this. I no longer focus on the worst-case scenarios; I focus on the best-case scenarios *knowing with God all things are possible!*

Remember what Wayne Dyer said, "If you knew who walked with you, on this path you have chosen, you will never experience fear or doubt again." Believe this! Whenever thoughts of doubt try to get in, I say, "Nope, I'm not going there! I'm trusting God!"

Dear God, thank You for Your faithful help in our times of trouble. Take away all thoughts of doubt, worry and fear. Amen.

KEEP CALM—YOU'RE ROLLING WITH GOD

"BE AT PEACE WITH EVERYONE IN YOUR LIFE...

... Including all your relatives."

This is an easy one, right? Honestly, this is where I try to be in my life, but it hasn't always been easy. But here's the deal, when you are at peace with everyone, that's when you enjoy a sweet life. When you're upset, you're miserable, and the moment you forgive and extend grace (pardon), you're happy again! And now a message from our meditation book, *The Imitation Of Christ:*

"You know well how to excuse and gloss over your own deeds, but you will not accept the excuses of others. It is better for you to accuse yourself, and excuse your brother or sister. If you wish to be borne with, bear also with others. See how far you still are from true charity and humility, which knows not how to feel anger or indignation against anyone but oneself.

It is easy to converse with the good and meek, for this is naturally pleasing to all. And everyone prefers to live in peace with those who agree with them and love them the best. But to know how to live peacefully with those who are stubborn and perverse, or indiscipline and opposed to us, is a great grace, worthy of much praise, and a sign of great strength."

"Father forgive them for they know not what they do" (Luke 23:34). Is what I keep in mind whenever I'm tempted to be unforgiving towards anyone. If Jesus can ask God to forgive the people who nailed Him to a cross, I can certainly forgive those who wrong me in any way. *"Be at peace with everyone."*

"Father, thank You for giving me Your peace and strength today. I choose to hold my peace and bless those who come against me. I choose to walk in love and forgiveness so that I can honor You in all that I do in Jesus name. Amen." – Pastor Joel Osteen

KEEP CALM—YOU'RE ROLLING WITH GOD

Day 309 — Live in God, Live in Love

I'M STICKING WITH GOD!

You don't go wrong with God! I feel silly telling you guys about hand soap, shoes and makeup showing up for me, when God has done such incredible things that I can't even write about, but I'm telling you, they're *huge*. All things are possible with God! It's mind boggling how God wants to be involved in every detail of our lives.

"How do you deal with annoying people?" was my question to Him. I hate when I lose my patience when dealing with a person in my life and I'm not my best, most loving self. His advice was to pause before reacting to anyone and take the time to listen for His input before doing anything. *Pause.* Such simple yet profound advice!

I've learned that this pausing is where we should be all day long. I started calling the space between my thought and my response to that thought, my "God space." So many thoughts come at us all day long that can really throw us off our grove. Thoughts like, *You should be offended what they just said to you. You should worry about this problem. You should do this crazy thing!* can waste our time and keep us focused on the wrong things.

Our emotions such as anger, sadness, fear, worry, hurts, jealousy and disappointments will hold us back and hold us down, not to mention other distractions, when we let them control us. The trick is to catch ourselves, go to our "God space" and seek His input before responding to them. Like I had a talk with Him about some sadness I was feeling, and it was because I was focusing too much on other people and what they were doing, instead of keeping my focus on God and what He would have me to be doing – *like finishing this book! LOL!* Everything is between God and us, not between us and anyone else. I'm following Oprah Winfrey's secret to her successful brand: "My choice to in every way, in every example, in every experience to do the right thing and the excellent thing..." I do my best, and God astonishingly takes care of the rest. This is the way to the sweetest life "where you know that even when the storms come, which they will, you can stand strong knowing this too, shall pass" because I KNOW I roll with God. *Grace and Peace.*

Dear God, pardon us for the times we may not get it right and give us the grace to do the same for others, as we keep striving to be the people You would have us to be. Amen.

KEEP CALM—YOU'RE ROLLING WITH GOD

Day 310 — Live in God, Live in Love

THE BEST MARRIAGE ADVICE EVER PART 2

It seems I have a new job lately: *marriage counselor!*

Here's some more advice for one of our most challenging yet most rewarding relationship. I'm telling you guys my secrets here, so please don't tell my hubby!

- Patience and prayer - In areas that I'm not 100% happy with in my marriage, I practice patience, and I pray asking God for help. Sometimes, believe it or not, *it's me who God has to change,* not my hubby. God gives me the wisdom to look at things from another perspective. Other times it's my hubby, but I don't nag him about it. I worry about nothing and pray about everything. *Patience and prayer!*

- *"You're right, Hon!"* I choose my battles and instead of arguing, I just say, "You're right, Hon!" He knows me so well by now, and he knows this is just my cue that I don't want to argue about something. On important issues to me, I stand my ground, though, but on other issues, "You're right, Hon!" and my life is at peace.

- *Find the right time to talk.* On issues that are important to me, I've learned to find a good time to discuss them. When both of us are upset is not the right time. I wait until he's in the best mood and guess when that is? Then I discuss whatever is on my mind.

- *How may I serve?* I look at my job as a wife to be my husband's helper, and I look for ways to make his life easier in any way I can. This allows him to do his job of providing for us even better. As I've stated before, we have no obligation to each other, but an opportunity to live our best lives together and I believe we're doing that. I try to be the best wife and when he sees me trying to be the best wife it inspires him to be the best husband. I also believe God sees our hearts and it's as if He's joined us to help us accomplish our goals and dreams.

- *I plan for the best marriage.* I tell my hubby whatever we have to go through, we'll go through it together. There's no talk of leaving each other, not even as a joke. I don't worry about the future or let people put ideas in my head of worst-case scenarios that has happened to other couples. I believe in the best possible scenarios, and I trust God will always take care of me. Everything is between you and God, remember?!? I give my best, and I know God will always give me His best, including the best marriage.

Our God, bless our marriages and other significant relationship.
May they fulfill Your purpose. Amen.

KEEP CALM—YOU'RE ROLLING WITH GOD

Day 311 — Live in God, Live in Love

MY MIND IS PLAYING TRICKS ON ME

I laughed at myself thinking of the worst-case scenarios of a situation I'm currently dealing with.

Then I thought, Nik, you're the one telling everyone every day to trust in God, and now you're here all worried? *What's up with that? Has God ever let you down?* And I reminded myself of all the times God has shown up for me. Then the perfect message showed up in my Facebook feed: "God has you in the palm of his hand. He has never failed before, and the good news is, He is not about to start now."

It's crazy how we allow the smallest little things to turn into the biggest problems ever in our minds. I believe God allows me to go through these dramas so that I can learn from them and teach you that there is a better way of living. We can have peace, joy and happiness despite our problems.

One of the best ways is simply by not worrying about tomorrow. Matthew 6:34 says, "Give your entire attention to what God is doing right now, and don't get worked up about what may or may not happen tomorrow. God will help you deal with whatever hard things come up when the time comes." My meditation book puts it this way, "It is vain and useless to feel either grief or joy for future things which perhaps will never take place."

I'm having the hardest time practicing meditation, trying to train my mind to stay in the present moment, not thinking about what's going to happen in the future. It's hard as heck, but that's where we all need to be more often, in the present moment where we've left the past in the past, we're not worried about the future, but we're having our constant conversations with God, *What do WE do here?* And allowing Him to direct our lives, one step at a time. Not the next ten steps, only the next one!

Dear God, keep our minds stayed on You and Your promises: "If God is for us, who can be against us? (Romans 8:31)."

KEEP CALM—YOU'RE ROLLING WITH GOD

THANKS, JOSHIE, FOR HELPING WITH THAT GOD WINK

Joshie, my son, recently dropped my phone and the screen got damaged.

I replaced the phone, but his dad insisted that I not let him play with the new one. When he asked for it, I explained, "Daddy, not me, said you couldn't use it anymore." We were in the U.S., and my hubby was in Nigeria and can you believe what this then four-year-old said, refusing to hear no: "LET ME TALK TO DADDY!"

I got his father on the phone, and he says to him, "Daddy, I'm sorry I dropped the phone, I won't do it again. Can I please play with mommy's phone?" And of course, he said yes! "He's so persistent!" I said to my friend one day, and she responded, "He takes after his momma." I'll admit it, I can be annoyingly persistent at times. So, when he asked me to go to sleep with him last night, he did not hear that I wanted to work on my book seriously. One of the last posts I had saved to be included in the book before he harassed me to go to bed with him, was the following: "Trust in the Lord with all your heart; and lean not to your own understanding. In all your ways acknowledge him, and he shall direct your paths" (Proverbs 3:5-6, NIV).

I had just read that these are the favorite bible verses of Trayvon Martin's mother, Sybrina Fulton, and they also pretty much sum up what I write about every day in these posts.

Saving the file, and putting my computer to sleep, I grabbed my phone to read my meditation book, thinking I neglected God that day by being so focused on getting the book done. I opened Jesus Calling and continued from where I had last left off and the Bible verse quoted for that very day was unbelievably: "Trust in the Lord with all your heart and lean not on your own understanding (Proverbs 3:5 NIV)." Another God wink when out of the blue, everything lines up a little bit too perfectly that I know it's God reminding me that His invisible Presence is always with me and is taking care of me.

Our Father, thank You for being a part of our lives. May we surrender every aspect of our lives over to You knowing that you have good things in store for those who love You. Amen.

KEEP CALM—YOU'RE ROLLING WITH GOD

Day 313 — Live in God, Live in Love

THE GOD WINKS CONTINUED

My God winks are when out of the blue, everything lines up a little bit too perfectly. They're special to me because they remind me that God's deeply involved in all my life's moments, more than I can possibly imagine. He's always with us and closer than every breath. *How sweet is that?* We're never alone. *Relax*, we roll with the Creator and Controller of the entire universe!

One Saturday, I called my friend, Sal, in South Africa to harass her over a book chapter I wrote to be included in another compilation. I had sent a draft to the person putting all the sections together but wanted my friend to read it and give me her feedback before I finalized it. I called Sal, my poster lady of my blog posts because she has stuck with me from the very first one over five years ago, and I cherish our conversations, if they're making any positive difference. *Does she get the message?*

One Saturday, she totally gave me goosebumps when I heard her say, "Nikki, I've stopped getting so emotional when the storms come. I've learned to calm down and have a conversation with God, *God, what do we do here?*" Coming from Sal, this was like a miracle because I would call her sometimes from wherever I happen to be in the world and say to her, "Sal, calm down. What are you doing?"

Hours after that conversation with her, trying to make up for all my appointments that I had missed with God for that day, I continued reading the chapter I wrote in that book over a year ago. These were my words in writing about a big problem I had to resolve:

"I dealt with everything as it came up one step at a time, trusting and having faith that everything would be okay and that God would perfectly direct me as to what decisions to make. I continued to enjoy life, not sitting around upset and worried the way I was on that day. Okay, God. We're here, what's the next step? is what I continually asked, and I trusted my feelings to guide me. So far they haven't let me down yet!"

And out of the blue, everything lined up perfectly. It sounds like Sal is getting the message! No meditation book that day, but using my words written over a year ago, God found a way to remind me how deeply involved He's in all my moments.

Our God, may we trust that You are always at work in our lives and Your plans for us are real good. Amen.

KEEP CALM—YOU'RE ROLLING WITH GOD

Day 314 — Live in God, Live in Love

"THANK ME (GOD) FOR YOUR NEEDINESS..."

"... Which is building trust-bonds between us. If you look back on your journey thus far, you can see that days of extreme weakness have been some of your most precious times. Memories of these days are richly interwoven with strands of My intimate Presence." - Jesus Calling

Case in point: Ms. Oversensitive got her feelings hurt again by some tough words from her hubby, but this time I didn't defend myself or argue with him about it, but I went to God for an appointment. After reading from my usual meditation book, I felt a little better. However, I stick with my appointments until I feel like I've touched base with God (my high five from Him). I then got a feeling to read some of my old posts and at about the third one, I remarkably read the following, quoted from another book, *The Imitation of Christ:*

"My child, stand firm and trust in me; for what are words but words: they fly through the air, but hurt not a stone. If you are guilty, think that you will willingly amend yourself. If your conscience does not accuse you, think that you will willingly suffer for God's sake.

It is a small matter that you sometimes bear with words, (did you get that? small matter!) if you are not as yet able to endure hard stripes. And why do such trifles go to your heart, but because you are yet carnal, and regard others more than you ought? But give ear to my word, and you should not value ten thousand words of others. Could they even so much as pluck one hair from you? If you trust in me and desire not to stand by your own judgment, you will be void of human fear."

The undaunted Nik was back rolling with God! My weakness at that moment was an opportunity to grow strong in Him. I'm still in awe of how deeply He's involved in our lives. Some harsh words from hubby was a chance to seek God's face and ask for His advice on what He would have me to do. I left that appointment happy and laughing a little at myself, like, Nik, what's the big deal if you hear some harsh words sometimes from the hubby/boss? By that evening he was telling our daughter, Julie, what a beautiful wife he has. LOL!

Our God, control our emotions so that we can always react from a calm, wise space no matter the challenges we face. Amen.

KEEP CALM—YOU'RE ROLLING WITH GOD

"NIKKI, I'M HONESTLY GOING WITH GOD...

...when I feel myself getting anxious or feeling unsure about the situation; I just say God, I'm rolling with you!"

I love this message from a Facebook friend. That's where I want all of us - *me included!* I've realized that God puts us through stuff to develop our trust muscles in Him. *God, I'm so on to You!* The more stuff I go through, the more I'm learning to trust Him and go to Him with everything.

Like today, I had a little of an anxiety moment that I stopped in the middle of my exercising to go and sit and have a conversation with God, after receiving a not too pleasant telephone call. I felt so much better after that talk with Him, reminding myself of how great God is to me and the times He has shown up for me in the past.

A few minutes later my assistant called saying a customer wanted to speak with me. This client was already approved for a loan, and he says to me, "I want to spend this money with you." That from him made me realize how God has always been there for me and I have to lighten up over the little stuff that I allow to upset me. It was as if God was saying to me, *Nik, have I ever let you down?* The trust muscles are building! Ain't worried about nothing!

"I will fear no evil, for my God is with me and if my God is with me, whom then shall I fear? Whom then shall I fear?"

Our Father, we welcome You into every aspect of our lives. May every moment bring us closer to You. Amen.

KEEP CALM—YOU'RE ROLLING WITH GOD

Day 316 — Live in God, Live in Love

"DOES JOSHIE HAVE ON HIS SHOES?"

Is what I screamed down at everyone, as we all rushed to get out in time for school.

Arriving there, I had planned to stay for the weekly school's assembly but realized my then three years old and Mr. Independent, had put on one of his sister's sock instead of his. "What do we do now?" I asked him because I couldn't take him inside with different socks on! Then I remembered that last week, as we were rushing out again, and I took him a pair of socks, but because he already had some on, I placed the ones I had in my purse! And voila, just when I need them, super mommy pulled out of her purse a matching pair of socks!

What is it about everything I need magically appearing for me? I wrote about Ms. Ashley who for three years faithfully picked up my daughters from school. God sent the perfect lady with even a brand new car. She was so grateful for the car that she told God that whoever needed a ride, He should let her know. Trying to pick them up myself was extremely stressful. I was not this God Maniac at the time, but in looking back, I see His hands in us finding Ms. Ashley. She was such a nice, Christian young lady and I know the three years the girls spent with her as helped shaped their character.

On the ride to school I asked everyone what they're grateful for and Ember, my then eleven-year-old daughter, replied in the sincerest voice, "Mommy, I'm thankful for everything." He's even sent me the best kids. I feel so close to God, and I want us all closer and closer to Him.

"It's about a relationship with God," and I believe the way there is through being our most loving selves: "I certainly don't pretend to consistently achieve a loving perspective of every situation in my life. One thing I'm very clear about, however, is that when I do, life works beautifully. And when I don't things stay stuck." - Marianne Williamson, *A Return to Love*

Dear God, may we be more loving today, reflecting Your love everywhere we go. Amen.

KEEP CALM—YOU'RE ROLLING WITH GOD

Day 317 — Live in God, Live in Love

"I AM NOT FORGOTTEN. GOD KNOWS MY NAME"

That was me singing on the way to my kids' Nigerian Independence Day celebration at school.

We each can sing this song with such confidence, the Creator of the universe knows our name. "You are loved to the max right this second. There is not one thing you can do to make God love you less and not one more thing you can do to make God love you more. That's the essence of grace, amazing grace. You're supposed to dance this unconditional love." - Rev. Ed Bacon

And I'm feeling extra loved by God. A few days ago, I wrote about missing my God winks, when out of the blue everything lines up a little bit too perfectly that I know it has to be God reminding me that His invisible Presence is always with me. You may call them coincidences, but they're my *love notes* from God. Here's how this God orchestrated event went:

Like really, really, really pushing myself to complete my book (hubby was wrong, I can work hard... sometimes) to send to my publisher. I debated about including a post that began, *"MY MIND IS PLAYING TRICKS ON ME,"* a popular rap song by the Geto Boys in the early 1990s. Talking to God about it, I got the feeling to include it for all my fellow rap fans out there. About 45 minutes later and having finished up all my selections, I decided to send a message to a friend saying, "No news is good news?" since we hadn't spoken in a while. I'm all the way in Nigeria, and she's in the Bahamas, and I was completely stunned when I read her response:

"No news is definitely good news. The only thing that's interfering at times is *my mind is playing tricks on me. LOL."* Wink! Wink!

Isn't God funny? I'm not forgotten, baby, God knows my name!

O Lord, thank You for all Your love notes, big and small, that remind us that Your Presence is always with us. Amen.

KEEP CALM—YOU'RE ROLLING WITH GOD

Day 318 — Live in God, Live in Love

"IN ANY MOMENT WE CAN DECIDE WHO WE WANT TO BE"

That was my message to an *Eat to Live* group I started on WhatsApp.

We've challenged ourselves to six weeks of eating healthy and exercising, and in any moment we get to decide to be focused, disciplined, under control, wise and determined individuals or we could go the other way

Early this morning, I had some important choices to make: *Do I become the old insecure, emotional, fretful, and paranoid Nikki, or should I be my fearless, strong, trusting in God self?* I'm happy to report I stayed on the high road with God.

Someone called asking me to pray for them, as they're about to deliver their baby and I told them they can choose, too, who they want to be, fearful or strong and courageous, trusting God from moment to moment. I encouraged them to imagine God holding their hand and praying, *God, I trust You,* holding His hands tight.

I told you the story of making the decision not to play the weak woman role and instead be a positive example for my daughters to follow. And the latest lesson I'm teaching them is discipline. "You don't go too far without it!" I now call them my super daughters and I was so proud when they voluntarily turned over their gadgets to me so that they can focus on some upcoming tests at school. I came home from work and met them testing each other at our dining room table and I woke up and met them up early again there studying. *Go, super daughters!*

In any moment, we get to decide who we want to be and I say let's choose to be our best selves knowing God is with us each step of the way. I'm on to God in that sometimes He takes us on some treacherous paths, but once we KNOW that we're never alone and that's He's with us every step of the way, we can relax, and happy enjoying every minute of our adventure with Him. I've given Him the lead role of my life, and I don't make a move until I ask Him about it first. He gave me the perfect advice when I was tempted to go down a bad path, *Nik, you can do better than that!*

Our God, strengthen us in our trials that we may become the people You have created us to be. Amen.

KEEP CALM—YOU'RE ROLLING WITH GOD

Live in God, Live in Love

"WE'RE NOT GOING BY THE ORDINARY RULES OF MAN"

I said to a new sales staff I spent the day training.

"We do our best and God will do the rest." I went as far as having her read Pastor Joel Osteen's devotional for the day, which confirmed what I was trying to teach her:

"'Not by might nor by power, but by my Spirit,' says the LORD Almighty." (Zechariah 4:6, NIV)

By His Spirit

In this day and age, we are equipped with so many wonderful resources in the natural: technology, education, abilities. It's easy to rely on our own natural strength for so many things.

We have to remember that this natural world is only temporary, but the spiritual realm is eternal. We aren't limited to the earth's resources; we have unlimited spiritual resources by the Spirit of God. There are some things in life that can't happen by human thinking and reasoning. There are things that won't be solved by natural power and might. But God is not limited by the resources of this world. When you open the door of faith in your heart, God will move through you in powerful ways by His Spirit."

And to illustrate this quite clearly to us, God had a customer to come and purchase a car from us that day. He kept saying to us, "This feels good. This feels good." Apparently, they went to many other dealerships, but he said he felt good buying from us. I insisted on them test driving the van before buying it and they refused saying that the test drive was not necessary. Like who buys a car without testing it first? But then again, we're not going by the ordinary rules of man!

We sell vehicles in an area surrounded by other dealerships, not to mention all the ones he passed close to his home, yet he supported us because he felt good about it. Do your part by working hard and giving your best and leave the rest with God. He's behind the scenes of our lives as our business Partner, Helper, Friend, Counselor, Strategist, and Father. We're not going by the ordinary rules because God is with us every step of the way, directing us on the best paths.

Dear God, grant us faith to rely on you in all our endeavors, remembering that we are not going by the ordinary rules of man. Amen.

KEEP CALM—YOU'RE ROLLING WITH GOD

Day 320 — Live in God, Live in Love

"DON'T FLINCH!"

I'm stealing this line from Pastor Joel Osteen.

I love him, and I highly recommend his church sermons' podcasts on iTunes.com and all of his books. But, not flinching, no matter what comes at us is where we should be, especially in regards to what people say. Just today so many things came up, and I reminded myself, "Don't flinch!" For example, someone called me screaming and amazingly I only listened to them thinking, Somebody's having a bad moment! And I moved on without letting it upset me one bit – unflinching, baby!

It's unbelievable how much time we waste getting upset and offended over what people say to us or about us. I'm much improved in this area, and it's like I'm happy running my own race and doing my own thing regardless of what anyone says or thinks. And if they do have something to say, it's just their opinion. It's up to me to take what they say and use it to my benefit. If there's something I can take from it to improve, I can run with it, or I can simply professionally ignore it, kindly and respectfully, of course! The world is filled with insensitive people and that's not going to change; we're the ones who must become unflinching and not allow them to steal our joy. Life's way too short! I don't want to spend more than five minutes upset with anyone over mere words. That's time I could be using to enjoy life instead.

And while we're practicing being unflinching, let's also practice this when any adversity, problem or challenge comes our way, as well, remaining calm and looking to God for direction, trusting that whatever He wants for us is always best for us. We hear Him much better when we're relaxed, calm and collected. *Don't flinch!*

Our Father, may our happiness not depend on the opinions and judgements of others. Amen.

KEEP CALM—YOU'RE ROLLING WITH GOD

Day 321 — Live in God, Live in Love

"HE USED YOUR DRAMA TO HELP ALL OF US!"

Was me to my friend, Danny, after I shared how God is teaching her all about messy love. I got a comment from someone on Facebook, which also totally summed up how I felt as well after I read the post I wrote about her: "Wow! I love this piece. I'm even experiencing this great joy inside me."

Honestly, I had the happiest day I've had in a long time after finally getting the lesson that God wants us to love others the way He loves us. None of us are perfect! We all have our areas we need to improve in, but we expect others to be all perfect and to fit into the boxes we've designed for them, doing what we want and expect of them. But the deal is that we all make mistakes. We all fall, and we all have our faults and weaknesses, but none of that matters to God. A big lesson I'm learning is to extend lots of grace to others (pardoning them without punishment) the same way God continually extends it to me when I mess up. Before we were even born God knows everything about us and He approves of us. We can each say with absolute confidence, "I'm the apple of God's eyes!"

We are all children of the Most High God, and nothing we can do can ever change that. Yes, we still have our issues, but God has taken each one of us as His personal project to shape us and mold us into the superhumans He's created us to be.

And just how God loves and accepts us unconditionally, let's accept and love others the same way. We're all growing and maturing on our paths with God. He looks at our hearts, and he's not writing down every time we do something wrong, and we should be the same with others. I told my husband today that because he's such a great man, he motivates me to want to be a better wife. I'm focused on the 10,000 things he does right, and I'm proud of him. I'm not so focused on when he messes up because I know his heart is in the right place – to be the best father and husband.

It may have taken a while, but I'm getting the lesson to be a gentler version of myself, giving people the space to make mistakes and to never stop improving with God helping and supporting us all the way. *Heads held high, fellow superhumans!*

Dear God, bring forth the fruits of Your spirit within us: "love, joy, peace, patience, kindness, goodness, faithfulness, gentleness, and self-control." Amen.

KEEP CALM—YOU'RE ROLLING WITH GOD

GOD SINGS A LOVE SONG TO ME

So, I'm driving to work, singing my heart out to God, playing one of my favorite songs, *I Wanna Know* by Joe:

> "I'd like to know what makes You cry
> So I can be the one who always makes You smile
> Anyway that I can please You let me learn So I wanna know
> Tell me what I gotta do to please You Anything You say I'll do
> Cause I only wanna make You happy From the bottom of my heart, it's true"
> At a certain point I felt God was singing back to me:
> "I'll take good care of you lady, have no fear, oh"

I smiled and said to Him, *I believe You!* And we had a beautiful time singing to each other, as I had the best drive ever to work. I know at this point you're probably saying, "Nikki has really lost her mind this time!" But as soon as I got to my office, I decided to have an appointment with God and of all my meditation books I have on my phone to read, I opened to the most unbelievable message that indeed confirmed that He was singing to me:

"God's greatness lives within me, creating ever more-expansive patterns of life and love. It sings to me, and I sing back, a continuous song, from my heart to the universe and the universe back to me." - A Year of Miracles by Marianne Williamson

The fantastic news here is that He's not only singing to me, it's a continuous song to you, as well. My hope is that these blog posts will open your mind and heart to listen to the love song He's singing to each one of us as if He's always singing...

"I'll take good care of you, have no fear, oh" As we sing back to Him:

"Anyway that I can please You, let me learn"

> *Our Father, may we all hear the love song You are continuously singing to us. Amen.*

Sign up to receive my **FREE** daily devotional email:
http://werollwithgod.com/sign-up/

KEEP CALM—YOU'RE ROLLING WITH GOD

Day 323 — Live in God, Live in Love

MAKE GOD YOUR PRIORITY

I had spoken earlier with my friend, Danny, about a 17-year-old young man who delivered an impressive sermon at her church entitled, *Make God Your Priority.* He was talking about how we keep God in the background of our lives when He should instead be our number one focus.

"Are we having champagne with our dinner tonight?" I had asked my hubby right before he left work. He said yes, and I was expecting us to have a special evening together. But, boy oh boy, was I wrong! Instead, he was terribly upset at me about a decision I made. He blasted me completely over it! After 14 years together I'm used to it, though, especially when I can completely justify my decisions as always being what I feel is best for my entire family at any given moment – including sometimes being a professional ignorer – kindly and respectfully. *He was not hearing that!*

Even though I tried to lighten the mood, he was still upset that I decided just to give him his space to cool off and it also gave me an opportunity to work on my book again. There were so many old posts about what a wonderful husband he is and that I'm not to look to human relationships for perfection that I decided to go to bed and snuggle next to him because he truly has earned my love and respect.

Early the next morning, I decided to read from exactly where I left off from the night before in my book, and it unbelievably ended with this prayer:

"Dear God, thank You for Your love. Help us to make You our first love and priority. Amen." In the entire book of 143,643 words, I only used the word "priority" 2 times and once again, out of the blue, everything lined up a little bit too perfectly that I KNOW it was God reminding me that His invisible Presence is a constant in my life. *Wink, wink!*

When we make God our priority, we can trust that His spirit will always guide us to make the best decisions. Nik, forgive your hubby, maybe he had a rough day. I'm back to calling him my pain-in-the-*** husband, and I'm his pain-in-the-*** wife.

Our Father, we dedicate our lives to You. Use us for Your purpose in the world. Amen.

KEEP CALM—YOU'RE ROLLING WITH GOD

Day 324 — Live in God, Live in Love

THREE WORDS FOR WHATEVER YOU'RE FACING: GREATER IS HE

This was the striking message I got from Tumblr.com, where I go to hear from God.

God is greater than anything we may ever face! This morning, I woke up thinking about someone I know God arranged to help my hubby and me with a challenge we faced. In a business dinner conversation, someone casually mentioned that we should do a Google search to find someone who could help us in a very particular area. I did this the next day and the first person I contacted agreed to meet us in his office for a free consultation. He ended up spending three hours with us for free, and that time with him helped to answer so many questions I had in regards to this problem.

In the meeting, he sensed I was a bit anxious, and I'll never forget the words he said: "Fear no one!" As soon as he said that, I calmed down, as though I heard directly from God.

"I have told you these things, so that in Me (God) you may have [perfect] peace and confidence. In the world you have tribulation and trials and distress and frustration; but be of good cheer [take courage; be confident, certain, undaunted]! For I have overcome the world. [I have deprived it of power to harm you and have conquered it for you]" (John 16:33, AMP).

Maybe a week after meeting with him, I needed to ask him another question. Shortly after sending him an email on a Saturday, he gave me his cell number to call him. He again blew me away when he said that at a certain point when we've done all that we can do, we have to turn things over to God. I did exactly that, and I remember saying to Him, *I'm turning this matter over to You.* Everything ended up working out beautifully.

I'll never forget that Christmas. Our family begged my hubby for us to travel, but he kept saying no. At the very last minute he agreed, and while vacationing, we met this gentleman and finally resolved the issues that were pending for months. *Greater is He. FEAR NO ONE.*

Dear God, thank You for working everything out for our good. Give us the faith to face our challenges confidently, trusting You infinity percent. Amen.

KEEP CALM—YOU'RE ROLLING WITH GOD

Day 325 — Live in God, Live in Love

"NIKKI, YOU MAKE IT SOUND SO EASY"

It was a message from a sweet friend one day.

I took her on a quick run with me to my home for food, but I savored every moment of our conversation about God. She wants this closeness with God that I write about. Here are my top two pieces of advice for accomplishing a closer walk with God:

- In as many decisions as you make every day, go to God for direction by listening to Him through your spirit. This will take you slowing down, calming down, and paying attention. Deciding to go home that day was a conversation with God. *Do I go?* I asked Him, and I got the feeling of peace that it was okay. I told my hubby recently, "Arguing with you was so last year!" This year, I plan to go to God instead and have Him direct me as with His insights and wisdom the best way to resolve conflicts.

- Have standing appointments, quiet times, with only you and God. For me, it's reading from one of my meditation books, and sometimes reading a little bit is enough to get my mind focused back on God again, like this short message one day: "Who is in charge of your life? If it is you, then you have a good reason to worry. But since I (God) am in charge, worry is unnecessary and counterproductive. When you start to feel anxious about something, relinquish the situation to Me. Back off a bit, redirecting your focus to Me. I will either take care of the problem Myself or show you how to handle it. In this world you will have problems, but you need not lose sight of Me." – *Jesus Calling* by Sarah Young

In fact, reading or listening to anything spiritual or uplifting is great in these appointments. If you pay close attention, He'll even direct you on exactly what to read or listen to. Let's live the sweetest life with God's constant direction."When I consider your heavens, the work of your fingers, the moon and the stars, which you have set in place, what is mankind that you are mindful of them, human beings that you care for them?" (Psalm 8:3-4)

Dear God, may we never stop seeking You and listening to Your direction for our lives. Amen.

KEEP CALM—YOU'RE ROLLING WITH GOD

Day 326 — Live in God, Live in Love

"GOD WILL USE YOUR ENEMIES TO BLESS YOU"

I said this phrase to a God connect, Danny. I'm amazed how God brought her into my life to help her deal with someone who showed up unexpectedly at her house one morning, and her life has since dramatically changed. "Your so-called enemy now, but one day, you'll want to kiss her," I said. In one of our previous conversations, she made me extremely happy when she said that if this situation brings her closer to God, she's okay with it, despite a big headache it has been. .

In one of my always-sacred conversations with Danny, I told her how this "enemy" had already become such a blessing to me. To encourage her to get closer to God, I agreed to read together with her Rick Warren's book, *The Purpose Driven Life*. It was in an appointment with God while reading this book (which I forgot I had downloaded over a year before this) where I was reminded by Him of the verse that has since changed my life:

"Let us strip off anything that slows us down or holds us back." – Hebrews 12:1 LB

I knew right away God was talking about my Facebook addiction with my constant check-ins. Talking to my hubby again, I told him how great I felt as if I'd been given a new life where I was enjoying every moment on a whole different level. So, her "enemy" had her reach out to me, and in trying to encourage her, I helped myself to a new life. I could kiss this person! I already see the difference in her, too, and I motivated her to let this situation push her to a new level of living where she's her best self for God.

Here's the deal: I shared with her the message from my last appointment with God from *A Year of Miracles*, which encouraged me so much:

"Today I remember that there is only one work: to be who I am capable of being, to do what I am capable of doing to make the world a better place. May my life be of use to something greater than myself, that I may feel the joy of being used."

Super wife, mom, and person are back, baby, all for the glory of God!

Dear God, mold us to be the people You would have us to be and help us strip away anything that is displeasing to You or holding us back. Amen.

KEEP CALM—YOU'RE ROLLING WITH GOD

Live in God, Live in Love

GOD, I HAVEN'T HEARD FROM YOU LATELY

I thought right before going to sleep.

I complained I wasn't getting my God winks as often as I would like and I was missing Him. The next morning, I asked again, *What should I read to hear from You?* I tried downloading a book, but the website refused to open. A few minutes later, unbelievably, I received a text message on my cell phone:

"My silence for a long time does not mean that I have forgotten you. My being hushed is a simple symbol, a promise that even if I am being quiet, I am here for you."

That got the God Maniac crying and extremely happy again. It reminds me of a post I saw on Tumblr.com: "One evening, I was pouring my heart out to the Lord saying, 'Lord, I'm so tired already.' The very next morning, I saw a girl wearing a shirt that said, 'Come to Me, I will give you rest.' God talks to us in every way possible. We just have to stop and listen."

Are you hearing from Him? Having a close relationship with God is the best! In working on my book again, I received the perfect message from a podcast. I doubt myself and wonder who would want to buy my book because I'm not a great writer. Then Elizabeth Gilbert spoke as if she was speaking directly to me, saying (and I paraphrase here) that it's about being authentic and touching hearts. We're not to worry about the numbers and who to market the book to; it's only about following your curiosity and seeing where it leads. Now with each post that's to be included, I ask, "Will this touch someone's heart, inspire, and encourage them to live their best life close to God?"

God has filled my life with such wisdom, happiness, love, peace, joy, gratitude, and contentment. The hurts and disappointments will still be there, but we can shake them off and hand them over to God, who *knows* how to use them for our good. And about the trials, problems, and frustrations that regularly show up? We can truly *refuse to worry,* knowing we have the best Back Up as our Helper and Partner – God. *What can mere mortals do to us?*

Our Father, may we always see our lives from Your supernatural, anything is possible, perspective. Amen.

KEEP CALM—YOU'RE ROLLING WITH GOD

Day 328 — Live in God, Live in Love

"GOD IS DOING TWO TRILLION THINGS FOR US"

That's according to my five-year-old sage, Joshie. He made my night with his God wink. He was looking in the mirror and came to me afterwards asking, "Mommy, why is my nose red?" I said, "It's because of you have a cold, but it'll get better." Five minutes later, he decided to play some music on his iPad, and the words of the first song randomly played were, "Like a red nose," and he exclaimed, "Mommy, that's a God wink!" I'm thrilled my son has his own personal God winks and reminders that His invisible Presence is a constant in our lives.

Here's the deal: this God who is doing two trillion things for us is always calling for us to be our highest and best selves in every moment. *Never stop improving!* Like my sister loves to say, "When you know better, you do better." I love how God is teaching me to be the best person. Regardless of what anyone does or doesn't do, my call from Him is to show up as the best me possible. I'm challenged to be my most loving, forgiving, kindest, wisest, calmest, and strongest self, always seeing the best in everyone *(even when I want to strangle them!).*

And that means we have to always catch ourselves, calm down, and continually seek God's wisdom. *God, what would You have me to do here?* Once we have His direction and what we believe He would have us to do, we can then confidently move forward with His strength backing us up to be the best people we can be for Him in the world. In doing this, we set a positive example for others to follow.

Dear God, pardon our sins. Grant us Your wisdom, insights, guidance, and strength as we seek to be the people you would have us to be. Amen.

KEEP CALM—YOU'RE ROLLING WITH GOD

Day 329 — Live in God, Live in Love

A PEP TALK FROM GOD

I'll never get over how intimately God is involved in our lives. One Saturday, I was nervous—really nervous—about speaking at my children's school that upcoming Monday, but God, knowing every thought we think, had the perfect encouragement in my 5 p.m. appointment with Him. I found a quiet spot, and the very book and page I opened to on my phone was astonishingly the story of Oprah Winfrey's first celebrity interviews. It so happened that she was given five minutes for each interview and I was given five minutes for my speech, so I totally took that as a God wink, no coincidence. In her book, *What I Know For Sure,* here's how Oprah described that day:

"There were throngs of local newscasters, entertainment/lifestyle reporters, each given five minutes to interview an actor from the season's upcoming lineup. I started to feel nervous. Uncomfortable. Inept. *[Me that Saturday reading this!]* Not good enough to be there with all these other reporters from much bigger cities with more experience than I.

For some reason—you might call it a coincidence; I call it grace in action—I was switched from the Priscilla Presley line to interview a young comedian who was starting a new show called *Mork & Mindy*. What followed were five of the most exhilarating, wild, off-the-charts minutes I'd ever spent in an interview, with the most uninhibited, out-of-the-box, free-falling-in-every-second celebrity/human I'd ever met. He wasn't afraid to be his many selves. I had a great fun playing with Robin Williams, and I learned in that instant to go where the interview takes you. He was all over the place, and I had to flow with it.

So when my turn came to talk to Miss Priscilla, I had received the lesson: You can't accomplish anything worthwhile if you inhibit yourself. If life teaches you nothing else, know this: When you get the chance, go for it."

Moral: Sometimes you have to leave your comfort zone and "go for it" like Ms. Winfrey said, knowing God is with you every step of the way. I did and had a great time speaking. They even invited me back again!

Heavenly Father, thank You for these growth opportunities, where we must leave our shells and try new experiences (like publishing this book!). Amen.

KEEP CALM—YOU'RE ROLLING WITH GOD

Day 330 — Live in God, Live in Love

BACK TO THE HARSH WORDS FROM HUBBY

"Have I not commanded you? Be strong and courageous" (Joshua 1:9, NIV).

This was exactly the tough talk I needed from God when this verse came clearly to mind after I thought about how silly I was allowing the words of my husband to upset me. I felt so ashamed that I was the one to apologize to him for becoming so emotional and carried away. As usual, there are many lessons I'm taking away from this experience.

I learned that I need to be more aware of my husband's moods because sometimes he may vent at me, but it's because he has a lot that's on his plate that may be disturbing him. And like God perfectly reminded me in this verse, *I'm to be strong and courageous.* I want to be an even better and more supportive wife by helping him more in whichever way I can to ease some tension from him. Also, I have to lighten up and not take everything he says to heart, forgiving quickly and allowing him to have his moments because he's only human. He's such a great husband and dad.

As far as these words from him, I must remember that someone's opinion of me at any given moment doesn't make me anymore or any less of a person. I'm to keep my focus on God and His unconditional love and acceptance of me always, no matter what.

I'm also looking at what was said and seeing if there's anything I can take from it to improve myself. And there was a lot. I'm working on being more focused and procrastinating less, so I've set up alarm reminders on my phone to help me stay more organized and on top of things. *Constant and never-ending improvement!*

Life will throw at us all sorts of stuff, but we have to keep this commandment in the forefront of our minds: "BE STRONG AND COURAGEOUS. Do not be terrified; do not be discouraged, the Lord your God will be with you wherever you go" (Joshua 1:6-9, NIV).

Dear God, toughen our skin! Help us not to be easily shaken by the opinions and judgements of others, no matter the words or challenges that are thrown our way. Amen.

KEEP CALM—YOU'RE ROLLING WITH GOD

Day 331 — Live in God, Live in Love

"NIKKI, NIKKI, HONEY"

That was my daughter, Ember, being funny.

She was imitating a little boy we watched in a video on a friend's phone, referring to his mom as "Linda, Linda, honey," when he wanted more cupcakes. We had such a great time hanging with this friend and her daughters, and they are a big part of the reason why I love my life in Nigeria. *God has surrounded us with the best peeps!*

I also got to speak to my fabulous friend, Marcela, who I couldn't stop thanking for all the help and support she's given me. She's a big reader of these posts, and I asked her if she's feeling the way I've been feeling lately, absolutely in love with everything and everyone on an entirely different level. She was feeling the same way. In fact, I love our conversations because she's like a guinea pig of how these posts are doing.

I shared how I told my hubby that it feels like I'm falling in love with him all over again. The funny thing is he hasn't changed one bit, but I've changed. I've learned to overlook 10,000 of his faults because God overlooks 20,000 of mine. I forgive quickly, and I love extravagantly, focusing on what I love about him, not the things that used to drive me crazy. His tongue is still like a razor, but my skin is becoming tougher and instead of getting upset, I look to see what I can take from whatever he says to improve myself and I run with it. I'm not waiting for his praise anymore, either; I'm quite happy doing my best in everything as a wife, mother and person because everything is between me and God, who never stops letting me know how loved I am by Him.

Moral: I'm having better relationships because my relationship with God is better. My appointments (alone times) with Him, for a few minutes a few times a day, have changed me dramatically. In each one, I get more of God's insight, wisdom, and perspective so that when I'm back into the world, I'm more at peace. I tend to be more calm, patient, loving, content, forgiving, and able to make much wiser decisions

I mostly read from one of my meditation books and lately I'm in love with, *A Year of Miracles* by Marianne Williamson. Since reading it, I'm experiencing tremendous miracles!

Dear God, thank You for Your love and for blessing us in so many ways, including all the special people You send into our lives. Amen.

KEEP CALM—YOU'RE ROLLING WITH GOD

A GOD WINK FROM PRESIDENT OBAMA

My God winks are when, out of the blue, everything lines up a little bit too perfect that I know it has to be God, reminding me that His invisible Presence is always with me.

You probably call them coincidences, but they're my God orchestrated events that show up all over the place. And one morning, it came through an interview of President Obama by Marc Maron in a podcast on iTunes.com.

That week, I totally got on my publisher's nerve, sending her emails in regards to the subtitle of this book. In thinking about it that morning, I started questioning the actual title, *We Roll With God*, debating whether or not to stick with the term *"Roll"* because it may be considered too slang and therefore people may not take the book seriously.

In listening to my usual podcasts, they didn't feel right, and I decided to look for something new to listen to. The first one that scrolled across the screen on iTunes.com was this interview of President Obama. It so happened that the day before, I had read an article on the internet about it, and I immediately downloaded it, taking it as my wink from God. So, there I was, questioning whether I should keep the name *We Roll With God* or not, and then listening to this podcast. As they wrapped up the interview, President Obama said these words as if he was speaking directly to me:

"I ROLLED with it." *Wink, wink!*

That was the confirmation from God I needed to advance confidently with my book title. If the President of the United States is using the term *"roll,"* it's good enough for my book.

Here's the deal: God's constantly speaking to us, guiding and directing us as to the right path to take, but we have to pay attention to all the cues and nudges from Him. Notice I wrote that listening to the other podcasts *didn't feel right.* All day long, I want us always asking ourselves, like Oprah Winfrey taught us, *Does this feel right?* And, making decisions based on what feels right because that's God's way of communicating to us.

Dear God, thank You for Your intimate involvement in our lives. Help us learn and pay attention to Your ever-present communications with us. Amen.

KEEP CALM—YOU'RE ROLLING WITH GOD

Day 333 — Live in God, Live in Love

MY APPOINTMENTS WITH GOD ARE THE BOMB

Here's how they went one day:

That morning, I decided to read from an old Oprah Winfrey magazine article, where she wrote: "Life is about recalibrating (adjusting). About continually asking yourself: what do I have to do to get where I need to be? How do I create the life I want? We have to make ourselves over daily, consistently, to keep moving forward. We are not meant to be stagnant."

And recalibrating/adjusting is what I've seemed to be doing lots of. Instead of feeling overwhelmed or frustrated by the changes going on around me, Oprah simply reminded me that this is what life is about and every day, I can bring all my valuable lessons from the past and make myself over daily to face whatever changes that may come my way. NEVER STOP IMPROVING!

The 12 p.m. appointment was reading three words from my meditation book: "Focus on Me." In other words, Nik: "Trust God from the bottom of your heart; don't try to figure out everything on your own. Listen for God's voice in everything you do, everywhere you go; He's the one who will keep you on track." *Woohoo...* I needed that one, too.

The 5 p.m. appointment found me in my car, having a quiet moment to myself after having to rush somewhere urgently. I opened my meditation book again on my phone to read: "You need Me in every moment. Your awareness of your constant need for Me is your greatest strength." This is so true.

I had run out of my office to make it where I needed to be at before 5 pm, when I hit a long line of traffic. I passed one exit, but asking God if I should turn off; I felt the answer was no. Got to another exit and this time, the feeling from God was to turn off. My GPS recalculated the route, and I made it on time. *God, I do need You every moment!*

Moral: make sure you're spending enough alone time with God every day. Sometimes I literally must run to Him when things come my way during the day.

Dear God, help us to keep our eyes focused on You in every moment, doing what You would have us to do, saying what You would have us to say and going where You would have us to go. Amen.

KEEP CALM—YOU'RE ROLLING WITH GOD

Day 334 — Live in God, Live in Love

NOT BITTER, BETTER

Early one Saturday morning, I spoke to a very special God connect, Danny. We both have no doubt that our getting to know and help each other was God working behind the scenes of our lives and on a Saturday, after our lengthy and deep talk, He reminded us that He's with us. A perfectly orchestrated God wink assured us both that's He's amid all our messiness, fighting on our behalf, and that we have to stay calm.

She said, "We're not getting bitter." And I responded, "We're not getting bitter, but better."

Right after speaking with her, I debated whether to work on the 15 pages of my book like I committed to with my publisher each day or go to work. The feeling I got from God was to work on the book first. I went to the file where I've been extracting the posts I would like to be included in the book to work on with the suggestions from the publisher, and of all the hundreds of posts I've written for years, I read the following words in one of them that got me all teary-eyed:

"Here's the deal: forget evil, it's all for our good. Let's continue to walk bravely with God knowing whatever He allows to happen to us is ultimately best for us. "God may kill me, but still I will trust Him" (Job 13:15, CEV). These events are all perfectly designed lessons to bring us out of our comfort zones and help us become our best selves—wiser, stronger, braver, more loving and closer to God. "Often it's said we can be bitter or we can be better." - Marianne Williamson, *A Year of Miracles*. The lessons seem never to end, but once we learn them, we see a whole new world opening before us. *God, I'm so on to You!*"

Out of the blue, and once again, everything lined up a little bit too perfectly! *Wink, wink!* God has brought me and my friend, Danny, out of our comfort zones. We've committed to improving our lives in every area, and we've challenged each other to be our highest and best selves for God.

I love this text message that came through on my phone: "Love just doesn't sit there, like a stone. It has to be made, like bread, and re-made all the time. Love is never static. It grows when we grow!"

Dear God, may our lives glorify You as You help us to love others the way You love us–unconditionally and with lots of patience. Amen.

KEEP CALM—YOU'RE ROLLING WITH GOD

Day 335 — Live in God, Live in Love

I DIDN'T KNOW WHAT TO DO

I was unsure in regards to a challenge that came my way. I'm usually so together, having constant conversations with God and making moment-by-moment decisions based on my feelings, cues, and nudges from Him. But in regards to this situation, He wasn't giving much help at all. I asked Him, paranoid, *What's going on here?*

At my 5 p.m. appointment with God that day, nearly about to give up, not knowing what to do, I opened one of my meditation books, *Jesus Calling* by Sarah Young. I read the astonishing message, as if God was speaking directly to me in that very moment:

"EXPECT TO ENCOUNTER ADVERSITY in your life... Anticipate coming face to face with impossibilities: situations totally beyond your ability to handle. This awareness of your inadequacy is not something you should try to evade. It is precisely where I want you— the best place to encounter Me in My Glory and Power. When you see armies of problems marching towards you, cry out to Me to fight for you. Watch Me working on your behalf, as you rest in the shadow of My Almighty Presence. 'He who dwells in the shelter of the Most High will rest in the shadow of the Almighty'– Psalm 91:1."

Could this be God telling me that my part was done and to leave the rest with Him?

I then went to my Tumblr.com where I go to hear from Him, and the perfect confirmation appeared in a post there: "He will cover you with His feathers. He will shelter you with His wings. His faithful promises are your armor and protection."— Psalms 91:4

If you notice, the Psalm scripture from Tumblr continued from the very Psalm quote I'd read in my meditation book. So, I went home and had the best sleep. The next day, it turned out that everything I had already prepared was enough, and by the time the expected big wave was to hit me, it was quite small. I know that it was only God doing His part to help me.

Here's the deal: "EXPECT TO ENCOUNTER ADVERSITY in your life," but know that our help comes from the Lord, the Maker of Heaven and Earth. *Simply do your best and leave the rest with Him.*

Dear God, thank You for being an ever-present help in our times of trouble. Fill us with courage and strength. Amen.
KEEP CALM—YOU'RE ROLLING WITH GOD

Day 336 — Live in God, Live in Love

"PAY ATTENTION"

The words got me excited, listening to Oprah Winfrey interview Paulo Coelho, the author of one of my favorite books, *The Alchemist*.

It was no coincidence that I found myself in Target looking to buy a charger for my phone, after the last one I had caught on fire, and I held this book in my hands, debating whether or not to buy it. Fast forward a couple of hours later, when I glimpsed a video of Oprah Winfrey on Facebook. I'm always eager to listen to whatever Ms. Winfrey has to say, and I immediately viewed it. Can you believe she was announcing that on her next show would be with the author of this very book? The one and only book that I happened to pick up and hold in my hand at Target a few hours prior.

Moral: See what I mean about paying attention? Of all the books in Target, my spirit/gut/intuition felt drawn to that particular one. I've already downloaded it and love reading and rereading it, but Mr. Coelho perfectly articulated something in the interview I watched the next day, which I've been feeling for a while. He explained that life is something like a scavenger hunt and we pick up clues along the way as to where to go next. And this is exactly what I'm finding. The clues can come from all over the place. From songs on the radio, books, TV shows, or even from a moving repair truck like it did recently for me. As I drove to a meeting with someone to see if he could assist us with a challenge, I got a glimpse of a repair truck with this person's last name boldly painted on it. That was my cue along with my feelings of peace and excitement that God wanted me to hire him to help us. He handled that problem expertly and is also helping us with some other issues. It was about 3 a.m. one morning when my hubby asked me to call my friend, Mabel, for advice on finding someone to help us with this issue. She connected us with this gentleman. *God and Mabel, I'm grateful for the hookup.*

Dear God, help us to PAY ATTENTION to Your nudges and clues, as we have the best life adventures with You as our Guide to our personal promised lands. Amen.

KEEP CALM—YOU'RE ROLLING WITH GOD

Day 337 — Live in God, Live in Love

"IF LOVING YOU IS WRONG, I DON'T WANT TO BE RIGHT"

It's the old line from my hubby that always gets me laughing!

But what's not funny is this love thing! I'm the God Maniac who often writes to love extravagantly and forgive quickly, but it's not easy all the time. I have some messy love relationships, and I get mad at myself that I'm not doing better in this area, but I always find the following quote (from a post I found on Tumblr) helpful to not be so hard on myself:

"Dear Human: You've got it all wrong. You didn't come here to master unconditional love. That is where you came from and where you'll return. You came here to learn personal love. Universal love. Messy love. Sweaty love. Crazy love. Broken love. Whole love. Infused with divinity. Lived through the grace of stumbling. Demonstrated through the beauty of...messing up. Often. You didn't come here to be perfect. You already are. You came here to be gorgeously human. Flawed and fabulous. And then to rise again into remembering." - Courtney A. Walsh

And, that's where I find myself often...messing up. I know that when I'm my most loving self is when I feel closest to God, but it's hard getting there sometimes. *Call me gorgeously human!* But like I always say, fall off the wagon and get back on. Practice. Practice. And more practice, remembering that everything's between God and us, not between us and anyone else because a life lived close to God is the best life.

Two more quotes I love:

"There will be misunderstandings; every family has its cross, its suffering. Always be the first to forgive with a smile. Be cheerful, be happy." — Mother Teresa

"FOR SOMEONE WE DISLIKE: The fault is probably mine, Lord, but I very much dislike Thy servant, N. Instead of thinking about the hundred ways in which he maddens me, I turn to Thee and ask Thy help for both of us. Give me the grace to meet him as a friend; give him the grace to conquer all his faults; and give to the two of us the grace of seeing each other as we are... equally friends of Thine." —Unknown

Dear God, control our minds and emotions, assisting us in getting it right more and more often, as we consciously live our lives pleasing to You in every moment. Amen

KEEP CALM—YOU'RE ROLLING WITH GOD

THE STORY DIDN'T END THERE

I shared my biggest regret one summer and a hurtful experience God counseled me through.

In an appointment with Him a few mornings later, I felt that He was asking me to share that story again in my daily blog postings. A book somewhat opened by itself on my phone, so I took that as my cue from Him that it was what He wanted me to read. The chapter spoke about how God can use the worst and most horrible events—Judas' betrayal of Jesus, as an example— and use them to bring about the best things.

This is exactly what happened to me. A hurt and disappointment were used by God to teach me (and you, too, hopefully) some valuable lessons. It is another miracle to report, as it has changed my thinking on so many levels. I'm so much happier and filled with more love and mercy in my heart thanks to this experience. *God, again, I'm grateful.*

Unbelievably, I went to work that day and the message for that exact date on my favorite calendar that I feel God speaks to me through read: "Just as the crushing of a rose brings out sweet perfume, so the difficulties of life release the sweetness within us. If we let them, they can bring out qualities such as love for others, tenderness, compassion, humility, and closeness to loved ones."

This was such a confirmation from God as, word for word, that was my experience. A "difficult" experience has made me more loving, tender, compassionate, humble, and closer to my loved ones.

Dear God, thank You for the difficulties and trials that You use to mold and shape us to become more like You. Amen.

KEEP CALM—YOU'RE ROLLING WITH GOD

Live in God, Live in Love

"BEING A SERVANT MEANS...

...giving up the right to control your schedule and allowing God to interrupt it whenever He needs to." — Pastor Rick Warren

This was what happened one day when I attended a wedding but didn't make it to the wedding, feeling God had another plan for me that day. It started with my little man, Joshie, falling asleep and I didn't have the heart to wake him up after we had spent two days that week traveling and I immediately rushed him back to school the next day. Then a lady came in where we were at the house of the wedding to breastfeed her five-month-old baby, and I got a feeling to ask her if she would have an appointment with God with me. She agreed, and I opened to her birthday in my meditation book to read to her. I got a God wink when the verse quoted for that day was a specific verse I had on my mind for the last few days. I first read it on the plane earlier in the week, which blew me away: "God may kill me, but still I will trust Him" (Job 13:15, CEV). This is so where I am in my life, trusting that God knows precisely what's good for me and humanity in any given moment. And even if that means killing me.

Next, I thought to give her one of the calendars that was left out for me by my friend, as she knows I love giving them away. This is the same calendar I feel God speaks to me through. I randomly opened the calendar to read to her, and I got another God wink with the verse quoted for that day saying:

"Do not let your hearts be troubled and do not be afraid." John 14:27 (NIV)

The day before, I was in Nigeria and had called my mom in the Bahamas, who was about to go into surgery. I had quoted this exact verse to her, telling her I believe this was the message I had received from God in regards to my anxious thoughts about her operation.

I gave the lady I was sitting with the calendar, and I had a great time talking to her about God, knowing I was exactly where He wanted me to be.

Dear God, may we be attentive to others, spreading Your love wherever we go. Amen.

KEEP CALM—YOU'RE ROLLING WITH GOD

BUT MOM, IT'S SO SO HARD!!"

I was venting to my mom in the Bahamas! There's someone in my life that's always driving me crazy! I know God has sent this person to me and they will eventually become one of my greatest teachers, but for now, I'm still in training. Everything they do seems to irritate me. They represent everything that I'm against, and I'm finding it tough to be my best self around them. I need some free therapy here, so here's the plan moving forward:

- Stay calm, catch myself whenever I'm losing my temper and ask myself if there's a calmer, more loving way to approach the situation.

- Remember the 80/20 rule. *Nobody's perfect.* Focus on the stuff I like about this person and kindly and respectfully try to ignore the other part.

- Fall off the wagon and get right back on, no matter how many times in one day. LOL!

- Don't sweat the small stuff.

- Remember Jesus' words: "If you love those who love you, what reward will you get? Are not even the tax collectors doing that?" To love the people who love us is easy, but when we could love those individuals who are not so easy to love, then we reach another level of living.

- Remember everything's between God and us. Whenever I'm my most loving self is when I feel closest to God. Try to stay there!

- More to remember from Jesus: "Father, forgive them for they know not what they do." Practice forgiving quickly and endlessly.

- Lighten up and don't be so hard on myself.

- Leave the past in the past.

Dear God, we hand every part of our lives over to You, including the hurts, frustrations and disappointments, knowing our reward lies with You when we strive to be the people You would have us to be. Amen.

KEEP CALM—YOU'RE ROLLING WITH GOD

Day 341 — Live in God, Live in Love

"MOMMY, JOSHIE LIKES MUSHROOMS"

Said my sweet, considerate, and smart daughter, Ember, when we discussed what she would cook for lunch for everyone. I had suggested something else, but there she was thinking of something her five-year-old, picky-eater brother would like. It made me so happy knowing that I have such a loving daughter that I bragged to everyone who would listen to the story of the mushrooms for Joshie.

Fast forward to my appointment with God that day, and look what word of all words showed up in my meditation book, *Jesus Calling*:

"If you must consider future events, follow these rules: 1) Do not linger in the future, because anxiety sprout up like mushrooms when you wander there."

The God wink I needed —when out of the blue everything lined up a little bit too perfectly that I know it's God. This life can get overwhelming at times, but this was my reminder that I handle nothing alone and God's my ever-present Helper.

Later that afternoon, a minute after going through a list of to do notes, I decided to have another appointment with Him before going out, and there I got another great wink:

"There's a better way to find security in life. Instead of scrutinizing your checklist (exactly what I was doing), focus your attention on My Presence with you. This continual contact with Me will keep you in my peace. Moreover, I will help you sort out what's important and what's not, what needs to be done now and what does not. Fix your eyes not on what is seen (your circumstances), but what is unseen (My Presence).

"You will keep him in perfect peace, whose mind is stayed on You, because he trusts in You. Isaiah 26:3." - Jesus Calling

And, how do I know these are communications from God that I'm writing about?

"I am the good shepherd; I know my sheep and my sheep know me..." (John 10:14, NIV).

Our God, take away all thoughts of fear and worry, filling us with thoughts of faith, hope and love. Amen.

KEEP CALM—YOU'RE ROLLING WITH GOD

Day 342 — Live in God, Live in Love

"GOD HAS A REASON FOR EVERYTHING"

This was from a wise friend after I shared with her some good news that a situation that I'd been dealing with for years had finally been resolved.

I told her I couldn't understand why it had to take so long to conclude. A few minutes after speaking with her, God answered me in a quote from Oprah Winfrey in an email: "Transformation happens when you dare to be awakened to greater heights. When you stay open no matter what. Letting each experience, especially the tough ones, strengthen you and add depth and wisdom."

And, that's exactly what happened in this situation as I see how I've become stronger through the years of dealing with it. When it first came about, I was always worried. Now, with the new confident me, when any problems come up I say bring it on because I know I have God as my silent Partner/Companion to direct me on exactly what to do to resolve them.

Speaking of Oprah Winfrey, I'm reminded of this interview with Rev. Ed Bacon, as this is the reason why I write these posts and why I can say confidently, *Bring it on!* to whatever comes my way: I know God is with me and I want you to know He's with you, too.

"You don't want everyone to be in church on Sunday?" asked Oprah Winfrey of Rev. Bacon. "No, I want everybody to know God. I want everyone to know the love that I know that fills their hearts so much that they are joyful and peaceful..." - Rev. Ed Bacon, Former Rector All Saints Church, Pasadena California

Here's the deal: pay attention to those feelings and trust your inner voice, as that's one of the ways God communicates with us. He's our silent Partner, and He's accessible to us in every moment. He's a 24/7 God and loves us unconditionally. *Can't beat this!* The Creator of the universe walks with us. Remember what Dr. Wayne Dyer said, "If you knew who walked with you on this path you have chosen, you will never experience fear or doubt again." *Don't ever forget this!*

Our Father, may our minds and hearts stay on You and not this world. Amen.

KEEP CALM—YOU'RE ROLLING WITH GOD

Day 343 — Live in God, Live in Love

I GOT KICKED OUT AGAIN

I'm forever getting kicked out of Facebook groups.

In the beginning, I used to be all hurt about it, but I've grown lots, and now I completely understand why Jesus told his disciples, "If anyone will not welcome you or listen to your words, leave that home or town and shake the dust off your feet." I realize that not everyone will understand or appreciate my posts and that's okay. That goes for life too. Sometimes people will like and understand you, and sometimes they won't. One reason why I love a friend so much is because she says to me all the time, "Nikki, do you! You can't live to please people!" And I've found that one day people may love you and the next day you're their enemy number 1.

Here's the deal: You must learn to shake the dust off your feet and keep stepping, being open to everything and attached to nothing. A friend may not want to be friends anymore, a spouse may not want to be married anymore, a parent or child may not even want to be contacted anymore! Do you spend the rest of your life crying over it? No, you dust off your feet, and you keep going. You must be tough in this life. People will disappoint you, but don't let that stop you from opening and loving again. I had a friend that stopped answering or returning my calls, and I was upset and hurt about it for a long time, but if I had decided not to trust friends again, I would be missing out right now on the best friendships ever.

I must say, though, the guy who kicked me out was kind compared to other ones. He must have been reading some of my posts about living kindly (lol). He sent me a private message explaining why he was removing me, unlike some that blast me in public or just remove me without saying anything. He just reminded me that whatever I do, I could choose to do it with kindness. And so can you!

Our Father, with You, we have all we need. May You always be our first love and priority. Amen.

KEEP CALM—YOU'RE ROLLING WITH GOD

Day 344 — Live in God, Live in Love

"I GUARANTEE THAT WE'LL STILL HAVE TRIALS...

...difficulties, hurts, disappointments, pains, challenges, and mistakes, but it's still a sweet life filled with joy and peace when we learn to keep our focus on God," was what I wrote in a chapter for another published book, *Sources of Wisdom*. Keeping our focus on God is the ultimate challenge of life, no matter what's going on. When we're there, trusting God, going to Him in those 1,000 daily decisions, that is when we get to enjoy the best life with Him guiding us with His wisdom. *How cool is that?*

I'm in Nigeria, in the middle of what some call a civil war, and instead of living full of fear, I remind myself that God's my protection wherever I am. I have no fear of bad news, refusing to worry about anything, knowing I handle nothing alone, and like we've done so many times in the past. God, our ultimate Helper, Strategist, and Adviser will help me navigate through anything that may come my way. Sometimes I must imagine He's holding my hand, moment by moment, to make it through those tough *times, but I always come out of those difficulties better/tougher/stronger/wiser than I was before them. This life is not for weaklings!*

My message today is simple: keep your focus on God. We're never alone; listen to His direction by paying attention to those feelings as He leads you on the path to the best life. When I feel excitement, peace, or joy, I take that as God's direction to move forward with those plans, but when I'm not at peace, or I have doubts, I take that as God saying don't do that.

Hurts, disappointments, and pains are all a part of the sweet life, too; it sure ain't pretty all the time. But when we keep our focus on God, staying on the high road with Him, forgiving quickly and endlessly and loving extravagantly, it has been my experience, repeatedly that He'll pay us back more than what was ever taken from us. "Blessed are those who mourn" (Matthew 5:4, NIV). Because once you come through that period of mourning, you will find a whole new world awaits you.

"For our light and momentary troubles are achieving for us an eternal glory that far outweighs them all" (2 Corinthians 4:17).

Our Father, keep our eyes fixed on You. May we never doubt that You are intimately involved in every moment of our lives. Amen.

KEEP CALM—YOU'RE ROLLING WITH GOD

Day 345 — Live in God, Live in Love

"STOP BEING SO EXTREME - DRAMA QUEEN. HAHAHA LIKE MY RHYME?"

It was like the universe came to my support and said, *Okay, Nik is in her weight loss mode. AGAIN! How can we help her this time?*

Universe: This book written by Jillian Michaels, *Slim for Life* should help (which it did), then arrange for her to have a long sit-down dinner with her friend, Marcela, who can convince her to stop all this extreme stuff. It may also be a good idea for her to start blogging about it again, getting her Facebook friends involved, too. And what about that interview with Oprah Winfrey and Byron Katie? That should get her to stop beating up herself so much, loving herself and her healthy body as it is right now.

You may think these are all insignificant happenings, but to me, it's like the universe responded to my issue. I'm amazed how every time I seem to face a challenge, extraordinary things seem to take place. The right ideas come to mind, the right people show up, the perfect stuff unbelievably appears. I've seen this happen so many times before. I now know and trust that God will go before me and everything and everyone I need will be provided. *That's faith, baby!* And I want you here with me, trusting God always and having no doubt that everything will work out in our favor. It's all about advancing confidently, and KNOWING God is our constant Companion. Jesus said, "Go, it will be done as you believe."

Whatever challenge you may be facing right now, slow down, calm down, and listen. Just know you have the Creator of the entire universe as your personal Adviser. Just take life one step at a time having those constant conversations with God; *Okay, God, we're here? What do we do now?* Pay attention to those feelings and go with the decision that brings you peace when you think about it. Calm down, already! *God has everything under control.*

"Just KNOW God is your constant Companion."

Dear God, thank You for being so attentive to our lives. May we seek You in everything we do. Amen.

KEEP CALM—YOU'RE ROLLING WITH GOD

Day 346 — Live in God, Live in Love

"WE ARE CONQUERORS, AND WE WON'T ACCEPT DEFEAT"

That was me motivating my daughters (and myself) one morning right before exercising together. I told them that we're superhumans, capable of handling anything that may come our way. *In this life, you will have trouble!* The challenges, problems, and frustrations will always be there. As I seem to make one step forward in an area, then three steps backwards, but that doesn't mean I'm going to give up trying. Like Shaun T says in my *Insanity* workouts, you must have endurance in exercising and endurance for your life.

Here's the deal: it's pretty difficult to endure some of the things God gives up to deal with, but I got some good advice from the eBook *Day By Day* by Charles Swindoll that freakily opened up on my phone:

"Moses endured—even in his eighties. How? The same verse tells us: by focusing his attention on 'Him who is invisible.' He fixed his heart and soul on the One who, alone, judges righteously. He continually reminded himself that his sole purpose in life was to please the Lord...to obey Him...to glorify Him...to gain His approval at all cost. Whatever it is you're facing, stand strong. Walk in confidence. Be sure without stubborn...firm without being unteachable...enduring but not discourteous...full of truth balanced with grace."

I'm at the point of my life where I simply follow God's leading. And let me tell ya, sometimes He leads me on some treacherous paths! But I continue to follow Him and what He would have me do from moment to moment, paying attention to my spirit, which I know is God's voice speaking to me.

Sometimes, I want to give up, asking why I must be my best self when others aren't being theirs, and He has a way of reminding me how blessed I am and that at the end of the day everything is between Him and me. I've learned to shrug off the disappointments and hand them over to God, who will correct them in His timing. That way, I can happily move forward living my best life and being the best version of me that I can possibly be. I don't have to control anyone else, only doing what God leads me to do. Supermom, superwife, and superperson is back, all for the glory of God!

Dear God, we can do all things through You who strengthen us. May we keep our focus on You, despite what may be going on around us. Amen.

KEEP CALM—YOU'RE ROLLING WITH GOD

Day 347 — Live in God, Live in Love

"LOVE LIFE"

This beautiful and important reminder was on a label in one of my favorite London supermarket, *Waitrose*. Our adventure with God continued surprisingly in London, where we enjoyed the cold, but not so cold weather.

Writing my blog posts have helped me tremendously in learning this valuable lesson of loving life. Yes, there will always be challenges, problems, and troubles in one form or the other, but when we stay close to God, trusting His guidance, He helps us with them all so that we can relax and truly love our lives.

"I'm happy this problem came up," I strangely said to my hubby that week when things seemed to be going wrong. It was good for me, as it taught me to be brave about everything, to listen to God on a moment by moment basis, to focus as He helps me discern what's important and what's not important and what I needed to do versus what I needed to trust Him to do. I built serious trust muscles, doing my best with my part and leaving the rest with Him.

I can, therefore, suck the enjoyment out of all my moments. I can't get over these fabulous adventures God takes me on. From one moment to the next, I don't know what to expect from Him. He has taken me beyond what I could have even imagined. The husband, children, close family and friends He has blessed me with have been remarkable. I love my life! I'm excited waking up every day to see what God has in store for me. I'm enjoying my life's adventure with Him as my most fantastic Guide, constantly paying attention to what He would have me to do.

"Have no fear of what this day will bring. Concentrate on trusting Me (God)," said my meditation book, and as I travelled there to London, I continually reminded myself of this.

Dear God, thank You for Your blessings and faithfulness. May we never doubt You. Amen.

KEEP CALM—YOU'RE ROLLING WITH GOD

Day 348 — Live in God, Live in Love

MY BIGGEST LESSONS OF THE YEAR

I had a great year where I accomplished my primary goal of a closer walk with God, and I wish the same for everyone on the entire planet. Here are some of my favorite lessons:

1. My appointments with Him are a must every day in assisting me with staying tuned into the best advice on what to do, where to go, and even what to say.

2. Trust my instincts/intuition/feelings/spirit. I'm talking endless conversations with God about everything!

3. Fear no evil. God goes with us and before us, and He's our protection.

4. Start being brave about everything, staying open to whatever God sends our way.

5. Forgive endlessly, staying on the high road with God.

6. Everything's between God and us, not between us and anyone else. Love extravagantly!

7. Hurts and disappointments are a part of life. Shrug them off and remember lesson #5.

8. Nobody's perfect. People put up with my stuff, and I should do the same with theirs.

9. Love is messy, and I'm gorgeously human, meaning I'll mess up sometimes.

10. Relax because God's deeply involved in our lives.

11. Everything can be used as an opportunity in learning to trust God more, really trust Him.

12. Be the best version of me, looking at my interactions with others from the standpoint of how can I improve in any area.
13. Teach my children to have a relationship with God.
14. Every bite is a banquet and every moment of life is to be savored.
15. Balance and not going to extremes (thanks, Marcela!).

Our Father, thank You for all the valuable lessons and experiences that we may rise higher and be the people You have called us to be. Amen.

KEEP CALM—YOU'RE ROLLING WITH GOD

Day 349 — Live in God, Live in Love

"I WISH I KNEW THIS NIKKI FIVE YEARS AGO"

I wrote to someone after he said that he wishes he had known me then.

Here's the deal: God is always calling us to move forward. I read from Rob Bell that if we're at the letter Z in our lives, God's calling us to Y and if we're at K, He's calling us to J. Maybe five years ago, I was at a Q, continually frustrated about my weight with a very low self-esteem. Just about every day I was upset about something, carrying so many people around with me with thoughts of unforgiveness, or just worried about all the problems I needed to resolve. Now I'm proud to report that I'm at maybe around letter L, where I've learned to be happy no matter the situation I may find myself. I'm content and bouncing around with gratitude with no thoughts of unforgiveness towards anyone, and I'm trusting God, confident that there's nothing He and I can't handle together

Constant and never-ending improvement is my new focus. Every moment we can work on becoming the people we would like to be. Only God's perfect! We've all made mistakes in the past, but one of my most important life lessons is to leave the past in the past and keep moving forward. God is our head lifter, and He's calling us to live our best lives with Him, but we can't do that walking with our heads down, depressed, and defeated over what happened years ago, or that person who did us wrong. We must keep going! The new Nikki is purpose-driven, and every day I set daily goals of what I'd like to accomplish. Some days I achieve them all, and sometimes I don't. But most importantly, I see my walk with God getting closer and closer. I fall off the wagon, and I get right back on, committed to doing better next time.

And even if you're at Z, God loves you completely and unconditionally right there. No other love required.

Our Father, thank you for Your love and commitment to us. Pardon us for all our sins and errors as we begin again to be the people You would have us to be. Amen.

KEEP CALM—YOU'RE ROLLING WITH GOD

"... YOU MUST RUN YOUR OWN RACE"

I'm so getting freaked out by *The Monk Who Sold His Ferrari* by Robin Sharma.

It's about a former lawyer who travelled to the mountains of India to discover so much of what I'm now learning through writing these posts every day. But, back to running your own race, I love this quote from the book:

"There is nothing noble about being superior to some other person. True nobility lies in being superior to your former self...All I'm getting at is that if you want to improve your life and live with all that you deserve, you must run your own race. It doesn't matter what other people say about you. What is important is what you say to yourself. Do not be concerned with judgment of others as long as you know what you are doing is right. You can do whatever you want to do as long as it is correct according to your conscience and your heart. Never be ashamed of doing that which is right; decide on what you think is good and then stick to it. And for God's sake, never get into the petty habit of measuring your self-worth against other people's net worth. "Every second you spend thinking about someone else's dreams, you take time away from your own."

This running of my own race has freed me. I no longer compare myself to anyone else.

I'm happy doing Nikki. It's now all about constant self-improvement and working to become the best version of myself. I want to be a better wife, a better mother and a better person living MY best life following my heart, doing what I feel God would have me to do. I just love doing me, no apologies! What more can I say?

Dear God, may we become the most beautiful versions of who You have planned for us to be. Amen.

KEEP CALM—YOU'RE ROLLING WITH GOD

"BE NOT AFRAID"

Was my God wink. I had one little thought, well a few little thoughts, about something that scares me, and I was astonished how God answered me within the next few minutes of thinking it. The feeling was to go and read a blog that I love. After I noticed there was nothing new that touched me, I still felt I should keep scrolling down some more, and there was my God wink: "I plead with you—never, ever give up on hope, never doubt, never tire, and never become discouraged. Be not afraid." -St. John Paul II

When I got home, God led me to another message in my meditation book:

"When anxiety attempts to wedge its way into your thoughts, remind yourself that I am your Shepherd. The bottom line is that I am taking care of you; therefore you needn't be afraid of anything. Rather than trying to maintain control over your life, abandon yourself to My will. Though this may feel frightening—even dangerous, the safest place to be is in My will."

I called my friend, Sal, to talk about my God winks and both of us were in awe of God—how He knows every thought we think and how He can speak so clearly to us. "My sheep listen to my voice; I know them, and they follow me" (John 10:27, NIV). Fast forward about an hour later, when I asked my assistant for the day of her birthday and read that date for my 12 p.m. appointment with God in my meditation book again, and the message for that date read:

"I am a God of both intricate detail and overflowing abundance. When you entrust the details of your life to Me, you are surprised by how thoroughly I answer your petitions. I take pleasure in hearing your prayers, so feel free to bring Me all your requests. The more you pray, the more answers you can receive. Best of all, your faith is strengthened as you see how precisely I respond to your specific prayers."

Thank you, Sarah Young, for this book, *Jesus Calling*, which has brought me so much closer to God and filled me with such wisdom, joy, peace, and hope.

Our Father, renew our hearts, minds and souls, removing all doubts and fears, filling them with faith in You always. Amen.

KEEP CALM—YOU'RE ROLLING WITH GOD

THE BEST MARRIAGE ADVICE EVER

I've been given lots of marriage advice through the years and here are some that have stuck with me (they apply to all significant relationships, by the way):

- *Focus on God!* Respond to difficulties from a calmer, kinder, respectful, patient and more loving space, allowing God to direct you with His wisdom. Rest with God while He fights on your behalf!

- The 80/20 rule - After complaining to my mom one day, she explained: "If your spouse has 80% good qualities and 20% not so good ones, focus on the 80% that's good. Focusing on the negative 20% only will make you miserable. Now when my hubby does something I don't like, I just constantly remind myself, *Nik, 80/20, 80/20!*

- Become a professional ignorer and choose your battles wisely. Keep the blinders on and the ear plugs in! Know what to ignore and what not to, both kindly and respectfully, having constant conversations with God.

- Lots and lots of patience. We too have stuff that others must be patient with us about. We are all on our own individual journeys with God. I'm now excited to see where God is taking both of us.

- Leave the past in the past. If you guys went through something and decided to go forward together, don't take old baggage with you! I told my hubby recently that all our years together have only been a warm-up/practice. *Our best days are ahead of us!*

- Forgive and *forget* quickly and endlessly. The universe is growing us all up. We all make mistakes. I used to spend days upset with my hubby, but now I remind myself what a great husband he is and I now focus on enjoying every day of our life together.

- Change from looking at your marriage as an obligation to an opportunity. You have no obligation, instead, you have an opportunity to live your best lives, raise the best kids, and there's no limit to what you both can accomplish doing it together.

- Be the best spouse you can be. In the final analysis, it's between you and God. Marriage is our important work from and for Him! Let's teach future generations to fight for their families, too!

Dear Lord, grant us grace to stay faithful, loyal and committed to our families no matter the challenges we face. You wipe our slates clean every day. May we do the same for our loved ones. Amen.

KEEP CALM—YOU'RE ROLLING WITH GOD

Day 353 — Live in God, Live in Love

"I'LL MISS YOU WHEN YOU DIE!"

I said to my sweet sister, Kelly, joking with her, since her son, Justin, always reminds us, "No one gets out alive!"

Growing up I always wanted to be like her. I wanted to dress like her, I wanted to be a mom like her, I wanted to talk like her. And now we're great friends! I called her one day and after feeling guilty that I hadn't called her in a while and said, "You can divorce me as your sister," and she replied, "I love you too much ever to do that, and no matter what you do I'll always love you."

She has become one of my go-to people when I need advice or someone to talk to and one Sunday I did just that after receiving confirmation that someone else who's been an important part of my life made it clear to me that they've been avoiding me. After calling them zillion times and have my calls go unanswered, I figured out so much! But lessons, lessons, lessons in everything and this lesson has been a good one. Ready for it?

Here's the deal: Our lives are like a journey walking on a path. On this life path, we will see people come and go – they die, they divorce us, they don't like our decisions, and they cut us off, we move, etc. That's life! Here's the trick, you must learn to enjoy the people on the path with you right now. *Got that?* This moment is all we have, and life is too short to be concerned who's not on the path with you. Simply enjoy the people who are there! Tomorrow they may not be there, so suck the enjoyment out of every moment. I don't want to spend more than five minutes upset with anyone on my path! I want to love them how God would have me love them—unconditionally—not on human terms, loving extravagantly and forgiving quickly!

Dear God, the people in our lives are blessings from You. May we never take them for granted. Amen.

KEEP CALM—YOU'RE ROLLING WITH GOD

"AUNTY NIKKI, LOOK WHAT ELSE I FOUND"

This was from a smart, little, sweetie pie God has brought into my life. We had the best day hanging out, celebrating all the academic awards the children received at school the day before. She was excited showing me something she read in the daily devotional for kids that I bought for her and her sister to have their own appointments with God. And I believe He wants me to share that important message with you today: "Give all your worries and cares to God, for He cares about what happens to you" (1 Peter 5:6, NLT).

This message was extra special to me because it was pretty much the essence of another post: I've given up all the worries to God, keeping my focus on Him, being the best person I possibly can be and surrendering the rest to God.

Our kids surprised us with their school results. Even though mommy was busy working or on Facebook posting, God took control, and I had the best time bragging to my mother-in-law how well everyone is doing.

"What matters supremely, therefore is not, in the last analysis, the fact that I know God, but the larger fact which underlies it—that fact that He knows me. I am graven on the palms of his hands. I am never out of his mind. All my knowledge of him depends on his sustained initiative in knowing me. I know him because he first knew me, and continues to know me. He knows me as a friend, one who loves me; and there is no moment when his eye is off me, or his attention distracted from me, and no moment therefore, when his care falters." - J. I. Packer:

We can relax and enjoy life knowing God is with us every step of the way.

"Always be full of joy in the Lord. I say it again—rejoice! Let everyone see that you are considerate in all you do. Remember, the Lord is coming soon. Don't worry about anything; instead, pray about everything. Tell God what you need, and thank him for all he has done. Then you will experience God's peace, which exceeds anything we can understand" (Philippians 4:4-7, NLT).

Dear God, thank You for Your Constant Presence in our lives. Help us to leave all worries and fears with You. Amen.

KEEP CALM—YOU'RE ROLLING WITH GOD

Day 355 — Live in God, Live in Love

"NOT BY MIGHT NOR BY POWER, BUT BY MY SPIRIT...

.. says the Lord Almighty" (Zechariah 4:14)

This is why Oprah Winfrey, who has changed the world in so many ways through her life and work can say, "That will be your single greatest gift: knowing there is a power greater than yourself and trusting that Force to guide you."

I'll never forget driving one day listening to Oprah Radio when she said, "It's all about instincts! Everything I do is based on my feelings. I'm sitting here right now because I had a feeling this would be a good idea." Here's a woman who is phenomenally successful teaching us to trust our Spirit to guide us in every step of our life. I don't know about you, but I'm going with Oprah. Before I make any decision, I pay serious attention to my feelings.

I was so happy meeting with a young man and we got chatting about God. I asked him, "How do you know when God is directing you?" I didn't expect him to know, but I was so amazed at his answer because it was exactly what I write all the time. "I go with the feeling that brings me peace," is what he told me. I said to him, "Lucky you! You learned this at a young age; I'm just learning this stuff now!" So imagine the possibilities if we all learn that God's spirit is within each one of us and it's not by might nor power, but by God's spirit that dwells within us that we are all capable of achieving greatness. *If all you can do is crawl, start crawling! God is with you!*

This is why I tell you there are no limits in life. Whatever you want to accomplish, you can! Believe this! Go with God, as He directs you on where to go and what to do. I recently wrote about a problem I had two hours to solve and out of nowhere the solution just popped into my mind. That was God helping me! And He's with you too! Every invention that man has ever made started simply in someone's imagination, including computers. Anything you're inspired to do, go ahead with it. That's what makes life interesting. Once you start, God joins in! Don't die before you die. Pursue your dreams. Do what you love and love what you do. I'm excited about writing more books! What are you excited about? Wake up every day enthusiastic about life, knowing God is with you all the way!

Our Father, bring out Your greatness within us. Use our lives for Your glory. Amen.

KEEP CALM—YOU'RE ROLLING WITH GOD

"MOMMY, CAN YOU COME TO SEE MY STARS TODAY?"

Asked Joshie, hugging and kissing me goodbye before leaving for school.

I said I would, and I was happy I did. My son is leading in the star count chart in his prekindergarten class! Leaving the class, he asked me twice, "Mommy, are you proud of me?" "I'm extremely proud of you!" I replied.

In fact, I'm extremely proud of all my kids and I have no doubt that it's not only my husband and I raising them, but we also have God as our Partner in that area too. And this is the Great News I have to share with you every day, that God is our Partner in every aspect of our lives. I go to God in my parenting decisions, and I lean on His wisdom by paying attention to those feelings I always write about. The decision as to whether to leave him in a smaller school environment or to move him to the big school with my other kids was a discussion with God, and I got the feeling of peace from Him to change schools. He's becoming so independent and kissing and hugging me goodbye is a significant step forward from us having to drag him in the car some mornings.

But I knew this was the best decision once I had a chance to sit in a classroom session with his teacher for about 30 minutes. The feeling of "YES!" this was the right move was there. I later found out that she loves God and she is so passionate about what she does. I trust her and the school, and I thank them for helping to nurture him to become this very studious and focused young leader. This is the same school that I mentioned before that God went ahead of me and had built in Nigeria because He knew we were relocating here from the US. It's the most beautiful school and it opened the first year we were here and for the very first time on my older daughter's birthday. *Wink! Wink!*

KEEP CALM—YOU'RE ROLLING WITH GOD

Day 357 — Live in God, Live in Love

"I SO DISAGREE!"

I argued with a Facebook friend after he questioned the credibility of a post I shared by another friend there who blew my mind when he wrote:

Post: LUKE 12:7: And the very hairs on your head are all numbered. So, don't be afraid; you are more valuable to God than a whole flock of sparrows." Just imagine. If the population of the world is 7 billion and let's say the approximate number of hair on every person's head is 200,000. It means that the total number of hairs in the world is 7,000,000,000 times 200,000. This gives 1,400,000,000,000,000. An incredible and mind blowing figure and yet God has accounted for each one of these hairs. How mighty is our Lord God? How awesome is our Creator?

Skeptical friend: Why would God number the hairs on every head?

Me: He knows every thought I think, every word I say before I say it, so why wouldn't He know the number of hairs on my head? I'm a believer! And that goes for each one of us! Check this out...The sun is 864,400 miles (1,391,000 kilometers) across. This is about 109 times the diameter of Earth. The Sun weighs about 333,000 times as much as Earth. What is impossible for God?

Like the stalker that got me away from the U.S. and my TV addiction to Nigeria. It was all a part of God's plan to get me here, I'm sure. I can see clearly now that my simple life in Nigeria (not driving, no TV, no electricity 50% of the time) put me in the space to begin writing every day and to meet a friend here who has been such a positive influence on me. God sent me to her for training! Her calmness and example of being the best wife, mother, and person have inspired me greatly.

"And everything is possible with God.""

RELAX... He has the whole world in His hands!

O God! Use our minds, hearts and hands for Your purpose. Let us shine Your light in all the dark places of the world. Amen.

KEEP CALM—YOU'RE ROLLING WITH GOD

"YOU GAVE ME GOOSEBUMPS!"

I said to a young lady I met in Burger King.

I had complimented her on her beautiful, black, natural hair and excitedly told how my daughters and I are transitioning from chemically straightening our hair as well. We chatted for a little bit, and I thought that was the end of our conversation. My kids and my mom wanted ice cream cones and while they ate their cones I just stood in front of the table where they sat. I got the feeling to go over and talk to the lady again to ask her if she would like me to email these posts to her but feeling a little awkward about it, I changed my mind.

Next, I felt as if I was being nudged by God to go and speak to her. Again, I ignored the feeling. Hey, I get shy sometimes! I then felt strongly that God was insisting that I go over and speak to her and this time I listened (My sheep know my voice). I walked over to her table and said, "Can I ask you a very silly question? I write a blog about my life with God every day, and I would love to email it to you." Her response caught me off guard: "Sure. I've been praying to God to send more spiritual people in my life!" And that was when I got the all the goosebumps, as she sounded totally sincere.

Was it a coincidence that she prayed for more spiritual people in her life and the God Maniac shows up in Burger King to meet her? I don't think so! And I now know why I needed extra time in my appointment with God that morning, why my son, Emmie, gave me such a hard time in getting him dressed to go to the doctor, why there was such a long line in the drive thru at Burger King that made us decide to eat inside in the first place. Our meeting was all perfectly planned. Relax, peeps...

Dear God, give us the wisdom to stay on the path You have designed for us.

KEEP CALM—YOU'RE ROLLING WITH GOD

Day 359 — Live in God, Live in Love

"WOW, I FORGOT ABOUT THIS QUOTE..."

"Lift your eyes to the Maker (God). Your eyes are to be fixed on Him, not this world." — Tumblr.com (via god-loves-u-sweetheart)

This one quote can dramatically change our entire lives. The hurts, disappointments, frustrations, sadness, problems, and challenges, I promise you, will all still come your way, but if you keep your eyes steadily fixed on God, you'll come through them all the better than you were before them. God will never leave or forsake us, no matter what comes our way.

A little while ago, my wonderful hubby said to me, "Nikki, if I lose you, I lose nothing." Last week, I was the best wife in the world and this week, if he loses me, he loses nothing. Okay, I was kind of hurt about it for a minute, but when I remembered this quote—that I'm to keep my eyes fixed on God—I shook off the hurt immediately. I know my hubby has a tongue like a razor and he may say things he doesn't mean when he's upset (no one's perfect). I'm using this as an example of how this life could be such a rollercoaster and circumstances are always changing, but God never changes. His love for us is constant and everlasting, and this is why we're to keep our eyes fixed on Him, not shaken by whatever comes at us in this world.

And in keeping my eyes fixed on God, I forgave and practiced being a professional ignorer (kindly and respectfully). Instead of becoming bitter, I became better—stronger and unflinching. What are words? "They fly through the air, but hurt not a stone" (*The Imitation of Christ*). I kept my eyes fixed on God, being the calm, strong, loving person He would have me to be, not the unforgiving, dramatic, crazy person that wanted to make an appearance.

God is our ultimate Friend. Through the biggest problems, He has directed me one step at a time, with brilliant solutions magically popping in my head or the right people show up with the perfect advice and assistance. And through the biggest hurts, He's helped my heart to heal. On the worst days of my life, He's figured out ways to let me know He was right there with me, holding my hand as I held His super tight. I sent hubby a text: "If you lose me, you may lose nothing, but if I lose you, I lose the best husband in the world."

Dear God, may we immediately hand over all disappointments, frustrations and hurts over to You. Amen.

KEEP CALM—YOU'RE ROLLING WITH GOD

GET ACCUSTOMED TO REFERRING EVERYTHING TO GOD

THIS IS WHERE I WANT US! Constantly going to God and seeking His incredible wisdom in everything we do, everywhere we go and everything we say. The customer I wrote about recently, who I advised to include God in on his decision about where to move to, sent me an email yesterday that he found a new place. He was excited about it and knew without a doubt that this was where God wanted him. I told him that doubt for me means don't from God because His answer is never "maybe" or "perhaps," it's always a big *YES!!!!* when He wants us to go in a direction. Here's the deal:

So, all day now I'm going to God, *Should I say this? Should I do this" Should I go here?* and I listen for His direction. If I feel peace or excitement, that's my cue from Him to proceed. N*o peace means no move!*

A question to Him yesterday was, *Should I go to work?* (Working with a hubby/boss certainly has its privileges!) The feeling from God was to go, and I was so happy I did.

"Worry about nothing, instead pray about everything." In this life, there will always be challenges, trouble, frustrations, but we must not get discouraged.

"The Lord replied, "My Presence will go with you, and I will give you rest." Exodus 33:14

In other words, we roll with God, and He's working behind the scenes of our lives, protecting us, fighting for us, helping us with our challenges and therefore we can relax and simply focus on doing our best with what He would have us to do and leave the rest with Him.

"Not by might nor by power, but by my Spirit," says the Lord Almighty (Zechariah 4:6)

"We aren't limited to the earth's resources; we have unlimited spiritual resources by the Spirit of God. There are things that can't happen by human thinking and reasoning.

Day 360 — Live in God, Live in Love

GET ACCUSTOMED TO REFERRING EVERYTHING TO GOD

There are things that won't be solved by natural power and might. But God is not limited to what we can see. When you open the door of faith in your heart, God will move through you by His Spirit. No matter what challenges or obstacles you may be facing today, know that you can live in complete victory by His Spirit!" – Pastor Joel Osteen

God, Thank You that we're not going by the ordinary rules of man. Help us to "get accustomed to referring everything to You." Amen.

KEEP CALM—YOU'RE ROLLING WITH GOD

"ARE YOU HAVING APPOINTMENTS WITH GOD?"

I asked a friend. She told me about something that didn't go as planned, and I also asked her the lessons that she had learned from the experience and it came out in our conversation that she felt she didn't need God and did everything without going to Him for input.

"I want to remember God every moment!" was the important statement from one of my favorite customers, and I've realized this is the best way to live. All day, I'm listening to God. As I work, I let Him set the agenda, paying attention to every God thought that comes to mind such as: call this customer, have a meeting with this staff, remind hubby about this matter, get this task done, etc. MY SHEEP KNOW MY VOICE. I'm learning to continually listen to God, working smarter with the best Adviser, Strategist, Helper, and Companion who's always with me. I allow my feelings, promptings and impressions from God to help me to decipher what's important and what's not.

And the appointments are helping me to get even closer to God. They're my quiet time with Him, and miraculously, He always leads me to the perfect messages. At my 5 p.m. appointment, the feeling was to read my post about my hubby telling me I don't work hard enough and I had a well-needed laugh with God about it because working with a hubby has its moments. About an hour later, I picked up that calendar again that I feel God talks to me through, asking Him, What do you have to say to me today? The date I randomly turned to said:

"If you ever wonder if anyone cares and sees the effort you make, always know that God does..."

"For God is not unjust to forget your work and labor of love" (Hebrews 6:10).

Super wife, super mommy, and super person is back in full effect! This morning, I was up at 4 a.m. to exercise and help make a Nigerian dish for my son, Emmie, to take to his class. He left for school bursting with happiness!

Dear God, may we never forget that our lives are partnerships with You. Regardless of what anyone else is doing or not doing, help us be the people You would have us to be. Amen.

KEEP CALM—YOU'RE ROLLING WITH GOD

"YOU UNFRIENDED ME"

I screamed at a very close friend. Not only did she unfriend me from Facebook, but her husband did, as well. After feeling pretty hurt all day about it, I went to God, and in talking to Him, I got the feeling to do the excellent and most loving thing: I bought some grilled chicken, brown rice, black beans, and corn, and showed up at their house with it for dinner. "You're not going to get rid of me so easy," I said to them, "I love you guys too much, so whatever issues you have with me, just get over it." We had a beautiful evening together, and by the time I got home, I noticed that I had already received new friend requests from them.

I write to be open to everything and attached to nothing, but some relationships are worth fighting for. These are people who have been so wonderful to me and my family, and I'll be the first to admit that sometimes I have so much going on with me in my life that I neglect some of the important people God has blessed me with. Note to self: don't take significant relationships for granted.

Nobody's perfect. Love people for who they are and where they are. Don't expect them to be exactly who we would have them to be. We're all on a different journey with God. I have another friend who is always complaining about her husband, and I asked her, "Tell me one other man you know who's a better husband than your husband?" She went back to someone she knew 20 years ago! I said, "No, someone you know right now," and she couldn't think of anyone. "See there, you have a good husband. Stop being ungrateful!" I told her. I want to be with my husband forever, and I want us to see our grandchildren together, and sometimes that means I must choose my battles very wisely. But again, that goes for all relationships.

Our Father, give us courage, grace and strength to forgive, love and to extend Your grace to others. Amen.

KEEP CALM—YOU'RE ROLLING WITH GOD

Day 363 — Live in God, Live in Love

THE STORY IS NOT OVER

I shared with you some messy love stuff I had going on. And it was a book that showed up from a Catholic Priest, on the worst day of my 12 years of marriage, which miraculously included the following prayer, that gave me the perfect message from God, proving again just how deeply involved He is in our lives:

"Heavenly Father, Please shine your light upon my family.

Give us strength to overcome all of the difficulties that we are dealing with now and protect us against any future problems we may encounter in the future.

O Lord, bring us together as we are meant to be. May the love that binds us only grow stronger as we fulfill the destiny you have laid out for us.

Grant my family forgiveness for any sins we have committed. May we also forgive one another Lord, as it is sometimes difficult to do.

Bless us Lord, as we humbly and confidently pray in your name. Amen." - *Oremus: He Lives Well Who Prays Well* by John Ifeanyi Okoro

Six months later and I was a super happy wife again. I'm learning to suck the enjoyment out of every moment hubby, and I spend together. Last Sunday, that meant laughing in our kitchen, drinking champagne, and eating boiled chicken.

In life we will have trouble. But just like every other time I'm faced with a challenge, I run to God, and He's always there, someway and somehow, to guide me with His wisdom. In this case, He taught me to keep my focus on Him, forgive endlessly, to stay on the high road, leaving the past in the past, work on rebuilding my marriage, and little by little our relationship is stronger than ever.

"Love just doesn't sit there, like a stone. It has to be made, like bread and re-made all the time. Love is never static. It grows when we grow!" – Amy E. Dean

I'm learning to trust God and lean on Him moment by moment to follow His will for my life. I do my best to make Him a part of every decision, in every aspect of my life and I'm super happy here and filled with peace. No more getting overwhelmed, worried or fearful. *I just do my best and leave the rest with God.*

Our Father, may we delight in doing Your will, especially when it is difficult doing so. Amen.

KEEP CALM—YOU'RE ROLLING WITH GOD

Day 364 — Live in God, Live in Love

"FOR YOU WILL NOT FORSAKE HIM WHO TRUSTS IN YOU TO THE VERY END"

This was from a random page I opened to in my meditation book, *The Imitation of Christ*, after my phone alarm alerted me that it was time for my appointment with God.

I was busy prepping onions and peppers when we were all in our kitchen together cooking dinner, and I shared this with everyone. Only one sentence was enough, a perfect little reminder that God is my constant Companion: "For you will not forsake Him who trusts in you to the very end."

In another appointment, I got the feeling to open my Wayne Dyer book, *The Power of Intention*. He wrote, "It is only discord acting within your own feelings that will ever deprive you of every good thing that life holds for you." Did you get that? "It is only discord acting within your own feelings that will ever deprive you of every good thing that life holds for you."

This life with God is the sweetest! The life where you have so much joy, despite all your problems and challenges, knowing that you don't handle them alone, and you know the Creator of the entire universe goes with you and before you wherever you go. And you're confident that whatever God wants for you is best for you, open to everything and attached to nothing.

Mornings, noon, and 5 p.m. are my times to focus on God, and that could be one sentence from a book or a simple prayer, Thank You, God. Join me and experience a sweeter and closer walk with God! I have a new Facebook friend who shares remarkable posts about Him. He wrote the following that has stuck with me: "... Progress only stops when you give up, so keep your head up and your heart in it, and never give up. It took me awhile, but it took progress, not perfection, to become the person I am today...never give up on progress! One day at a time."

Our God, thank You for creating a new me! May we never stop seeking Your guidance and input for our lives. Amen.

KEEP CALM—YOU'RE ROLLING WITH GOD

"BREATHE EASY?"

It was a sign outside our hotel's fitness center.

I was not allowed to take my coffee inside, so I was sitting in the reception area, sipping my delicious coffee latte and enjoying every moment of my vacation in Dubai. *We can certainly breathe easy when we're rolling with God.*

"God is able," read another sign on a bus that we passed on the way to the airport to see my mother-in-law before coming to Dubai. We were called and told there were not enough seats for us all on that flight, but I was relaxed and confident knowing God is able, and mysteriously, we all got on that flight.

So, breathing easy is about knowing we don't handle anything alone. God is our Helper who is not only with us at every moment, He incredibly goes before us so that anything we need will be there for us when we need it. I've seen this happen repeatedly in my life. We all have our crosses to bear, but God will help us to carry them so that our burdens are light and easy.

I'm trying to remember God in every moment, listening for His guidance as to what He would have me to do. I love my appointments with Him where I read something from one of the many books that inspire me. I pay attention to my feelings as to which to read and I always come away from them feeling better about my life. In one alone time recently, a book entitled, *The Happy Family* by the Jehovah Witnesses, reminded me that family life is about service to each other, using Jesus' life as an example, *as He spent His life in service to others.* I hate ironing, but that morning I asked everyone, "What can I iron for you?"

Dear God, may we relax and enjoy our lives, wonderful adventures with You. Amen.

KEEP CALM—YOU'RE ROLLING WITH GOD

Day 366 — Live in God, Live in Love

"LIVE AS HUMBLY AS YOU CAN"

That was my message from God one morning leaving a store. I was thanking the gentleman who paid after me for the kindness he showed the lady who was behind him and he responded (I paraphrase here):

"We have to live life as humbly as we can, doing God's will. We're not here to judge anyone but to leave all the judging to God. He is the only one who can judge us. No one is perfect."

This was truly a message for crazy lady here from God Himself. This stranger perfectly articulated my latest lesson from Him. I want to judge all the imperfect people in my life instead of focusing on what God would have me to do, which is to love them.

A couple of days ago, frustrated and angry, I go to work on the final editing of my book, and there was another perfect message on the screen from my meditation book this time:

"You know well how to excuse and gloss over your own deeds, but you will not accept the excuses of others. It is better for you to accuse yourself, and excuse your brother or sister. If you wish to be borne with, bear also with others. See how far you still are from true charity and humility, which knows not how to feel anger or indignation against anyone but oneself." - *The Imitation of Christ*

Here's what I wrote in that post: Can you imagine getting to a place where you do not feel anger, insulted, offended or annoyed by anyone for what you believe is unfair treatment by them and having such feelings only against yourself? Wow, what a wonderful life that would be, but is that even possible humanly speaking?!?"

Well, God is truly trying to get me there, and I want to challenge you to get there with me. We're to love others, stop judging them. Everyone is on their own path with God.

We must be professional ignorers, otherwise, we will go through our lives always offended, insulted and frustrated. When others disappoint us, we have to shake off the hurts and disappointments *immediately* and keep walking humbly with God, extending grace (pardoning without punishment), forgiving endlessly, becoming better instead of bitter and loving extravagantly.

We can do this! *Superhumans* we shall be, all for the glory of God!

Our Father, mold us to be more and more like You every day. Amen.

KEEP CALM—YOU'RE ROLLING WITH GOD

Sign up to receive my FREE daily devotional email: http://werollwithgod.com/sign-up/

Follow me on Facebook: https://www.facebook.com/We-Roll-With-God-241974312487814/

Email me: support@werollwithgod.com

About the Author

Nikki Bless is the official God maniac! Her mission to bring humanity closer to God—one person at a time—is what fuels her to tell her personal stories of faith. As an avid blogger and writer, she enthusiastically shares her message that we are never alone, and He is with us every moment of every day.

She is a proud wife of her wonderful husband of fourteen years, Emmanuel, and a prouder mother of her four fantastic kids: Ember, Julie, Emmie, and Joshie. Along with talking and writing about God, she loves spending time with her family and friends and travelling whenever she can. She currently lives between Nigeria and Miami, Florida.

To connect, visit her website at www.werollwithgod.com, by email: support@werollwithgod.com, follow her on Facebook: Nikki Bless or Tumblr.com: https://www.tumblr.com/blog/werollwithgod

www.ingramcontent.com/pod-product-compliance
Lightning Source LLC
Chambersburg PA
CBHW062242300426
44110CB00034B/1120